To two very nice people
our sincere best wishes
Rev & Mrs L. L. McCormick

2 Timothy 2: 15

Table Grace

We bless Thee, O Lord, for all Thou hast been to us and for all Thou hast bestowed upon us. We thank Thee for the gift of this food before us. May it strengthen our bodies. Use us in Thy service, for the Redeemer's sake. Amen.

THIS IS GOD'S DAY

This is
God's Day

BY

REUBEN K. YOUNGDAHL

AUGUSTANA PRESS
ROCK ISLAND, ILLINOIS

THIS IS GOD'S DAY

Copyright, 1956, by
AUGUSTANA BOOK CONCERN

Library of Congress Catalog [Card Number: 56-10136]

Second Printing

[PRINTED IN U·S·A·]

AUGUSTANA BOOK CONCERN
Printers and Binders
ROCK ISLAND, ILLINOIS
1957

Dedicated
to my son
Stephen Mark

Foreword

THE CONVICTION that every day, whether Lord's Day or weekday, common or special, is God's day is given vigorous emphasis in this, the latest devotional book by Dr. Reuben K. Youngdahl.

It is, indeed, characteristic of all the books which the pastor of Mt. Olivet Lutheran Church of Minneapolis has written, that they bring the riches of God's grace and the resources of Christian faith and love to bear upon the actual day-by-day experiences, problems, needs, and aspirations of men and women in every walk of life.

In the messages of This Is God's Day, there is an awareness always of the kind of day the reader may be facing and the speaking of a sure and winsome word of invitation, encouragement, admonition, or challenge to help him face the day with God, seeking His grace and help and walking in His way. There is an insistent call to claim by faith the joy and the victory God intends for His children.

Spiritual lessons for daily living are made vivid and unforgettable by the many apt illustrations, which are often drawn from the writer's personal experiences and observations as pastor and world traveler.

DANIEL NYSTROM

JANUARY 1

A New Day Dawns

I lift up my eyes to the hills. From whence does my help come?
Psalm 121:1

This is the day of beginnings. As we travel life's road we are prone to walk with downcast eyes, fixed solely on the earth and our immediate surroundings. Both our physical and our mental vision are blurred by the bright lights and deep shadows of the picture constantly before us. The passing events of the day absorb our attention so completely that we have become spiritually shortsighted. We are concerned about wars and rumors of wars, about tensions between classes and races of men, about storms and earthquakes. Consequently we are enveloped by a murky fog rendering poor visibility in every direction. Many of us are not only worried but desperately afraid, and wind and wave threaten disaster. We are like Peter who, walking out on the waters to meet Jesus, suddenly cast his eyes down upon the angry sea, and began to sink. Just so we are helpless and without hope.

"Whence does my help come?" are words that match our inarticulate cry.

On this day let the Psalmist give the answer: "My help comes from the Lord, who made heaven and earth."

Peter turned to his Master and cried out, "Lord, save me." And Jesus did.

If we make God our refuge, this new year will be the happiest ever. But we must meet certain conditions. We must forget the things that are past—the old failures, disappointments, prejudices, and hates. We must stretch forward to the future and enter this new year with courage, hope, humility, and faith. Transformed and regenerated by a power beyond ourselves, we can become new people, for the place of true happiness is within. The only One who can create it for us is God, and He is so willing to help all. He may not shield us from sorrows, but He will strengthen us when they come. He may not give all of us sunny days, but He will keep our faces alight even in deep shadows. He may not spare us from life's battles, but be sure He will bring us from every battlefield more than conquerors through Him that loved us.

Today hear God's voice saying, "This will be the happiest year you have ever lived, if you will but follow Me."

TODAY'S THOUGHT: *God needs every single voice for His celestial chorus. To those out of tune He gives a new voice.*

1

JANUARY 2

Great Expectations

For thou, O Lord, art my hope, my trust, O Lord, from my youth.
Psalm 71:5

God alone knows what is in store for us this coming year. But of one thing, we can be certain—it is and will be the year of our Lord. Time belongs to Him. It can be a good year if we want it to be. It can be a difficult year if we choose to make it so. Men can reject God's blessings, if they wish, but they cannot escape His judgments.

With faith in God we can face this new year optimistically, seeing an opportunity in every calamity. The pessimist, meanwhile, sees a calamity in every opportunity.

A man facing a major problem explained why he refused to give up. "There are no hopeless situations. There are only hopeless people in them."

This is God's promise: "Now to him who by the power at work within us is able to do far more abundantly than all things that we ask or think." This promise comes from a Gentleman who has never gone back on His word. Man's greatest expectations can be realized. The secret is to hope for the finest, the highest, yes, the impossible. Gratefully receive God's blessings day by day, confidently believing that more will follow. For God wants every good thing for His children. But be vigilant, and accept His gifts.

Think today of the promises you can carry into the new year. One of the greatest is: "Lo, I am with you always, to the close of the age." In His presence there is abiding joy and happiness.

A man stepped aboard a commercial airliner on a gloomy and foreboding day. The DC-6 climbed slowly through a heavy cloud bank, and then suddenly the sun was shining. The pilot's voice reported over the public address system, "We are flying at an altitude of 15,000 feet. For several days it has been raining at our destination. But up here the sun is always shining."

"Many times since then," that passenger remarks, "when things go wrong and no solution appears on earth's horizon, the words of that pilot flash across my mind: 'up here the sun is always shining.'"

As you live in the presence of God, the sun of righteousness will bring you optimism, hope, blessings, and sunshine for daily living.

TODAY'S THOUGHT: *Walking God's way, we can find a rainbow shining through every tear.*

JANUARY 3

Faith Is Like a Lodestar

So that the law was our custodian until Christ came, that we might be justified by faith. Galatians 3:24

Faith often appears as insignificant as a little mustard seed; yet faith has tremendous potential. It matters not how tiny faith is in its beginning. For if we nourish and keep it growing steadily, God assures us of marvelous things. Faith can become a growing force in adding meaning and quality to life not only for us but for countless others whom we may touch.

Too often we expect results without being willing to pay the price. To become educated, one must go to school day after day, and faithfully carry out the assignments. To grow spiritually, one must follow the same pattern of conduct with regularity and diligence. First, man discovers the need of something beyond his present state. Then, in casting about for the answer, man suddenly realizes that God is able to give what he needs. That realization becomes our mustard seed. It is our newborn faith. But it must not stop there. Man must continue to seek and to grow by practicing the Presence. His faith builds into a bulwark. He gathers inner reserves of strength and peace as deep as the mighty ocean is deep.

Growing discouraged, some people just quit. Who knows all the little, exaggerated discouragements that clouded their way and caused them to give up? Certainly they miss the blessings and reward of those who "hold fast."

Ought we not remember, too, that faith is like a lodestar? Storms may come, but somewhere behind the clouds that star remains constant. It never falters, never moves from its relative position. Like that is faith, the lamp of human hope. It looks beyond the immediate present with the assurance that in God's own time our difficulties will pass away, and skies will be blue again.

Let Christ inspire us! Think of His temptation. Think of His trial. Think of His courage and the victory it brought Him. He might have had earthly wealth, position, popularity. He chose instead to humble himself, to become obedient to the cross, to create from that instrument of criminal torture the symbol of salvation.

He gained the victory for each of us. He proved that if we have faith in God, all things can work together for good.

TODAY'S THOUGHT: *Faith is the hand that takes His hand, the ear that hears His words, the heart that loves Him.*

3

JANUARY 4

God Has the Power for the Faint

There is none like thee, O Lord, and there is no God besides thee. 1 Chronicles 17:20

We would be happier if only we remembered that it is not the ship in the water, but the water in the ship, that sinks it. We would be wiser if we kept fresh in our minds the thought that it is not the Christian in the world, but the world in the Christian that destroys him. We ought daily to seek God's strength to be in the world without being of the world.

We can trust this promise of God: "He gives power to the faint, and to him who has no might he increases strength." Do you know this source of power? Are you acquainted with Him who is able to help when you feel depressed and spent? Whenever you have exhausted your resources, God is always there to take over, if you will only seek His help. When you do, you discover how foolish you have been in neglecting Him so long, since all that time His power was available.

Each of us has the choice of what to do with life and what to desire from it. Consider two men playing the piano. The first plays beautiful harmony while the second achieves nothing but discord. Yet would any person be foolish enough to blame it on the piano?

In a sense life is the same for all. Discord and harmony both are there. Play it correctly, and it produces peace and serenity. But play it falsely, and it creates tension and strife. Here, too, life itself is not to blame.

Of course, this does not mean that a Christian walks clear of hardship or trouble. But it does mean that he has God as a partner who helps him to use whatever adversity comes for constructive purposes.

The story is told of a biologist who watched an ant carrying a burden of straw. It seemed far too big for the little creature. Then he observed it came to a crack in the earth too wide to cross. For a moment the ant stood still as if wondering what to do. Then it put the straw across the crack and walked over it. It illustrated a fact we ought never forget: a burden can become a bridge.

TODAY'S THOUGHT: *Patience is honey gathered on the wings of sorrow and trouble.*

4

JANUARY 5

Life Is a Co-operative Venture

So far as it depends upon you. Romans 12:18

Our daily relationships with people are a significant factor in our happiness. Life was meant to be a co-operative venture. No matter how few our talents may be, each one of us is important to God and to each other. God expects us to respect and honor every living soul as a child of His. Confronted by human need, we ought to stop to help, even as Jesus did. If the hurts of our world are ever to be healed, we need more twentieth century good Samaritans willing to make sacrifices. We ought to stop whatever we are doing, when a chance to bind up the wounds of anyone in desperate need comes our way.

Do you dare pray this prayer at evening: "O Lord, treat me tomorrow as I have treated others today"?

God planned that we be joined together in a fellowship of love.

Watching people knit has always fascinated me. This skill is as old as recorded history. The knitter interlaces loops of thread or yarn, linking one loop to the next until the fabric is complete. Love is a loop that knits Christians together. Being thus connected we Christians form a fabric that warms and beautifies the entire world.

Add a plus to your living. Too frequently we try to get by with as little effort as possible. A salesman summed up his success in three words: "And then some . . ."

"I discovered at a very early age," he said, "that the difference between average people and outstanding people can be expressed in those three words. The world's great did what was expected of them—and then some. They met their responsibilities in life with a cheerful smile—and then some. They were faithful to their friends, dependable in any emergency—and then some."

The cross is a giant plus sign. May it ever remind us that Christ gave His life for our salvation. Today He is asking, "What will you do for Me?"

TODAY'S THOUGHT: *Daily duty is as much a part of religion as daily devotions.*

JANUARY 6

The Great Serve Others

Because you have been faithful in a very little, you shall have authority over ten cities. Luke 19:17

After one has decided to go God's way, what then? The decision is worth little unless it is followed by action. When waves wash a lobster high and dry on the rocks, he has neither sense nor strength enough to return to the sea. If the tide fails to reach him he remains ashore and dies, though the slightest effort could bring him to the water.

The lobster teaches a lesson. Our lives will not get anywhere, if we do not act on inspiration. Too many of us sit idle, waiting for a mighty gust of wind to carry us out to smooth waters.

When asked what made him outstanding in his field, John Wanamaker replied, "Thinking, toiling, trying, and trusting in God." If we possess this abiding faith in our heavenly Father we, too, will try and try again. We will find courage to push forward past obstacles, discouragements, and mistakes.

Abraham Lincoln's birthday prompted the publishing of a cartoon showing a log cabin close to the foot of a high mountain. On the summit was the White House and against the mountainside rested a ladder. Its bottom rung touched the cabin and its top one reached the executive mansion. The caption was: "The ladder is still there."

Everyone has the opportunity to live a great life. I am measuring true greatness by the influence of your life upon your fellow men. If but one life is transformed because you lived a life of love, your contribution to the world will be felt. The secret of greatness is to keep climbing day by day. With God providing the power and strength, you can overlook disappointments and conquer discouragements. As you climb you will meet those who need your help. Whether you are a ten-talent or a one-talent man, you can add something to life. No matter how rich or poor you are, God has a place of service for you. The day to seek that place is today!

TODAY'S THOUGHT: *Taste the joy of salvation and soon you will taste the joy of serving others.*

JANUARY 7

Christ Paid Our Debts

For in Christ Jesus you are all sons of God, through faith.
Galatians 3:26

Christ died on the cross to redeem us. We do not seem to realize the tremendous price He paid to conquer the old Adam in our souls. The cross of Calvary enables us to turn the pliant clay of our lives over to the Father for Him to remold and shape after His will.

Man does not have the power to free himself from sin's consequences. Each day he writes a record, and each day there is error in that record. No one is perfect; all have sinned and come short of the glory of God. Whatever man attempts to do has the fatal flaw. However good a life he tries to live today, nothing can ever make up for yesterday's sins. How, then, can he pay for the deeds omitted and the sins committed?

Many years ago a Russian soldier, heavily in debt, prepared a list of his obligations and groveled over them in deep despair. He scribbled in large letters under it, "Who will pay these debts?" With head in his hands he fell asleep. His commander chanced by and read his scribbling. He signed his own name below the question. And on awakening the soldier found himself freed from his debts.

The soul's way to freedom from debt is as simple as this. At the end of every day we should prepare a list of all our known wrongs, adding those committed in ignorance, our unintentional sins, too. Unlike the Russian soldier, however, we need not write, "Who will pay these debts?" For we have the right to turn to Christ who has redeemed us by His blood, forgiving all our past, and cleansing us from all unrighteousness. There is only one name under heaven whereby we must be saved. Only His name gathers sufficient meaning to make us trust the promise that He is willing and able to forgive. "There was no other good enough To pay the price of sin; He only could unlock the gate Of heaven, and let us in."

As we seek His forgiveness every day and follow His will, our hearts are in heaven and heaven is in our hearts. Life becomes more joyful.

TODAY'S THOUGHT: *The future of every believer is brightened with the radiant colors of hope.*

7

JANUARY 8

Two Roads Stretch Before Us

Stand by the roads and look, and ask for the ancient paths, where the good way is; and walk in it. Jeremiah 6:16

There are two ways open to us. We can enter the narrow gate and follow the hard way which leads to life, or we can enter the wide gate and travel the easy way which leads to destruction. Some people are like the man who built his house upon solid rock. They are able to weather the storms, no matter how severe. Others are like the man who built upon the sand. When the storm comes and the winds descend, they are destroyed because they have a weak foundation.

The Master speaks about the righteous and the wicked, the believers and the unbelievers. These lines of difference still stand. We are either for God, or against Him. If we willfully insist on being our own architect in this life, we are destined to failure. God offers His help to every one. It is up to us to choose His way and find the abundant life.

How thoughtless we sometimes are with the gifts of God! A certain man owned a violin. It was very valuable and could have been sold for a large sum. But the owner was not aware of the fact. Instead of selling it to a master musician to play and appreciate properly, he used it as a doorstop in his modest home!

With the Holy Spirit's assistance, each of us can open the door of our hearts, permitting God to draw forth music from our lives. In His hands our will is a valuable instrument. But we can also shut the door or force Him out. If we do, we miss the glorious adventure He intended for us.

Who doesn't feel sorry for the motorist who stopped a farmer at the forking of the road to ask where the roads led. "Where do you want to go?" countered the farmer.

"Oh, it doesn't make any difference," was the motorist's reply.

"Well, then," answered the farmer, "it doesn't make any difference which road you take." Many of life's travelers have no destination for their trip, and many a man no purpose in his life. The farther we go, the plainer is the truth—it makes all the difference in the world which road we take. One road leads to Christ, to life eternal, and happiness; the other leads to the devil, defeat, and death.

TODAY'S THOUGHT: *The God who planned our world can surely be trusted to direct the building of our little lives.*

JANUARY 9

God Will Surely Help Us

Be still before the Lord, and wait patiently for him. Psalm 37:7

Some children were asked to write down their idea of God. One answer went something like this: "God is a very old gentleman who lives in heaven above." A child's superiors always seem old to him, while God is the oldest of all.

It is tragic when people carry this conception of God into adulthood, putting God so far away as to be detached from them. They think He views them impersonally and makes no claim upon them.

God is too distant to many people. They think He is too aloof to help with their problems, too old-fashioned to understand this age of radar, jet propulsion, and atomic fission.

With God bowed off the edge of the world, no wonder worries loom as big as Mount Everest. Barriers to happiness become unconquerable. But in God's vocabulary there is no such word as "cannot."

If problems plague you, and stand between you and happiness, remember they can be conquered. Come to the knowledge that God is great enough to help you.

For centuries Mount Everest was unconquered, challenging men to climb her. Finally a team of men took a long look, started climbing, and made it. Man's indomitable courage and faith won out.

Our problems may not change, but our attitude toward them will, if we but face them squarely, lay out a plan, and work toward a solution. If you have a mountain of worry on your hands, take it apart, work it out piece by piece and conquer it.

A pamphlet bore a picture of Mount Everest. At the top of the mountain was written a bold, "Conquered," and down the mountain were the words, "Step by step." Indeed it was conquered step by step. And so, by God's help, your problems can be solved day by day.

TODAY'S THOUGHT: *Many a big change is the result of a little improvement made every day.*

JANUARY 10

Christian, Guard Your Heart

Be glad in the Lord, and rejoice, O righteous, and shout for joy, all you upright in heart! Psalm 32:11

Dwight L. Moody once asked, "Suppose a man advertised that he took photographs of the heart. Would he have many customers?"

We all need a photograph of our hearts. We need to look within to see if Christ has room enough, or if other gods are crowding Him out. What kind of heart do you have?

A little boy well versed in Christlike things was watching the cook prepare potatoes for dinner. She took a large one, beautiful to behold, and cut it in two, but discovered that it was hollow and black inside, filled with dry rot.

"Why, Maggie, that potato isn't a Christian!" the boy exclaimed.

"What do you mean?" asked the maid.

"Don't you see, it has a bad heart!" the boy replied.

To be a Christian is more than going to church, participating in worship, and listening attentively to sermons. To be a Christian, you must be not only a hearer of the Word, but also a doer. You must live the gospel day by day. Consistently you will say "No" to the things of the world, and "Yes" to the things of God. Constantly you will be alert, praying that you may not yield to temptation. The more Christian you become, the more active the evil one will be in his schemes to conquer you.

A common plant called Matador, meaning murderer, grows in Brazil. Its slender stem creeps along the ground until it comes to a vigorous tree. With a powerful clinging grasp, the plant entwines itself around the victim tree, growing larger and closing in more tightly. Up it climbs as high as the tree. Finally the plant lifts its head above the strangled treetop, a conqueror completing its work of death.

Like that lethal plant the evil one works slyly among the children of God. It is our hearts he wants to conquer. He, too, hopes to claim one victim after another.

Watch and pray that you enter not into temptation!

TODAY'S THOUGHT: *What do you listen for—the cries of the world, or the voice of the Lord?*

JANUARY 11

We All Hunger for Righteousness

Blessed are those who hunger and thirst after righteousness, for they shall be satisfied. Matthew 5:6

There is no food that satisfies except the food which God gives—the spiritual food of the gospel. Like the prodigal, you may try to fill yourselves with the husks which the swine eat, but you will not be satisfied. You may try to gain satisfaction from hard work or your ability to get money; you may throw your life into pleasures and sins; but in vain.

Still you will feel a craving and a yearning and a hungering for something more. At life's end you will not ask for worldly things. You will not beg to see the labors of your hands. You will not want to count the money you have accumulated. Nor will you be interested in hearing the praises men have sung about you. You will want only one thing. You will say, "I want God, for I am starving."

From time to time it is well to stop and think what our values really are. We do not willfully lose some of the good things God gives us. We just lose them because we have been too busy to stop and think. How often we have wasted the time which He lends us! How many misused days and months lie behind! How many warnings and teachings have been disregarded! How many calls to repent have gone unheeded!

Each day Jesus of Nazareth has been passing by. Have we been too busy to recognize His presence? Too busy to answer His call as we see Him in the needs about us? Too busy to hear His cry for help that comes from all parts of the world, to aid many of His children who are starving because they have not food to eat? Who are cold and naked because they have not clothes to wear? Who are discouraged because they have not houses in which to live? Who are lonely because they think nobody cares? Who are living in darkness because we have failed to bring them the message of Him whom we know to be the Light of the world? Are we, indeed, too busy?

There are too many people living in false security because they feel they have not intentionally committed sins against God. Let us not forget that there are sins of omission. There are things we fail to do, and that displeases God, too. May we live humbly each day, asking the Master to direct our every word and deed.

TODAY'S THOUGHT: *When you give yourself to Christ, you give your life and breath, your every thought and action.*

11

JANUARY 12

Sin Blots Out Beauty

He who commits sin is of the devil; for the devil has sinned from the beginning. 1 John 3:8

One day an artist was examining some paintings. He found one that was hideous and coarse and badly painted. He decided to remove the unsightly painting from the canvas and use the panel for other purposes. While he was engaged in the exacting removal of the color he noticed other colors emerging from beneath the coarse picture. Excitedly and with great care he worked until he beheld a face, the lovely features of the Christ Child. It had been painted by one of the famous masters, but callously someone had blotted out the image of Christ with his own ill-inspired work.

Many times in my travels around the world I have entered beautiful temples where repairmen have uncovered fine mosaics. Through the centuries these had been covered by one layer of plaster after another, and only recently have men removed the plaster to reveal the original masterpieces.

Made in the image of God, our lives are like these pictures. They are so marred by our daily sins that every feature of Jesus Christ is blotted out and no longer is there beauty to behold. But as we repent our mistakes, Christ restores the picture to its original. He gives us the chance to begin anew an unblotted page.

We must remember that we remain in His grace as we live according to His will. Whatever we do or say ought to be in the name of Jesus. Our words, our works, every aspect of our living must be such as our Savior can approve.

In all things we should be motivated by the great love of God. In all things we should be ruled by the will of God toward the sole end, that in all things we glorify God.

Our lives have come from God. They belong to Him. Each day we should keep them pure and holy, knowing they are meant to be dedicated temples to Him who is the hope of the world.

TODAY'S THOUGHT: *The beauty and serenity of a holy life is a powerful influence in the world.*

JANUARY 13

Man Seeks Living Water

Make every effort to supplement your faith with virtue, and virtue with knowledge. 2 Peter 1:5

After being buffeted and driven hither and thither by a storm, a ship, still far from any port, was without water. Fainting from thirst, its crew hailed a passing vessel with the cry, "Water! Water!" The answer came back. "Let down your buckets where you are. You are surrounded by fresh water." It was then they discovered they were off the Brazilian coast in the outflow of the Amazon River, which pushes its tide of living water one hundred miles out into the Atlantic.

Every person is filled with wants, longings, desires, and hopes both for the body and for the soul. There are thirsts for the friendship and love of God, for forgiveness, immortal life, happiness, and heaven. The larger the soul, the greater are its thirsts.

Yet God can satisfy them all. We do not have to seek elsewhere to find these satisfactions. Wherever we are they are about us, near at hand, if we will but let down our buckets in the right places, and if we seek our riches not in the physical but in the spiritual sphere.

The world can never satisfy the soul. The world offers wealth, power, and pleasure. But these do not satisfy the spiritual desires of man. Seeking satisfaction in worldly things is like trying to quench our thirst with the salt water of the sea. The more we drink, the thirstier we become. We may even sicken and die from such drinking. What the world has to offer is like a mirage on the desert, an inviting oasis of burning sand. Solomon tried all that the world could give, and under the most favorable circumstances, too; yet he found it all to be vanity and vexation of spirit. Alexander conquered the world, but did not satisfy his spirit.

We are acquainted with the wages of sin. Many of us are even willing to pay the price. Yet, we do not realize that good things of the spirit can never be bought. The rewards of goodness cannot be purchased, and these rewards are the only ones worth having.

How different is eternal life! This is God's treasure which He gives to us.

TODAY'S THOUGHT: *Those who love God have spring forever in their hearts, though winter may surround them.*

JANUARY 14

Death Walks Before Us

Even though I walk through the valley of the shadow of death, I fear no evil. Psalm 23:4

Most of us have experienced the death of friend or relative. For a time afterwards we were very solemn indeed. The passing of a life impressed us deeply because we were reminded again that "we have not here on earth an abiding city," that our best insurance is preparation to meet our God. But, "time will rust the sharpest sword," and after a while when the grave had been closed and the turf started growing green, we began forgetting those reminders of eternal life.

Each day we should remember that death is before us. It should not be a sorrowful idea, the thought that we must leave this world. It should be a happy thought, reminding us of the fact in which we can all believe, that we shall live in another world forever and ever. Our immortal soul, which makes us feel and know and love, cannot go to sleep, nor can it die. The very nature of our souls requires some kind of eternal existence. Herein is the key to the way of light or the way of darkness. For we are taught of God that either our souls dwell with Him in perfect happiness, a state called eternal life, or else they are away from God in a condition of living misery called eternal death.

When Jesus said, "Truly, truly, I say to you, if any one keeps my word, he will never see death," He was clearly not speaking of the death of the body. Before long He himself was to die a cruel death upon the cross. He spoke of the soul. He tells us that those who keep His sayings shall pass from the church on earth to the church in paradise. He promises that when we lay aside our body in death, it will merely be to put on the resurrection body, because we are entering the gates of the King's palace.

Each day we should live close to God, keeping our house in order and constantly prepared. We know not the moment we shall be called home to God. If we reverence the sayings of Christ and follow His commandments; if we penitently confess our sins and receive His forgiveness; if we trust His promise that because He lives we shall live also, then we can know peace, realizing there is a rainbow in our future. It is the rainbow of everlasting life.

TODAY'S THOUGHT: *Many long for heaven, not merely to see the mansions, but most of all to meet the Master.*

14

JANUARY 15

The Devil Makes Us Proud

God opposes the proud, but gives grace to the humble.

James 4:6

Whom the devil decides to make his prisoner he first makes proud. The rest follows naturally.

There is a legend telling how a certain man came disguised to a church, asking to make his confession to the minister. As he unfolded his crime the minister shuddered with horror. When he had finished his tale of woe the minister, not realizing it was Satan that sat before him, told him that he could find pardon if he humbled himself before the crucified Savior. Then the fiend rose in rage, and scornfully refused to bow himself before One who had trained in a carpenter's shop, lived as a homeless teacher, and died on the cross like a common criminal.

It is the devil behind our pride who keeps some of us back from the cross today and prevents our enjoying the peace which comes from leaving sin's path. Many people would rather adopt a purely intellectual religion, a palliative religion for educated minds, than accept a faith which tells them they are sinners, that Jesus Christ died for them and that if they repent, His life will be their ransom. They do not understand this; rather, they despise it.

If you have sinned in this way, fling away your pride, become as a little 'child and you will surely find peace for your soul. If you were a criminal condemned to die this day, would you be consoled by the treasures of wealth? No, you would care for none of these things. The one thing you would think of and long for and ask for is pardon.

You are courageously trying to face yourself. You are endeavoring to carve out a new road, even to form a religion without a Savior. Take heed. There is no other road to the new Jerusalem, but by the way of Calvary's cross. It alone will bring you to God.

TODAY'S THOUGHT: *Is something blacking out your sunshine? It is probably the shadow of yourself.*

JANUARY 16

You Must Change Inside

Look up and raise your heads, because your redemption is drawing near. Luke 21:28

As a publicity stunt at a barbers' convention a committee went to the city's Skid Row and picked out the most sorry looking man on the street. They gave him a bath, a shave and a hair cut, and dressed him in an elegant manner. He was as fine a looking gentleman as you could possibly find. The manager of the hotel where the convention was being held was very impressed with the change. He decided to try to help the man.

"Now that you have been made over," he said, "I am going to give you a chance to begin again. There will be a job waiting for you tomorrow morning. What time can you start?"

"Suppose we make it eight o'clock," the man replied. The next morning eight o'clock came and went, but the new employee did not arrive. The hotel manager waited until noon, then six o'clock. Following a hunch he went to the district where the man came from, and found him sleeping on some old newspapers in an alley, most of his fine clothes hawked for rags, the rest soiled and rumpled.

"I certainly was disillusioned," the hotel manager said. "The barbers may be able to clean up a man on the outside. But you can never make anything of a man unless you change him from the inside."

External changes are not enough. Only God can change a man to make him better. But a man must have the desire to accept the plan for change which God offers. There are some things that God does for man, and some things that man has to do for himself. God provides the power, but man has to choose to go into partnership with Him. He will even provide the will to choose through His Holy Spirit, if a man will surrender and quit saying, "No."

Your partnership with God will prosper in the measure you use the things you have been given to the best advantage. If we follow His leads, God will bring about a wonderful change.

TODAY'S THOUGHT: *If you have never made a mistake, you have never made anything.*

JANUARY 17

Prayer Has Power

With thanksgiving let your requests be made known to God.
Philippians 4:6

"What is prayer?" A woman once wrote this question on a little deaf and dumb girl's slate.

"Prayer is the wish of the heart," the little girl wrote with her chalk.

This is the promise of Scripture: We can ask anything that is the will of our Father, any wish that we hold in our heart. God will always answer prayer, just as a loving father will always answer the requests of his children. Sometimes God says "Yes" and sometimes He says "No." Whatever the answer, it is for our own good. We must have faith enough to know that God is concerned about us and that He would never allow us to receive anything bad for us. He loves us too much.

What is prayer? Prayer is power. A great benefactor lived such a vibrant life and had such joy that he was a tremendous influence on all who knew him. After his death, a man visiting one of the institutions he founded, remarked about his wonderful character and asked the secret. A staff member led the inquirer to a little room. There stood a small altar and before it the carpet showed two ragged holes worn by this man's knees.

"That," said the staff member, "was the secret of his power."

Why do so many lives today lack that which matters most—spiritual food?

The Japanese can dwarf trees. They take a cherry or maple tree and dwarf it so that it will never grow taller than 12 to 18 inches. They cut out the tap root and the tree lives only by its surface roots. It lives but it cannot grow.

Leave prayer out of your life and you cut its tap root. True, it is possible to exist, but not really to live. Life will lose its meaning. There will be no vibrancy, no trumpets in the morning, no celestial songs at night.

What a difference it makes when we spend one brief hour in the presence of God to tell Him the wishes of our hearts and to receive His power!

TODAY'S THOUGHT: *If we spent as much time in prayer as we do in complaining, we should have little to complain about.*

JANUARY 18

In the Presence of the Father

If any one serves me, he must follow me; and where I am, there shall my servant be also. John 12:26

Fear is one of man's worst enemies. It will shroud his heart with gloom, if he allows it to take effect. But fear never troubles a trusting heart. In the brightness of faith the darkness of fear cannot enter.

A traveler saw a fisherman's wife wading in the water and leading her little boy by the hand. He was very much afraid and clung to his mother desperately. With great patience she encouraged him, and assuring him that he would be all right, she led him in and out of the water again and again. At last, made fearless by her training and encouragement, the little lad toddled down to the water alone.

"What were you doing?" an onlooker finally asked.

"Drawing out his fear," the mother answered.

We all need someone to draw out our fear. Each of us has the privilege of walking every day hand in hand with the Master, the only One who is able to help us. If we want to be with Him there is no need to worry.

I like the story of the doctor who was sitting in his study. He wanted to be alone to concentrate, because he was reading about some of the latest medical discoveries. Then by his side he felt the presence of his son. Unconsciously he handed him a coin, and continued to read. Still the boy stood there.

"I don't want money," said the boy.

"What do you want, Son?" the doctor asked.

"I only want to be with you, Father," said the son.

Do you long to be continually in the presence of God, or do you come to Him only when you are seeking? Does His friendship mean so much that never would you want to forsake Him?

Walk each day with God, knowing He has traveled the pathway before you. He will draw out all fear as you realize He is able to conquer anything.

TODAY'S THOUGHT: *Some of us pray daily to our heavenly Father, but continue to live as though we were orphans.*

JANUARY 19

Free for the Accepting

For every one who asks receives, and he who seeks finds, and to him who knocks it will be opened. Matthew 7:8

Some people make the mistake of thinking that pleasure and happiness are synonymous. Pleasure is temporary while happiness, once attained, is permanent. Though happiness is available to every one of us, we cannot have it if separated from God. He stands by, waiting for us to accept Him.

Have you ever seen a picture of a happy miser? The only ones I remember show bitter, miserable persons who lived shut off from society, alone in a littered old house.

Many times, however, we have seen pictures of poor men who are happy. Though their clothes may be patched, their happiness shines through kindly eyes, because the key to happiness is within every man's reach—millionaire or pauper. The door to an abundant life can be unlocked, if we but reach for the key and use it. God has made all the preparations for us. Everything we can possibly need, everything worth while in life, is waiting if we will only use the key.

Once a little boy raided a jar of jam. With a small boy's thoroughness, he gorged on the sweet preserves until you could hardly tell which was the jam jar and which was the little boy. His mother caught him in the act, but as she opened her mouth to reprimand him, he beamed impishly. Remembering a little saying she had taught him, he recited hopefully through jam-smeared lips, "Remember, Mommy, God helps those who help themselves. You told me that yourself."

It is inextricably a part of God's plan of salvation that worthwhile things do not come without effort. The wonderful grace of God is free, to be sure, because it is the result of Christ's death on the cross. But we must choose that gift of grace or we will never possess it. Once we have truly received that grace, it proves itself by flowing out in loving service to our fellow men. God showed His compassion for us through Christ, the source of our joy and happiness. When we have accepted what Christ offers, our search ends and a new life of happiness and peace begins.

TODAY'S THOUGHT: *He who chooses the path chooses the place it leads to.*

Perfect in His Image

The fear of the Lord is the beginning of knowledge.

Proverbs 1:7

At kindergarten two little girls were given a lump of plastic clay to take home and make whatever they wanted.

"I know what I am going to make," said one little girl. "I am going to use my clay to make a little devil."

"Well, then, I'm going to mold a little angel," countered her playmate.

You can do what you want with your life. You can turn it over to the evil one and become a bad influence, or you can surrender your life to God and become an influence for good. God gives you the choice. Every man decides what he will make out of his life.

There is a legend about a prince who had a crippled back. Being very proud, he was troubled because he was not like other people. He decided to seek a skilled sculptor.

"I want you to make a statue of me," he told the artist, "but you must show me with a straight back. I want to see myself as I might have been."

When the perfectly erect statue had been completed, the sculptor suggested it be placed at the palace gate.

"No," said the prince, "I want it in a secluded place in the garden where I will be the only one to see it."

Each day the prince strolled through the garden and paused to gaze at the statue, at the image of the man he might have been. Each time he left he seemed inspired, inspired to become like that man. As the months passed a change became apparent.

"Look," the people began to remark, "the prince's back is growing straight! He is more noble looking than before."

The prince became the man of his dreams.

As we look to Jesus day by day, we become more and more like Him. And finally in glory we shall be made perfect in His image.

TODAY'S THOUGHT: *Perfection is not doing unusual things, but doing the usual things unusually well.*

No Care Too Small to Take to God

God is our refuge and strength, a very present help in trouble.

Psalm 46:1

Each day we make mistakes, only on some days they seem to pile higher than on others. If we do not seek forgiveness from time to time, they will become burdens great enough to break our spirits.

Often we are like little children solving arithmetic problems on a slate. We try one method, and if it does not work, we cross it out and try again. Soon the slate is so smudged that we cannot read the figures at all. Then like little children we start crying, and things get worse. We simply cannot find the right answer when suddenly the teacher comes along. If the situation is hopeless, he washes the slate with a sponge, blotting out all the mistakes and helping us solve the problem correctly.

So it is in life. The Christian who has faith in God need have no concern. When we are in difficulty, the Master comes into our lives with hands of tremendous power, striking out the trouble. The ever living Christ was born to inspire us and lift us to the glorious life for which we long.

A great king of long ago employed many of his people at weaving. He said he would be kind to them, and he urged them to send for him when predicaments arose. It would be no trouble, he assured them, for he would be happy to straighten out their problems. They had many problems, too, but one woman at the factory worked cheerfully without a worry. Once when the silks became tangled and the weaving unlike the pattern, the other workers began to quarrel violently. Suddenly they turned on her.

"Tell us why you are so happy at your work, when we are always in difficulty," they demanded.

"Why don't you send for the king?" asked the woman. "He told us that we might."

"We do send for him every morning and night," they replied.

"The difference is," said the cheerful woman, "that I send for him just as soon as I have a little tangle and he fixes it before the pattern is in one big mess."

No matter how insignificant your problem seems, God is willing to help.

TODAY'S THOUGHT: *With God as our guide, we can scale the steepest mountain in our life.*

JANUARY 22

Your Link to Power

That your faith might not rest in the wisdom of men but in the power of God. 1 Corinthians 2:5

Imagine seeing on the far side of a great chasm something you desperately want. You can see it, but you cannot reach it. It is there, you are here, and there is no way to cross the chasm. You cannot possess this coveted object without some kind of bridge.

Can you picture the world without bridges? Suppose you are walking to the store. Your cupboards are bare, and it is time to prepare a meal for your hungry family. You are on your way to buy food when suddenly the sidewalk ends, and a deep ravine yawns in front of you. You must cross it, or your loved ones will go hungry; but there is no bridge.

Or suppose you are driving along a smooth, wide highway, when abruptly it comes to the brink of a canyon. Your heart sinks because the appointment that awaits you in the next town is the most important of your career. But it is impossible for you to keep that appointment without a bridge.

A traveler, no matter what he is seaching for, needs a bridge to carry him over deep gorges and valleys, over swift, wide rivers. Primitive man wandered up and down until he found a means of crossing from one bank to another. The first bridge was a tree that just happened to fall across some stream. Today's giant bridges span unbelievable distances and are wonders of engineering skill.

But the most important bridge in the world today is the one linking you to God's almighty power. Without that bridge you are stranded on one side, with His blessings on the other. That bridge is the bridge of faith spanning even the last valley of the shadow of death.

The Norse mythologists said the rainbow was a bridge by which mortals who were worthy might go to walk with the gods. But if any unworthy foot touched the bridge, it would give way and the unworthy be lost forever.

Well, we have that bridge. And because it is braced and made secure in a way that the Norsemen never dreamed by two wooden beams in the form of a cross, the unclean and the unworthy may safely pass over to walk with Him in light. By faith we receive the power of Almighty God to cross over to the other side.

TODAY'S THOUGHT: *Faith will give you wings to fly above the corroding cares of this day.*

JANUARY 23

With a Prayer in Your Heart

Ask, and it will be given you; seek, and you will find; knock, and it will be opened to you. Matthew 7:7

We need to learn when to pray. In one sense we should always pray, not only in church, not only when we awaken or when we retire at night, but all day long we should be in communication with God. A Christian who believes in prayer is able to speak to God anywhere and under any circumstance. There would not be as much sinning, nor would we be yielding so often to temptation, if prayer were brought into every relationship of life. The man who brings prayer into his business does not tell a lie over the counter. A man with a prayer in his heart has a difficult time telling a bad story. Let people who lose their tempers easily, and say words they later regret, pray more often. By so doing their words will bring blessedness rather than bitterness. What strength and courage we lose because too seldom do we turn to God in prayer.

On the night before the Battle of Hastings the Saxons spent the night feasting and singing, but the Normans spent their time in prayer and worship; and to them went the victory. The Roman Legions never undertook a war or any serious matter without consulting an oracle. Ours is not the heathen's oracle. Ours is the living God, and whenever we are in dire need, or difficulty, or danger, we should pray to God about it.

Quiet, humble prayer, practiced with diligence and sincere faith, will turn your life into a deep, rich, exhilarating experience. In our hearts prayer creates serenity, and strength, and light in the most extraordinary way. For from an inner depth we had not known, within ourselves these things "shine forth as the sun in their heavenly Father's realm."

But it is not only in troubled times that we should turn to Him. Whenever we make an important decision let us pray about it as Jesus prayed before choosing His disciples, and as the apostles prayed before choosing the one to replace Judas.

Let us bring prayer literally into every part of our lives. More homes would be happier, and more workers contented, if they spent more time with God in prayer. Our right choices would far outnumber the wrong ones, if before each decision we took it to the Lord in prayer.

TODAY'S THOUGHT: *Pray to God as you begin your work that it may come to a good end.*

23

Cleansed by Jesus' Blood

Blessed are the pure in heart, for they shall see God.

Matthew 5:8

Who are the pure in heart? Those who are sinless and free from evil? Too many people shy away from this verse of Scripture, because they think it does not include them. On the contrary, this beatitude is not for the sinless. It is for sinners who have been forgiven by the grace of the Lord. The pure are those who have been purified. Their robes have been washed white in the blood of the Lamb.

There is a beautiful story about a certain artist and his pupil. The latter had worked hard at his picture. He had grown weary and discouraged, because there were so many faults in his work. Try as he would to correct them, it just seemed impossible, and finally he fell asleep at the easel. While he was asleep the master came and, correcting the pupil's mistakes with his own hand, he finished the picture.

So it is that, when we strive for holiness, when we do our best only to be disheartened by failure, the Master will come, and with His own hand will correct our mistakes and finish our work.

What is the reward for those who are pure? They shall see God. The impure, the sinful, those who live intentionally according to their own will instead of His, cannot even see Him, much less enjoy Him. They do not understand His nature. They do not know the meaning of His character. The selfish cannot understand love.

When will we see God? We need not wait until eternity, for we see Him here and now. What a privilege to see God, His glory, His goodness, and His love. How it sharpens the vision, widens the horizon, and expands the soul. How pitiful are those who have no desire to live this kind of life, and who have no appetite for God.

There is the pathetic story of a sick woman who went south for her health. In every letter home she told of wonderful luxuriant growth wherever she looked, and of the abundance of food upon the table. Yet each letter continued to say: "If only I could eat, I would soon recover here. But I have no appetite." She died in the midst of plenty, not from lack of food, but lack of hunger.

God has provided spiritual sufficiency for us all. If we refuse to accept His gift, we shall suffer. If we accept, we shall live.

TODAY'S THOUGHT: *Rivet your life to God and His church, for they will never fail you.*

24

JANUARY 25

On Wings of Faith

He who believes and is baptized will be saved; but he who does not believe will be condemned. Mark 16:16

Robert Louis Stevenson was depressed. His health had been failing, and trouble surrounded him. "I must get out my wings!" he said. There is a way to fly over any mountain of difficulty. God has given us the opportunity of having faith that will enable us to overcome any situation, no matter how impossible it might seem.

A crippled man is tempted to give up, but not Sir Walter Scott. He rises to victorious heights. A man is put behind prison bars and is tempted to curse God and die, but not John Bunyan. He uses his time to write Pilgrim's Progress. A man is born in a log cabin in abject poverty. He could easily say there is no hope for him, but not Abraham Lincoln. Diligently he applies himself to the means at hand —to become President of the United States.

We can miss months of victorious living, if we keep our eyes on the trouble which seems to be ahead. We forget that with God there is a way out of any difficulty. We magnify the trouble, and minimize the power of God.

Have you ever wondered how a small and frail creature like man can control a powerful horse? It is said that the horse's eye has an unusual ability—it magnifies the image. Man looks larger to the horse than he is because of this magnification. So it is with some of us human beings. We magnify things out of all proportion and constantly cringe in fear, when Christ meant that we should live in faith.

Oh, that we might have the faith of a little child! Kara, a little orphan girl in India, had a wonderful faith. Kara's greatest wish was to go to live in the home of her missionary teacher. The teacher had no money and no room, but promised to pray over the matter. The next day the teacher received a gift of money from America and sent for Kara. Kara, however, met the messenger halfway. Later she explained, "I was praying, too. I thought I might as well start."

The secret is not to look at the trouble, but to look to Him who is our help in time of trouble. We should be far happier, if we did not look at tomorrow's difficulties, but rather at Him who creates tomorrow.

TODAY'S THOUGHT: *Blessed is the night of trouble, for it reveals the stars of faith and hope.*

JANUARY 26

All the Way to Heaven

Unless one is born anew, he cannot see the kingdom of God.
John 3:3

An old shepherd offered a prayer in church which indicated sorrow over his backsliding: "Lord, I got into the thorns of the briars and was scratched and torn and bleeding. But, Lord, it is only fair to say that it wasn't on Thy ground. I had wandered out of Thy pasture."

Like that honest shepherd, we find ourselves in difficulty only when we go our own way. The man who follows the Lord will always find sufficient strength and power to carry on. What God demands is the total consecration of every single one of us to His way of life.

Suppose a doctor making his rounds met a patient who told him, "I'm quite willing to follow your directions on those matters which seem to me to be good, but in other matters I will follow my own directions. I'll decide which of your orders I want to follow."

What would the doctor do with such a case? Surely he would not accept that patient; he would leave him to his own devices, saying, "I can do nothing for him, unless he puts his life into my hands without reservation, and unless he follows my instructions explicitly."

That is consecration. God, the Great Physician, must have our case placed in His hands without reservation. His directions must be explicitly followed, if we are to expect a cure. There is no problem God cannot solve, no burden He is not willing to bear, no fear He cannot conquer, if only we put complete trust in Him. Knowing how great God's love is should be enough to persuade us to trust in Him above all things.

"How much do you love me?" a mother asked her child.

"All the way to the stars and back again," the child answered, looking through the window at the starry sky above.

God through Christ has loved us all the way to heaven and back again. With His care there is nothing to fear.

TODAY'S THOUGHT: *The things that we love form the framework of our lives. Therefore, love God first and best.*

JANUARY 27

After the Storm, the Rainbow

Suffering produces endurance, and endurance produces character, and character produces hope. Romans 5:3, 4

In France, in 1812, three-year old Louis Braille was boring holes with an awl in a heavy piece of leather in his father's carpentry shop. The sharp awl slipped, and the resulting accident blinded him. Seventeen years later this totally blind youth invented the Braille System so that the sightless could read. We know full well how much the Braille System has benefited thousands of blind people around the world. Thus a tragedy in one man's life brought help to succeeding generations of the blind. He turned the dark cloud inside out and found the silver lining.

A physics teacher told his class that they could see much farther at night than in the daytime, because the stars are millions of light-years away. A nature lover pointed out that the woods may not be as lovely in the winter as in the spring, but we can see farther. So often we find that in hours of darkness and the wintry experiences of life, we are able to see more clearly the really important things of life. If only we are patient, God will show us the purpose of our difficulty.

The Christian remains cheerful through trials and in so doing exerts a powerful influence on others. I know a woman who is poor and heavily burdened, yet she is unfailingly cheerful. Long ago she resolved that she would never sadden anyone else with her troubles. She has laughed many times when she wanted to cry. She has tried to smile in the face of every misfortune. She closes every visit on a light-hearted note. This woman is much happier now than when she bemoaned every difficulty that came her way. Said Abraham Lincoln: "Every man is as happy as he decides to be!"

Here is a good resolution: I will bear my burdens, but never impose them on others. If I must fall in life's battle, let me fall with a smile, knowing that the God of power will lift me up again. Then I will understand when Jesus says, "Be of good cheer, I have overcome the world."

TODAY'S THOUGHT: *Some men owe the nobility of their lives to their uncounted difficulties.*

No Task Is Too Small

There is nothing better than that a man should enjoy his work, for that is his lot. Ecclesiastes 3:22

Desperately in need though the world is, it will never be saved by a few big lights, but by a multiplicity of lesser lights. God intends each of us to contribute our part to help dispel the world's darkness. We must not spend our time complaining about the insignificance of our particular talents. We may be vastly more important in God's plan than we dare dream.

An old legend tells about God creating the world. The story says that God gave to every living thing an angel to bless it and guard it. There was an angel for man, one for birds of the air, one for beasts of the forest, one for trees, and one for flowers. Every living thing, even the common grass, had its angel. But the angel of the common grass was not pleased with its commission. It was jealous because God had given to it only the common grass, while the other angels had beautiful flowers, tall trees, brilliantly colored birds, and other things that seemed so beautiful. Humiliated and full of envy, this angel went about proclaiming emphatically, "The old homely grass can just grow by itself. I will not take care of it." So the season passed, the leaves of the trees shriveled, the flowers died because the grass held no dew, and the cattle of the fields passed away because there was no grass to eat.

One after another of the angels threw themselves at the feet of the Lord God and begged His aid. At last man himself lifted his eyes to heaven and cried, "O Lord God, take me away, too. For my beautiful world is dead."

It was then that God turned to the angel of the common grass and asked, "Was it a great thing or a small thing that I asked you to do?"

In shame the angel of the common grass dropped to God's feet, asking forgiveness.

If we think that the task assigned to us is too small, let us remember that using it to glorify God's Name is greater gain than earthly fame.

TODAY'S THOUGHT: *Everyone on the team must do his best, the water boy as well as the captain.*

JANUARY 29

Every Believer a Minister

Truly, truly, I say to you, he who believes in me will also do the works that I do; and greater works than these will he do, because I go to the Father. John 14:12

Every one of us was meant to be a messenger of God. We all have a task to do in order that the world may be won for Him. In a sense we are apostles, sent forth to help each other draw closer to God.

Too many people think that only ministers are called upon to do this work. Ministers have their special tasks, but every Christian is a soldier in the great arena of life. The kingdom of God will not come nor will His "will be done, on earth as it is in heaven," unless every one of us is willing to take his place on the battlefield, and do the special job God has in mind for him.

The minister of a fruitful church was once asked, "How do you account for the fact that your congregation is so effective in winning souls for the kingdom? How can one minister do such a wonderful work?" His answer was this: "It is not my preaching just one sermon a Sunday to my congregation. Rather, my people listen to what God says through me, and then go out and preach the sermon by their living each day of the week. So, you see, we really have hundreds of preachers in our church."

As members of the Christian church, it is the duty of each and every one of us to help build the church, and strengthen the kingdom by setting a good example for others. We who are believers are called upon to show the unbelieving what it is to be a Christian. We who are of the church must indicate to the world by our living that we have been with Jesus. Daily we must, by power of God, resist sin in all that we do and say.

TODAY'S THOUGHT: *Speak up for the Savior; even if you cannot say exactly the right thing, say something.*

JANUARY 30

Success Within Your Grasp

Believe in the Lord your God, and you will be established; believe his prophets, and you will succeed. 2 Chronicles 20:20

Many people fail to do the little they could do, because constantly they complain about not being great people, not having great talents, not being able to make great contributions to life. Only a few are permitted to become great men, and make a name for themselves in the world, but every one of us can act his part honestly and honorably to the best of his ability. We can use our gifts, and not abuse them. We can strive to make the best out of our life, whatever our limitations. All of us can be truthful, honest, and faithful in the smallest things. All of us can do our duty in that particular area in which God has placed us.

Success is not what you do, but what you do with what you have. The significant life in the sight of God is not only the one which does something great or brilliant, but it is every life that does as well as it can.

Some soldiers are ordered to retreat in the thick of battle, while others are commanded to stay behind at their front line post and, if need be, to die there. So it is with us. Some are called to high places and others to low places, but in God's sight all are significant. Some have five talents, some only one. And we must all remember that we did not create these talents, they were given to us. We are only asked to use them wisely that they might continue to produce. Wherever we are, that is our place of duty, and if we try to do it well, we can be sure God is with us.

A famous philosopher once said, "We do not choose our own parts in life, and have nothing to do with these parts. Our simple duty is confined to playing them well. Happiness lies in yourself and in being master of yourself."

One becomes master of himself only as he allows God to come into his life to make everything that he does significant. God will grant His power to you today.

TODAY'S THOUGHT: *The man who thinks he can be happy without God is doing some foggy thinking.*

JANUARY 31

Take My Life

Create in me a clean heart, O God, and put a new and right spirit within me. Psalm 51:10

A mother had cut a bouquet of flowers for a friend in the hospital, and sent her little daughter to deliver it. When halfway there, the child decided that she would rather keep it for herself. She saved the bouquet, but to ease her conscience she took one flower to the sick woman. A few days later she took a second flower to the hospital.

Do you think this child obeyed her mother? No, indeed. She could have obeyed only by giving the entire bouquet to her mother's friend. God has asked that we give our entire life to Him. You shall love the Lord your God with all your heart, soul, mind, and strength. How often do we break off a little love to give Him now and then, and keep the rest for the world. If we are to find happiness and joy, He demands strict obedience.

"Would you advise a young Christian to do something for the Lord?" a man was asked.

"No," was the reply, "I would advise him to do everything for the Lord."

Many people wonder why things do not happen to them, why their lives are not filled with the riches which God so abundantly promised. They go through the motions of faith without putting them into practice. They may observe religious rituals. They may attend church. But they forget that going to church does not make a man a Christian, any more than taking the automobile to the garage repairs its knocks. To repair the automobile a mechanic must work on it. If a man is to be made whole, he must place his life in the hands of One who has the power to heal. This is the only way he can hope to mend his life.

Never forget that certain conditions must be met, if you are to live more abundantly. An athlete trains diligently to become a champion. A musician must practice for hours and days, for weeks and years, to become great. And every day without fail man must seek the presence of Christ to become truly Christian.

TODAY'S THOUGHT: *Seek first a job to do, then seek God's grace not only to begin it, but to continue working patiently at it until that job is done.*

FEBRUARY 1

You Can Emerge Victorious

The Lord is near to the brokenhearted, and saves the crushed in spirit. Psalm 34:18

Each of us should have the will to win, bending every effort to emerge victorious in life's race. Too many have what psychologists call a "defeatist" attitude. They start each day fearful they are going to be defeated.

A football coach watched his team bungle its plays. He knew the boys had the ability, but they did not seem to have the spirit. At the end of the first half, defeat seemed inevitable. As they trooped into the locker room the boys' shoulders drooped; they were a sorry lot. The coach called them together, gave them a pep talk, and reminded them of the strategy he wanted them to use. Together they went over the diagrams of the plays.

"Keep one thing in mind," he told them. "You have the ability to win. If you play your best, you will not be defeated. It is all up to you. Let's go out and get that victory."

Back on the field, no one could believe it was the same team. They were fired with new hope. They knew their coach had confidence in them, and they went on to score a decisive victory.

We Christians have a leader who can inspire us to victories beyond our greatest expectations. If only we will come to Him when we are dejected, He will show us the plan He has for our lives, as it is outlined in His Holy Word. Patiently He encourages us, saying, "With my help you can win." No matter what blocks seem to stand in our pathway, He will lead us across the goal line if we but heed His advice, and let Him call the plays. His ultimate goal for every one of us is victory over death.

England in 1940 faced what seemed certain disaster. Yet one man, Winston Churchill, rallied English morale to its highest point in history. If enough of us were inspired to do the same in our little islands of influence, many of today's groundless fears and "defeatist" attitudes would vanish. Be on the alert, for today you may meet someone who needs to be encouraged and inspired by the story of Jesus' victory over death.

TODAY'S THOUGHT: *If we are happy about the little day-by-day victories in our lives, how much greater ought our happiness be in Jesus' victory over death.*

FEBRUARY 2

God Sees Your Possibilities

As for me, I am poor and needy; but the Lord takes thought for me. Psalm 40:17

In one of England's cathedrals sunlight streams through a very special stained glass window, depicting facts and personalities of the Bible and the glorious truth of Christianity. Visitors are told that the craftsman who made the window used broken glass which other artists discarded. The craftsman had had a dream of beauty, and had accepted the challenge of using something rejected and worthless to fashion a masterpiece.

Whenever you begin to think that you do not amount to anything, remember that God wants to pick up the broken pieces of your life. The Master who commanded even the waste bits of bread to be gathered that nothing be lost will take your talents and abilities and mold you in His likeness.

Many of us miss happiness along life's way by depending too much upon ourselves. We ought to be honest like Mr. Moody who said, "I have had more trouble with D. L. Moody than with any man I know." The Bible challenges us to turn our lives over to God to see what He can do with them.

A stranger settled in our community. He was a lawyer and rarely left his legal files and books. The only recreation he allowed himself was an evening walk. Always alone, he paced along with his head down, a look of depression on his face. One day, falling into a chance conversation with a painter who had a studio in town, the lawyer confessed that he had made a tragic mistake in his life, and that it worried him deeply. The artist said nothing. But some weeks later he invited the lawyer to his studio, and asked him to judge a portrait he had painted. The lawyer was surprised to see a portrait of himself, standing erect with steadfast gaze.

"If you see that in me," he said, after standing silent for a few minutes, "then I can see it, too. If you think I can become that man, then I can, and I will."

And he did! Think of the possibilities God sees in you.

TODAY'S THOUGHT: *God is looking at us through the eyes of love. Try for one day to look at others like that, and you will want every day to be like that.*

FEBRUARY 3

Prayer Rules Out Oppression

Therefore confess your sins to one another, and pray for one another. James 5:16

Recently a friend told me of a certain business man, one of the most active in his city, a man with a happy, vibrant personality. My friend asked him how he always managed to be so cheerful.

"I notice that you face any problem unruffled, no matter how difficult it is."

"I have learned," the business man replied, "to set aside a little time each day to be alone with God. Usually I shut myself in my office, and refuse to accept any phone calls. I spend the time talking to God and letting Him talk to me. An amazing calm comes into my soul, no matter how full of stress the particular day is."

Countless people have learned this business man's secret, and have discovered how glorious life can be. Many others, however, are cut off from the source of power, living by their own strength, rejecting the help of Him who stands ready to assist in every time of need.

We need to take more time to talk to God in prayer. We need to notice the beautiful things around us every day.

Another man tells how he gets a touch of the lovely into his l i f e whenever he wills. He may spend time in a garden, admiring the flowers, or drop into an art gallery, or merely place a beautiful rose on his desk where he can see it. Thus, he does not become oppressed by the numerous duties of life, and remembers constantly that life is like a growing thing.

Sometimes a rose in a vase may mean more than any other touch of beauty in a room. I remember reading of a woman who had a rose within sight whenever possible. Her father, a country pastor, had presented her with a rose not long before he died. Giving her the flower, he said he expected her to make her life and character as beautiful as that red rose. He wanted her to live and bloom, bringing sweetness and beauty to others, just as roses do. As that daughter grew up, worked her way through school, and finally raised a family of her own, she always kept a rose before her, and lived as her father had wished.

So our heavenly Father desires that we show our love for Him by living inspired lives. The life of Jesus is our perfect example.

TODAY'S THOUGHT: *Many a person who thinks twice before addressing his fellow men does not bother to think at all before addressing his God.*

FEBRUARY 4

Nature Proclaims the Resurrection

There will be a resurrection of both the just and the unjust.
Acts 24:15

The Master stood one day in a situation where He was face to face with the decay of death. Suddenly He said to Lazarus, "Come forth," and a miracle occurred.

Today some of us are walking corpses, living entombed by our sin, bound hand and foot by the winding cloths of evil habits. To us the Master gives the same command, "Come forth." Unless we hear and obey, we shall never realize the wonders of living, nor what this resurrection experience can mean.

All of God's beautiful world is preaching resurrection. Every budding tree and springing flower, every singing bird, is a preacher from God saying, "Wake thou that sleepest, and arise from the dead." Arise from what or to what? Your own heart can answer that question. Perhaps already you are certain the life you now live is worthy of one for whom Christ died and rose again from the dead.

What is your chief aim and what do you live for? Some of you answer that your principle pursuit is happiness, and that since God would have us happy, there can be no sin in that. Are you quite sure you are not confusing pleasure with happiness, putting one in the place of the other? The pursuit of pleasure alone does not bring happiness. Pursuing pleasure, we love to do those things which we ought not to do, and we neglect those things which we ought t o d o. We choose a thing not because it is right, but because it gives us pleasure.

Life lived with Jesus Christ means something different. It means that we learn to deny ourselves, and to seek God's will rather than our own. It means that we do not ask whether a thing is pleasant, but whether it is right. We desire not to do as we like, but simply to do our duty. This is the true and happy life.

TODAY'S THOUGHT: *With God as our gardener, we cannot help but to grow a better tomorrow.*

FEBRUARY 5
Life Must Be Well Rooted

But these have no root, they believe for a while and in time of temptation fall away. Luke 8:13

An old Greek was approached one day and asked by a visitor, "I have observed how happy you are despite your many years. How did you attain it?"

The old philosopher replied, "Look over there, and see the fine trees and orchards which I possess. Well, I have them because I planted them as a young man. In youth I laid the foundation for my life. I did not wait until I was old to begin to build for this day."

Have you ever watched the trees bending almost double in a heavy wind? Did you not marvel that in spite of the wind's power not one of them was uprooted? How could they stand the strain?

If you have ever dug up an old stump you know the answer. Roots in every direction anchor the stump to mother earth. It takes plenty of ax swinging and grubbing to unearth it. Roots are the secret of why trees stand in the wind. But trees do not begin to grow roots after they have matured. Far from it. When only seedlings they prepare for the future, in the very beginning of life, sending out their roots.

Roots are the secret of human greatness. The way in which a man faces the winds of discouragement, despair, and defeat depends upon his roots. Those who have roots of faith, courage, perseverance, love, and understanding have the strength to live heroically. Great men, like giant trees, have deep roots.

We need to develop our faith life, sending out new tendrils day by day. We need to decide our life's direction. If we are wise, we will follow the Master's plan, asking Him for guidance along the way. An old story tells of a university professor talking to a group of his students about the game of life. "But how are we going to play the game of life?' one of them asked. "We don't know where the goalposts are."

How can we hope to win by playing according to our own rules? Men have tried it before and always have failed. There is only one way to win the game of life. It is to seek and follow God's way.

TODAY'S THOUGHT: *The great God who set in motion the solar system is infinitely more interested in an individual man's movements. One verse proves that: "What shall it profit a man if he gain the whole world but lose his soul!"*

FEBRUARY 6

Winners Never Quit

For thou didst gird me with the strength for the battle.

Psalm 18:39

There is an old Dutch proverb which reads, "No May lasts seven months." If life were smooth sailing all the time, it would be stale and uninteresting. We appreciate the calm doubly after a storm. We need to learn the lesson of fighting on through the battle to victory.

If ours is to be a victorious life, we must remember that a winner never quits and a quitter never wins. The challenges of life are almost always stepping stones to higher ground. Bobby Jones once told Grantland Rice, "I never learned anything from the games I won. All I know about golf I learned from the matches I lost."

When apparent defeats come we should remember the truth spoken by the Apostle Paul. "In everything God works for good." Remember how earnestly Paul prayed that his tormenting physical affliction cease. He had a "thorn in the flesh," a baffling, mysterious thing which seemed to hinder his doing God's work effectively. Annoyed and pained by this affliction, he could not see how any personal good could possibly come of it. Finally God said to him, "My grace is sufficient for you, for my power is made perfect in weakness." It was at that point that Paul said, "In everything God works for good with those who love him."

Many times when we survey the record our lives have written, we see how God has been ever present, using for good everything that happened. At the time perhaps we were prompted to say, "Why did God allow this?" We did not know then. But in looking back, we realize that God never allows anything to happen to harm His children.

No matter how difficult or how big your problem may seem right now, do not try to handle it all at once. If you do, it will press you to the earth. Begin to solve the problem by taking one step at a time. If you fail, try again. Ultimately you will find the right solution, and God will be constantly with you, giving you the strength to conquer your failures and the guidance to lead you out of your problem. With this assurance in his heart, a child of God can face life unafraid.

TODAY'S THOUGHT: *Watch the way a man faces discouragement and you will know the depth of his faith.*

37

FEBRUARY 7

All Men Must Face Death

He will swallow up death for ever, and the Lord God will wipe away tears from all faces. Isaiah 25:8

The Lord told us to be ready always. For at any moment He may appear again, this time to end our waiting and hoping, and to lift us out of trials and temptation. Or at any moment death may cut short our earthly pilgrimage. Therefore, for each one of us it is true in one way or another that "the end of all things is at hand." That is to say, the things which belong to life.

The end of earthly greatness, wealth, and pleasure is at hand. No one will live on earth forever. This was not God's choice for us. It was man's when he chose to sin. So it is that, no matter how mighty a man may appear to be in the eyes of the world, there is one enemy who is more than his match, the enemy which all men must face, namely, death. Whether rich or poor, learned or unlettered, it is all the same when the shadow of death appears.

All earthly friendships must one day end. Then comes the parting and separation until the glorious reunion above. Have you ever gone to a great railroad station, or a busy international airport, or the pier of an ocean liner just to observe? There husbands are saying good-by to wives, children parting from their parents, friends bidding each other adieu. The whole world is much like that, full of partings and farewells.

Morover, the end of opportunities is also at hand. We should be sure to make use of our opportunities, because once they are lost they do not return. The Greeks, indeed, were wise to write upon the walls of one of their temples, "Know your opportunity." God has given everyone a place in the world and a chance of doing work for Him. We must redeem our time, complete our task before it is too late.

Then, too, the end of our trial and waiting is at hand. Now we see in a mirror dimly, but in a little while we shall be able to understand more clearly. Now we are all tried and tempted, but in a little while we can take leave of our earthly Calvaries, our places of crucifixion, for the joys of Paradise. We must prepare ourselves for this great adventure, which commences the moment life is ended. In this world's training school the Christian must learn that flowers cannot grow where weeds are allowed to flourish.

TODAY'S THOUGHT: *Science can teach us to control nature, but only God can teach us to control our lives.*

FEBRUARY 8

Be Subject to God's Will

For you have need of endurance, so that you may do the will of God and receive what is promised. Hebrews 10:36.

God is on duty 24 hours a day We can go to Him at any time. Always He answers our prayers, but He does so at the time He thinks best. He is never reluctant to give us His gifts, but demands that we be persistent in our asking. And we must be satisfied if He tells us to wait.

Think of the Apostle Paul. After his conversion he wanted to go out and preach. But God was not ready for Paul to proclaim the Gospel. There had to be a training period and so Paul had to wait three years.

When life puts you in a corner like that when you are eager to be doing, or God tells you through a time-consuming illness or frustration to wait, what happens? Do you give up? Too many people just quit. They are not willing to accept God's time table in answering their request.

There was once a man, intent on taking his life. His pastor pleaded for him to wait just one more day. The man was ready to throw up the sponge, because he could not find a job. However, the very next morning, he landed his job. He felt eternally grateful that he had followed his pastor's advice and not given up. Soon he readjusted himself to society, and today he is making a real contribution to life.

It is most important for us to cling to this faith. For ultimately all things do "work together" for them that seek God and His will. God is not hiding from us. If we seek Him with our whole heart, we shall surely find Him.

Do not be a quitter and give up. Whenever life faces you with major problems or decisions and you are tempted, think of a certain little boy on the skating rink. He was spending more time upon the ice than on his skates.

Finally someone said, "Sonny, you had better stop. You might fall down some time and hurt yourself."

The little lad replied, "Listen, Mister, I didn't buy these skates to quit on. I bought these skates to learn to skate on."

We need some of that spirit as life hems us in a corner.

TODAY'S THOUGHT: *Every player in the game of life ought to be ready for the moment when his signal is called to carry the ball.*

FEBRUARY 9

We, Too, Have Gethsemanes

We rejoice in our sufferings, knowing that suffering produces endurance, and endurance produces character, and character produces hope. Romans 5:3, 4

One day I walked a short distance down the road from the city of Jerusalem until around a bend of the road I saw clearly the Mount of Olives. Just ahead of me the Garden of Gethsemane nestled on a low rise of a foothill to that storied mountain. I thought to myself, "One cannot reach the heights without going through the valleys."

We shy away from the troubles and burdens of life, and tell God we cannot understand why they needs must come. We forget that some defeats are more triumphant than victories. In the early thirties, when a grasshopper plague was laying waste the Midwestern states, someone asked a farmer what he was going to do with the pests.

"Well, they took most of my crops," he said. "They have just about eaten everything. But, you know, I've gathered about ten tons of them and have stored them in the barn. I am going to feed those grasshoppers to the chickens this summer. I figure if I can't raise a crop, I'll raise chickens. I think I am going to come out ahead!"

Jesus did not lead an easy life. Constantly, He had to bear the taunts of His fellow men. He passed through many Gethsemanes, but He knew that these were incidents on the way to glory. He said, "And for their sake I consecrate myself." He taught us to take honey from the carcass, and to benefit even from our failures. For example, we ought not merely to endure our sickness. We should get gain out of it. Theodore Roosevelt once called his critics, "the unpaid guardians of my soul." There is not a single disappointment or defeat that will not yield a profit if we invest it in the right way.

If something happens to you today, something disagreeable and hard to take, the Christian's reaction is not, "How can I escape it, or how can I bear it?" The Christian asks rather, "How can I use it?" He makes of it a scaffolding with which to build a more abundant life.

TODAY'S THOUGHT: *To think a problem insoluble is to make it so.*

FEBRUARY 10

Prayer Must Reflect Faith

Hearken to the sound of my cry, my King and my God, for to thee do I pray. Psalm 5:2

Do you believe in this great promise, "If you ask anything of the Father, he will give it to you in my name"?

"How can that be true," you say, "when so many prayers remain unanswered?"

This is the reason: simply because some prayers are offered without faith. Our Lord never worked a miracle unless the asker showed faith. So with our prayers. We must not only wish that our prayers would be heard, but be sure they will be, even though at the time we may not know the best means of their being granted.

Some prayers are unacceptable because they are not offered in the right way. Like foolish children, we have prayed for something hurtful for us to be granted, and in His great mercy God does not grant our request.

Prayer must reveal a responding love. We do not ask our favors of a stern task-master. We go instead to a friend. If you are afraid of God, you cannot pray to Him aright. If you love Him, however, you are certain that even your ill-considered requests will be understood.

There was a little boy whose mother lay ill in the hospital. The child fancied that his mother did not love him, for otherwise would she have left him? So he determined to send her a letter to find out. Quite unable to write, he scrawled all over the paper, as little children will, and then begged his friend to carry it to his mother. The messenger laughed at the strange letter, claiming that no one could make it out.

"Mother will understand," said the child.

When Eddie's note was given to her she recognized at once the work of a child's fingers, and understood the meaning.

As often as not our prayers are put together like Eddie's scrawled note. Yet, if we are sincere as we turn to God in prayer, we can be confident that He can make out our request and understand. What a privilege to carry everything to God in prayer!

TODAY'S THOUGHT: *When thoughts of God rise up in the hearts of men, that may be a form of prayer.*

FEBRUARY 11

God Grants Pardon and Peace

Peace I leave with you; my peace I give to you. John 14:27

How wonderful it is to have faith in a changeless God, one who is the same yesterday, today, and tomorrow. The works of our hands will perish and decay. The hopes and plans of our hearts are often destroyed. Those dear to us are maybe taken from our midst in order that we who remain may fix our affections on things above and not on things of the earth. The change and decay and uncertainty of all earthly things should lead us to seek first the kingdom of God and His righteousness. They should lead us to reach for those imperishable gifts from an unchanging God. Pardon and peace, faith and joy, hope and life eternal—these gifts never change. The gifts and boons of the world soon pass away, while God alone and His proffered blessings remain.

We live so far removed from the time when God revealed himself to man in the flesh that to many of us the picture has become dim and obscure. Innumerable changes have occurred in the world since the cross of Calvary, so many in fact, that we are prone to think of God as having changed also. Men have grown to think light of sin, and they live as though God too winks at sin. They think of God as the old man upstairs, grown indulgent with age. But what a fatal and mistaken thought this is.

God's justice is unchanging. Today's God is the same God who said yesterday, "The soul that sins shall die. The son shall not suffer for the iniquity of the father, nor the father suffer for the iniquity of the son: . . . the wickedness of the wicked shall be upon himself."

The Son of God was crucified on Calvary so long ago that some of us have forgotten that our sins helped nail Him to the tree. Whenever we are tempted to think lightly of sin, we would do well to kneel at the foot of the cross, and look into the eyes of our suffering Savior. "He himself bore our sins in his body on the tree, that we might die to sin and live to righteousness. By his wounds you have been healed."

TODAY'S THOUGHT: *Man could not, unaided, climb out of the pit his sin has dug. But Christ's sacrifice on Calvary, what was it but Christ leaping into that pit to lift man out?*

42

FEBRUARY 12

Are You Sympathy-Starved?

Render true judgments, show kindness and mercy each to his brother. Zechariah 7:9

Thousands of people in the world are starving for want of a little sympathy. Often many of us say, "Oh, we wish we could do something for them. But the task is so big, and the little that we could do won't make much of a difference, anyway."

We forget that it is not the value of a gift that makes it precious, but the spirit in which it is given. A wilted dandelion, gathered by a loving child for his parent, is much more than the rare and costly orchid from the rich man's greenhouse. All that some of the sad and lonely people in the world needs is to know that you have not forgotten them and that you will help as much as you can. Often as I travel about the world people have turned to me and said, "But nobody cares!" They suffer from a lack of "belonging." What courage and hope would be theirs if they only could believe that they were not forgotten. If our world is ever to know peace, we must be far more unselfish than we have been.

In one of the great battles of an ancient war a hero had received his death wound. They put a private soldier's blanket under his head, and it gave him much momentary relief. He asked what it was.

"It is only a soldier's blanket."

He insisted on knowing to whom the blanket belonged, and they told him it was the blanket of a soldier named Roy.

"Then see that Roy has his blanket this very night."

The Master said, "I was hungry and you gave me food, I was a stranger and you welcomed me, I was naked and you clothed me, I was sick and you visited me." If you want to do something for the Master, do something for your neighbors who are His people. Stymied in other directions, we can still show kindness.

A man visited a hospital and began talking to one of the most wretched of the patients. Suddenly the sick man burst into tears. As soon as he was able to speak he said, "Forgive me, sir, but I cannot remember anyone speaking more kindly to me than you. I have lived with a broken heart."

Live close to God and He will give you medicine with which to heal the broken hearts which you may touch along life's way.

TODAY'S THOUGHT: *How wonderful it would be to live close enough to God to hear His every whisper!*

43

FEBRUARY 13

His Love Is a Fact

As the Father has loved me, so have I loved you; abide in my love. John 15:9

At a certain orphanage the infant mortality rate has been notably reduced, not by any wonder drug, but by a method that has been tested and tried for years. An attending nurse holds each motherless child for an hour each day, in order that the little one may feel that it really has a mother. This tender loving care cut the death rate of the orphans less than a year old almost in half. It seems impossible, but it is true.

Yes, love is the best medicine in all the world, for it can help master any kind of suffering. All of us have experienced a shower of love during a period of sickness. The cards, letters, and visits we received assured us that we were not alone. We knew that others were thinking of us, and this comforting knowledge of love helped us to brave our difficulty and gave us courage when it seemed the odds were stacked against us.

Doctors have known for a long time that love has more power than drugs. Hatred and resentments combine to disease the body and destroy the soul. They directly oppose the creative spiritual power of love which aids the forces of healing.

But most important of all is the assurance of God's love as He keeps sending us His message of hope in times of tribulation. He wants us to know that we belong to Him and that He is deeply concerned about our lot in life, whatever it may be. Not a day passed in Jesus' life on earth but that He evidenced His great love for man.

During an afternoon call a woman asked her pastor to read to her from the Bible. He chose the familiar words, "Lo, I am with you always," and then remarked, "What a lovely promise that is."

"My dear friend," the woman replied, "that is not a promise. That is a fact."

Let us always remember that the love of God for us is not merely a promise, but the declaration of a glorious fact. His presence is an inspiring certainty that can lead us out of the shadows of any darkness into the light of glorious living.

TODAY'S THOUGHT: *We spend large sums and long hours for the things of the world. Yet we are known to complain of having to spend a brief hour considering the things of God.*

44

FEBRUARY 14

Charity Means Love

But concerning love of the brethen you have no need to have any one write to you, for you yourselves have been taught by God to love one another. 1 Thessalonians 4:9

Old Rip Van Winkle is not the only one to open his eyes wide, amazed by change. As one travels about the world, it is surprising to observe the changes that have taken place since the last visit. Miracles have literally occurred, as undeveloped countries have with one great leap caught up with progress. Factories have been built, roads constructed, and great engineering feats performed. But above and beyond these, changes that have taken place in human life are the one thing that alone is immortal. Love lives on forever. Whereas all material changes have the fatal flaw, only love will last when the east sun is dead and the stars snuffed out.

Paul puts love ahead of all the Christian graces. Without true charity one cannot do any good deed. With it, even something as seemingly insignificant as a cup of water has value. "Love never ends." Love reigns immortal, as the last of the multitudinous seas dries up, because love is divine. "God is love." The more we seek grace to love Him and our fellow men, the more godlike we become.

The Jesus-way differs from all other religions because it is the gospel of love. Other religions may teach men to fear god. In them the deity is made out a cruel and arbitrary tyrant, intent on destroying his people in return for their wrongs. Heathens bow before their deity all atremble, since he is about to let loose a swift arrow of vengeance. They try to please them with bloody sacrifices and by inflicting sadistic tortures. One's heart breaks over the black darkness in which they live and the sad, beaten look on their faces. For their's is a life devoid of hope and joy.

At the heart of our gospel is God on the cross for us, His erring children. It shows the Master going about doing good, healing the sick, opening the eyes of the blind, comforting the sorrowful, and at last dying that His people might live. The whole of the gospel is in these words: "You shall love the Lord your God with all your heart, and with all your soul, and with all your strength, and with all your mind; and your neighbor as yourself." Apply this acid test of your faith: Do you possess love?

TODAY'S THOUGHT: *Where there is but little love, we see the faults of others through a magnifying glass and our own through the big end of a telescope.*

FEBRUARY 15

Get Down from Your High Horse

I commune with my heart in the night; I meditate and search my spirit. Psalm 77:6

No one has any way of knowing what a day may bring forth. This is something for which to be devoutly thankful. We can be certain of one thing. No matter what may happen, whether the hours are to be filled with joy or trouble, we possess a Savior who is the same yesterday, today, and tomorrow, and who gives us the power to face life with a smile.

An old Christian prayed a prayer that each of us could well use each day: "O God, I do not ask for poverty or riches. Whatever may be Your will for me, give me also a heart humble enough to accept what pleases You to bestow."

God promises us His power and strength. He tells us that if we pray to Him with sincere and penitent hearts He will give everything we need. Furthermore, He assures us of courage to live every day with hearts that know a peace the world cannot give.

Every day presents a new page in our book of life. In spite of yesterday's troubles that page can be spread with hope. With the Good Shepherd guiding, we shall not be led astray. No matter what happens if we follow closely, we shall have a greater store of hope at the day's end than when it began.

Some years ago at a practice of Handel's oratorio, "The Messiah," the soloist sang the strain, "I know that my Redeemer liveth!" Her notes were clear and beautiful, but before she had finished the old conductor stopped her, saying, "My good woman, I don't think you really believe that your Redeemer lives."

With a look of amazement at his daring, the soloist turned to reply, "Why I most certainly do believe it."

"Well, then sing it from your heart," he said.

Once again she began the beautiful refrain, and forgetting herself she sang out of her own experience. When she finished there was a hush. The old conductor said quietly, "You really do believe. You have just told me that."

If we truly believed that our Redeemer lives and is ever-present, what is there possibly to fear? Of whom shall I be afraid? We have it on God's promise and Word. What is left is for us to accept and believe it. Joy will come with such a faith.

TODAY'S THOUGHT: *The believer's song of salvation drowns out the croak of fear from his heart.*

FEBRUARY 16

Detours May Be Necessary

Be patient in tribulation, be constant in prayer. Romans 12:12

Sometimes, when driving along the highway at a pleasant clip, we come occasionally to detour signs. We grumble impatiently, and pause to glare at the barrier in the road as if it were to blame. The detour usually is rough and dusty, and lengthens our trip provokingly. Yet the route change is most unavoidable and if we only are patient, it soon brings us back on the highway.

Life's highway likewise has detours. Perhaps sickness intervenes, or we miss a goal we had set our heart on. Yet if we but follow God's directions, we will overcome the difficulty, however insurmountable it may seem. Though we have been forced to exchange the smooth road for a rough one, where we inch forward only with bump and jolt, the highway may show up at the next turn. For us, as for Christ, the way of the cross leads home.

Lives lived always in unclouded sunlight are not always the most beautiful, just as trips without detours are not always the most rewarding. When touched by rays from the Sun of Righteousness, even a life filled with sorrow and struggle can yet inspire many. What blessings stem from such lives! Like their Master, the Man of Sorrows, they were full of threatening clouds. But they were lighted by a rainbow at long last.

The life of Helen Keller knew two such black clouds. Her double handicaps were blindness and deafness, with accompanying dumbness. But indomitable Helen also had a rainbow, namely, her faith in God. Faith guiding her, she learned to read and write and do many things for herself. She even learned to speak in the curious tones of one who has never heard sound. After graduating from college, she devoted herself to helping the handicapped by lecturing and writing, and stabbing others awake to see their need.

Helen Keller did not allow handicaps to thwart progress. She wrote , "I thank God for my handicaps! Through them, I have found myself, my work, and my God."

TODAY'S THOUGHT: *Too much sunshine can turn a life into a desert.*

FEBRUARY 17

God Alone Grants True Success

A faithful man will abound with blessings, but he who hastens to be rich will not go unpunished. Proverbs 28:20

One of the greatest personal tragedies that can befall us is to walk through life with our eyes closed and unseeing. We thereby miss the many opportunities of serving God and our fellow men. If we but open our eyes and look about, we shall see many who need our help not only with their big problems but with the little ones, too. No day will pass but that we shall find opportunities for service. Wherever a man's path takes him he can find someone who will need him.

George Bernard Shaw once said, "There is no doubt that Christianity is the best way of life. If we could only just get someone to practice it."

What a different world we would then have! What a different commuity ours would be, if those who go to church on Sunday morning would live the gospel they have heard in their daily associations.

We would be different individuals, too. No one can be truly successful, and at the same time find joy within himself, unless he works for something bigger than himself. Much physical illness is really caused by people simply being self-centered. People think only in terms of their own problems, bemoaning their lot. Rather than feeling grateful for what they possess, they look only at the things they do not have. They try to get and hoard everything for themselves, and fail completely to be concerned about their neighbor who has less.

One day a young man said, "Watch me. I am really going out and make some big money. I am going to make it early so that I can retire at forty. Then I will look around to see what else life might have that is worth doing."

Well, he made his fortune! But at forty he found himself in a hospital, the victim of a complete breakdown.

His doctor told him, "The trouble with you, young man, is that you have taken too much from life and given back too little. You are obsessed by self. No one can possibly make that way of life work."

The physically and spiritually healthy person is the one who follows Christ and forgets self, thinking of others.

TODAY'S THOUGHT: *There is nothing wrong with a one-track mind, as long as that track leads to life eternal.*

FEBRUARY 18

Faith Looks Beyond

He who believes in him is not condemned; he who does not believe is condemned already, because he has not believed in the name of the only Son of God. John 3:18

Faith is a solid foundation, holding our lives steady whatever winds may buffet. It is anchored to Christ, the Rock of Ages. Faith gives peace even when "sorrows like sea billows roll." It gives songs in the darkest night. No matter what happens, having faith we can say, "It is well, it is well with my soul." Whatever thunderbolts the world may hurl at the soul's inner castle, the faithful souls resist because they know a strength beyond and above their own. That unlimited strength God will supply.

A Christian is not promised a life free of trials and afflictions. He is promised that there will always be a way out. Those who truly believe can never be defeated. Someone there is who watches over them. The Father's hand of love will never be withdrawn in tribulation's testing. He will steady us and keep us from a breakdown. However overwhelming the difficulty, He will supply the needed strength.

Think of the infinite love of Jesus. It is pictured for me in these simple lines, "Wide, wide as the ocean, High as the heavens above, Deep, deep as the deepest sea, Is my Saviour's love. I, though so unworthy, still am a child of His care. For His Word teaches me, That His love reaches me everywhere!"

Too many of us focus on our immediate troubles, rather than on the rifts and the blue skies that show through, giving promise of a sunny day. When will we learn to look beyond our Calvaries to God's Easter, which comes to all who have faith?

A man studied violin under a famous teacher. He was an experienced, powerful personality with a very gentle face.

"Always remember," the master told his pupil, "that to play good music you must keep your eyes on a distant star."

To live a blessed life, you must keep looking beyond the horizon, knowing that if you but walk arm in arm with the Almighty, every day can be more wonderful than the day before.

TODAY'S THOUGHT: *Faith never fails. It levels all boundaries, surmounts all obstacles, and flies beyond all limitations.*

FEBRUARY 19

God Is Ours and We Are His

Lo, I am with you always, to the close of the age. Matthew 28:20

It is so important that we cling to the faith that tells us no man walks alone. One of the most trying sicknesses is loneliness. Man has this promise from God: He will be a friend that sticks closer than any brother. He will never leave him nor forsake him. Though man may flee to the ends of the earth, God will be there before him.

Man just cannot get along without God. We are faced with problems demanding solution. We may think we are strong enough to handle these situations by ourselves. But it is then that God must humble us and teach us that, unless we seek His strength, we cannot hope to make it.

We ought to remember that God belongs to everybody, and that it is our responsibility who know Him to share His message with all the world. Many people suffer today simply because they do not know the gospel of Jesus Christ and all that it means. In Bombay, India, for example, a 32-year-old father took his two-and-one-half-year-old daughter to a stone altar where his particular sect worships its mud god. Taking his healthy child by the heels, the father then kept hitting her head against the stone altar until she died. Think of it, it is almost 2,000 years since Christ lived and taught, and still such cruel practices persist! Have we listened to His entreaty, "Go and make disciples"? Unless we accept those marching orders, we can never fully know the peace that He gives.

Can it be that we think only of the security and well-being of ourselves and our own loved ones? No wonder we are not inspired to share with others!

One night a mother was putting her little girl to bed. The girl looked out of the window and saw the moon.

"Mother, is that moon God's light?"

"Of course, my dear."

"Doesn't God ever turn off His light and go to sleep?"

"No," the mother said, "because God loves us so much He always stays awake to watch over us. He never sleeps."

The little girl snuggled deep in her comforters. "I'll not be afraid ever to go to sleep if God always stays awake."

When faith assures us of His presence then we, too, will have nothing to fear.

TODAY'S THOUGHT: *Christ can set you free from every fear that would destroy you.*

FEBRUARY 20

We Have a Pattern for Living

The steps of a man are from the Lord, and he establishes him in whose way he delights; though he fall, he shall not be cast headlong.

Psalm 37:23, 24

For all sorts and conditions of men, and in all circumstances, the Master has given us a pattern for living. His life is a perfect example to humanity. The gospel story has little to say concerning the first thirty years of Jesus' life. They have been called "the hidden years." About all we know of Him in those years is that He who later humbled himself even to the cross worked with Joseph, His father, at the carpenter's bench. For years He lived all unnoticed and unknown by His world. He who was destined to be the Lord of lords and the King of kings, by His faithfulness at humble tasks taught the world the sacredness of life's duties and the dignity and worth of labor.

We can learn from this to be content to do our duty wherever God may put us. We should work on, humbly and faithfully, unseeking of men's praise.

Jesus as a man was like us in all things, except that He had no sin. He faced the same trials and troubles. He lived the sort of life any man must live who works for daily bread. His example, therefore, is not one just to be praised and to be observed from a distance. It is a living pattern to be followed closely in our everyday life.

The Master never really laid aside His power or His sonship with God while He dwelt among us robed in the veil of flesh. But He never used these vast powers for personal gain or advancement. He spoke with authority. He healed the sick and raised the dead. He pardoned the sinner. Yet, despite this power, He remained humble. He never sought place or preferment. Always He remained meek and lowly in heart.

Here we have a true test with which to try our religion. If we are stiff-necked and proud, feeling superior, strutting of position and wealth, it reveals a weakness in our life. Let us always remember that Christ, the only perfect Man, was meek and lowly of heart. Let us follow in His steps.

TODAY'S THOUGHT: *No man can successfully lead a double life, being puffed up and proud before men while feigning humbleness before God.*

51

FEBRUARY 21

Salvation Is the Only Security

Blessed be the Lord, who daily bears us up; God is our salvation.
Psalm 68:19

Modern man has found what he has been searching for, a new god whom he has chosen to call "material security." Many have fooled themselves into believing that if they can only accumulate "things," and pyramid "things" on which to perch, then they will know security at last. As a nation we have invested billions of dollars in planes to carry the atom and hydrogen bomb to any part of the world. We have erred in thinking that security can be manufactured. But in spite of all these inventions of man's creative genius, we are today more fearful than ever. Too long have we depended upon our own strength. In spite of man's vaunted genius, he has not the capacity to compete with God, who alone can satisfy our every need.

One day Jesus presided at a campaign report meeting. The seventy disciples had returned from a missionary journey, and came to give Him an account of their activities. Sent out to witness in behalf of the kingdom of God, they were overjoyed with the results. "Lord," they said gloatingly, "even the demons are subject to us in your name!"

The Master saw at once that their emphasis was in the wrong place. Here they were exulting over the demons being subject to them, whereas they should have been happy because by the grace of God, they were children of the heavenly Father.

So the Master turned and said, "Nevertheless do not rejoice in this, that the spirits are subject to you; but rejoice that your names are written in heaven."

People frequently ask, "How can I know that I am saved?" Man, you could not save a straw on that great and awful day. Your salvation does not depend in the most infinitissimal minutiae on what you have done or on what you have failed to do. However, God can save you. If you have faith in the Lamb of God, who takes away the sin of the world, you can be sure beyond all peradventure that you are saved, indeed. Instead of being a "hope so" Christian you can be a "know so." "Nothing in my hand I bring." No human addition whatsoever is needed to make your salvation sure. It is all of faith "lest any man should boast."

TODAY'S THOUGHT: *Our faith alone can give us solid security and a refuge against "that day."*

FEBRUARY 22

Sin Can Cut the Power

Depart from evil, and do good; seek peace, and pursue it.
Psalm 34:14

A farmer and his household waited expectantly for the first family car to be delivered. They were all elated when it finally arrived. But after they had driven it for a few months, some trouble developed. Since no one in the family knew the least thing about mechanics, the car seemed doomed to uselessness. The motor that once purred so smoothly and served so well now could not climb even the slightest grade in low gear. Finally a neighbor hit on the trouble: particles of dirt and sediment were clogging the fuel line. He unscrewed the small pipe leading to the carburetor, and attaching it to a tire pump he ingeniously blew out the dirt. His idea worked. The car soon was running normally, and gave promise of delivering all its old power.

Several times after that this same trouble developed. But now they knew the cause and how to clear the clogged pipe. No car can run with normal power as long as there is dirt in the fuel line.

Now our Christian life is like that car. So-called "small" sins become the clogging dirt in the power line. Pride, selfishness, greed, and lies—these are the things that keep God's power from reaching us. These and other so-called little sins must be conquered, if our Christian life is to progress smoothly again.

God has made available to us the power sufficient to surmount any hill of difficulty on life's roadway. If we move on our own strength alone, we shall fail. In His strength, however, we can surely succeed.

Some automobiles today are supercharged. When you press the accelerator to the floor, an added carburetor gives an extra spurt of speed, enabling you to pass every other car on the highway.

We, too, can have that added power. God has promised it to us in needed quantity to defeat any enemy or surmount any obstacle in the world.

Why move along at this "slow dying rate," when impowered by God you can fly past the pestilential swamp lands of sin and its ugly cities of greed, on to the shining city of God.

TODAY'S THOUGHT: *Sin is like quicksand. It will suck us below the surface and suffocate us, if we fail to grasp God's proffered hand to pull us up on salvation's solid ground.*

FEBRUARY 23

We Would Be Generous

Zaccheus . . . said to the Lord, "Behold, Lord, the half of my goods I give to the poor." Luke 19:8

A small boy entered a cash-and-carry store. He held in his hand a clean milk bottle in which two dimes and two pennies had been placed.

"I want a bottle of milk," he told the cashier, "but since I am going to the movies, can I leave the bottle here until I get back?"

She told him to put it on the counter beside the cash register. Two and one-half hours later he returned, and the cashier handed him his milk bottle. He could not understand what had happened for it was almost one third filled with nickels, dimes, and pennies. The only explanation the cashier could offer was that people, seeing the bottle with its coins on the counter, concluded that it was a collection for a worthy cause. So, without even as much as asking what the cause might be, they dropped their change left when paying their grocery bills.

Basically, we are all blindly and sentimentally generous, for we have learned that in giving and loving only can we find satisfaction. Not every one is engrossed in chasing the almighty dollar. There are many, many who know values out and beyond a hoard of coins or things.

A government officer related about the time when he was traveling through the great Smoky Mountains of Tennessee. The depression was then at its lowest dip, and the government's relief program was making allotments to impoverished farmers for seed and stock and needed improvements. Another government officer told him about a woman who, though living all alone, had yet managed to make a living from her scant two acres of ground. She was asked, "If the government allowed you $200, what would you do with it?"

The woman thought for a moment and finally said, "I reckon I would give it to the poor." It is just this kind of love which you find in the hearts of all who really appreciate what God has done for them. God so loved us the He gave the best that heaven could boast of, His lovely Son, Jesus. He has given us all that we have. He requires only that we keep giving until He stops giving to us.

TODAY'S THOUGHT: *The man who is stingy with the little that he has is only fooling himself, if he thinks he would be generous if he had more.*

FEBRUARY 24

Fill That Empty Heart!

Therefore choose life, that you and your descendants may live.
Deuteronomy 30:19

A young couple sitting in the bus station one day listened to the music coming over a public address system. Suddenly they heard a beautiful hymn. People were impressed as the young couple sat in deepest reverence with folded hands and bowed heads. But after the hymn concluded, the man stood up and said, in a rather loud voice, "Well, now that our souls are taken care of, let's go out and paint the town red. Boy, what a good time we will have!"

There are too many people who think like that. For them religion is meant to be cooped up on Sunday and, compartmentalized from everyday living. They lose out on the joyous abundance God intended for them all, because they do not bring Him into every area of their living.

Our Master once told about two men who built houses. One of them built his upon the sand. As long as the skies were cloudless, his house stood as well as the other. But when the storms came and the winds blew and the rains descended, the house fell because it was built without foundations on the shiny sand. The second man built his house upon the ugly rock. His house weathered the storms, all because it was built securely on solid ground.

So when one builds his spiritual house he ought to make sure that he has a foundation that will stand, whatever the weather, and for every day of the week. Besides building on faith's foundations, he should open the door and invite God to be a permanent guest. The trouble with many of us is that we allow God into the front vestibule of our house only, but do not give Him the full possession of our life. We are afraid to give ourselves totally to God, fearing that He will put a strait jacket on us, and restrict our style of living. Some of us have given Him only one room, that which is called Sunday. Sadder still, some of us thrust Him out entirely. But like the empty house of Jesus' parable that does not stay empty, but becomes overrun by sin far worse than the first, empty lives are a standing invitation to mischief and evil. Do you wonder that He is dissatisfied, and we remain insecure, until we turn to Him and pray, "Lord, may my life be wholly given to Thee."

TODAY'S THOUGHT: *Promote your conscience to first sergeant, and do not let your life step out of line.*

FEBRUARY 25

God Knows the Way Ahead

Then Moses and the people of Israel sang this song to the Lord, saying, "I will sing to the Lord, for he has triumphed gloriously; the horse and his rider he has thrown into the sea." Exodus 15:1

We need to heed the hymn writer's advice who said, "Keep thou my feet; I do not ask to see The distant scene,—one step enough for me." Life cannot be victorious until we wake up to the truth that God sees all, that He knows all, and that if we put our trust in Him, He will lead us safely on our journey, one step at a time.

Once when flying in an airplane over a beautiful river, I saw a boat slowly sailing on the water below. The captain of the vessel below could see no farther than the next bend of the river. But from my vantage point of 15,000 feet in the air, I could see the entire course of the river. In fact, I could even see the mouth of the river emptying into the open sea, the ultimate destination of every stream. I could see at a glance what the captain was seeing only bit by bit.

Day by day let us remember that God in His heaven can see the entire pathway before each one of us. We do not know what will happen next. Nor should that concern us so long as we walk life's pathway hand in hand with God. He will direct us safely around the mysterious bends and over the rapids until we at last reach our destination.

So many people ask, "Why can't I feel with assurance the presence of God with me? Sometimes I try so hard to find Him, but always there is a wall between us."

To begin with, I do not need to search to find God, because He is never lost. It is God who seeks and finds me. He never hides from me. I am the one who hides from Him. Well did the old saint put it who said, "Whoso advances one inch through doubtings dim, God will march one mile in blazing light to him."

There is a spring in the cleft rock which is Christ from which God daily would refresh us. It is always available. Let us make sure that we do not choke up the water of life with our sin and refusals.

TODAY'S THOUGHT: *It is our responsibility to mark out a sure path to heaven for all those we love who follow us.*

Peace Is Worth Its Price

Let us then pursue what makes for peace and for mutual upbuilding. Romans 14:19

Time and again Jesus reminds us that the kingdom of God and all that it includes is worth more than all earthly possessions added together. Now, He does not literally mean that we must sell our possessions and then give the proceeds to the poor in order that we shall inherit the kingdom. Instead, God asks us to give proportionately of what He gives us. God asks for and expects a total consecration of self. It is in this deep, personal sense that we are to give Him all that we have. I ask you simply, Is the best that He gives worth that much? Unnumbered souls have tried it before you, only to affirm that you will be forever restless, until you have made the great commitment.

Jesus indicates to us that it is worth the price. We say we will be satisfied with only a few shares of the kingdom of God. We are willing to go only a part of the way in keeping His commandment. We do not want to give our all because of the inconvenience involved. We say we want to share just a little of His glory. But if we will not go for all, we cannot have any of it.

What is the best that Jesus has to offer? Is not the finest thing in living that of finding what can satisfy the deepest hunger of our souls? Let us throw away the flimsy baubles which in clinging to us jeopardize our very soul. Let us become as a little child now before God. Everything depends on our being honest with Him. It is not only Ananias and Sapphira who found death by "holding back the price."

What is it that disturbs us most? What is the thing that brings more unhappiness into our lives than anything else? Is it not the fact that we live contrary to the will of God? We sin, and as long as unresolved guilt keeps hounding our consciences, we are miserable. If we persist in letting it pile up without repenting and getting it cleansed away by the blood that removes every stain, we make ourselves likely prospects for the psychiatrist's office.

Jesus has offered us that which alone can satisfy the soul's deepest hunger. He alone can give us what matters most—the forgiveness of sins. Millions have tried Him and found that "He is able!" If each day we will but turn to Him to seek it, we shall surely find it.

TODAY'S THOUGHT: *First seek forgiveness, then faith and fellowship with God follow hard on its heels.*

FEBRUARY 27

Work Hard for Him

Be strong, and show yourself a man. 1 Kings 2:2

A character in a current novel said, "Wind me up, I have run down again."

No one can continue to live without a source of strength and power. The only power that completely satisfies is the power of the Lord, renewed in us every day as we call upon Him. The best things in life, however, do not remain with us unless we keep using them. Just as batteries need recharging to keep giving their needed spark to keep the auto operating, so Christians need to read God's Word every day and remain in constant prayer, in order to receive the energies for victorious living. It is in meditation with God that we discover a fundamental law, that peace and joy become ours as we share them. Our own faith life develops from a willingness to serve.

One of the best ways to happiness is to become attached to some cause greater than yourself. It is thus that the petty problems which irritate so are swallowed up.

Florence Nightingale once said, "If I could describe my life, I would simply show you how a woman of very ordinary ability has been led by God in strange and unaccustomed paths to do in His service what He has done for her. If I could tell you everything you would see how God has done all and I nothing. I worked hard, very hard, and that is all. I have never refused God anything."

Jane Addams is another Christian woman who gave her life to a cause. She moved to Hull House in Chicago's immigrant section, and opened her home to slum children. There she spent 40 busy, happy years working tirelessly to obtain better living conditions, better schools, and better recreational facilities for her neighbors. The secret of her personal happiness and greatness, too, was that she poured out her life for others.

We would be ever so much happier, if we only asked God each day for grace to do a great deal of good, and to forget that we ever did it. Then we would be His partners, not only in helping others, but in helping ourselves. We would discover the peace, the power, the inner joy, that comes to those who love and serve God. "I feel as if I had swallowed sunshine," is the lovely way one of His followers described this inner joy. That could be you, friend. Why not try Him?

TODAY'S THOUGHT: *A Christian life that yields no life of service is like a leafy plant that bears no fruit.*

FEBRUARY 28

He Made Us His Heirs

So that we might be justified by his grace and become heirs in hope of eternal life. Titus 3:7

"Ask for anything you wish and I will give it to you," the king told a favorite nobleman.

The man deliberated for a long time. Should he ask to be made the commanding general of the realm's large army? Or should he ask for gold and jewels? Or should his request be for a sizable portion of the kingdom so that he might become a powerful land-holder? Finally he thought, "No, instead I will ask for something which will give me all these things." So he announced to the king his choice: "I would like to have your beautiful and gracious daughter as my wife." The marriage made him at once heir to all the wealth and power of the kingdom.

In choosing Christ, we are made heirs to the wealth and glory of the Father's kingdom. We become possessors of all that He is and has. His resources are unlimited and inexhaustible. His protecting love and care will follow us into every avenue of life and finally lead through the valley of the shadow to the eternal kingdom above.

A father decided to send his young son by train to a distant city to visit relatives. As they were driving to the station, the boy revealed his anxieties about the trip. He had never been away from home, and he naturally wondered what would happen when he reached his destination. He soon found that his concern had been unnecessary, for when he boarded the train, the conductor asked if there were anything he could do for him. Someone else showed him to the dining car and assisted him with his meal. When he arrived at the city, a friendly man in the station put him in a taxicab, which took him at once to his relatives' home. The boy just could not understand; he thought the whole thing was a miracle. Several years later he learned that his father had made all these detailed arrangements for him. He had talked aforehand to the conductor, and he had carefully laid plans for the boy at his destination.

Even so our heavenly Father cares for us. Through faith we have been made heirs of His eternal kingdom and joint heirs with Jesus Christ. Even the death of a loved one puts a period to one of the most burning of all our Lord's prayers: "Father, I desire that they also, whom thou hast given me, may be with me where I am."

TODAY'S THOUGHT: *What higher hope can anyone aspire to than the hope of eternal life?*

FEBRUARY 29

Faith of Our Fathers, Holy Faith

Therefore, since we are justified by faith, we have peace with God through our Lord Jesus Christ. Romans 5:1

Faith is always a vital force, a certain strength. Without faith, nothing difficult or important is ever done, whether it affects an individual or a nation. We take pride in saying that we can do marvelous things with our intelligence and manual skill. Yes, but these achievements are possible only when our intelligence and skill are awakened, inspired and guided by faith.

A 14-year-old boy was caught in a Minnesota blizzard and badly frozen. He lost both legs, his left hand, and most of his right hand, and it seemed that this young man's life was all but ruined. Still he would not give up. With tremendous courage he worked and studied until he completed his education. Then he became a newspaper editor, and later was selected as the speaker of the House of Representatives in his state. From the legislature he went to the presidency of a bank.

Most people in his predicament would have given up, but not this brave youth. He moved the mountains of handicap and discouragement, and showed a dauntless and indestructible faith in summoning the courage to do so.

Faith is the mightiest weapon man has at his command. The achievements of generations of believing men and women shine before us an ever present challenge.

The history of our country includes many classic examples of people whose faith enabled them to overcome their difficulties. Think of the pilgrims who crossed a stormy ocean in a creaking wooden vessel which no modern traveler would think of boarding. When they landed here they drew up a compact which began, "In the name of God," and closed with, "Amen." Or remember the pioneers who rode west on the danger-infested wilderness trails. They had a few material possessions, but they had faith in themselves, and a dream for this sprawling country.

Although we today live surrounded by luxury, many having every advantage, yet something seems to be lacking. Is it not that we need a return to the faith of our fathers, a faith that is a vital force for good?

TODAY'S THOUGHT: *Faith ought to be contagious, spreading like smallpox from man to man.*

MARCH 1

A Bridge Built by God

And he said to the woman, "Your faith has saved you; go in peace." Luke 7:50

Do you know the story of the Tacoma Narrows Bridge over Puget Sound in the State of Washington? It was the third longest bridge in the world, a suspension bridge with a main span of 2,800 feet. From the day of its opening the peculiar heaving movement of the bridge attracted attention. Motorists came from miles around to drive over "Galloping Gertie" as the bridge was nicknamed. That ribbon of steel gave passengers the sensation of riding a bucking bronco. The bridge stood for four months, then on November 7, 1940, it fell, crashing into the waters of the Sound far below. Fortunately no lives were lost.

That morning as a 40-mile an hour wind whipped the waves the bridge began to heave up and down, soon developing into a twisting motion. Steel and concrete moved as though made of rubber, until finally the main span tore away from the piles which supported it. Then like a zipper the steel girders ripped apart from the floor and the Tacoma Narrows Bridge disappeared into the foam below.

Such are the bridges that men build, bridges that appear strong and stable, but in some of which there may be a fatal flaw. We must not lump together all the world's great bridges and condemn them, for many have stood for decades and may stand for many more. But in Tacoma Bridge's design there was a flaw, something that human minds with all their engineering skill had not detected. This flaw contains the lesson we must consider here.

When we speak today about the bridge of faith, linking man to the power of God, we are not speaking of a man-made affair. This bridge was conceived in the mind of God, and built by the Son of God as He died on Calvary's cross. No matter what the outside pressures, whether fears, temptations, or disappointments, the span extending from God to man is indestructible. Only by traveling on man-made bridges of self-sufficiency are we doomed to defeat. Though clouds may gather and winds blow, we can walk surely over the strong bridge of faith to ultimate victory. But we must not fail to take advantage of the opportunity given freely by God. In foul weather and fair, we must step confidently onto the bridge of faith by confessing Christ and Him crucified.

TODAY'S THOUGHT: *Only by walking a bridge of faith can man come home to God.*

61

MARCH 2

The Lord's Miracles

Though he had done so many signs before them, yet they did not believe in him. John 12:37

All nature is a miracle. Every natural change is a manifestation of the power of Jesus Christ. The seed sown in weakness is raised in power. The corn or wheat thrown into the earth, apparently to die, is given back to us in green blade, and ripening ear, and bread. In all this wondrous change we see the outstretched hand of the Master working a miracle. We learn that as God gives us our daily bread, so God himself is the true bread from heaven which feeds our souls. There can be no life without Him.

Every growing vine, with its clustering grapes, also teaches us a lesson. God's rain falls upon the vine, and is absorbed into the stem and the branches. Finally there comes the bloom and the fruit, and another miracle is complete, caused by the outstretched hand of Jesus. He is the true vine, and we are joined to Him as the branches. Unless we abide in Him, we cannot live.

Every day we see the great miracle of the Lord. If we have eyes to see and ears to hear, wherever we look there are manifestations of His power.

The greatest miracle of all is the capacity of God to raise up fallen human nature, and to put new strength into mankind. We see that miracle performed in the lives of the early disciples, especially in the life of Peter. Three times he denied his Lord. But God's great power changed him into a pillar of the church, willing to stand fast in the faith among the rulers of his day, willing to be cast into prison, willing to die for Him whom he had once denied.

We see Saul, the Pharisee, taking pride in his learning, living a strict and disciplined life, yet not knowing the truth that sets men free. We see him changed into a living Paul after his conversion on the Damascus Road. Once a proud man, he now insists upon being called the chief of sinners, for he has seen the light. Indeed it now shines within him. He realizes he has not the capacity to save himself, and so he turns to the Lord, the only one who is able to give him peace.

God can work the miracle in every one of us, if we will but yield our lives to Him.

TODAY'S THOUGHT: *The joy of salvation can set your spirit soaring.*

MARCH 3

A Pulpit Everywhere

Let your light so shine before men, that they may see your good works and give glory to your Father who is in heaven.

Matthew 5:16

Is our faith real? Whitewashing a pump will not guarantee pure water. A lip service profession of faith is not going to change lives. The cleansing must come from the wellspring—from within. If God controls our lives, we are bound to be different.

The inscription on a highway plaque in a small Minnesota town reads, "On September 1, 1894, a forest fire swept over this area and 450 people lost their lives." As one reads this sign, he cannot help asking himself, "What do you suppose started that fire?" Then he begins to think of repeated warnings he has read, and he concludes that a single match carelessly thrown away can start a forest fire. One match seems insignificant, but think of the tremendous potential.

Sometimes we look at our lives and say, "My little life doesn't count for much." But it is then we should remember the little match, the one that wiped out an entire forest, and caused the death of 450 people. A Christian light of one candlepower could be an influence that might win 450 people for God's kingdom.

The most influential pulpits of America are at your workbench, your home, your schoolroom, your factory. At whatever place you work, there is your pulpit. In fact, wherever you are at any given moment is your pulpit. Every day people are watching, observing the things you say, seeing how you live, how you react to circumstances, whether with God's help you have the courage to battle against temptation. They are watching to see if your faith means anything. You are the ministers of your church. You are important.

Consider this harness maker. He could have said, "I just make bridles. That means very little. What good am I to society? How can my job be a pulpit?" Then one day he saw a runaway horse and wagon. A terrified little boy was sitting in the wagon, careening dangerously down the street. The harness maker managed to dash out and grab the bridle, and as he stood there trembling, he said to himself, "I am glad that I put my very best into that bridle, because it likely saved the life of this lad." This harness maker's bridle shop was his pulpit!

TODAY'S THOUGHT: *This is no time for silence, speak and live for the Savior.*

63

MARCH 4

The Challenge of Defeat

Rejoice not over me, O my enemy; when I fall, I shall rise; when I sit in darkness, the Lord will be a light to me. Micah 7:8

It has been said that a bird with a broken but mended pinion never soars as high as it once did. But a bird with a mended pinion can know the joy of victory. It can come through its testing courageously, and so successfully withstand the full onslaught of the temptation to give up.

So it can be for God's children. Most of us are struggling with some kind of broken pinion, perhaps in the form of a handicap that prevents us from seeking the goals of our ambition. Instead of complaining about our handicaps, let us seek to discover the compensations which accompany them—courage, vision, understanding, and priceless other qualities. Let our broken pinions become a teacher to keep others from the crippling power of sin. Let them become an inspiration for increased effort.

No human soul need accept defeat, if he refuses to surrender to the problems of life. Our setbacks, and truly they are temporary, need not be a burden designed to cast us down, but rungs on the ladder to God. Defeat may serve, as well as victory, to check the soul and let the glory out.

With what attitude are you facing life? A three-year-old girl tried to move a table. After she had struggled for a long time, her mother sought to discourage her by saying she could not move a table as big as she.

"Yes, I can. I am as big as it is," replied the child.

There is a great difference between two ways of looking at a job. To say, "The task is as big as I am," is to invite defeat. But to say, "I am as big as the job," is the first step toward victory. With God, you are big enough to handle whatever problem may face you.

TODAY'S THOUGHT: *The only man worse than a quitter is the one who cannot bring himself to begin.*

MARCH 5

The Story of the Mustard Seed

If you have faith as a grain of mustard seed, you will say to this mountain, "Move hence to yonder place," and it will move; and nothing will be impossible to you. Matthew 17:20

Some time ago I received a gift which I shall always treasure. It is called a mustard seed remembrancer, and it received its name "remembrancer," from the old royal court. A remembrancer was a man hired to remind the people of important events taking place.

The little mustard seed remembrancer has an interesting history. There was once a couple in Missouri whose lives were tense, anxious, and fearful, as many lives are in our world today. This husband and wife simply could not find any joy in living. One day they heard a message of faith delivered by a certain pastor in their town, and his message found lodging in their hearts. They started reading their Bible, and soon concluded that it would be helpful to find some reminder of this newborn faith and what it enabled them to do. Faith had transformed their living, yet they were very conscious of the fact that there were days in their Christian lives when faith grew weak and dim.

In any Christian life there are moments of tribulation and doubt. This is why we need to employ certain techniques as we seek to make our faith grow stronger. But let us continue our story.

Reading the Bible one day, this Missouri couple came to a verse in Matthew which gave them the answer they were seeking. "If you have faith as a grain of mustard seed . . . nothing will be impossible unto you." So what did they do? They went looking for mustard seeds and found some. They came upon a process whereby a mustard seed could be encased in a transparent ball. People could wear them on key chains, or around their necks, or carry them in their purses. The little mustard seed could be seen through this transparent ball. And thus goes the story of the mustard seed remembrancer.

Every one of us can keep in our minds an image of the seed. Then, if fears start crowding in and we become anxious about what we must face, we can remember the promise that if we have faith as much as a grain of mustard seed, nothing is impossible—abolutely nothing.

TODAY'S THOUGHT: *Looking through eyes of faith, we see life in its proper perspective.*

MARCH 6

Harmony after Calamity

By day the Lord commands his steadfast love; and at night his song is with me, a prayer to the God of my life. Psalm 42:8

Ice glazed the sidewalks of the city, as a moving van loaded with trunks stopped in front of a house. A wide-shouldered, husky man jumped down, and went to see if it was the right address. Twice he fell on the slick walk, and could barely keep his footing. It was the right house, so he returned to the van, and ordered the heaviest trunk put on his back.

A passer-by thought, "How foolish!" He felt sure the man would fall, and the trunk would come down upon him, perhaps even seriously injuring him. But instead the strong man's feet were steady. He did not slip once. His burden was heavy enough to give him solid footing.

Some burdens of responsibility are blessings in disguise. If we would see the good in what seems adversity, we should discover that lessons can be learned from every circumstance.

The great composer, Beethoven, had a horror of deafness. You can imagine his feelings when he realized he was losing his hearing. When the first symptoms of deafness became apparent, Beethoven knew anxiety bordering on despair. In spite of the best medical attention his plight grew worse, until at last he could converse only by writing. But the significant part of the story begins here. Beethoven wrote his finest music after he was deaf to all sound. Out of calamity came great harmony.

This is the comment of a violin maker who enters the forest himself to select the wood for his instruments from the north side of the trees. "I never awaken in the night and listen to the wind without thinking of the great, storm-tossed, groaning, and slow-toughening forest trees—learning to be violins."

Whatever enters your life today, if you allow God to help you, some good can come of it.

TODAY'S THOUGHT: *When the night looks blackest, the dawn must be very near.*

MARCH 7

A Few Simple Rules

Blessed is the man who fears the Lord, who greatly delights in his commandments! Psalm 112:1

On awakening each morning, why not turn to God and say, "Take over, Lord, this is your day"? How different our lives would be, if we dedicated every day to Him! Then we would be sure of His seeing us through our difficulties, both great and small. The Lord has grace to conquer all our fears. When the way seems darkest and the fight the most severe, if we are still, we will hear His voice, "Fear not, my child, for I am near."

Here are a few simple rules to follow in daily living. They will never fail for they are drawn from divine resources and, though sorely tested, have never failed throughout the centuries.

"Be anxious for nothing!" Deliberately refuse to be bothered by the worries and fears which surround you. Do not let concerns overwhelm you. In the storms of life, look not at the waves, look up into the face of Jesus.

"Be thankful for everything!" When troubles surround you, do not take inventory of them. Instead, begin a mental listing of all the things you have for which to be thankful.

Thanksgiving and praise are almost synonymous with singing. Carry the melody of a victorious hymn in your heart, and hum it often. Constantly remind yourself that no power on earth can possibly defeat you as long as He cares for you. Repeat to yourself the words of the Twenty-third Psalm, and study their meaning. The Lord belongs to you. He is your shepherd. With Him by your side, there is no evil you need fear. His strength surrounds you. Though you must walk through the valley of the last shadow, He is there with you. Keep singing praises to Him who has promised never to forsake you.

"Be prayerful always!" Prayer is one of your finest privileges. It will connect you with life's greatest source of power. Remind yourself that though the night is dark, the morning is coming, and God will be there, and you will be triumphant because of Him.

"Cast all your care upon Him!" You belong to Him. You are a child of the King.

TODAY'S THOUGHT: *As a child clings trustingly to the hands of its parents, so a man ought to cling to his heavenly Father.*

MARCH 8

Letters from the Master

But he answered, "It is written, 'Man shall not live by bread alone, but by every word that proceeds from the mouth of God.'"
Matthew 4:4

How great is our consecration to Christ? Do we love Him always, or only when we find ourselves in difficulty? Is our faith merely a spare tire kept for emergency? Unless our faith is real, we cannot hope for the blessings we desire. The answers to our problems can be found in God's Word, if only we will use it as a guide for daily living.

A missionary worked several years in a small town in East Poland, then went home on furlough, leaving his Bible with the people there. When he returned, they arranged a reunion with great celebration. The missionary said, "Instead of the usual congratulations, we will recite verses from the Bible."

One man raised his hand, and asked the missionary if he meant chapters instead of verses.

"Chapters?" the missionary asked in surprise. "Could anyone recite whole chapters of the Bible?"

Soon he discovered that many of the 600 townspeople could recite not only whole chapters, but whole books as well.

"We had to memorize it," the people explained. "If our Bible had ever been lost, where would we have gotten another?"

Too often we fail to appreciate what we have until we lose it. We have in the Word of God a pattern for life, teaching us how to live in this world and in the world to come. It is written so that anyone can understand, even a little child, and it describes the kind of person we must be to find peace and happiness. It speaks of gentleness, humility, kindness, selflessness.

It is a book of power, telling of a Savior who can forgive our sins and cleanse us of all our unrighteousness. It assures us that He will be our companion every hour of every day. It comforts us with the promise that never need we be alone, if we believe in Him. It offers security for every waking moment, and for that inevitable day when we must walk through the valley of the shadow of death.

How much time do you spend each day reading the Bible? There is a message in it. The books are personal letters addressed to you.

TODAY'S THOUGHT: *God's Word is one Book where the author stands beside you as you read it.*

MARCH 9

Power for Transformation

The Lord will rescue me from every evil and save me for his heavenly kingdom. To him be the glory for ever and ever. Amen.
2 Timothy 4:18

It seems impossible that the oyster can produce a pearl—but it does. It seems impossible that from a tiny shriveled seed can come a glorious flower—but it does. It seems impossible that from a cocoon can come a butterfly—but it does. It seems impossible that God can completely transform a human life—but He can!

Look at the early disciples. In all history one of the most convincing evidences of God's power is the personal transformation of this group of men. After they knew Christ, their faith swept away hesitancy, cowardice and fear, and replaced them with confidence, courage, and hope. Yet at His crucifixion they were defeated and afraid, and ran away and hid themselves. After the Resurrection, however, they became dynamic evangelists, willing to give their lives for the cause. They were a motley crew before Christ called them, but with Him they lived and moved with great confidence in a new world. Faith in Christ can transform men today in just such a miraculous manner.

Though we cannot walk and talk with Him in person as the disciples did, we have His promise that He is with us always, that He will never leave us nor forsake us. We can talk to Him in prayer. He speaks to us as we read His Word, where we even find letters concerning our particular problems. It is in the Bible that we can discover the power God has put at our disposal. There, too, we learn of the forgiveness He offers the penitent, the faith He offers the doubter, and the courage He offers the desperate.

A few minutes spent each day searching the Scriptures will reveal their unlimited resources, and will convince us of our daily guidance. When problems appear, we are more aware than ever of our need. Therefore, we must study His Word regularly, to be ready when emergencies arise. We need to fill up a reservoir of faith so that, whatever life's day may bring, we can say triumphantly, "I know Him and am confident that He is able to keep me."

TODAY'S THOUGHT: *Trust God to guide you from here to eternity.*

The Meaning of Freedom

Now the Lord is the Spirit, and where the Spirit of the Lord is, there is freedom. 2 Corinthians 3:17

A class of young people was once asked, "What is freedom?" Quickly a bright youngster replied, "Freedom is doing whatever you want to do."

That is what many people in the world today think, but how sadly mistaken they are. They think freedom is the right to do anything they feel like doing, regardless of how it effects them or anyone else. The Bible tells a story about a young man who felt that way, too. Tired of parental restraints, he asked for and received his father's permission to take his inheritance and go into a far-off country.

It was not long, however, before he found he had made a mistake. What he thought would be hilarious freedom turned out to be hellish slavery; for, though all unaware, he had lost the real liberty he possessed. Fortunately, he was wise enough to come to his senses, and return home to the freedom of his father's love.

You cannot have the freedom when you are bound by sin and death. Paul assures us that to be free is not to do what one wants to do, but rather to do what Christ desires us to do.

Man is the servant of someone, and if he is not the servant of God, he is the servant of someone else. Yet only in God do we find true freedom from sin, from fear, and from our enemy.

One cannot progress unless he grasps the meaning of freedom; without God there is no progress. Life is like a locomotive speeding smoothly along the rails. Let it leap from the rails, spurning restrictions, refusing restraint, and it is not free. It is wrecked. The flower blowing in the breeze is rooted in rich soil, obeying nature's law of place. As long as it remains where it is, it is free, but let it be uprooted and loosened from the earth, and speedily it dies.

A rootless life heads toward destruction, while a life in God brings freedom and fulfillment. Some of us create our own prison walls by not accepting or believing what God offers. Mark Twain once told the story of a man many years in prison, who walked out one morning only to discover that the doors never had been locked. Jesus offered the door to freedom for every one of us, when He says, "You will know the truth, and the truth will make you free."

TODAY'S THOUGHT: *Some say religion clips their wings, but true believers know that faith gives them wings.*

MARCH 11

Blessings Instead of Punishment

According to the riches of his glory he may grant you to be
strengthened with might through his Spirit in the inner man.

Ephesians 3:16

An eleven-year-old boy disobeyed his parents one day, and was
quite unreasonable with them when discussing the incident. At
the time, the parents were so disturbed that they decided to wait
until the next evening to issue punishment. They thought it better
to let the fires of their tempers cool. The following afternoon a
stamp album ordered previously by the boy arrived in the mail,
and when the boy's father came home he brought some long awaited
additions to the lad's chemistry set. These had been given to the
father by a family friend.

When the boy surveyed the two prized packages he had wanted
for so long, he began to cry. Overcome with grief, he turned to
his parents and said, "I have never felt so bad in all my life. I wish
you were the kind of parents who whipped their children when they
were mean. It is an awful feeling to know you have hurt your
mother and father, and then have them act so kind and good and
fair that they do not take things out on you. I would rather have
been spanked last night when we were all angry, than feel like this
now. I feel worse than after any punishment I have ever received.
You love me, that I can tell."

This incident reminds us how God deals with His children. Every
one of us is guilty of sin. We deserve punishment. Yet our heavenly
Father keeps showering His blessings upon us. When a man comes
to his senses, he becomes penitent, like that little boy. He turns to
God and tells Him that he cannot understand how He can be so
good. God does not expect anything in return for His goodness, except that we honestly resolve to mend our ways and be different.
He reminds us of something Isaiah said long ago: "Let the wicked
forsake his way, and the unrighteous man his thoughts."

Life offers so much—so much more than we have yet found. You
will have a plus to share, if you maintain your partnership with
God. Think straight. Let God help you live according to His commands, work hard, and everything will come out all right. God
knows our every need.

TODAY'S THOUGHT: *Are you wearing the harness of life like
a heavy awkward yoke or like a bright and shining crown?*

MARCH 12

God's Greatest Gift

No one can receive anything except what is given him from heaven. John 3:27

Few of us hope for greatness, or expect it; but all of us have great dreams. Sometimes, as life goes on, we have to modify our dreams; but we are better people because of those dreams—of goals to which we aspired.

Often we think of greatness only in terms of places, like the Great Continental Divide or the Grand Canyon. It is natural, too, to think of famous men as great. Yet some of the greatest personalities of all live and die unknown. These are the unsung heroes of life, and to them God will give a reward. We all need to remember that the great heart of God beats in everyone, and that life has wonderful possibilities for every individual who keeps his heart tuned to the Almighty. In fact, God's power is the one power in the world that can save us.

We are deeply concerned in this atomic age about the explosive forces that destroy. How quickly our anxiety would vanish, if we realized that Christ in the heart of every individual could bring peace to the world. Each person becomes great as he allows God to enter his life and make him a part of His army of righteousness that will build this world brotherhood.

"What is the greatest gift of life?" we ask. "I can only live it once, and I want to be sure that I live it to the best advantage."

Life's greatest gift, of course, is that God is in you, that you are created in His image. Indwelt by Christ, you are healed and saved. God's power offers vast possibilities for growth and development, even for greatness.

When George Nicholls, a famous member of the English Parliament, was a boy working on a farm, he attended a meeting where the speaker remarked, "Who knows whether some lad in this meeting will become great?" The speaker mentioned names like Livingstone, Gladstone, Curie. Mr. Nicholls looked around, discovered that he was the only boy present and thought, "That must mean me." At that moment he decided that, by the help of God, he was going to make good. There are countless opportunities for greatness waiting for everyone who gives his life to God.

TODAY'S THOUGHT: *Do not despise your talents or your means. No matter how small they seem, combined with God's they provide unlimited resources.*

MARCH 13

Every One a Witness

Repentance and forgiveness of sins should be preached in his name to all nations. Luke 24:47

A man just returned from Paris was asked his impression of the French art galleries.

"They have the finest collection of frames that I have ever seen," he said.

Fascinated by the ornate, glittering frames, he had missed the masterpieces! So often our lives leave the same impression. We surround ourselves with luxuries. We possess everything that money can buy. People get an impression of what we have, rather than of what we are. Do people see what you own, or are they impressed by the one who owns you? Every one of us is meant to be a living witness for God, and people should know how much we love Him. Man is rich only if his soul is rich.

A little girl who had been reading the Beatitudes was asked which one she would like most to fulfill.

"I would rather be pure in heart," she answered. She went on to explain why: "If I could be pure in heart, I would have all the other good qualities Jesus talks about in these verses."

What a different world it would be, if all of us sought to be pure in heart. Then, much of our fellow men's suffering and privation would disappear as we faced our obligations to them.

We all have an unconscious influence on someone else. Your neighbor next door may be passing through a severe crisis, perhaps even suspended between life and death. A kind word or a gentle touch of the hand may determine the destiny of his soul.

"Out on the highways and byways of life, many are weary and sad," are the lines of a gospel chorus.

You may be the only one having the opportunity to help them. Your life could make an impact for good. Say, when people see you, will they see only a picture frame? Or will they see a radiant life that demonstrates your concern for others even as God is concerned about you?

TODAY'S THOUGHT: *Make someone happy today, and you may gain a memory that through long years will make you happy in remembering.*

MARCH 14

One Day at a Time

Therefore do not be anxious about tomorrow, for tomorrow will be anxious for itself. Matthew 6:34

A man went to visit a friend at a nearby farm. He stayed so long that it was night when he left the house, and his friend loaned him a lantern. After walking a few feet in the dark, the man realized a storm was brewing, and that even with the lantern he could see only a few feet ahead. He returned quickly to the house.

"Haven't you got a stronger light?" he asked dismayed.

"It will light your way home," the friend replied.

"But I can't see my house from here," the man retorted.

"It will light your way one step at a time, and bring you safely home," concluded his friend patiently.

We have been given the Bible, the Word of God. It is the Light that leads us home, one step at a time. God has not promised to reveal the whole future to us, nor is it necessary to know everything in order to be happy. Sometimes it is better not to know what is going to happen, for no man has strength to face his entire future in the course of a single day. "Let the day's own trouble be sufficient for the day." As we learn to live one day at a time, we find that God's grace is completely adequate. Why will we not trust His promise, "as your days, so shall your strength be."

Faith builds your morale, brightens your outlook, and makes the future glorious. Faith teaches us to look in the right direction. It keeps our eyes focused upon Him who is the answer to every problem.

In the early days of the West, ministers served a circuit dotted with preaching stations. Riding horseback, they had to cross countless flood-swollen rivers. They found if they fixed their gaze upon the swirling waters, they could easily grow dizzy, and be swept away. But if they fixed their gaze upon a big tree, some mighty rock, or the summit of a hill, they would ride through in safety. Man will be victorious in life, if in faith he fixes his eyes, not upon the shifting scene about him, but upon the eternal love of God.

TODAY'S THOUGHT: *Make your life a prism, to catch the rays of God's love, and reflect them on those who need your help.*

MARCH 15

A Philosophy of Living

For he who finds me finds life and obtains favor from the Lord.
                                            Proverbs 8:35

A man was once traveling west on a train from the eastern seaboard. It was late in the afternoon, and the sun had nearly reached the horizon. The man's seatmate turned to him.

"Sir," he said, "will you please lower the shade of your window. The sun hurts my eyes."

"Lower the shade?" replied the man. "I can't do that. This is the most magnificent sunset I have ever seen. If I lower the shade I will be shutting God out."

This story is a parable of two attitudes toward God. Some people look upon Him as a sort of annoyance. They would rather be alone, apart from Him. Others know Him as a person of tremendous beauty. They see in His every act something wonderful to behold.

Another man was touring the West by bus. Though it was his first trip, he was unaffected by the glory all about him. In fact, he was openly critical of such beauties of nature as the Grand Canyon and the Painted Desert. The bus driver, after hearing for some time this constant flow of cheap criticism, could stand it no longer.

"Listen, Mister," he said, "if you haven't got it on the inside, you cannot see it on the outside."

The bus driver was right; it is the kind of philosophy you build in your mind, and the kind of faith you have in your heart, which counts. If you have it on the inside, you will be able to look above your difficulties, and see those things which are beautiful, helpful and inspiring. Then you will live each day knowing that the longer you live, the more wonderful life becomes.

A young doctor asked John Dewey on his ninetieth birthday what good his philosophy did him.

"The good of it," the great man replied quietly, "is that you climb mountains."

"Climb mountains?" the doctor asked unimpressed, "Why is that good?"

"You see other mountains to climb," was the reply. "And when you are no longer interested in climbing mountains to see other mountains, life is over." The Christian will find this doubly true.

TODAY'S THOUGHT: *At dusk each child of God stands at the brink of a beautiful tomorrow.*

MARCH 16

Faith to Follow Through

Love the Lord, all you his saints! The Lord preserves the faithful, but abundantly requites him who acts haughtily. Psalm 31:23

A small British village is located on one of the most dangerous harbors on the entire English coastline. After several drownings, the villagers resolved to get a lifeboat to help in such emergencies. But first they built a boathouse. It cost more than they expected, and by the time they had completed it the money ran out, and the lifeboat was never purchased. Today the house stands, well-built, gleaming with fresh paint, ready for use—but empty.

Many lives are like that! We dream fine dreams; we have good intentions; make promising beginnings, but fail to follow through. Our lives are empty and useless, while all about us great areas of human need call for our attention and seek our help.

To be a true Christian there must be an open confession, and an enlistment in the army of Christ. "Son, go work in my vineyard," is His command.

At the beginning of the Reformation a monk by the name of Martin of Basel came to the knowledge of God's truth. But he was afraid to make a public confession, afraid of what might happen to him. So he wrote on a piece of parchment, "O most merciful Christ, I know I can be saved only by the merit of Thy blood. Holy Jesus, I acknowledge Thy suffering for me. I love Thee, I love Thee." Then he removed a stone from the wall of his cell and hid the piece of parchment behind it. It was not discovered for more than 100 years.

About the same time there lived another monk by the name of Martin Luther. He, too, found the truth of salvation by grace alone. But he said, "'My Lord, I will confess Thee openly before men. I will not shrink from confessing Thee before kings." The world knows what followed.

What about you? Will you make your life count by having the faith and courage to follow through?

TODAY'S THOUGHT: *God readily reveals His will to those who are willing to obey it.*

MARCH 17

The Danger of Delay

The appointed time has grown very short. 1 Corinthians 7:29

The man who advised us never to put off until tomorrow what we can do today was wise. I have heard America called a nation of procrastinators. We seem to like the proverb better when it goes like this: Never do today what you can put off until tomorrow.

Students from grade school on up prove that proverb every day. Some students prepare their assignments every day, while some of their classmates keep putting off their study until the day before a big examination, and then sit up half the night cramming for the test. Their test scores may not show the difference, but in terms of actual knowledge those who study day by day are really learning their lessons. What is worse, this habit of putting off work can continue after school days. On the job or at home it is the person who does today's work today that is able to take advantage of a sudden opportunity.

Putting off that extra little job may mean the loss of a golden opportunity; but putting off accepting Christ may mean the loss of eternal life.

"It isn't surgery that kills people," Dr. William Mayo said, "It's delayed surgery." And it is not usually hard times that wreck businesses, but the failure to call in expert advice soon enough. A powerful banker made this comment about business failures: "Oh, if they would only tell us their troubles sooner!" God is seeking us, He is waiting patiently for us to come to Him with our troubles. He has promised if we cast our burdens upon Him, He will care for us.

When we have found the joy of accepting Christ as our Savior, we will stop worrying about the future, and happily live and work one day at a time. I like these words of J. Hudson Taylor, "Don't have your concert first," he says, "and then tune your instruments. Begin the day with the Word of God and prayer, and get in harmony with Him at the very beginning."

When our spirits are in harmony with God, we shall know that every single minute can be used for good.

TODAY'S THOUGHT: *If time were not precious, why would it be given to us one moment at a time?*

MARCH 18

Concentrate on the Love of God

Return to the Lord, your God, for he is gracious and merciful, slow to anger, and abounding in steadfast love. Joel 2:13

A London shop displayed a vase of beautifully arranged artificial flowers. They had been made so carefully that it was easy to mistake them for living ones. Somewhere in the bouquet there was a real flower, and a notice on the vase challenged passers-by to pick out the living blossom.

Too frequently we Christians look and act much like the world. In watching us, people cannot tell that we have committed our lives to the Master. We wish not to be apart from the crowd, and we do not like to be embarrassed. Many times, like Jesus' disciple Peter, we mingle with the world without revealing our discipleship. We deny our Lord, and swear by our actions that we have never known Him.

There is too much empty, meaningless worship today. Many of us have allowed our faith to become a form rather than a force. We go through the rituals of religion without putting our hearts into it, then wonder why there are no results.

In Japan a religious sect was observed as it went about its rites. To perform one of the devotional acts, the worshiper ran around the sacred temple 100 times, dropping a piece of wood into a box at each round. With the tedious rounds completed, the worshiper went home tired but very happy, convinced that he had done a worthy service. Was this exhausting ritual a worthy service?

Real devotion to the living God will always result in acts of love. We cannot be connected with such a dynamic power without being devoted to it.

Fritz Kreisler wrote, "I have not the slightest consciousness of what my fingers are doing when I play. I concentrate on the ideal of the music that I hear in my head, and try to reproduce it as closely as I can. I do not think of the mechanics at all."

As we concentrate on the love of God flowing into our hearts every day, we shall be compelled to serve our fellow men. As we serve others, we shall find the joy and peace we are seeking.

TODAY'S THOUGHT: *Think of the lives of others as a cup, and fill that cup with drops of kindness, one by one, until it overflows.*

MARCH 19

We Are the Future

(You) have put on the new nature, which is being renewed in knowledge after the image of its creator. Colossians 3:10.

During World War II a young man and his wife were talking together outside a a London air-raid shelter. It was night and they stood together watching the searchlights beam into the sky, and listening to the drone of enemy planes in the distance. It became to them an old story, repeated numberless times. And who knew how many more like them were yet to come? Finally, breaking the poignant silence between them, the man turned to his wife and said, "What future is there in all of this? What hope for tomorrow? I feel adrift. All of us are washed up."

Quietly, surely she said, "The future is not in this. It is in us."

Difficulties come to us all. Whether or not they will defeat us depends on our attitude toward them. Many times we are tempted to give up, to quit. Whenever we do, we lose. But if we resolve to meet each difficulty squarely, and with God's help and strength try to conquer it, we are always victorious.

In naval annals there is a story of a certain cruiser anchored in a Pacific harbor with ships of other flags. Suddenly a furious tropical storm broke. At the first blast of wind the cruiser captain hoisted anchor and steered straight to sea into the teeth of the gale. It was tough going. For two days the vessel's fate was in doubt. Later, however, when the battered ship limped back to its moorings, there were the other vessels piled high upon the shore, all of them victims of the storm. Only the ship which had gone forth to meet its fate head-on survived!

There is a great truth in this story. The future belongs to those who go forward, who dare to face up to difficulty. It belongs to those who seek to conquer, rather than to those who hope to ride out life's furies at anchor. If we accept the challenge, and use the power which God gives us, we shall find a way out.

A legend often repeated concerns the story of the creation of the bird. When the Almighty had started to place wings upon the birds' little bodies, they complained about the burden they would have to carry around all through life. But these burdens became their wings. How often in life we discover that those things which seemed to be burdens turn out to be blessings!

TODAY'S THOUGHT: *Our prayers and God's mercy are like two buckets in a well; as one goes down, the other comes up.*

MARCH 20

The Gospel Is Sunshine

Every one then who hears these words of mine and does them will be like a wise man who built his house upon the rock.

Matthew 7:24

Have you ever thought of how democratic sunshine is? It shines with equal radiance into the cottage of the poor and the palace of the rich. It falls upon the rose bush, bringing the buds to burst into beautiful flowers, and on the ragged cactus, too.

The gospel is like sunshine. It is available for all. No sinner has fallen so low that he cannot be reached and cleansed by it, if he will only look up and see. No saint has ever risen so high that he does not need the daily sunshine of the gospel.

The Master came into our world to be the Savior from sin. His coming brought joy and hope to the fallen who repented of their wrongdoing. Do you remember the day Jesus spoke these words: "Take heart, my son; your sins are forgiven"? A palsied man was brought to Him for healing. Our Lord, who always sees beneath the surface of things, perceived that the man's soul was more needy than his body. He first gave to him that which he needed most—forgiveness of sins.

Even if sin has crippled and scarred one's body, one may yet be happy because of the peace that comes from hearing the Master say, "Your sins are forgiven." No matter what life's outer circumstances are, when guilt festers within happiness is fled. Music turns to discord. Every time he shuts his eyes, his conscience points an accusing finger. Yet no man need despair. The secret is to become truly penitent, to feel sorry for what has happened, and to engage your "advocate with the Father, Jesus Christ the righteous." He is also the Great Physician and will apply His healing touch to the place of need. Hear the assurance in His voice as He says, "Go your way. Be of good cheer. Your sins are forgiven you."

One day a little girl asked her mother, "Where does Jesus live?"

The mother answered, "In heaven."

She was right. But she would have been just as right if she had said, "Here with you, in our home, and in your heart wherever you go."

Keep Jesus there, and day by day greater victory will be yours.

TODAY'S THOUGHT: *Never go it alone! Take Christ with you into every day.*

MARCH 21

Look to the Lamb of God

The Lord redeems the life of his servants; none of those who take refuge in him will be condemned. Psalm 34:22.

The only sinless person who ever lived was the Lord Jesus. If we are honest with ourselves, we shall have to admit that no one of us can face God and say, "I have never done anything wrong." Nor can anyone ever conclude, "I have done enough good things in my life to save myself."

What is the meaning of salvation? If you were to visit Norway you might find a little church in whose tower is the carved image of a lamb. Some years ago during the building of the church, there was a man working on a scaffold on the tower. He slipped and fell from it, and as he was falling to the ground, it appeared to those nearby that death was inevitable. But it happened that at that same moment a shepherd was bringing his sheep along the little road which ran close beside the church. The workman fell on one of these sheep, and while the animal was crushed, its body broke the workman's fall and saved his life. When the church was finished, the townspeople decided to carve a lamb in stone and place it in the tower. They wanted to memorialize the incident. Most of all, they wanted all who would ever see it to be reminded of the Lamb of God "who takes away the sin of the world."

We all need the forgiveness which our Savior has provided. If you have ever been in critical condition in a hospital or have had a loved one for whom the doctors ordered a blood transfusion, you know how this fresh blood had the power to supercharge one, and perhaps even save a life. In like manner the Master gives of himself. Because of the old rugged cross there is a transfusion available to all, to save us and to heal. And not only is a life saved, but a new power is given.

One New Year's Eve I sat in a hotel in Tel Aviv, Israel. Suddenly, just before midnight, there was a power failure, and the lights went out. I had never realized before how inky black the midnight darkness could be. Twenty minutes later the lights came on. I knew then how much light meant to me.

God is willing to heal the line sin breaks. Man must make the decision, and snap on the switch of faith. Of one thing you can be dead certain: If you choose God, you choose victory.

TODAY'S THOUGHT: *Do more than wish for eternal life. Prepare for it.*

MARCH 22

Seek the Faith of Our Fathers

So faith comes from what is heard, and what is heard comes by the preaching of Christ. Romans 10:17

God promises the Christian daily victory. This is what He said: "Whatever is born of God overcomes the world; and this is the victory that overcomes the world, our faith." All who are in God's service know that this is so.

It was faith which enabled Noah to stick with building the ark despite the hoots and jeers of his countrymen. They thought him peculiar. It was faith which braced Abraham in offering his son as a sacrifice, which strengthened Joseph to resist temptation, and Moses to resolutely turn from Egypt. It was faith which carried Joshua through a host of enemies into the promised land, and comforted Daniel in the lions' den. It was faith which transformed the disciples from cowards on Good Friday, when Jesus was crucified, into unflinching saints who rose up to fight against the sinfulness of a pagan world. It was faith that gave the Christian martyrs courage to let their bodies burn rather than their souls perish. It was faith that enabled Martin Luther to stand against the heirarchy of the church and fearlessly point out its wrong, even as he magnificently said, "Here I stand, God help me. I cannot do otherwise."

It is this faith that inspires Christians today to leave home and family to go to the far corners of the world. As ambassadors of love, they bring the light of Christ into the sin-darkened hearts of the heathen.

But you ask, "Why is there so much evil? Why is it always the world that seems to gain so many victories?" The answer is that too many of Christ's soldiers are A. W. O. L., have turned in their uniforms and no longer fight the good fight of faith. They are wearing the world's crown of roses instead of Christ's thorns.

If the world is ever to know peace, it must be as true faith in Christ rules the hearts of men. Fight the good fight of faith. You can be more than conqueror through Him who loved you.

TODAY'S THOUGHT: *With faith, our vision of peace can emerge a reality.*

MARCH 23

Accept Today's Opportunity

Walk while you have the light, lest the darkness overtake you; he who walks in the darkness does not know where he goes.

John 12:35

A double painting hangs in an art gallery of Paris. The first picture depicts an outraged father banishing his disobedient son from the house, with the rest of the family weeping in the background. The second picture shows the same cottage and the same humble room. But the father is lying on his deathbed with the mother at his side. In the open door stands the returning prodigal, looking for a sign of forgiveness. But the father is too weak to speak the words of forgiveness, and the son remains outside. The boy's opportunity had passed; it was too late for him to be received again into his home.

What a different picture we see in the cross, and how different is the message we receive from the Bible! The door to the Father's house is always open for anyone who believes in Him. It is never too late. God is always alert to the call of His children. There is room in heaven even for the penitent thief. Only those who completely harden their hearts, who turn deaf ears to the call of God, will be without a safe place for their souls on the great and terrible day. Nor is this of God's choosing. Only man can close his ears to the voice of God. Man himself is responsible if he repeatedly says "no" to the call of the heavenly Father. He turns into a living "no."

We should be alert to our everyday opportunities to grow in grace and in the knowledge of our Lord Jesus Christ. The more of ourselves we invest in others, the more vibrant our faith in God becomes. The more time we spend doing good, the less time there is for us to be tempted to do wrong.

Think of those wasted moments of life, wasted because of the love we did not give and the powers we did not use. Many of us have missed happy hours along the way, because we withheld our love, and refused to give even as God gave for us.

"Why has God made me like this?" a cripple once asked her pastor.

"My friend," said the pastor, "God has not made you. God is making you. Each day is a day in the School of Life."

TODAY'S THOUGHT: *God sometimes digs ruthlessly into our lives. For it is in the deepest pits that the finest gems are found.*

MARCH 24

How to Grow Strong

And as your days, so shall your strength be.

Deuteronomy 33:25

Just as storm, rough weather, and hard training make a man strong and hardy, so sorrow and misunderstanding, if used in the right way, can help to make a man a strong Christian. The troubles that seem to overwhelm us should carry us closer to our God who has been our help in ages past, who is a very present help in time of trouble, and our hope for years to come. The fair winds of prosperity are by no means the most advantageous in our journey to heaven.

When troubles do come, we must prepare to meet them prayerfully, with willingness to endure hardship as good soldiers of Jesus Christ. Unless we face adversity confident of victory through God's strength, adversity can overwhelm us. We must never forget that "all the water in the world cannot sink the ship unless it gets into the ship."

Man fights an unrelenting battle against sin. The one who tries humbly and earnestly to follow after Christ finds that he has engaged in a daily struggle. He must fight the good fight of faith. As long as he resists the evil one and recognizes temptation, subtle as it may be, all is well. But when he carelessly lays aside his protective armor, the unlooked-for danger appears on the scene and proves his undoing.

It is interesting to know that David, standing before Goliath, was a man after God's own heart. He was actively engaged in two kinds of battle, the mental battle of the striving Christian, and the combat of a good soldier on the field. He could not be defeated, because the resources of God were then, and are now, greater than those of man. But when David tarried in Jerusalem as others went out to fight, and spent his time in idleness and luxury, temptations came which led to adultery and murder. "The devil finds some mischief still for idle hands to do." Fight the good fight of faith, and you will be victorious.

TODAY'S THOUGHT: *It is better to attempt great things, and succeed with only a part of them, than never to venture forth.*

MARCH 25

We, Too, Will Be Tempted

Watch and pray that you may not enter into temptation; the spirit indeed is willing, but the flesh is weak. Matthew 26:41

The first temptation that Jesus had to face was one of the flesh. He was faint with hunger, and the devil tried to induce Him to misuse His power and satisfy himself. Jesus met the temptation by showing that He could subdue the flesh to the spirit, and that man does not live by bread alone, but by every word that proceeds out of the mouth of God.

The devil tempts us in a thousand ways. He appeals to our natural appetites, or he tempts us to use our talents for the wrong things. Some people he tempts to work for their own selfish ends, without thinking about the needs of others. He tempts others to be extravagant and to live beyond their means. To them he is ever whispering and commanding that these stones be turned into bread. He leads people to think they need more comforts, more luxuries than they have. So by degrees he leads them away from the place where they are happy and persuades them to seek another kind of world, a delusion of happiness.

One way to resist temptation is to remember that the life is more than meat, and the body more than clothing. The strength which Jesus showed He gives to the humblest of His followers. Read the story of the army of martyrs. Call to mind how brave men, women, and children suffered hunger and thirst, cold and nakedness, the horrors of prison, the agonies of the arena, rather than purchase comfort at the price of sin.

Thanks be to God, there are still martyrs among us now walking the streets of today. There are men and women sorely tempted by the power of sin, but who act strong in His strength. He showed us the example when He gained the victory in the wilderness long ago. The children of God learn that great lesson, too, that truly to live one does not live by bread alone.

TODAY'S THOUGHT: *Accept the challenge of temptation, and through Christ's power grind it beneath the sole of your shoe.*

MARCH 26

Have Complete Confidence in God

The Lord is my helper, I will not be afraid; what can man do to me? Hebrews 13:6

"What is the outlook?" friends asked a man who was facing great trouble.

"The outlook is dark, but the uplook is wonderful!" he replied.

The hymn writer gave us sound advice when she said not to look about us, or behind us, or within us, or ahead of us, for that would make us wretched. She told us, instead, to look up into the face of Jesus. There we can find peace in a world of turmoil, forgiveness of our sins, an erasing of the besmirched record of the past, a fadeless hope for the future.

We have been created to travel the sky road, which is the high road that leads somewhere. Only when we disobey the heavenly vision shall we find ourselves traveling a dead end. No matter what our situation may be, God can make something out of our lives, if we will only place them in His hands.

I read once that several of the world's greatest violinists felt they could not play well, unless their favorite violins were in their hand. Fritz Kreisler, however, could take any violin and make it sound superb. So God can bring beautiful harmony out of every life placed in His hands. But we must put our lives in His hands. This we do when our confidence in God becomes unshakable.

Late in life an old woman accepted Christ as her Savior, and was thrilled with this new partnership. She talked about it constantly.

"You seem very confident about this salvation of yours," a friend said to her. "I wouldn't be so sure if I were you. What if the Lord lets you slip through His fingers?"

"Oh, no," replied the old woman, "I don't have to worry about that. I am one of His fingers."

In a sense she was right. Every one who has accepted Christ as the Savior is a part of Him. We shall never be separated from Him. We can have complete confidence that we shall be with the Lord forever.

TODAY'S THOUGHT: *The heart that worships and trusts in God alone will never know earthly anxiety.*

MARCH 27

You Have Spiritual Potential

Be strong, and let your heart take courage, all you who wait for the Lord! Psalm 31:24

One morning an interesting editorial appeared in the newspaper about a golfer who had refused lessons from a professional, and yet prided himself on breaking 100 once every 50 times he played. The editorial indicated how foolish the man was. Had he been willing to take lessons perhaps he could have made 100 every time he played the game. Then it went on to tell about a self-taught musician who could play, "Hail, Hail the Gang's All Here." Yet if the same man had taken lessons from a professional teacher, he might have mastered a symphony.

The editorial writer concluded that there is much latent power in every individual, but we refuse to pay the price for something which could transform us and make us so much more than we are.

There is not a single person in the world who lacks the capacity to become more than he is. This is true in every area of life, especially the one which is our spiritual self. A writer of Scripture said this of Christ: ". . . to all who received him, . . . he gave power to become . . ." One cannot have this power for living, however, unless there are deep inner wells. They are much more significant than any outward circumstance. Some people spend their time building up fortune, fame, and reputation. But one touch of death's cold hand, and these will vanish like a vapor. Moreover, they render us vulnerable. The devil, the world, and our own flesh can attack us, and we be utterly defeated.

In medieval days, when people were besieged in their castles by enemies, they always had a deep well hidden within the walls of the fortress. They reasoned this way . . . the enemy can pollute or fill up the wells on the outside, but regardless we shall have our protected inner well clear and pure.

Those putting their trust in the grace and mercy of God build up reservoirs of strength. They can outlast the siege of evil and overcome in crucial times. In these critical times God needs soldiers of great strength. Every one of us can add our part to God's answer to the evil, totalitarian powers seeking to destroy the dignity of the individual, to annihilate Christianity, and to conquer and rule the earth. Let us use our God-given talents for Him!

TODAY'S THOUGHT: *If your life is in your hands, turn it over to Christ.*

MARCH 28

Look Toward Heaven

Not every one who says to me, "Lord, Lord," shall enter the kingdom of heaven, but he who does the will of my Father who is in heaven. Matthew 7:21

Let us look up and build for heaven. We ourselves construct our future, and we must build high, if we would build for eternity. We must build, not as the foolish people of Babel who built in pride, but as humble workers building in partnership with God.

Have you learned the lesson of the ivy growing around a mighty tree until it deforms the trunk? Do not let the world get too tight a hold on you. Closing upon you, it can deform your life, and make you unfit for heaven. People entirely satisfied with this world will never look off to heaven. When their arms clutch tightly an idol, they cannot be lifted to worship God. When their eyes turn downward into the mistaken treasure-mine of position and pleasure, they cannot look up to see the harbor lights of heaven. Some of us have our eyes so fixed upon the mirror of selfishness that we can see nothing but our own reflection. Others have lived so long groping about in the dark places of the earth that they cannot see the light. They are like fish in the waters of a subterranean cavern, who, though they still have eyes, have lost the capacity to see.

Hope of heaven should comfort us in time of trouble. The godless man who loses his friends, his money, or his health feels that he has lost all. There is nothing for him but despair. The Christian, however, may lose all things yet still take comfort, for he has the hope of heaven—the truth, the glory, and the good—which never can be taken away from him. He has Christ within, the hope of glory. To die is merely to move into another room of God's great household. It is to inherit the place which the Master went on before to prepare for every one of us.

Thank God this day for the fadeless hope that is ours.

TODAY'S THOUGHT: Hope is the only cure for the ills of mind and body that men suffer.

MARCH 29

God Will Never Go Away

Jesus answered him, "If a man loves me, he will keep my word, and my Father will love him, and we will come to him and make our home with him." John 14:23

I can remember that as a young child occasionally I drove my mother to distraction by some of my antics. I was the last in a family of ten children, so when I arrived, she had already had a full, busy life raising such a large family. Usually she was the essence of patience, but every once in a while after becoming especially distraught she would say, "Sometimes I get so discouraged I could go away and never come back again." The thought was innocently spoken, but having heard it, one could not easily forget it.

One day when I missed my mother, I went calling through the house, "Mother!" But no one responded. Wondering what had happened, I went to the window and waited. Minutes seemed like hours, but presently I was filled with relief as Mother came out of a neighbor's house and strode home across the lawn. When she came in, I began to cry, "Mother, I thought you had gone." How relieved I was that she had not left me! And how obedient I was after that. I realized how terrible home would be without Mother!

Sometimes in our spiritual lives we have experienced a like situation. And the way we have acted we could hardly blame God, if He went away and left us alone in this vast universe. But this God came to earth to save us.

So often people wonder whether God will forgive them. Do you remember *Les Miserables* and the story of Jean Valjean. He had been a galley slave. When he was released, he felt that society would never forgive him for having committed a crime. Men refused to employ him. He was turned away from their doors until finally he went to the bishop's house. The kind man took him in and gave him the best place at the table. When Jean Valjean stole the silver, and the police brought him back, the forgiveness of the bishop broke Jean Valjean's heart. The bishop treated him as a brother, had faith in him, and offered him help in living a new life. Had he earned it? No! It was purely by grace that he was given a second chance.

So God's grace each day is our personal opportunity.

TODAY'S THOUGHT: *If we can kindle a glow of hope in the life of another, we are doing God's work.*

MARCH 30

Men Must Live as Brothers

Any one who hates his brother is a murderer, and you know that no murderer has eternal life abiding in him. 1 John 3:15

As a soldier in battle never knows when a bullet may hit him, just so in the battle of life we can never know when death's angel may cross our threshold. Life is like that. We ought always be prepared. For at the time we least expect we may hear the whisper, "Come along!" Indeed we would be wise if every day we stood guard against temptation and prayed without ceasing, so that whenever our number is called, whether early or late, we shall be ready because of the mercy and grace of our Savior.

We should be very careful how we live. God expects us to love one another. The very foundation stone of our faith as Christians is love for God and for our fellow men. "For he who does not love his brother whom he has seen, cannot love God whom he has not seen." No man dare presume to call himself a Christian, unless he loves his neighbor and is charitable toward him.

This love should be practical. To say we love our fellow man, and yet do nothing for him, is pure hypocrisy. One of the chief marks of loving charity is to think gently of another's faults. Love covers a multitude of sins. What a different world it would be, if we tried to save our fellow man instead of dragging his faults before the eyes of the world. Whenever we are tempted to judge harshly, we should remember how much God has forgiven us through our Savior, and how much pardon we ourselves need each day.

If we do not forgive our fellow man, how will we fare on Judgment Day when we ask the Judge to forgive us? There are some people who look at a beautiful picture and see only the speck of dust or the crack in the canvas. There are some who look at their neighbor, and see only the weak points in his character or that broken place in his spiritual armor. Let us not go about with a magnifying glass, searching for the faults of our fellow men. If we must use the magnifier, let us turn it upon our own lives.

Happy is the man who has wiped away the tears of someone who has sinned or is in trouble. He shall not be forgotten by God, who shall wipe away all tears from his eyes.

TODAY'S THOUGHT: *We need never expect mercy, unless we ourselves first show mercy.*

MARCH 31

God's Word Will Direct You

And the Word became flesh and dwelt among us, full of grace and truth; we have beheld his glory, glory as of the only Son from the Father. John 1:14

Each Sunday as we worship, we join other Christians to strengthen our resolve to do God's will, and accomplish the tasks He has set for us to do. We confess our sins and we give thanks for His forgiveness. We admit our shortcomings, but we rejoice in the Almighty power of God. The church is the power station, giving direction to our lives from day to day. It stands as a great witness to the whole world. But merely to attend church is not enough. We need to bring the church to our homes, and carry it into our lives. It is important that we read God's Word each day, and so gain strength for the tasks at hand.

When, in the Lord's Prayer, we ask Him to give us our daily bread, we pray to receive food not only for our bodies but also for our souls. We ask not so much for the comforts of life as for His eternal peace in our hearts. We do not seek the world's pleasures but the blessings of heaven, which God alone can give. So we pray to Him, recognizing that He is not only the ruler of life, but the giver of the only gifts that bring us peace and joy. God spreads His Word before us as a map by which we steer our course. With certainty He points to the destination, and tells us the way we must take to reach our goal.

If you wished to travel to some distant point and had no idea of how to get there, you would be foolish to start without some directions. It would be absurd to think that, by going in any direction whatsoever, you would reach your destination. Oh, it is true you could travel in that manner, but only to get farther and farther away from your original goal. The results of it all could be tragic.

Today many people think they can get along without God. They feel no need to pray to Him or to seek His guidance. They take no time to read His Word in order to find direction in living. Yet they wonder why they are missing the joy which they are seeking.

There is only one road that leads to abundant life. It is the Master's way. In the Word God gives us new strength and understanding. If day by day we put into practice the eternal truth, our souls become temples worthy of eternity.

TODAY'S THOUGHT: *You will never know the wisdom of His Words until you have lived by them.*

APRIL 1

Trust Your Master Unreservedly

Commit your way to the Lord; trust in him, and he will act.
Psalm 37:5

We are often so inconsistent in our thinking. We board a train and ride comfortably to our destination without the slightest worry, in spite of the fact that we have never met the engineer. We take a complicated prescription from our family doctor to the pharmacist whom we do not know, and have complete faith that this chemist will put up the right medicine with which to combat the particular illness. We climb aboard an airplane, and with supreme confidence travel to distant parts of the world in an engineering miracle, with a pilot at the controls who is a total stranger to us. Yet, we can quibble about faith in God who desires to direct our lives, or to believe in God who never fails those who turn to Him.

The truth is that no person can organize a successful life without a living faith in the power of Almighty God. Even though that faith be ever so feeble, anything is possible. When faith is nourished, it will grow strong and flourish. It can become such a power as to remove mountains, i.e., surmount any problem, and triumphantly rise above any cross planted athwart the highway of your life.

Faith is also the channel by which the power of God can enter our lives to give us the abundant life. A saint lay on a bed of illness, broken and depressed. The turning came when her whirring mind grasped the thought that even a hollow straw floating on the ocean has the mighty sea flowing through it. "Into my broken finiteness could flow infinity," she repeated. And her yielded faith permitted God's healing power to move in. All of us know people who are bearing tremendous problems. We ask them curiously, "How do you do it?" Then we learn their secret, "Simply by quietly trusting in God."

Faith gives victory. It gives us the final push to reach the finish line and win the race. If a runner keeps telling himself, "I cannot do it, I am going to lose!" he can hardly do anything but fall behind. But if he keeps saying to himself, "I am going to win!" most often the victory is his.

Let us live with the enthusiasm and zest that comes from a faith in a loving God who keeps His promise of victory.

TODAY'S THOUGHT: *Today is filled with golden, irretrievable moments. Let us wisely spend them.*

APRIL 2

Power to Become

For to me to live is Christ, and to die is gain. Philippians 1:21

We should always keep in mind the difference between making a livelihood and making a life. Jesus too had a livelihood—He was a carpenter. But that was not what He was living for. Andrew, Peter, James, and John had a livelihood—they were fishermen. But that was not what they were living for. Paul was a tent maker by trade, but that was only incidental to his real aim for life. Suppose you and I were to ask Paul for the reason for his life. We find his answer in our Bible: "For to me to live is Christ, and to die is gain."

We know, too, how extremely important a good beginning can be. Yet even more necessary is to keep becoming. God has given each of us the capacity to grow, and every day we should seek to increase our stature. Did you know that science has proved that the brain will continue to develop even after 60 years of age, if only we continue to use it? Yes, indeed, God has given us the capacity of a growing edge of both mind and soul, if only we maintain the desire. Resources unlimited are available within, if we will but follow the plan of our Master Builder.

Let us remember, too, that though we are children of today, we are also citizens of eternity. It is by making every day of our earthly lives significant, cramming them with a thousand unremembered deeds of love, all according to the unfolding will of God, that we shall escape the boredom and exhaustion of futility that make many old before their time, and render them walking corpses while they live, and glad when they find their grave.

Victor Hugo strikes my note in writing to a friend: "I feel immortality. . . . Winter is on my head but eternal spring is in my heart. . . . For half a century I've been writing . . . but I have not said one-thousandth part of what is in me. When I have gone down to the grave, I shall have ended my days' work, but another begins on the morrow."

Have you tuned in to learn God's purpose for your life? Are you living so close to God as to know beyond all doubt what you are living for? Stop this moment to gain eternity's perspective of the real values that can create the inner peace we seek. "Go down, son," said Martin Neimoller's father repeatedly, "go down to the last day of your life and let it your keeper be."

TODAY'S THOUGHT: *I will resolve to grow each day in grace.*

APRIL 3

On Tiptoe for Christ's Coming

Our soul waits for the Lord; he is our help and shield.
Psalm 33:20

One day Saint Paul prayed this brief prayer which is a model for those who love the Lord and await His soon return: "May the God of hope fill you with all joy and peace in believing." A little later on we find him writing to Saint Timothy saying, "Henceforth there is laid up for me the crown of righteousness, which the Lord, the righteous judge will award to me on that Day, and not only to me but also to all who have loved his appearing."

Let us think about Paul's personal circumstances at the time of this prayer. This brave soldier of Jesus Christ had nearly finished his earthly warfare. About thirty years had passed since on the road to Damascus he had seen heaven's light, and heard the voice through the blinding light say, "Saul, Saul, why do you persecute me?" From that soul-shaking moment on he had fought the good fight. He had kept the faith. He had run with patience the race set before him. And the secret of this great victory he puts very simply. He kept "looking to Jesus."

Think of Paul's suffering. He had endured stoning and dank prison cell, hunger and nakedness, perils by land and sea; and as he now writes, he was a prisoner at Rome chained to a soldier. Wherever he moved hand or foot, there was the clank of the chain, and the grim presence of the Roman guard, to remind him that he was awaiting death. Yet he could say, "I am already on the point of being sacrificed."

What was the secret of his life? How come he did not fear death? It was because he longingly awaited the coming of Jesus and the crown of victory. For him death was the sweet chariot to bring him into the immediate presence of his Lord. He longed for the reward of an everlasting peace which he knew would be his. His imprisonment could only end in the glorious liberty of the children of God.

We who have faith to believe that "in everything God works for good with those who love him," can share Paul's poise and confidence, since for us, too, that day will be filled with peace and joy of believing.

TODAY'S THOUGHT: *Faith gives you to look at life through the eyes of Jesus.*

94

The Humility That Begets Courage

The reward for humility and fear of the Lord is riches and honor and life. Proverbs 22:4

The assurance that Christ is ever present with us should naturally result in certain changes in our lives. If we really lay hold of this fact and know His very presence, great things are bound to happen to us.

First of all, we become very humble. That the holy Son of God, the King of kings, and the Lord of lords chose to be born in an earthly manger, to be raised in a poor workingman's home, and as an itinerant teacher had no place to rest His head, indicates how much He humbled himself. Following in His footsteps, we have reason to be anything but proud. Yet, how difficult it is for us to remain humble! As we become successful and prosperous, we come to think more highly of ourselves than we should. But even as bacteria shrivel and die before a gamma ray, so the virus of pride must give way to the presence of God. Judas could not endure the power of sacramental love unveiled in the upper room, but slipped out into the night. Jesus and base pride are not compatible.

The knowledge of the Lord's presence should also make us courageous. Let us hold to the faith that, "If God is for us, who is against us?" There is no temptation that He cannot conquer. There is no sorrow too heavy for His shoulder who is beside us to help. There is no difficulty that we cannot overcome, if we hold His hand as we walk life's way. Let us remember that when the strident sounds of the world would drown out the whisper of God, we ought to turn to Him, confident that He still is able to bring us to a quiet place apart, where we can again clearly hear His voice. And, having heard this call, become victorious.

Our Lord's presence makes itself known by making us kind to one another. His early followers were characterized in these words: "See how they love one another." It must break the heart of God when He sees His children quarreling among themselves, being petty in their judgments, and selfish in their living.

There is a legend telling of an old cobbler saint who made shoes for the poor without payment. The angels kept his supply of leather undwindling. God provided the means for the doing.

TODAY'S THOUGHT: *Only members of God's kingdom receive, free for the asking, resources unlimited.*

APRIL 5

My Jesus Ever the Same

Extol the Lord our God; worship at his footstool! Psalm 99:5

What a source of comfort it is to know that God's lovingkindness is unchanging! The same gentle eyes which brought repentant Peter to tears, which wept for friend Lazarus in his grave and over sin-stricken Jerusalem, those eyes look down upon us today, too. The same hands which held little children, which healed the sick, which cleansed the lepers, which strengthened the crippled, are reached out to us now. He stands before us with the same invitation as of old: "him who comes to me I will not cast out."

God's tender loving care is unchanging. God never unlearns being gracious. He may lead us along on a very rough way. He may even plan a heavy cross that He wants us to bear. But the prime thing to know is that, planting our feet in His footsteps, we are on our way to heaven. Whatever may happen in these our lives, that are on top today and in the deepest trough of despond tomorrow, of one thing we can be absolutely certain: God cares.

"Troubles," say the Arabs, "come in on horseback and go off afoot." But when difficulty comes, let us remember that the toughest steel has been heated again and again. Heated and hammered, heated and hammered, in a seeming purposeless pattern. Yet it emerges a keen-edged blade. What we sometimes call mistakes God uses to make the blessings which shape our lives and make us the better people. "Hope in God, for I shall again praise him," says the psalmist. He is never too busy to take notice of the lilies of the field. Even the tiny sparrow does not flutter to the earth unnoticed. No matter what happens, He cares. You can count on God's forgiveness. Because of the sacrifice of Jesus Christ on the cross, God has pardon for all who are truly repentant. So every day seek that old path and walk in it. Hold firmly to the faith that, "If we confess our sins, He is faithful and just and will forgive our sins and cleanse us from all unrighteousness."

Moody loved to tell of a windmill he saw in a barnyard with the word printed across: "God is love." "What," he asked his host, unable to veil his alarm, "do you mean His love is as fickle as the veering wind?" "Oh, no," answered the sturdy man of the soil. "I mean whichever way the wind blows, God is love."

TODAY'S THOUGHT: *The tested Christian would rather walk in the darkness with God than to walk alone in the sunlight.*

APRIL 6

"What You Are Speaks So Loudly . . ."

Truly, truly, I say to you, we speak of what we know, and bear witness to what we have seen; but you do not receive our testimony. John 3:11

We are God's ambassadors, sent into this world to speak up for Him. Day by day we should seek God's will so as to discover our appointed task. "For this cause I have come into the world, to bear witness to the truth," said the Lord. Too few of us realize why we are here, or what we were born to do, and the reason why God preserves us alive, and why all of the blessings have been showered on us from His open hand.

He did not send us into this world just to make money, or to seek so much pleasure, or to attain this or that ambition. He is eager that our higest ambition should be in the spiritual realm. Every living soul has a task in God's great plan. Every day we preach a sermon by the way we live. We must remember how important can be the example of our lives to others.

As I travel abroad, especially in the far corners of the world, I have discovered how closely watched is everything the missionaries do as they minister to those, still strangers to the light of the gospel. When I have spoken to those converted to the faith they have said, "We watched how the missionary lived. That was enough of a sermon for us to want to become Christian, too."

Someone has well said that it is astonishing how much good goodness makes. Like a stone thrown into a pool causing a myriad of concentric circles to flow swiftly from the center until they die on the surrounding shore, so is a good deed in a naughty world.

What a different world, if every one of us sought to widen the sphere of his influence! If we took our cue for every act directly from God, it would not take long for His message to encircle the world and bring it out of darkness into light. One hero example in a battle creates a host of other heroes, while the influence of one single coward in a moment of danger can panic a crowd.

Daily ask God for strength to follow our Lord and Savior, the only perfect pattern. With our hearts giving and giving, and never counting the cost, our light will so shine before men that they will see our good works, and with us glorify the Father who is in heaven.

TODAY'S THOUGHT: *You are a representative for your Redeemer, all day, every day.*

APRIL 7

Hold to Your Childhood Faith

I will look with favor on the faithful in the land, that they may dwell with me; he who walks in the way that is blameless shall minister to me. Psalm 101:6

One evening in a children's hospital a nurse entered the room of a four-year-old boy with tuberculosis in his thigh. The doctors had been considering amputation. Looking out of the window at the colors splashed across the sky by the setting sun, the boy seemed awed by the beauty of it all. He turned to the nurse and said, "My, but the sunset is beautiful!"

"God is painting the sky," the nurse said, and left the room for a moment. Returning on tiptoe she saw the little fellow still gazing at the beautifully painted sky, and then heard him say, all unaware of any human presence: "God, if you can paint the sky, you can heal my leg. Thank you, God! Goodnight!"

All of us need the simplicity of faith of that little child. People have much more faith than they give themselves credit for. We come into the world with this gift from God already in our hands. And as children we use it heart and soul. But in growing older either we let it die from lack of use, or we use it so seldom it is no longer effective. We must use or lose the faith that God has given us.

We have every reason to believe in Jesus. His touch brings healing and salvation. He never touched anyone who was not made whole. Jesus was one person with no failures in His record. Someone has suggested the fact that no one ever died or remained dead in His presence. True, He conducted no funerals. He occasioned resurrections only.

No matter what your problem or concern, He has power plus to help. Too frequently we lose sight of life's value because we do not realize the tremendous price God put on it. Take that talent, even if it be only one, and turn it into good. With His help, we can conquer in any situation. There is a girl who took her facial deformity and, by living one of the most beautiful lives in the community, turned it into a mark of distinction. In spite of her appearance, she was determined to live the abundant life.

That possibility is open to you, too. Offer what you have to God. If it is sorrow, let Him make from it a song.

TODAY'S THOUGHT: *Faith forms the first line of defense against man's foes, visible and invisible.*

APRIL 8

Give Your Life to God

I have been crucified with Christ; it is no longer I who live, but Christ who lives in me; and the life I now live in the flesh I live by faith in the Son of God, who loved me and gave himself for me.

Galatians 2:20

Wise and happy is the person who gives his life to God. So many put the commitment off to a future date. They intend to lead a new life, but never find time actually to set about doing it. They could be likened to a man who, fantastically enough, put off eating, drinking, and sleeping day after day, until his body collapsed and he died. So often we think of a life with Christ as a life that restricts, that cheats us of life's joys. What we do not understand is that every day we fail to live with God is a lost day.

To worship God is man's most blessed privilege. It brings supreme joy. It smites down evil within him, and raises up the good and makes man godlike. Daily communion with God re-creates God's image within.

When Moses came down from beholding God, his face shone with an awful and shining glory. Paul said, "And we all, with unveiled face, beholding the glory of the Lord, are being changed into his likeness from one degree of glory to another." Finally, we have the promise that, "We shall be like him, for we shall see him as he is."

Staying close to God gives us power to do what never we would otherwise be capable of doing. No man knows how much he can endure until he is tested. A garage mechanic found his wife pinned under his automobile; bunching his back under it he lifted the car, pulling her out from under with the one free hand. He could never in God's world have done anything like that under normal circumstances. Unsuspected strength is ours if we are in communion with God. We draw from His vast reservoirs of power.

The secret is to know that His strength is available. In an old story of the crucifixion of Jesus, Pilate's wife is asking the Roman centurion the question, "Is He dead yet?" To this the centurion replies, "No, He is not dead." "Where is He then?" asks anxious Mrs. Pilate. "He is not gone," the gruff soldier replies, "He is set loose in a world where no one can stop Him!"

TODAY'S THOUGHT: *Knowing how stubbornly fought is every inch of advance in righteousness, think of the changes the gospel has wrought in 2,000 years, and with what remarkable results in human lives!*

APRIL 9

Get Off That Teeter-Totter!

You are the salt of the earth; but if salt has lost its taste, how shall its saltness be restored? Matthew 5:13

Whenever you pass by a playground, I imagine you are as fascinated as I by the children on the teeter-totter. It is hearty and wholesome recreation for them. But there are all too many mature people who live just that way. One minute they are up, and the next they are down. Living the teeter-totter way of life finds a man high in his ideals, in his ambitions, in his hopes for a short while, then tragically dip to the lowest earth level again. Look at that poor wretch slipping down, down, grasping things temporal which, like the poppy's flower, you grasp only to have it go to pieces in your hand.

There are too many of us who are fence straddlers in our world. When will we learn that we cannot serve two masters? We prove by our living what kind of faith we have in our hearts. In the beginning the devil does not conquer us by having us commit big sins. Instead he creeps into our souls by gaining our gradual submission to little sins. These act as spreading cancer cells, eventually destroying the very life in our spiritual veins.

In an experiment a scientist put a frog into a pot of boiling water. The frog's instinct of self-preservation reacted quickly. He immediately jumped out of the boiling water. Then the man put this same frog into a pan of water which he heated slowly. The frog became sluggish in the gradually rising temperature eventually boiling to death. People are slowly enmeshed in sin's evil snare, gradually losing ground until finally they succumb. They face spiritual death now, and eternal death forever, all because they do not stay alert.

If you plant a healthy tree, it will grow and bear fruit. But if it is diseased, it will soon wither away, only to be thrown into the fire. The Master cautions that not everyone saying, "Lord, Lord," not everyone who confesses his Christian creed, and not everyone who goes to church on Sunday, shall inherit the kingdom. Only those that prove their sincerity by doinng the will of God will gain heaven at last. The Holy Spirit's change wrought within us is bound to be evidenced in a change in the things we do and say. Otherwise our faith lacks vitality and meaning and is spurious.

TODAY'S THOUGHT: *God gets some of His greatest work done through the most ordinary people.*

100

APRIL 10

Keep Walking Toward Your Savior

I sought the Lord, and he answered me, and delivered me from all my fears. Psalms 34:4

Said a young man to a minister, "Finally I have found out what is wrong with myself."

"What did you find out?" asked the pastor.

His friend replied, "I have been keeping the wrong company."

"What do you mean, you have been keeping the wrong company?"

"I have been keeping company with myself."

He had made the discovery that he was his own worst enemy— the enemy urging him to doubt, persuading to dependence on his own strength rather than God's. After prolonged, deep thought he had come at last to the conclusion that without God he had degenerated to a spineless jellyfish lacking will power and the "git" to do good.

"I can do all things in him who strengthens me." That was Apostle Paul's faith. And it is the faith by which anyone who claims it can conquer today. That faith brings us into partnership with a power from which not even death can separate us.

An artist once painted a picture of Jesus as He healed the blind man at Jericho. After completing it he showed it to his friends asking them, "What impresses you most about this picture?"

"I like the color and the background," answered one of them.

Another said, "I like the faces, they're alive and strong."

"You've all missed the point," the artist commented. "Look," said he pointing to a white cane lying by itself in the background. "That blind man is walking to Jesus, having dropped his cane. So confident is he that the Master will heal his sightless eyes that he has let the cane drop from his eager hands."

With a faith and confidence in the Lord like that, anyone can conquer. Of the lepers we read, "As they went they were cleansed." Faith is the bridge over which we walk into a living relationship with the Almighty God.

TODAY'S THOUGHT: *A great peace of heart comes to all those with an unfaltering faith in an unfailing God.*

Banish Discouragement

Forgetting what lies behind and straining forward to what lies ahead, I press on toward the goal for the prize of the upward call of God in Christ Jesus. Phillippians 3:13, 14

There is an old fable about the devil's wedge. It seems Satan announced he was going to retire from business, and would sell all his tools at public auction. The evening before the sale, people came from far and near to see what he had to sell. The chief tools were malice, envy, jealousy, and deceit. But in one corner lay a wedge-shaped tool, marked at a higher price than the others. Someone asked the devil the reason for the excessive price.

"That," he said, "is the most useful tool in my whole collection. It is worth more than all the rest put together. When nothing else will work, I can use this to pry into a man's heart. That tool is Discouragement."

Remember, this is the devil's favorite tool, and do not permit yourself to be discouraged. The last key on the choked key ring may be just the one that opens the door. Do not give up now. Who knows what is just around the corner for you? Hundreds of people miss great rewards simply because they are unwilling to walk just a bit farther, to work just a little harder. Mark Twain missed a fortune by throwing down his pickax and bucket and quitting the claim. The very next bucket his partner panned was "pay dirt."

Theodore Roosevelt was blind in one eye. Yet he practiced at marksmanship until he became not only a good shot, but one of the best big game hunters of his day.

As a young man Winston Churchill stammered and lisped. He was tempted to give up, but instead launched a frontal attack against his speech problems. He made himself one of the world's greatest contemporary orators.

Franklin Delano Roosevelt was a victim of polio, but he underwent physical therapy until his body was strong enough to allow him to lead a near normal life. As a young lawyer he was appointed Secretary of the Navy, and then in stages he climbed to the top of the political ladder. In the heart of World War II, he told his discouraged countrymen, "The only thing we have to fear is fear itself." Life tied to God's power can overcome anything!

TODAY'S THOUGHT: *The hero of heroes is the one who faces life with courage, opposes wrong, and upholds right regardless of its personal cost.*

APRIL 12

Foster a Forgiving Spirit

Forgive, I pray you, the transgressions of your brothers and their sin. Genesis 50:17

Some years ago there was an outbreak of anti-Semitism on one Eastern college campus. A Gentile attacked a Jewish student with such violence that, fearing he had killed him, he fled in panic. The law never caught up with him, and therefore he was never punished. He lived incognito in a distant part of the country. After some years he prospered, even being elected as an officer of his company. However, when a serious problem arose in the business, an emergency call was sent East for a specialist. To his horror who should the specialist be, but this Jew he had nearly killed!

Bent and crippled though he was, the Jew sensed the situation at once. He said quietly, "I know what must be going through your mind. Let me just say that, as far as I am concerned, the whole affair is a closed incident. I did spend two years in a hospital, which gave me a lot of time to think things through. More than ever I determined to make good, not only for myself, but for others like you, who for some strange reason or another, do not think that Jews are entitled to the full advantages and opportunities of our American democracy. My deformity became a driving force, and while it seemed for long an insurmountable handicap, I now tell you honestly that I bear no ill will toward you. On the contrary, I intend to throw all of our resources behind your organization to make it possible for you even to undertake a large expansion here."

Think of how transformed our world would become if, instead of harboring hatreds, each one of us would give back a forgiving spirit. How much happier we should all be. How much further advanced our world would be, too! But better than all this, we would be doing God's will.

You ask, "How often should one forgive his fellow men?"

Jesus answers, "Not seven times, but seventy times seven.'

TODAY'S THOUGHT: *Man needs a greater might than atomic power for constructive purposes. Most of all he needs atoning power.*

APRIL 13

Give That You May Live

You shall give to him freely, and your heart shall not be grudging when you give to him; because for this the Lord your God will bless you in all your work and in all that you undertake.

Deuteronomy 15:10

A little boy had five whole pennies all for himself. How happy he was as he skipped down the street wondering how to spend them! He ran into a little candy shop to buy something he had always wanted. On the shelf was a glass jar filled with red, green, and yellow candy balls. Carefully he counted out his five pennies, and placed them on the counter. The five candy balls he put into his pocket, and hurried away to the Christian community center, hoping he would not be late for story time.

"I'm here," he announced as he ran through the door. "I love the missionary stories."

"And just in time for the story, too," said the missionary.

Now it happened that the story this day concerned the little boy who gave his lunch to the Master. Jesus took the loaves and fishes and, having blest them, fed many, many people. The boy in listening to the story almost dropped off his chair when he heard the teacher say how willingly the little lad in the story had given Jesus his lunch. He glanced up at a picture of Jesus and the children on the wall. The boy wanted, like those children, to be near Jesus and to be loved by Him. But what did he own that he could give? Then he remembered his five candy balls. Quickly he put all of the five sticky balls into the teacher's hand saying, "Give them to the other little kids."

By this spontaneous little act he passed happiness around to all, and received much more himself.

The greatest example of giving the world has ever known is found in the story of the cross. A sinless Christ is giving himself that others might live. In losing His own life He is offering the opportunity of saving all those who believe in Him. This unselfish sacrifice must be the example that we follow.

The Dead Sea is parable enough of the one who just takes and never gives, without our demonstrating it in life, too. We must give to live.

TODAY'S THOUGHT: *Anyone can give without loving, but no one can love without giving.*

APRIL 14

God Is Unchanging

This God—his way is perfect; the promise of the Lord proves true; he is a shield for all those who take refuge in him.

Psalm 18:30

The world and everything in it is full of change. Only God, our Creator, from whom comes every good and perfect gift, is unchanging.

One who travels about in the world has this fact brought home with emphasis. In the Bible you read about the city of Capernaum. In visiting the Holy Land, all you can find there are the ruins of some of the buildings. Yet He who predicted Capernaum's doom, Jesus Christ, remains the same yesterday, today, and forever. If you seek Nineveh's site, where Jonah preached, you will not find one stone upon the other. The great city has been obliterated. Yet the God who called upon its people to repent is the same as ever. Silence and desolation preside over Pompey's darkened rubble-lined street, where once rang out men's careless laugh and merry songs as if to say, "Let us be merry, for tomorrow we die." Yet the God who let this worldly way of these fair but sinful homes fall back in judgment on their heads remains the same.

Turning to look at ourselves, we can see change everywhere. Many of us have revisited the place of our childhood after long years of absence. There is the old school where we spent our boyhood. Perhaps we even found the very desk on which we carved our name. There is the old hill down which we turned our sleds, and over there our favorite haunt, the corner drugstore. But how different things are now. The once familiar places look so strange and unnatural. And what of the people? Of those who formed our world, who smiled and surrounded us with warm security, few if any remain.

Yet the God that we loved then, and the God that has kept us through the years, remains constant. His love still surrounds us and dwells within our hearts. Long ago the psalmist prayed, "Lead thou me to the rock that is higher than I." All of us need something constant, something immovable, to which we can attach ourselves. Let us never forget that, although the world about us may change from day to day, the Rock of Ages still remains. Forever its cleft will be a hiding place for man's soul.

TODAY'S THOUGHT: *Every time we look up, God's light is shining, always from the same place with the same brilliance.*

APRIL 15

My Utmost for His Highest

Blessed is the man who walks not in the counsel of the wicked, nor stands in the way of sinners, nor sits in the seat of scoffers.

Psalm 1:1

Not long ago a 63-year-old office worker made headlines for the first time in her life. It happened that one evening, as she was baby sitting, she was running the water into the bath tub to bathe the 19-month-old boy who was her charge that evening. Suddenly a faucet blew off, and gushing scalding water sprayed over the bathroom. With hands over the open pipe, she tried to talk the child into leaving the room, but he would not go. So she held back the scalding water and screamed until neighbors rescued the little boy. Even then she would not leave for the hospital, until a substitute had been sent from the the baby sitting bureau for which she worked.

Weeks later, just out of the hospital, she wrote, "I did not know the little boy before, but I love children, although I have none of my own. I have always felt nothing was worth doing, unless it was done to the best of my ability. There have been many reverses in my life, and I have been able to meet and conquer them only by saying, 'I can, and I will, with God's help.'"

The writing in her letter was thin and shaky because her hands were still wrapped with bandages. This lady, in doing her assigned task, had risked permanent injury in meeting that agonizing emergency. All through life faith in God had made this unbelievable spirit of dedication a part of her very nature.

Experience had given her a motto by which to live and, whenever facing a task seemingly impossible, she would repeat, "I can do it, and I will, by the help of God."

Never once had she found His strength wanting for the need that she faced. Such confidence in God is bound to present its unfailing reward.

TODAY'S THOUGHT: *With our faith serving as the starter, God will provide the power for forward progress.*

APRIL 16

Reflect God's Light

You are the light of the world. A city set on a hill cannot be hid. Matthew 5:14

One day a little 10-year-old girl was asked by her mother to take a bunch of flowers down the street to a shut-in old lady.

When the girl returned from her errand of love the mother said to her, "Now smell your hand."

She did inquisitively and discovered that her hand smelled like the flowers she had brought to this lady.

"Flowers always leave some fragrance in the hand of the giver," the mother pointed out.

It is that way in life, too. Every kind deed we bestow on someone else leaves us a sweeter person.

Just as there are two kinds of people in the world, consider two substances, both of which are carbon. One is black and dirty and comparatively worthless. The other is pure and sparkling and beautiful—a fit ornament in a king's crown—the diamond.

Why is the one beautiful and the other so unsightly? Because one gives back the light that strikes it, while the other absorbs the light and keeps it to itself. How vastly different they are in value. One is a precious gem, sparkling and glistening and reflecting a myriad of colors. The other is dark and ugly, and of little practical value. This one absorbs all the good. The precious gem, however, a glittering diamond, reflects and gives to all its share of the beautiful things of life.

Not only does an unselfish spirit give us peace and satisfaction, but it has its practical way of helping, too.

An Indiana farmer, whose prize corn took the blue ribbon at the state fair, was asked why he always shared his best seed with his neighbors. "It is a matter of self-protection. The wind blows up the pollen and swirls it from field to field. If my neighbor grows inferior corn, it will steadily degrade the quality of my corn. Therefore, I see that they only plant the best!"

We live in a world in which we are all dependent upon each other. When we help others, we are helping ourselves.

TODAY'S THOUGHT: *There is a perfume called happiness which we cannot give to others without getting some on ourselves.*

APRIL 17

Pray Just Any Place

Give ear to my prayer, O God; and hide not thyself from my supplication! Psalm 55:1

It is wise to set aside certain times and places for prayer, and we are fortunate if we have a place apart, regularly to be alone with God. But we should not forget that we can talk to Him any time during the day wherever we might be. Sometimes when we need God's help, we cannot find a quiet sanctuary in which to escape the noises of the world. Remember that you can pray right where you are, and God will hear.

People coming from small communities into large cities are often bewildered by the crowded streets and subways of these teeming urban centers. One such newcomer, a man of great physical stature, disliked very much being jostled by others. His annoyance mounted every time he had to enter a subway car to join, as he put it, "his fellow sardines."

"Usually," he said, "I made the trip home in the later afternoon, sharing the subway with swarms of pushing, perspiring, weary people at the end of a long exhausting day. The scream of the wheels on the rails when we took a curve, and the roar as we sped through a local station, grated on my soul like sandpaper." Then one day he noticed a fellow passenger hanging onto a strap in the midst of a swaying multitude with his hands lifted in the attitude of prayer.

"This thought struck me," he said, "these men and women are God's children, and life is pressing hard on many of them, too. What better way could I spend my time than in praying for them and for myself? Thanks, friend, for the valuable lesson!"

This man's experience can be for us a helpful lesson. From the moment he decided to pray on the subway, and put that decision into practice, all the dread of the trip disappeared.

"Many times," he said, "I have stepped out of the subway with my mind and heart at peace, and with a deep inner calm that passes all human understanding. Life is all different for me now," he continued, "for I have learned that we can pray in any place and get results! Didn't Jesus make the first, the fourth, and the last word on the cross a prayer?"

TODAY'S THOUGHT: *The more we pray, the better we know and love our God.*

APRIL 18

Seek the Riches of Salvation

Make haste to help me, O Lord, my salvation! Psalm 38:22

A man of faith who faces a difficult problem never says, "This is impossible. After all, I am only human. This mountain has me stumped." Walking hand in hand with God, he knows that there is not a single obstacle in life that cannot be surmounted. It is only when discouraged through lack of faith that we say, "What is so wonderful about life anyway?"

Many people today are living lives of utter boredom. Sure, they wish they could get more out of life. But what to do about it? Others are caught in a treadmill of routine existence, and their material resources are never sufficient to satisfy their personal insecurity. What they really need are the inner resources which come from the Friend who promises all things, whatsoever we need.

A well-known educator, a man of great intellect and Christian spirit, was discussing the typical American family which he dubbed "the Joneses." He went on to say that Mr. Jones builds his life around three things: Pleasure, Money, and Power. Mr. Jones of Main Street, America, feels that the most valuable things in life are those with the costliest price tag, those with the "mostest" physical thrill, and those that give a feeling of power over others.

Do we not all face just these temptations every day? How many of us are not looking in the wrong places for our riches? Often frustrated and frantic in our search for satisfaction, we grab at anything, and when these fail to satisfy we know not where to turn. Seeing our world collapse around us like a house of cards, we resign ourselves to despair. Our perspective becomes so cramped and narrowed that we lose sight of the true values of life. We are lost in the maze of things, all because we have forgotten that human power in no way can measure up to divine power. We ought to keep looking up, no matter how high and unscalable the mountains of difficulty may seem. We cannot afford to overlook the fact that "with God nothing is impossible."

Great things await us just beyond the summit that once seemed so impossible to scale. The secret of those who attain is that they made the upward climb step by step. And the first step to take is the step of faith.

TODAY'S THOUGHT: *Those who walk arm in arm with the Master find every mile to be a miracle mile.*

APRIL 19

Look Ever at the Bright Side

Happy is the man whom God reproves. Job 5:17

Mary was a poor colored woman who earned her living by scrubbing. Her life was most difficult, and she had every reason to complain. But despite this she was a joyful Christian personality and an inspiration to all who knew her.

"Oh, Mary," a depressed friend said to her one day, "it is all right to be happy now, but I should think the future would worry you. Suppose you were sick a spell and could not work. Or suppose you were to lose your job and couldn't find another one. Or suppose . . ."

"Stop it," Mary interrupted. "I don't ever do any supposin'. The Lord is my Shepherd, and I know that I shall not want. It is all those 'supposins' that make you so miserable. And I think you would be a lot better off, if you gave them all up and just trusted the Lord!"

Yes, the believer is always cheerful. He grows sour and unhappy only when he forgets, and starts supposing things will go wrong. He is generally serene and peaceful when he remembers to trust in God's protecting care. We would be far wiser to concentrate on the pleasant things that happen to us than on unpleasant that never do happen.

A young soldier back from overseas carefully avoided relating his experiences. He always said that nothing had happened to him, but one questioner was especially persistent.

"Something must have happened," he said. "Now tell me, in all your experiences, what impressed you most?"

"Well," said the young man after careful consideration, "I was most impressed by the number of bullets that missed me."

Our lives would be happier, if we filled our thoughts with the number of dangers that threaten us but fail to materialize, if we would concentrate on God's goodness and great care.

Think over the events of the day. Think of the problems that appeared and later vanished. Then resolve to live one day at a time, looking to God for the answer to every need.

TODAY'S THOUGHT: *Turn to God as you start each day and you will go your way as carefree as a lark.*

APRIL 20

Cross Over to God's Side

Whoever confesses that Jesus is the Son of God, God abides in him, and he in God. 1 John 4:15

A friend of mine tells of crossing the George Washington Bridge one morning in a heavy fog. As he neared the New York side, suddenly he saw the shadow of the Empire State Building looming through the mist, towering darkly upward over everything. The giant structure reminded him of the power of God towering over man as he travels through the mists and uncertainties of life. When we possess faith that bridges the chasms of doubt, God's available power will loom large, and the mists of uncertainty will part. We do so need God's power to bridge the difficulties athwart our pathway to peace.

From high school geometry we remember that a straight line is the shortest distance between two points. That is why men build bridges. They want to get from one place to another without taking the long way around. Even if we live in the heart of the desert, or in country so wild there are no railways or highways, we must cross bridges frequently. A bridge, according to a school boy's definition, is something that water flows under. Of course that is not true in all cases. But it reminds us of the many things that can be washed under the bridge—old regrets, sins, fears, worries, the traits we despise so in ourselves, all the habits we have longed to break with.

Webster defines a bridge as a structure erected over a depression or obstacle. Our unforgiven sins can be the obstacle separating us from God, and the temptations of the world can be a valley of depression in which we wander away from God's well marked roadway. But faith can be the bridge carrying us over that obstacle of sin or across that valley of temptation.

Bridges link one side with another. They can connect us with a country more desirable than the one where we are. Every Christian ought to build the bridge of faith to carry him from the human side, which is helplessness, to God's side, which is power. It is over on God's side that we alone can find victory and peace.

TODAY'S THOUGHT: *Since Christ is the only source of transforming power, we strive in vain without Him, whether we are building a life or a nation.*

What Is There That to Keep You Must Give?

*A new commandment I give to you, that you love one another;
even as I have loved you, that you also love one another.*

John 13:34

There is something that concerns us from the moment we are born until the day we die. If we possess it, we are vastly rich, no matter how little we may have in our pocketbooks. This something makes the world go round. It is the language anyone can understand. It is love.

When we say love makes the world go round, we mean that it is a universal subject and at the same time a universal power. But love is effective only as we are channels through which it can flow into other people's lives. It is something we cannot keep for ourselves unless we share it with our fellow men.

Shakespeare said, "For if our virtues do not go forth of us, it is as though we had them not." It is true—you cannot have the gift of love in your heart and keep it to yourself.

There must be "through roads" to travel in life. Before the Civil War a town was thriving near Red Rock Mountain in Maine. Today all that remains of the town is a few tumble-down walls, almost hidden by foliage. Here is the reason for the town's desertion and decay: surrounding mountain ridges made it impossible for the town ever to get a through road.

The deserted village is a parallel of what happens to human lives that are selfishly bound up with their own interests. These lives are without a road running through the mind and heart into the lives of others. Such lives decay for want of service and love. Where there are no "through roads," lives crumble.

Is the love of your life earth-bound? Is it lavished on personal satisfactions? Then yours is purely a selfish love. It is not really love at all.

What is the love of your life? Is your love a growing thing? Do you have so much of it that you cannot keep it all to yourself? Then yours is a true love, a selfless love, and a living one.

TODAY'S THOUGHT: *Every act of love adds another jewel to the crown of the soul.*

APRIL 22

Take Your Troubles to God

God reigns over the nations; God sits on his holy throne.

Psalm 47:8

A man is wise if he builds up his spiritual resources to provide strength when trouble comes. If we give God our best during the bright days of our lives, we will not need be concerned in the dark and cloudy day.

A little girl was continually afraid during thunderstorms. Her mother told her always to pray when she was afraid. But at the end of a particularly noisy storm she reported that, although she prayed all the while, she was afraid; it did not help a bit.

"Well, then," advised her mother, "try praying when the sun is shining, and see if that will take away fear." A few days later another storm came up.

"Mother," confessed the little girl, "praying while the sun shines is the best way. I wasn't afraid at all in the storm today."

This is a good lesson for us. Too frequently we stay away from our Master until the storms of life drive us to Him for protection. Then we wonder why we lack the faith we need. Fox-hole religion is doomed to disappoint. One man painted the words, "Christ is Lord," on the dial of his watch to remind him that no matter what time it is, God is still here, an ever-present help and friend. Only by so believing can we know the joy-filled life. Only by so believing will we do the will of God. Only with such a faith we can withstand the storms of life.

"How can you bear so much sorrow?" a Christian woman was asked.

"I don't bear it," was her prompt reply, "the Lord bears it for me."

"Oh," said her questioner, "you must take your troubles to the Lord."

"Yes," replied the Christian, "but I do more than that. I leave them there. Most people take their burdens to Him, then take them back, and are just as worried and unhappy as ever. Only by leaving them with Him can we find perfect peace."

TODAY'S THOUGHT: *The best place for your crushing burdens is the strong, broad shoulder of your heavenly Father.*

APRIL 23

Satisfy Your Soul's Hunger

Jesus said to them, "I am the bread of life; he who comes to me shall not hunger, and he who believes in me shall never thirst."

John 6:35

In order to discover the real happiness we are seeking, our one important need is to realize the necessity for living deep instead of shallow, fast lives.

In the novel, *Grand Hotel*, by Vicki Baum, a middle-aged man had just come from the doctor. Afflicted with an incurable disease, he had been told that death was imminent. Directly he decided to go out and see life and all that it had to offer. He went to the finest hotels. He visited world-famous clubs. He lived as much as the world thinks "living" really is! Yet he came to the end of each day completely dissatisfied. So he asked his friends, "What is the matter? What is life after all?"

They replied, "That kind of living merely passes time. It is not real living, for it does not satisfy the deep hunger of your soul. And there is no true living unless that hunger is satisfied."

As Jesus defines the term which He coined, the "kingdom of heaven," He is defining life. He says, "The kingdom of heaven is like treasure hidden in a field, which a man found and covered up; then in his joy he goes and sells all that he has and buys that field."

Here is the background for that story. Many times in the history of Palestine, foreign invaders overran this little land. The people had few soldiers. Nor did they have banks or steel safes as we have today. Their only safeguard for their treasures was to put them in a box which they would hide in some part of a field known but to themselves. Many times the husband would not so much as tell his family where the box was hidden. And then if he died, or was carried away a prisoner to wear his life out as a slave in a distant land, the treasure was lost. Years later by merest accident it would be discovered, turned up perhaps by a plowshare in the hand of some renter. Can you not see this renter bartering away his all in order to possess this field and claim the treasure?

So it will be with us when we really discover what God can mean to us. We will be willing to say, "Take my life, Lord—yes, all of it—and let it be consecrated, Lord, to Thee."

TODAY'S THOUGHT: *Let God's love shine in at the windows of your life to chase away the gloomy shadows of sin.*

114

APRIL 24

Do Not Miss Your One Chance

Today, when you hear his voice do not harden your hearts as in the rebellion. Hebrews 3:15

In East Africa a group of natives, having made a long arduous journey seeking medical care, walked right past a government hospital to reach the mission hospital. When asked why they had walked the extra distance to the mission, when the government hospital had exactly the same medicine, they replied, "The medicine may be the same, but the hands are different."

Sometimes we forget that the most important gospel is written by our lives. Helping hands are the most beautiful ones and the most effective. Every day all of us are given varied opportunities to serve God.

Think of the unexpected opportunities to witness and to serve, opportunities that present themselves by the strangest coincidence. Take, for example, the time Jesus was sitting by the well in Samaria. Tired and thirsty, He was taking a few moments to rest, when a woman He had never seen before came to draw water at the well. He started a conversation with her. The incident might have ended with their talk, but Jesus knew how to capitalize on a seemingly casual opportunity. Because He accepted the challenge of the moment, not only was the woman changed, but an entire community was transformed by her witness.

If the kingdom of God is to grow, we must not overlook the random opportunities we have to help others. We must be ready to serve Him at all times. Daily life is so crowded with casual encounters that we need to take advantage of these opportunities to witness for the Master. There is always a field that is "white for harvest" right before us. Even today you may pass someone who needs your help desperately, someone your life can influence. Do not miss your chance to be that hand of love that leads another into a more wonderful way of life. Serve God untiringly and discover that the investment you make yields tremendous dividends.

TODAY'S THOUGHT: *God promises to forgive us if we repent, but He does not promise another day in which to do what we put off doing today.*

APRIL 25

God Never Fails

Cast your burden on the Lord, and he will sustain you.

Psalm 55:22

It must have been a wonderful experience for those two men walking the lonely road to Emmaus when Another joined them. Wrapped in sorrow they did not recognize Him, but were cheered by His companionship. He seemed so interested in everything they had to say, and they did so need sympathy that day. They were fresh from witnessing the crucifixion of their Lord, but had not yet heard the news of the resurrection. Heavy-hearted, they saw little worth living for.

They told their new-found Friend all that had taken place in Jerusalem. Sensing how lonely they really were, He explained why these things had to happen. Later the men admitted to friends that their hearts burned within them as He spoke of these things. Then when He made as if to leave them, they persuaded Him to join them for a bite at the inn for it was toward evening.

Finally they made the discovery that He was Jesus, the Friend whom they thought they had lost, but who was alive again. Joy swept through their consciousness. Jesus had arisen from the dead! Now they had faith to know that with God anything was possible. Now they were willing to risk their own lives as never before on behalf of His kingdom.

That same faith is still manifested today. The star of a certain famous stage play told friends that he was too nervous to sleep the night before the opening performance.

"So I got up and dressed," he said, "and went to the nearest church, just to sit there. Soon all my nervousness vanished. It had been smoothed away. God has been good to me," he continued, "and my career has been so crowded with love that I keep turning to Him continually. Others may fail me, but God never does. He is my constant help in every part of my life."

Whether it is in the great or small, faith helps in the success of any undertaking. Faith is the most constructive force in all human existence—the more we have of it, the stronger we will be in facing any situation.

TODAY'S THOUGHT: *Some men live as if faith were being rationed in the most miserable pinches.*

APRIL 26

Practice Prayer

If you ask anything in my name, I will do it. John 14:14

Prayer is always a provocative subject for thought. Think of the power we have been promised through prayer. Through it all the resources of God are available to us. Absolutely anything is possible, if we have faith.

A recent poll indicated that only 25 percent of church people in America believe firmly in prayer and practice it daily. Often we talk about what prayer can do, but seldom do we exercise this wonderful God-given privilege.

Of course, a large number of people "say their prayers," but that is an entirely different proposition. People who are merely going through the motions of prayer expect little from it and receive less, because prayer grows in meaning as we practice it.

Frequently people say, "I try to talk to God, and my prayers do not even reach the ceiling of my room. The words are hollow and meaningless. Why then should I continue to pray?"

It is comforting to know that many of the saints in history suffered discouragement at some time or other, and had the same doubts which we experience. Even such spiritual giants as Moses, Elijah, Jeremiah, and Paul knew moments of depression. They, too, felt that evil was going to triumph, yet all of them learned differently. In a letter to Timothy Paul said, "Be urgent in season and out of season." In other words, continue your devotions whether you feel like doing it or not. Keep praying even when the results seem discouraging. For if you do, ultimately God will reveal His answer. Perhaps you will not receive what you are seeking, but you will receive what is best for you according to God's will.

Let us not forget that prayer grows in meaning as we grow in the actual practice of it. There is no better testing ground for prayer than one's own personal life. "Ask, and it will be given you," He has promised. "Seek and you will find; knock, and it will be opened to you." What a thrilling thing is this promise from God—our God of all power.

TODAY'S THOUGHT: *Let prayer pervade your life.*

APRIL 27

Swallow Your Pride

The patient in spirit is better than the proud in spirit.

Ecclesiastes 7:8

If we have faith to believe in Christ, our Savior, our sins will be forgiven, and our past forgotten. Each day is a new day and we can do with it what we will. With His help every one of us can win the victory. If we have faith and hope and love, we have the ability to conquer through Him who loved us. Our heavenly Father has saved us, and can transform us into people with whom others will enjoy living.

Often we are unaware of the things that prevent us from living victoriously. We are too proud to admit our failures, and shy away from words like "repentance" and "obedience" as from a contagious disease. Too often we forget love, the one quality which makes all the difference in the world. It can triumph when all else fails. But we must allow love to pervade our lives, and give us the vision to depend not upon ourselves but upon God. Because we think we can go it alone, our lives so often end in failure.

Pride and prayer are incompatible. Pride is arrogant, intolerant, and ignorant of the great fundamental truths—simplicity, humility, and human decency. Pride goes before a fall.

Prayer and victory are compatible. A man must allow God to use him as He will, even to making him a door mat, before he can win the victory.

At one city's centennial celebration, a member of the city council arrived in elegant attire on the opening day. His chest swelled with pride as he marched up to the keeper of the grandstand gate.

"I am councilman so and so," he said haughtily.

The gatekeeper eyed the councilman's fancy clothes deliberately.

"Fellow, pay your dollar, and I will let you through," he said.

Realizing he was not to receive special privileges, the councilman quickly came to his senses and meekly paid the admission. Had he stood on his rights, the crowd would have rapidly filled the seats, leaving him snarled up in red tape.

There is a tremendous difference between living an important life and living a self-important life.

TODAY'S THOUGHT: *Look beyond the trees to the stars, and measure your stature accordingly.*

APRIL 28

With Eyes Open to the Treasures of the Spirit!

For where your treasure is, there will your heart be also.

Matthew 6:21

A man and a woman died about the same time. The woman was the most fabulously dressed woman in all of Europe. She had a thousand dresses, but her eyes were blind to the needs of others, and her ears deaf to the calls of the needy on life's Jericho road. Every day as she looked out on life the artificial paint on her face hid any possible glow of human kindness from within. One day she died and, though she had a thousand dresses, was able to wear only one to the grave, and had to leave all the rest behind.

About the same time the man was buried. Now, he had only one suit. It was a shiny blue serge with a worn red collar on it. The man's name was William Booth, the founder of the Salvation Army. Although he had only one suit, he had literally lived a thousand lives. There is a tremendous difference when the amplitude of God's love surges through a human soul and mind, overflowing with its warmth and strength to every other life it touches.

What a satisfaction and security comes over us when we know the partnership we can have with Christ the Lord. He is ready to be present in our every need, if only we have eyes to see Him. For many of us religion is such a superficial thing. Some folks treat it as something for emergency use only, a spare-tire religion.

A man in a little rowboat was caught in a storm. As the waves were beating against his little craft he cried out, "God, I haven't called upon you for 15 years. But God, if you'll save me this time, I'll promise not to bother you again for another 15 years!" Many of us are like that. We make prayer an emergency hatch, and God our broker in trouble. We even think we are bothering Him when we call upon Him. Yet, all the time God stands by, ready to come into our lives to bring us good. But do you not suppose He has a special heart for His regular customers?

A day by day partnership with Almighty God is the only guaranteed way to peace. We can go anywhere, we can do anything, so long as God can go with us. With His presence to guide, we have nothing to fear in the unknown tomorrow.

TODAY'S THOUGHT: *With faith as a broom, we can make a clean sweep of life.*

APRIL 29

Dwell in God's Presence

But seek first his kingdom and his righteousness, and all these things shall be yours as well. Matthew 6:33

One early morning before yet the mist had cleared, Christ appeared to the disciples as they returned from fishing. They had been out all night and had caught nothing, when suddenly they saw the Master through a rift standing on the shore. Knowing their discouragement, He spoke words to this effect: "Put down your nets just where you are."

Human reason would have answered, "Lord, that is ridiculous. We have been fishing all night long. Furthermore, only a fool would try this close to shore."

But He persisted, "Let down your nets where you are."

Here is something for us to consider. Despising the place where we stand, we keep thinking if we could only be in a different location, or among other people, we would find what we are seeking. God is as near to us in our present circumstance as He could be in any other. We may be missing the chance of our life only because we are whining and complaining, "Lord, I am not in the right spot for blessings to come to me." With God, we can make the best of any situation. Let us put down our nets, right where we are!

God's blessings are infinite. The disciples obeyed the Master. They overcame their doubts, and put down their nets where they were. They caught so many fish that their tiny boats could not contain them. Sometimes it frightens me as I think of the tremendous unused powers of God, the tremendous unrealized possibilities that every single life holds out.

Four things can happen to the person in whose heart that Presence abides. He is given vision to see things clearly. He is given imagination to dream of things that can be. He is given courage—courage to act boldly, and make these things come true. He is given faith—faith to know that we are linked with a power that will help us through every hour of our life, even the tragic and the bitter.

The door is open, and everyone has the opportunity of following through to Him. That door opens to plenty. It opens to partnership and it opens to peace—peace that includes far more than material blessings. The promise that we can possess those inner qualities can alone bring happiness and peace to our souls.

TODAY'S THOUGHT: *If you look at life through glasses of faith, you will see that God's glory surrounds you.*

APRIL 30

Swell Faith's Mighty Tide

Make a joyful noise to God, all the earth. Psalm 66:1

Faith in God is not just an insurance against personal calamity. All sickness and death are caused by sin. However, if religion were a magic cloak that we could use to protect our families, everyone would reach for it immediately. We would seek religious belief as we seek any other safety device, not necessarily because we loved God, but just to play it safe. Thus religion would lose its true nature, and faith its real character. Is it not "the conviction of things not seen"?

God has not promised that we or our loved ones will be spared the flood waters. But God does assure us that, when we have to pass through the flood, He will hold us by the hand. Faith in God does not mean that He will step down from heaven to prevent causes turning into effects. It may be necessary for our fullest development that we suffer. But be sure that He suffers right along with us. He always stands at our side in the fiery furnace of a trial, to lead us triumphantly through, and to help us out of our difficulty, with not so much even as the smell of burn on the garments of faith.

The ebb tide of doubt is in our world, while the incoming tide of faith is being dammed in many places. But every added believer builds up the swelling tide of faith in this wide world until eventually the tide pounds away any dam, and it crumbles before the sea. One of the reinforcements we need is patience. We need a vision of His master plan, of course. But beyond that we also need the patience to keep marching along the road until the goal is reached. Only the farmer who in faith plants seed in the spring can see a harvest gathered in the fall. Only by faith can we believe what we do not see. And the reward of faith is to see what we first only believed.

Some time ago a popular song proclaimed, "You've got to have heart, lots and lots of heart." But the song does not tell us how to get that heart, nor can the world ever give us the answer. There must be heart at the center of faith. The object of faith is not *what* we believe but *Whom*. It is God alone who has the power, and the kingdom, and the glory.

TODAY'S THOUGHT: *All who enlist in God's army will have an increasing measure of God's power.*

A Change from Within

Put on the new nature, created after the likeness of God in true righteousness and holiness. Ephesians 4:24

A little colored boy was watching his mother bleach clothes. Tired of being ridiculed because he was black, he covered his face with soapsuds and lay down on the lawn to wait for the hot sun to turn him white. He was a disappointed little boy when he looked into the mirror several hours later, and heard his mother admonish him, "Silly boy, don't you know you can't make a white person of yourself by trying to bleach from the outside?"

Similar experiments are tried over and over again around the world, as men hope by education and change of environment to reform wayward people. Thoughtless, even we Christians fail to realize that a man is not made over by going to church, or mingling with "nice people." Christianity is a change wrought not from the outside, but from within.

Pulling a little boy out of a mud puddle, and sending him to play on the lawn, may keep him from getting into further trouble; but it will not clean his face, hands, and clothes. First he must be washed and then dressed in clean clothes. Too many people think that all we need is reformation. But reformation will never blot out one's past. No matter how many good works we do today, we cannot earn forgiveness for yesterday's sins. Only the blood of Jesus Christ, God's Son, can cleanse our sin-spotted record. Only the acceptance of Christ's holiness will enable us to pass out of death into life.

"How do you know you are saved?" the skeptic asked an aging Christian.

The old man walked a few steps, then dropped one of the bags of potatoes he was carrying. "How do I know I have dropped this bag?" he asked in return. "I haven't even looked around to see if it is sitting behind me."

"You're right," the skeptic said, "but you can surely tell that the weight is less."

"Yes," replied the Christian, "that is how I know I am saved. I have lost the weight of my sin and sorrow, and know a wonderful peace in my Lord."

Trust will put a like satisfaction in every believer's heart.

TODAY'S THOUGHT: *Those who would change the world must first themselves be changed.*

MAY 2

Trust the Unerring Pilot

By steadfastness and by the encouragement of the scriptures we might have hope. Romans 15:4

One day, as I was traveling from Florida home to Minnesota, a parable occurred to me. We were air-borne on a crisp morning, and had climbed into a sky where the sun was shining in all its glory. It was as smooth a beginning for a trip, and as beautiful flying, as one could wish for.

Suddenly I thought, "Life, too, at its beginning, is like that. At birth we are entirely dependent on those to whose care we are entrusted. Loving parents care for us, and make our decisions. They feed and clothe us, and watch over us when we are sick. Our responsibilities are few."

But things do not remain that way very long. As if to punctuate my thoughts our plane, winging its way northward, ran into an overcast of storm clouds, and the journey suddenly became rough. There were moments when we broke through into clear sky, and others when suddenly we plunged again into darkness. The clear spaces were smooth, but in the darkness we were buffeted by turbulence, until we wondered if the storm would ever cease. Soon, however, our plane, gaining altitude, climbed into clear skies and flew effortlessly with the cloud bank far below.

I continued thinking. "All of us must face difficulties. We are living happily when suddenly we are jolted by unexpected problems. We wonder how we will ever get through them. Then, as in this storm, life becomes a succession of contrasting days, some filled with happiness, others filled with heartaches. Yet we find that, if we trust the Pilot, inevitably we emerge into sunlight."

The end of the journey had a lesson for me, too. Here above the clouds I felt peace creep into my heart for soon I would be home, happily reunited with my loved ones. Our plane descended toward the city completely enveloped by the overcast. One last time we had to pass through the misty barrier. But with our pilot's unerring guidance we broke through the veil, and home and family hove in sight again.

So it shall be at the end of our days. For the Christian the last of life will be the best. With the Lord as our guide, we shall go through the valley of the shadow to the wonderful city of God.

TODAY'S THOUGHT: *Think of faith as an electric eye, opening doors that would otherwise remain forever closed.*

MAY 3

Invest Your Life

He who finds his life will lose it, and he who loses his life for my sake will find it. Matthew 10:39

Our life is like a great book. To grow and develop, we must read beyond the first page. Too many people make a good beginning, then stop, forgetting the importance of growing in life.

Let us look beyond the first page of life today and see the great horizons, the depth, the breadth, the height—the really important dimensions of life. It is not the length of life that is most significant, but what we do with the time that God gives us.

How do we invest our lives? Are we eager to make them count for Christ our King? Do we live deeply, or do we skim lightly over the surface of things, pushing back important tasks to finish those that will give us only temporal blessings? How wisely are we redeeming our time? In this jet-propelled age of ours we are all conscious of the passing of time. Each minute that ticks away can never be recalled. Though our lives and our talents may differ, we have one thing in common—24 hours a day, 168 hours a week. If we are too busy to spend a part of every day in the presence of God in order to grow spiritually, we are busier than God intended us to be.

Every one of us is seeking to master our lives, but few of us are willing to put forth the effort that is necessary for that self-mastery. The following is a statement made by the biographer of George Fox, the founder of the Society of Friends; "George Fox was completely master of himself because he was completely a servant of God."

Today we are seeking to defeat the godless power of Communism. Have you ever compared your devotion to the kingdom of God to that of a Communist to his party? He may be called on to attend as many as seven or eight meetings a week, and he gives a large proportion of his income to support his party. Does our devotion to Christ match his passion for his cause? His thinking is based on false premises. We are possessors of the truth that sets men free. Why not resolve today to dedicate your life anew to Christ and His kingdom?

TODAY'S THOUGHT: *God does not demand of us genius or eloquence, but faithful use of our ability and deep devotion.*

MAY 4

Pray for Courage

Why are you afraid, O men of little faith? Matthew 8:26

Frequently people ask, "What shall we pray for?" "In everything . . . let your request be made known," we are told. But too many of our prayers are solidly selfish, dealing only with physical needs. We are admonished to ask for those things requisite for the body a well as for the soul, but sometimes, putting the body first, we stop there. Like little children asking for money, and then spending it foolishly on trifling objects, we seek unworthy gifts from God instead of desiring those things necessary for our salvation.

The one great object of our prayers should be the attainment of holiness, that we may do such things as are pleasing in God's sight. He has promised His Holy Spirit to those who ask. Surely that is His supreme gift and the one for which we should long. Our prayers can be wings, lifting us above the world. Yet the grind of daily life drags us down, and we need by prayer to clasp God's hand, if we are to escape ruin. Weak and faltering as our prayers sometimes are, we must have faith that, if we but touch the hem of Christ's garment, we shall be made whole again.

Pray for courage never to be ashamed of your Master or your faith. Too many people deny their Lord rather than meet the ridicule of godless companions.

When a certain girl left home for college, her parents told her to read her Bible and pray before retiring at night. The first night in the dormitory she turned to God according to her custom. At once some of the other girls laughed, and scornfully said she was wasting her time. Rather than take the easy way out she persisted, praying for courage to be a witness to the girls about her. Within a few days a large group had become her best friends and joined her each night in devotions. One courageous girl, her soul clothed with grace, had transformed scornful laughter into humble prayer. "The king's daughter is all glorious within."

Holding fast to our faith we, too, can be witnesses, brushing off our intrepid spirit on the heart of others.

TODAY'S THOUGHT: *A trusting faith in the heart is the first step; to speak of that faith to others is the second.*

MAY 5

Thank God for Your Mother

Every one of you shall revere his mother and his father.
                                                Leviticus 19:3

"What kind of woman was your mother?" the slave master asked the young African whom he had recently purchased.

The boy hesitated as if he did not care to answer.

"Come on, tell me," said the master, "what kind of woman was she? Was she tall? Was she thin? old? young?"

After hesitating a few moments the boy lifted his face, his eyes glistening. "She was beautiful!" he said, his voice breaking.

That young lad became one of the finest servants the master had ever had. Later in life he told his master that, if he had done him any good, it was due to the inspiring influence of his mother.

We who have enjoyed the privilege of loving, Christian mothers should thank God often for them. Truly, home is where Mother is, and without her, there is a continual void. A wonderful mother is the one who tells us about God, and what He can do for our lives. She teaches us that we have two homes—one that we share with our family, and the other, our church home, where we worship God. We learn from her that the church is not just a building of wood or brick, but a place that our heavenly Father fills with His glory; that it is a power station where we are charged with energy and strength and courage to keep going.

It sometimes comes to me that God must be much like a Christian mother. A pastor disciplined his son for staying out late one night and bringing his mother a night of wakefulness and worry.

"I don't see why Mother has to stay awake on my account," the boy said finally.

"Well," his father replied, "God made mothers that way, that is all I know."

So it is with our heavenly Father. He is always on the alert, always concerned about His children, always answering their needs, always willing to guide them into pathways of more abundant living. There is not a single soul He does not love. There is not a single soul for whom He has not given His life. He offers a beautiful friendship to all who choose to walk life's way with Him.

TODAY'S THOUGHT: *There are times when a person would pay a million dollars for one faithful friend. Yet, how many have accepted the freely offered hand of our heavenly Father?*

MAY 6

Be Loved into Goodness

For I am sure that neither death, nor life . . . nor things present, nor things to come . . . will be able to separate us from the love of God in Christ Jesus our Lord. Romans 8:38, 39

Jesus has defined love to the whole world by the way He loved. He taught us that, great as it is to be a Christian and be certain of it, it is greater still to show it by your life. Too many people mouth creeds and pray prayers as evidence of faith and loyalty to Christ, only to leave church and turn a hate-contorted face to others. This inconsistency on our part is not acceptable in the sight of God. It will not help us build a community of understanding and hope for the future.

Jesus' plan was to love people into goodness. He was ready to point out sin and its consequences whenever He saw it, but He would never condemn the sinner who was penitent. When a mischievous young lad got into trouble, a wise old saint commented to those who tried to correct the lad, "You'll just have to love him out of it."

We would do well to remember that, just as no bacillus has been discovered that can survive the sunlight, so no evil can survive the sunlight of God's love out-poured in the hearts of men.

Jesus employed love in dealing with Mary Magdalene and Simon Peter. He would have used the same method on Iscariot, if Judas had only given Him the chance. But I am not inferring that sin is a trifle and of no consequence to God.

A woman once visited a friend whose children were very lively and apt to misbehave. In trying to quiet them, the woman said, "Your mother won't love you if you are naughty." This is the reply she received: "Mother doesn't always like us, but she always loves us, no matter how bad we are."

There is a difference between love and its limitations. God's love for us remains constant. He loves the sinner, even though He is disturbed by the sin. Many people read the text, "Thou, God, seest me," and picture a God with prying eyes watching them, waiting for them to do wrong so that He can punish them. A preferred and more accurate interpretation of that text is: God loves us so much that He cannot take His eyes off us.

TODAY'S THOUGHT: *Love given out in generous measure will heal anything.*

MAY 7

Dig Deeper

And let steadfastness have its full effect, that you may be perfect and complete, lacking in nothing. James 1:4

A farmer dug a new well to water his horses and cattle. The well supplied all their needs until one summer a drought came. There was not enough water for the cattle, and with much trouble to himself the farmer had to drive them to surrounding brooks and springs for the life-giving water. One day a stranger stopped at the farm and noticed the abandoned well. The farmer told him what had happened.

"Why don't you dig the well deeper?" the man inquired.

"I can't," replied the farmer, "for then I'll have to dig through a layer of rock and flint."

But the man persisted, "Even though that be necessary, it will pay you. Blast out the rock. If you go just a few feet, you may strike water again, and save yourself the trouble of bringing your cattle so far to satisfy their thirst." The blasting was done and, to the farmer's amazement, there gushed forth a stream of sparkling cold water—a veritable gold mine to his homestead.

Many of us experience periods of spiritual drought and barrenness. There is no water in our well, and so we turn away from it. We dig as far as rock and then stop. We lack the persistence to go farther. Likewise too many of us Christians are not willing to pay the price. We do not dig deep enough to get the results which always come to those who follow God's plan.

Once we have set our feet on God's way, let us resolve never to allow our steps to stray from it. When Rudyard Kipling was a boy he went with his father on a sea voyage. One day there was a great commotion, and a sailor came to tell Mr. Kipling that his son had crawled out on the yardarm. "If he ever lets go he will drown," reported the sailor.

"But he won't let go," answered the father confidently.

How wonderful it would be, if our Father in heaven could be equally confident that his children here on earth would never let go of their Christian faith.

TODAY'S THOUGHT: *Who ever loses faith in the sun when storms hide it? Why then does your faith in God falter when someone deceives you?*

MAY 8

Accept God's Help Today

Strengthen the weak hands, and make firm the feeble knees.
Isaiah 35:3

Do you ever grow discouraged and think God has forgotten you? Do you ever feel lost even in a crowd? Have you ever wondered whether or not God really cares? Then it would be well to remember such passages of Scripture as the one where Jesus tells us that the very hairs of our head are numbered. Moreover, it would be well for us to recall that no two people have been created alike. You are different from anybody else in the entire world.

We do not need more outward comforts and conveniences in the world today. Rather, we need inner strength from God, and the blessed assurance that His love will follow us to the ends of the earth.

There is no time like today to enter into a partnership with God. Everything has to have a beginning. All things do not crowd upon us at once. Our characters grow very slowly over a period of years. One does not become good or bad suddenly, but over a period of time. You can grow away from God, or you can draw closer to Him. Our faith was meant not only to secure our future, but to give us power for living each day of our life.

Many a great man has revealed that his strength was in reality the power of God working through him. Robert Morrison was on his way to China as a pioneer missionary when someone questioned his ability to penetrate a country so vast. "I do not expect to do great things," said Morrison, "but I expect God will."

God's infinite power is available today, tomorrow and every day. But there is no reason to put off accepting that power, for the supply is unlimited; God will supply power for every purpose.

A picture of a 79-year-old man who had suddenly become a millionaire appeared in a newspaper. Discovery of a clerical error in a land office in 1908 gave the man mineral rights valued at five million dollars on his 160 acres in Alberta, Canada. This was his reaction to the news: "It is too late to do any good."

Why wait to the end of life to receive the blessings of heaven, when heaven can be enjoyed while we live here on earth?

TODAY'S THOUGHT: *We rejoice in the beauty of earth, yet sin lurks here. How vastly more beautiful heaven must be!*

MAY 9

Introduce Christ to Your Friends

He put a new song in my mouth, a song of praise to our God. Many will see and fear, and put their trust in the Lord. Psalm 40:3

When God becomes the actual Ruler, the guiding Spirit of our lives, there must flame up within us the desire to tell others about His wonderful love. It is a message with such amazing meaning that it is too good to keep within ourselves. The wonderful things God does for us, He can do for others also. But He needs our efforts to bring His message to them.

It is not always easy to persuade somebody about the Christian life. Your faith alone cannot save another's soul, for the latch opening the door to each man's heart is on the inside. Each individual makes his own choice. He can decide to keep the door locked, or he can open it. However, God can use our life's example to persuade others to be His followers.

Bill and Tom were two strong healthy lads in the same grade in school. Bill was known as the troublemaker both in class and in the neighborhood, while Tom had the reputation of being kind-hearted. Bill knew Tom was an easy mark, and whenever trouble started, Tom always got the worst of it. Whatever happened, Tom refused to get angry, for he had as much forgiveness as Bill had mischief.

Then suddenly Bill became ill, and none of his playmates came to visit him—that is, none except Tom. Whenever he was most depressed, faithful Tom would be sure to stop by to encourage him, telling him to hurry and get well so he could come out and play again. Young Tom's thoughtful kindness made a lasting impression on Bill, and when he recovered the two were the best of friends. But there was one obvious change in their relationship. No longer was Bill the rough and tough boy that people disliked.

The consistent witness of one young boy had won the victory. Kindness and goodness had triumphed over selfishness and hatred. Many times we have vainly tried to argue our friends into the fold of the faithful, only to discover that it is our day-in and day-out living that wins out. The most effective sermons are not preached in pulpits but by people who manifest their faith in their living.

TODAY'S THOUGHT: *Do not be shy about telling others of Christ; simply say, "He is wonderful!"*

MAY 10

Look Ahead to Land

Arise, shine; for your light has come, and the glory of the Lord has risen upon you. Isaiah 60:1

Florence Chadwick was attempting to swim from Catalina Island to the California coast. In a boat by her side sat her father, urging her on. He had a blackboard and would write messages upon it to raise her hopes. Within a mile of her destination, she called to her father, "I'm cold and losing strength."

Quickly her father wrote upon the board these words: "Look! There is land ahead!"

Later on, having successfully completed her swim, she had this to say: "I saw the land ahead. That was all it took. The numbness left me. The cold vanished, and I had strength to go on."

Never has God intended that we project ourselves into a future colored by our fears. He has meant that we should live one day at a time, and leave tomorrow with Him. God has intended that by the wings of faith we should look far into the future. He wants for us the confidence that there is land ahead.

One never knows what is just around the corner. In 1700 there was no "Messiah," no "Hallelujah Chorus." Handel was broken in health, and his creditors were pressing him. Little did he realize that just around the corner he was to write an oratorio that would thrill and inspire untold millions.

John Milton, the poet, was going blind. Little did he realize that just around the corner was inspiration for two of his greatest works: "Paradise Lost" and "Paradise Regained." Beethoven was becoming deaf. Little did he realize that around the corner were his "Fifth Symphony" and the "Ninth Symphony," that would forever articulate man's highest aspirations.

It was Good Friday. They nailed Jesus to the cross. The disciples ran and hid. Little did they realize that just around the corner was Easter and victory!

If you really have faith in God, you will know that just around the corner for you are God's greatest surprises.

TODAY'S THOUGHT: *Those who are optimistic today, will find a wonderful opportunity tomorrow.*

MAY 11

Open Wide the Door of Your Heart

O magnify the Lord with me, and let us exalt his name together!
Psalm 34:3

One day a king was about to choose a prime minister. Seeking the wisest man in his kingdom, he narrowed the selection to three candidates. He brought them into a room to which there was a door with an intricate lock. He said that to the first man gaining access to the room beyond the door he would give the position of prime minister. Two of the men sat down and used their time to work out formulas on how to take apart the lock. The third man simply approached the door, turned the knob, and walked out. The door was open all the time!

As we read this little story, we cannot help think of the many people who are losing out on the glories of what Christian faith can mean. They sit down and try to work out all kinds of complicated formulas to solve the mysteries of human life and of the universe.

God has given faith in our hearts with which to answer the puzzles of life. He wants us to believe in Him, to trust Him. This fact made all the difference in the lives of the disciples. Remember how afraid they were on Good Friday? They ran away and hid. They were not witnesses to the Resurrection simply because they were trying to save their own skins. Moreover, they were afraid to return back to their old friends and their businesses. Had they left all to follow the Master? Perplexed and terror stricken by the day's strange events, they were sure that everything was doomed.

Then what caused their change of attitude? What sent them out to give their lives, to die as martyrs? Tradition says that Peter pleaded to be hung on a cross with his head down and his feet up. because he did not feel himself worthy to die upright as his Lord had died. What caused this onetime turncoat to become so courageous? It was because he had seen the risen Lord with his own eyes. In that Resurrection he had seen victory over any circumstance. He knew that in Christ there was power to defeat any foe. For him Christ became an open door to victory.

Such a faith is ours today, if we will but grasp it. We can wrest victory out of doom, the kind that is known deep down in the heart, when our faith is fixed on Him who goes before.

TODAY'S THOUGHT: *Do not dismiss a task as impossible until you have tried it.*

MAY 12

Concentrate on Christ

My eyes are ever toward the Lord, for he will pluck my feet out of the net. Psalm 25:15

If we are to conquer sin, the devil, and our own flesh, we must keep our eyes forever on our leader, Jesus Christ. It was when Peter followed "afar off" that he found trouble and subjected himself to the conquering temptation. The army with perfect trust in its commander watches his movement and follows him through any dangers because it has faith and believes the commander leads to victory.

When King Henry of Navarre fought a crucial battle, he asked the soldiers to watch the white plume of his helmet and to follow wherever it led. So in our battle with the forces of the world we must keep our eyes on Jesus. Wherever He leads, though it be through pain and loss and sacrifice, though it take us through the agony of Gethsemane and to the cross of Calvary, we must follow. Keeping their eyes on Jesus, gave brave men and women and little children the strength to fight the battle through the years and, in spite of terrible persecutions, to hold fast to their faith. In every area of our living we must watch our Leader, sure in the faith that He will carry us through.

There was once a lady about to undergo a serious operation. The doctors feared that the first sight of preparations for the operation would overwhelm her with fear. They were surprised, however, how very calm she was. She made one request. She asked that she be allowed to hold a picture of Christ crucified and so, strengthened by looking to Jesus, she was able to bear her trial. Here lies the secret of all the martyrs, ancient and modern.

If we are to conquer, we must obey orders. Success in battle depends upon the soldiers' implicit obedience. Most of us like to go our own way, and choose our own situation, instead of taking commands from our Leader, Jesus Christ. Sometimes we must suffer hardship and loss. It is not always easy to be a Christian. Yet there come no rewards to those unwilling to pay the price. The price is not too great when one remembers that we deal with something that lasts, not for a lifetime, but for eternity.

Can you say today, "Lord, I will go where you want me to go. Lord, I will do what you want me to do"?

TODAY'S THOUGHT: *God whose wisdom is infinite will put the right man in the right place.*

MAY 13

Rejoice in Life

He asked life of thee; thou gavest it to him, length of days for ever and ever. Psalm 21:4

A good motto for life is, "Serve God and be cheerful." Service to God and happiness go hand in hand. No one can find genuine satisfaction in living, if he forgets God, while no one who has God as his partner can ever be unhappy. Our Master would lead us in the way of sunshine and rejoicing. However dark life's outward skies, there can be sunshine within the soul.

As Christians, we have reason to rejoice every day, and to be thankful both for the Lord's blessings and for His promises which yesterday, today, and forever stand sure. By His first coming, Jesus gave us the possibility of the redemption of our souls. He gave, too, the means by which we can grow in grace. Remaining constant in our faith, we can know the hope of eternal joy.

Before Jesus' coming all was darkness in the hearts of men. It is true that people of old had their learning, their art, and their pleasures. But theirs was not the happy life, for a black shadow lay across their path, a shadow of fathomless mystery. Life was a flower which bloomed for a moment, only to fade away and die. People began to realize, with growing terror, that old age brought the grave, and that the grave faced them with the unknown. They knew of nothing beyond. These people had no hope. There was no joy in believing in the cold, passionless gods of wood and stone, gods who neither cared for them nor gave help or comfort.

Such was man's life without God. No wonder then that many a proud Roman who had nothing for which to live or even to hope would choose a day on which to enter his room, open a vein, and quickly and painlessly bleed to death. Many an ignorant pagan philosopher, maintaining that real joy lay in not having been born at all, said that the next best thing was to stop living as quickly as possible.

How altogether different is the Christian's thinking. "Rejoice in the Lord always," he says. "Again, I will say, rejoice." "For to me to live is Christ, and to die is gain."

Jesus came and changed the world's outlook. He altered man's ideas of life and death, and now we are filled with hope on hearing His promise, "I am come that they may have life."

TODAY'S THOUGHT: *With Christ as our companion, we soon learn to take life as it comes.*

MAY 14

One Step at a Time

I have fought the good fight, I have finished the race, I have kept the faith. 2 Timothy 4:7

A contractor, just new in the business, dreamed that one day he would build a tremendous building, a monumental structure that would be his crowning achievement. Yet in his heart he knew that it could only be after years of accumulated experience and wisdom that he could fulfill his dream. However, sooner than he ever expected, opportunity beckoned.

One day, without ever expecting to get the contract, he submitted his bid for the construction of a large building. To his amazement the committee selected his bid as the best! Never had he handled an assignment this size, and the thought of it momentarily staggered him. But he gritted his teeth, and in spite of inexperience began construction.

Summoning every skill he knew, he worked hard. He solved problem after problem with increasing patience and judgment. He spared no effort. He demanded of himself fantastic physical and mental energy, and became a human dynamo, a driving force inspiring every worker to maximum effort. Relentlessly he put into that building his very sinews and blood, and with each passing day he felt the tingle of an inner exultation.

When the building stood completed, many there were who applauded him for his fine job. Someone asked whether or not its size had ever frightened him.

"I can't tell you how frightened I was for a while," he related. "I was afraid to begin. But I was more afraid not to, so I just went ahead and tackled it."

"And wasn't it such a tough job after all?"

"Yes, and no," he said. "It was work. It wasn't easy. But I learned one important thing from this experience. The world's biggest jobs consist of many smaller ones. Do the work one step at a time, and somehow you finish the greatest task."

Too many of us fail because, in contemplating a project, we allow our dread of failure to prevent our doing the little jobs of which the larger consists. One kind, understanding deed added to another, builds a noble Christian character. Live each day with Christ, and you will pass through any valley to His eternal kingdom.

TODAY'S THOUGHT: *The place where we stand is not nearly so significant as the direction in which we are moving.*

135

MAY 15

A Simple, Childlike Faith

Therefore, since we are justified by faith, we have peace with God through our Lord Jesus Christ. Romans 5:1

The opposite of happiness and joy is not sorrow. It is unbelief. People are born to believe. They need faith in something, for no one can live on doubts and uncertainties. Repeatedly to question God's promises with the words, "Is this true?" is like coming to the table at mealtime saying, "Is this food?" If a man just kept questioning, and never sampled the food, he would surely starve. We all must venture in faith.

Do you have any idea how much we miss in life because we do not take God at His word? He has told us, "All things are possible to him that believes." I can never understand why we will put our faith in mere man, and then hesitate to trust God. Faith ought to be the working principle of our daily life.

Stand on a street corner some day soon, and watch a child cross the street with his mother. Probably he has been unconcerned walking along the sidewalk. But at this corner, when he must cross the street, he grows uncertain. The traffic is heavy; cars go whizzing by. Realizing that he cannot make it alone, he reaches up and puts his hand into his mother's. He is willing to depend on her judgment, and together they cross the street in safety.

Or you may notice somebody's son standing on a high step, calling, "Catch me, Daddy!" The father holds out his arms, and the child jumps down with complete confidence that his father will catch him and break his fall. Unless our faith is like the faith of these children, we cannot enter into the kingdom of God.

Faith in God is a vital force. It is a mountain mover. In our day of doubt and despair, faith is indispensable. Men and women awakening each morning to face up to this trying world must have something beyond themselves to turn to. It has always been so. Never forget that with faith nothing is impossible; faith is a mountain mover made for a difficult world.

TODAY'S THOUGHT: *Why talk about miracles! Be one!*

MAY 16

Determination Yields Dividends

My help comes from the Lord, who made heaven and earth.

Psalm 121:2

Determination is a desirable personal quality for, indeed, success in any field demands determination. To be an accomplished musician, one must have the determination and patience to seek the best teachers, and to spend hours practicing every day. To be a fine athlete, one must train and obey the rules of the game. Yes, the successful person is determined to do well; he has stick-to-it-iveness.

Great accomplishments have resulted from determination. Day after day during his voyage to America, Columbus made the following entry in his log: "This day we sailed on." And after Admiral Perry's struggle to reach the North Pole, a boy wrote in his diary, "I have decided to be the first man to reach the North Pole." Years later he became not only the first man to fly over the North Pole, but the first to fly over the South Pole as well. His name— Richard E. Byrd.

The president of a great corporation was asked what was his coat of arms.

"A pair of shirt sleeves," he replied.

God has decreed that man should work. He has endowed each of us with talents to become successful, if we work determinedly. The amount of success is not as significant as the fact that we have done our best. Too many people survey their limited talents, and decide to bury them in the ground, saying, "My life isn't important. I'll try to save what I have."

In saving our lives, we always lose them; but in doing our best with what we have been given, we save them without ever failing. In the battle of life, every man must seek peace with constant determination.

"I'm going to live until I die, and then I'm going to live forever," said an 82-year-old Quaker.

"Oh, God, help me to live while I am alive," said another. We must have sufficient determination to live each day with God, for then we shall find the peace that passeth all understanding.

TODAY'S THOUGHT: *Patience is one key to peace of mind.*

MAY 17

Avail Yourself of God's Gift

If you knew the gift of God . . . you would have asked him, and he would have given you living water. John 4:10

When we do not allow Christ to pour out His love upon us, not only do we miss out on the victorious living which He intended for us, but we actually sadden Him. He wants us to enjoy the kind of happiness that only He can give. By our lack of response and by our unbelief, we shut out the warm light that could bring beauty into our souls, even as the thick ice of the glacier shuts out the sunshine from the mountain side.

God has done everything in His power to give us a happy life on earth, and the assurance of everlasting life in the world to come. We do not gain salvation by what we do. Unaided, we cannot lay out the plan that will enable us to find peace in life. That was done a long time ago.

A minister was conversing with a fellow passenger on the train. The minister remarked how happy he was since he had been redeemed.

"I, too, am saved," commented the other.

"May I ask you," said the minister, "how long have you been saved?"

"Over 1900 years ago," answered his companion, "when Jesus died for me on Calvary's cross to deliver me from all my sin." By that sacrifice everyone is saved who chooses to accept it. How sad it is that so few of us live as if we knew of that sacrifice!

"Love so amazing, so divine!" we sing. Still there is one thing even more amazing, the unbelief that thrusts it aside!

A lawyer once canvassed the entire United States, looking for a man who was the heir of a large fortune. He finally found him living in a poorhouse in the far West. If the heir had only known what had been willed him, how different his life would have been.

The greatest fortune any of us can have is the knowledge that Christ died for our sins. Yet so many of us do not understand the implication of the promise, "For God so loved the world." Put your name where the words "the world" occur, for it means you, and anyone of His children. God loved you and me so much that "He gave his only Son that whoever believes in him should not perish but have eternal life." How rich we are!

TODAY'S THOUGHT: *Why should anyone of us fear loneliness, since Christ is always walking at our side?*

MAY 18

Smile at Adversity

Let not your hearts be troubled, neither let them be afraid.
John 14:27

If you have ever traveled in Norway and sailed up its beautiful fjords with mountains rising right out of the water to their sheer heights, probably you would learn a lesson for living. You looked ahead and saw the channel appear to narrow, until it looked like a blind end, as if you were foolishly sailing smack dab into the mountain. Approaching closer and closer, you even became frightened, thinking that the bow of the steamer would strike the cliffs ahead. But just when forward progress seemed impossible, the channel opens up, and the steamer can sail around a bend into another fjord even more beautiful than the one behind.

So it is in the pilgrimage of life. Some days we come face to face with iron gates of difficulty, temptation, sin, or death itself. It seems impossible to get through. If we maintain our faith and trust in God, however, we learn that in His own way and in His own time, God will swing open the gate and let us pass through our difficulty into His joy.

We are too easily tempted to quit. We spend our time complaining about the things we do not have, or worrying about what may never happen. In the process we lose the resources available to meet the present difficulty. We need to accent the positive, and to think about our many blessings rather than our difficulties.

Take a look at yourself. Soon you will discover how very rich you are. You live in a country that promises liberty and justice for all. You are a sacred personality created in the image of God. You are destined to be eternal by the mercy and grace of the Lord. You have the opportunity of living a life that never ends.

Whenever we are tempted to complain, let us sit down and take time to count our blessings one by one. We will not have come very far before we will have discovered that we are far out ahead the richest and the most wonderfully blessed people in the wide world.

TODAY'S THOUGHT: *Make light of your problems. But if you fail at this, at least you can keep them in the dark.*

MAY 19

His Master's Voice

And all the crowd sought to touch him, for power came forth from him and healed them all. Luke 6:19

"During a serious illness, something truly critical, the child who has been taught to obey stands a much better chance of recovery than the spoiled child who has been allowed to do as he pleased." This statement was made by a famous child specialist to a father, whose child had just come through a critical illness.

Although the specialist referred to our children's physical bodies, the advice is much more significant in referring to their souls. So often, as we teach them the Ten Commandments and the laws of God, we forget that the question of obedience may mean the safety or loss of a child. If we walk God's way, we shall discover the way of safety. If we listen to the voices of the world and follow them, we shall walk the broad highway that leads to destruction. And if we wander too far away, we may never have the opportunity to hear God's voice again.

Once a little girl was asked if she always came when her mother called.

"Yes," she answered, "but sometimes I go so far away I can't hear her call."

God is always seeking His children. No power in the world can silence His call. But God cannot force us to come back into the range of hearing. Every man decides which way his soul shall go.

God offers us abundant blessings every day. Yet many times we refuse them because we think we should have something better. This was the case with the Indian princess who was given a basket and told that she could pick the finest ears of corn in a certain row. The only rule was that she must choose as she walked along; she could not retrace her steps. Admiring the quality of the corn, she felt one ear after another, then left it on the stalk thinking that better ears lay ahead. Suddenly to her dismay, she found herself at the end of the row empty-handed.

The greatest possible blessing is to hear His voice and follow Him. He will lead us into green pastures, there to find life abundant. If we heed His whisper deep within, we will never go through life empty-handed.

TODAY'S THOUGHT: *God holds the key to the complicated and entangled maze which modern life has fast become.*

MAY 20

Looking Upward

Our days on the earth are like a shadow, and there is no abiding. 1 Chronicles 29:15

We need to practice the upward look. We are so prone to walk with eyes cast down upon the earth that we become blind to everything but our immediate surroundings. As life crowds in with its insistent pressing claims, a feeling of utter helplessness creeps over us. We come to the same realization as the prophet of old who said, "Where there is no vision, the people perish."

What causes these moments of frustration? We are completely absorbed by current events, and we lose sight of eternal values, of eternal truths and insights. Picturing our nebulous little lives in a world dwarfed by a vast universe, we feel helpless and alone. Wind and wave threaten disaster and, like Peter, taking his eyes off Jesus while walking out to Him on the water, we begin to sink.

David, the psalmist, experienced a similar feeling, and in his despair he learned the meaning of the upward look. He was tormented by these questions, "Is there no way out of this horrible dilemma? From whence comes my help?" Fortunately, he was able to answer his own questions and in so doing he answered ours, too. He looked up beyond the hills to God. The thought came to him that the God who flung out those granite mountains remains capable of pushing aside the mountains of difficulty standing athwart the highways of life. He knew the formula and writes it down for us: "My help comes from the Lord, who made heaven and earth."

We shall never be helped by looking within ourselves, where we find only failure and shortcomings. In ourselves we possess no man-made power or strength sufficient to help. But if we look up, up to the cross, we shall see Christ, our Savior from sin.

We cannot be helped by looking around us. For if we do we see nothing but confusion—the babblings of the world's pilgrims, seeking peace where there is no peace. But if we look up, we are carried into the presence of Him who gives a peace beyond all human understanding.

We cannot be helped by looking forward, for then fears will assail us. Only by looking up do we find the Guide, able to chart tomorrow's unknown way and bring us safely to our destination.

TODAY'S THOUGHT: *You will find very few unbelievers in fox holes and on rubber rafts.*

MAY 21

Doubt Not, Want Not

O fear the Lord . . . for those who fear him have no want!
                                                    Psalm 34:9

Two men were given identical pieces of land, and told to clear and cultivate them. The land was secured to them by every possible legal instrument. The transfer of the property was publicly registered, and they were given deeds. One of the men set to work to bring his land under cultivation. He labored at his farm day after day, without stopping. The other man left his farm every few days to go to the courthouse to ask whether the land was really his. He felt sure there must be some mistake. He kept doubting the legal documents which he had been given. The first man never doubted his title.

It is not difficult to determine which of these two men made the greater progress in his work, and which was happier. The one had a faith, and the other doubted.

Many of our problems in life are caused by our own doubts. We fail to take God at His word. In His last will and testament He declared that we are sons of God and joint heirs with Christ. He promised us His presence at all times to give the added assurance that His promises are true. Why will we not take Him at His word?

"If you pray for bread and bring no basket to carry it," Dwight L. Moody used to say, "you prove the doubting spirit which may be the only barrier to the boon you ask." "Where," asked a minister to his drought-threatened farm folk who had come to pray for rain, "where are your umbrellas?"

Some people doubt God because they do not understand just what His promise is. He has given us His word that He will take care of us. What we do not realize is that the protection He offers us is protection "in" and not protection "from" all strife and danger. We are set down to live our lives in this world, and as long as it is a world of sin and sorrow we shall be faced with difficulties. But God can keep them from caving in our spirit, since He will himself provide the inner braces.

TODAY'S THOUGHT: *How long do we have to live before we will realize that what we see teaches us to trust God for what we cannot see?*

MAY 22

Build a Temple to God

He who plants and he who waters are equal, and each shall receive his wages according to his labor . . . If the work which any man has built on the foundation survives, he will receive a reward.

1 Corinthians 3: 8, 14

The secret of a happy, useful life is to be busy with the Master's business. It consists of seeking to know His will for us each day, and then doing all to the glory of God. When Boniface landed in Great Britain, he came with the gospel in one hand and a carpenter's rule in the other. Thus he taught the Britons not only to build houses, but also to build good lives directed by God.

Sometimes man forgets about God and, living recklessly, spends his time pursuing wealth and material happiness, only to find himself at last in deepest misery.

There was once a great and gifted poet. But he had not yet learned the secret of a good life. For one day he wrote sadly, "I have just completed my 36th year." Then he added, "My days are in the yellow leaf; the flowers and fruits of love are gone." What a sad record of a wasted life to which "things" brought no ultimate, lasting pleasure.

If the Master is with us in whatever we do, then we are assured of finding happiness, and we can say with Paul, "But one thing I do, forgetting what lies behind, I press on . . . for I have learned, in whatever state I am, to be content." What a contrasting attitude this is from the man who landed in prison for the eighth time. This was his viewpoint: "The past deserts me, the present torments me, and the future terrifies me."

In His great mercy God has forgiven us our sins. If we are truly penitent, we can forget about them, since God has. In His great mercy God has promised us a future home. Since He has gone ahead to prepare it, we know it will be a glorious place for "he has done all things well." God has promised never to leave us nor forsake us. What is there possibly for us to fear?

TODAY'S THOUGHT: *However disappointing my yesterday and bleak and drear my today, I know that with Christ I can look forward to a bright future.*

Courage, Storm-Tossed Voyager!

He made the storm be still, and the waves of the sea were hushed. Psalm 107:29

A little boy and his father took some friends to sea in their fishing boat. Suddenly a storm came up, and whitecaps dashed over the vessel, rolling it in the heavy seas. Wet with spray, the passengers huddled together, while the skipper-father with a firm hand on the wheel skillfully rode out the storm. Someone asked the boy if he were not afraid. The lad looked up in surprise to answer, "Why should I be afraid? My dad's the pilot of this ship."

I stood one day by the shore of the Sea of Galilee. I thought of the time when Jesus' disciples in their terror, caught in a fierce storm at midsea in their fishing smack, forgot that the Master was aboard. We forget, too, when troubles and anxieties beset us. For to every one come times of great tempest, when trouble and sorrow sweep in. Maybe some dear one is snatched from us by death. Or we ourselves are flung on a bed of pain. It is then, when the waves would overwhelm our soul, that we must not be afraid. Let us remember that the Master is still with us. Though it may appear that He is unconcerned or that He is unmindful, we have a thousand and more assurances from Calvary down that we belong to Him. Let us believe with all our hearts that He never slumbers nor sleeps, and that He knows our need even before we ask Him.

One of the great Romans was once overtaken by a storm at sea. The captain of the ship was terrified, but said the conqueror, "Why do you fear for the ship? Do you not know that it carries Caesar?" We Christians should remember that with us in our ship as we cross the waters of a troubled world is the Master himself. If we trust Him, our Pilot, we can be at our best. He steers a true course. He promises to lead us through all dangers. What are wind and wave to Him who leads out the stars on their course? He does not alter His course when temptations surround us. He only asks us to listen to Him, and to trust Him. As He leads victoriously along the way, He pours joy into our hearts and conviction into our souls. Our faith is indeed the victory that overcomes the world.

TODAY'S THOUGHT: *Is the going tough? Why not try God?*

MAY 24

Doing a Bit More Than Is Expected

Let each one test his own work, and then his reason to boast will be in himself alone and not in his neighbor. Galatians 6:4

It was Jim's first intercollegiate competition, and he had practiced long and diligently for the track meet. A friend offered a word of advice, "If you do not win first place and the gold medal, you may win the silver one."

"I never try for second place!" Jim replied quietly, with steady, clear eyes. This youth's ideals were high, where they belonged. But unlike Jim, many of us set our ideals far too low. The goals we set should always challenge, and call for the last desperate spurt above and beyond anything we have done before. We should never be content with our work, no matter how impressive our accomplishments or how great our influence on others. Always new goals should loom. Our talents will be wasted, if we stop and say, "Well, I've done enough." We should be plodding persisters, not easy quitters. In every area of life we should do more than is expected of us.

A group of students was observing an eminent surgeon stitching up a wound after an operation. He always tied three knots where most other doctors usually tied two. This was his explanation:

"The third knot is my sleeping knot. It may not be necessary to tie it, but it is that much safer, and I sleep much better because of it."

This is only one example of the satisfaction and peace that come from doing more than is expected of us. It is also true of going the second mile. Those who go out of their way to show kindness and love to their fellow men, not only bring blessings to others, but receive deep and abiding satisfaction themselves. They find that, the harder they work for good, the more wonderful life becomes.

Too many people are just "getting by," and are pitching their lives to the low "mean" average. To be a Christian demands that you give everything you have. In this manner, the longer you live the more you will want to do, because you will have a greater appreciation of what God has done for you.

TODAY'S THOUGHT: *Your job may be small, but it is no less important. The jigsaw puzzle without its tiniest piece is not complete.*

MAY 25

Live Your Faith

These all died in faith, not having received what was promised, but having seen it and greeted it from afar, and having acknowledged that they were strangers and exiles on the earth.

Hebrews 11:13

Some thoughtful person said, "You don't have to be in a key position to open the door of opportunity." This statement applies perfectly to our faith. You need not be a church *officer* to serve in the army of the Lord. Everyone has been called to serve. Everyone has some job to do.

Many times the Christian witness of a person with few talents is more effective than that of the brilliant leader who is not truly dedicated. The witness of an average Christian layman is particularly effective, since people expect ministers to preach the gospel; and so they are doubly attentive on hearing a layman express his beliefs.

A high-caste Hindu habitually watched a convert to Christianity who lived across the road from him. The convert had no idea that her actions were being observed. A the end of the year this Hindu became a Christian, and is now one of the leaders in his congregation.

"If Christianity can make anyone live as that woman lives, it must be true religion," he said. "If she had made one wrong step, I think I would still be a Hindu."

Think of the influence you have each day on those about you. What kind of witness are you for Christ and His kingdom? Do people desire to follow after you? Do you by your living make them want to love the Lord? Think of what could happen, if all those who call themselves Christians would really dedicate themselves to their faith?

Two visitors, riding in a taxi down Constitution Avenue in Washington, D. C., passed a building on which was this inscription: "What's past is prologue." One of the passengers asked the driver what it meant.

"That," said the driver, "is government language. It means, 'Brother, you ain't seen nothin' yet!'"

The world has not begun to see what could happen, if the army of the Lord really started marching. Why not start today?

TODAY'S THOUGHT: *Christ has two homes, one in heaven, the other in the heart of one who loves and serves Him.*

Claim Your Inheritance

For I decided to know nothing among you except Jesus Christ and him crucified. 1 Corinthians 2:2

An unruly boy, who had given his parents nothing but trouble, finally ran away from home. After he had gone, his father wrote him many letters, pleading with him to return. But the boy stubbornly refused; in fact, he ridiculed his parents for their pleas. Then one day he received a telegram saying that his father was dead, and that the rest of the family wanted him to be present at the funeral. His first thought was to refuse, but he finally decided to go. The least he could do was pay final respects to the father for whom he had shown so little respect.

The son sat through the funeral service without any show of emotion, and the friends he met at the house afterward felt the chill of a hard heart.

Finally the family was called together in a special meeting, and the father's will was opened and read. With unbelieving ears the wayward son heard that the father had remembered him along with the rest of the family. He was to receive the same inheritance as the other children who had not gone astray. This realization broke his heart, and he repented his misdeeds. But for days he was confounded by the fact that his father had loved him in spite of his rebelliousness.

Like this truant's longsuffering father, God loves us to the end of the world. But we must come to God in order to receive our heritage. God's treasure awaits every one of us. He has named us in His will, making us fellow heirs with Christ. Our salvation is secure, but we must be willing to accept it.

Think of the cost of our salvation to God. A downtown store displayed a crucifix in its window, and there was a little sign below which read: "This beautiful crucifix on easy terms."

That is exactly the opposite of the meaning of the cross. You cannot take up a cross of any kind on easy terms. Christ paid the price. The terms were suffering, sacrifice, pain, anguish, and death. God's love was revealed on Calvary's tree. It cost God his own Son to assure us of salvation.

The price has been paid in full. Let us claim our inheritance.

TODAY'S THOUGHT: *When you stand at the gateway of death, with the password Christ on your lips, the eternal doors will swing open and a wonderful Friend will greet you.*

Flee the Prison of Constricting Walls

Put on the whole armor of God, that you may be able to stand against the wiles of the devil. Ephesians 6:11

It was a thrill to visit Istanbul, Turkey, there to stop and see the mosque of Saint Sophia. Recognized as one of the most beautiful churches in the world, Saint Sophia is a Christian church, now altered to be a temple to Mohammed. All the Christian inscriptions and symbols have been painted out and replaced by Moslem ones. If you stand under the great dome, however, you can see a faint picture of Christ with His arms outstretched in blessing. It too, had been blotted out, but is reappearing as the paint peels off. As you view the reappearing figure, you cannot help but think, "Christ is coming back." "He cannot be hid." Down through the centuries men have tried to blot Him out, but He is on His way to take His throne to reign as King of kings and Lord of lords. The powers of evil will be defeated, and the kingdom of righteousness prevail.

As we face every day the choices between good and evil, let us remember that we shall win the battle of life if we will choose God. Time passes all too quickly. While it is day we should give our lives to Him, for the night is coming when no man can work. Our moments of opportunity may soon be taken from us.

If you cage a bird from a migrating flock, interrupting, frustrating the God-given instinct which is guiding it and the other birds to the distant home, it will try desperately to escape. But when the season for migration is past, this songbird will not even step outside the open cage. His instinct for flight is gone.

In the same way, decisions for Christ may be delayed until there is no desire to serve Him. If we allow sin to surround and confine us like a cage, we will be unable to follow Him when He calls.

"Today, when you hear his voice, do not harden your hearts."

TODAY'S THOUGHT: *The finest armor against temptation is an enveloping awareness of God's presence.*

MAY 28

Believe in God for Life

The heavens are telling the glory of God; and the firmament proclaims his handiwork. Psalm 19:1

The Bible promises a wonderful life, if we will accept the help God offers, and walk His way each day. We discover how much more satisfying life is when we follow our loving heavenly Father's plan.

The dirty-faced boys about five years old were sitting huddled together on their front steps with their fishing equipment strewn about. They were digging into a can, and finally pulled out an angle worm.

Eavesdropping, I expected their conversation to be about fishing, the best kind of bait to use, or what the probable catch would be. But these boys had other things to discuss.

"Do you believe in God?" one little fellow asked the other.

They spoke so softly that I missed the answer.

Then the first boy continued, "Well, I believe in God. Do you know why? Because if you don't believe in God, you won't go to heaven when you die."

The boy was right. Yet he was forgetting something. Too many people think of faith only as some kind of emergency vehicle to help them cross the final valley.

To be sure, if we believe in Christ as our Savior, we can be positive of life everlasting. But faith in God means ever so much more than that. It means we shall have peace our life through. The man who accepts God comes to the realization that, "We love because he first loved us." Moreover, the power of His love keeps persuading us to be kind and loving toward others. Then we will pray for others, sharing with them our means and spending our energy for others. As we follow His pattern of living, a joy sweeps into our consciousness that is a foretaste of heaven. Who can challenge this statement, "Having faith in Christ is a wonderful way to live"?

TODAY'S THOUGHT: *How much better it is to finish one small task for Christ than to make big plans for service and never even begin them.*

MAY 29

Stay Within Earshot!

Let me hear what God the Lord will speak, for he will speak peace to his people. Psalm 85:8

How many times do we become so absorbed with insignificant things that we come to miss entirely the things that matter most, the really important things in life? Stevie had just finished his first months of school. At the end of this time his handwriting had improved very little, and his mother was anxious to know the reason for his failure.

"Stevie," she said, "it doesn't seem to me that your handwriting has improved at school."

"No, it hasn't, Mother," he replied, "but you should see how good I am at sliding down the slide."

Stevie had found the call of the playground more attractive than the call of desk and copy book.

Every day siren voices call for our attention. As we answer them we may find momentary pleasure. But only when we answer the voice of God shall we find lasting peace and joy. It is best to guard our ears so that the voices of the world do not drown the voice of the only One who can give us life.

Two Christians were arguing over the joy of hearing God's voice and of following Him.

"I have never felt any compelling call to give my life to Christ," said one.

"Are you sure you are within hearing distance?" was the somewhat disquieting reply.

The voice of God never ceases to call, but it is possible for us to wander so far away from Him that we cannot hear. If man persistently refuses to listen, eventually he will become deaf to the voice which brings salvation and everlasting life. We should be careful to stay in the presence of Him who is our finest friend.

The little girl had just asked grace at the dinner table: "Come, Lord Jesus, be Thou our guest . . ." Then suddenly she said, "Oh, but I don't want Jesus to be our guest!"

"Why?" asked her mother.

"Well," said the child, "a guest is one who only comes sometimes, and I want Jesus to be here all the time."

TODAY'S THOUGHT: *Even as no man can sail the seven seas without a compass, so no life is complete without a God-sensitized conscience.*

MAY 30

A Day of Loving Remembrance and Re-Education

A book of remembrance was written before him of those who feared the Lord and thought on his name. Malachi 3:16

Memorial Day originated as a day dedicated to those who gave their lives for their country during the Civil War. Lincoln gave the day its dominant theme when he pleaded in this familiar speech, "That we here highly resolve that these honored dead shall not have died in vain." The day assumes its rightful significance when first we realize that to live in the grateful memories of those left behind is not to die.

We know that mere words will never suffice to express the feelings in our hearts for the men and women who made the supreme sacrifice. How easy it is to forget the dead, or to remember them only with a sense of loss rather than with warm gratitude.

Days set aside to honor the dead and place flowers on their graves are as old as history itself. Similar customs were observed by the Greeks and Romans, and even the civilizations that preceded them.

But, to be truly significant, this day must be more than a day of memory. It must be a day of dedication. We must resolve to live so that we give thanks to those who died that we might live.

World peace begins at your and my home today. As an Italian father remarked, when an American soldier was visiting his home at the close of World War II, "We have learned to swim like the fish under the sea; we have learned to fly like the birds of the air; but we have not yet learned to walk the earth in peace with our fellow men."

Yes, our attitude toward our neighbor shows whether or not we are sincere in offering to help God build His world of love and brotherhood. Only as we give all people an equal opportunity, regardless of color or creed, will God's kingdom ever be built on earth.

As we follow Jesus day by day, and seek His will in all our relationships, we shall begin marching in the greatest army the world has ever seen. The army of Christ alone can eliminate the horrors of war. This day let us resolve to prove to God that our lives have been worth saving.

TODAY'S THOUGHT: *What a wonderful world this could be, if the peace of God reigned in every heart!*

Recruited for the Lord's Army

The earth is the Lord's and the fulness thereof, the world and those who dwell therein. Psalm 24:1

General William Booth revealed the secret of his success. "God has had all there is of me," he said. "There have been men of greater brains than I, men with greater opportunities; but from the day when I caught a vision of what Jesus Christ could do with the poor of London, I made up my mind that God should have all of William Booth there was. If there is anything of power in the Salvation Army today, it is because God has had all the adoration of my heart, all the power of my will and all the influence of my life."

What a different world this would be, if every single person who called himself a Christian were willing to dedicate himself in that spirit to the work of Christ. Some have greater talents and re-sources than others, but even the least of us can say, "Lord, take my life and let it be dedicated unto thee."

Each of us has much to do every day. There are definite duties connected with holding a job, making a home, or going to school, and we are expected to do the very best we can. We accept certain duties, too, when we confess to be Christians. It is then our duty as a soldier in the army of Christ to witness for Him. There are all too many indifferent soldiers in Christ's army today.

"Mother, do you love Jesus?" the little girl asked, for she knew that her mother was supposed to be a Christian.

"Yes," answered the mother, "why do you ask?"

"Well, you often speak of Daddy and Auntie and your friends," the child replied, "but you never speak of Jesus. I thought, if you loved Him very much, that some time I would hear you talk about Him."

Yes, if we love Him, we must tell others of His grace and power. Think what Christ did for us. Think of the sacrifice upon the cross. Think of the bridge He built with the sturdy cross beams across the valley of the shadow of death, so that we might be assured of eternal life. Can we afford to be indifferent to God's great love? There is something you can do this day for Christ. As you serve, you will find abiding satisfaction in living.

TODAY'S THOUGHT: *Train yourself to see God in the poor, the lonely, the afflicted.*

JUNE 1

Jesus—Our Flawless Example

Christ also suffered for you, leaving you an example, that you should follow in his steps. 1 Peter 2:21

The power of example is surely one of the greatest forces in all the world. People are more likely to do what they see others do rather than what they hear them teach. The example of the good and righteous person is often the power that more than any other makes people act differently than they otherwise would.

Think of the tremendous influence that good mothers have had in moulding great men. Yes, a good example inspired by love to Christ, will perform miracles

Once a great painter was engaged to paint the Last Supper. He took ill just as he began his work and, unable to continue, he called his most promising and devoted pupil, a youth who dearly loved him. He asked him to paint the picture, so that it would be completed at the appointed time. The young man hesitated to attempt so great a subject in behalf of the famous painter and exclaimed, "Master, what shall I do?"

"Do your best, my son," was his answer.

Fired by love for his teacher and with the examples of the master's work all around him, the youth painted diligently until he was finished. When the old man saw it, he bowed his head and said humbly, "I shall never paint again." The pupil had become the master. This is how da Vinci's Last Supper was painted.

Like Leonardo da Vinci we, too, have many models to imitate, but they all stem from one source. Jesus Christ is the example of all that is noble, pure, and unselfish. The pattern which He has given us is not only flawless, but a living one. "The best way to export an idea," said the nuclear physicist, Dr. Urey, advocating international student exchange before a United States Senate hearing, "is to wrap it up in a person."

Whenever a hero dies, all we can do is carve the story of his deeds upon the tomb. They become dead memories. But when Jesus died and rose again, His example lived and was even stronger after His death than before. When He lived, few believed in Him, but after He died, millions have followed Him. If His life is your pattern, you will find a joy "unspeakable and full of glory."

TODAY'S THOUGHT: *Happy is the man who, looking ever to Jesus, holds as his highest hope one day to have faith's vision of his Savior become glorious sight.*

JUNE 2

The Man with a Hope

Let thy steadfast love, O Lord, be upon us, even as we hope in thee. Psalm 33:22

When one of the greatest of the ancient conquerors came to his throne, he distributed to his friends most of the wealth left by his father. One of his companions asked what he had kept for himself.

"The chief of the possessions," said Alexander, "hope."

With the aid of hope, Alexander the Great conquered the world; but he was not able to conquer himself.

Unlike Alexander, we Christians can be more than conquerors of the external. Through Christ who loves us we can overcome, not only the world, but our own human flesh whose frailty remains our constant enemy. Realizing that we are sons of God, and that we possess the certain hope of everlasting life, we Christians can conquer all, the external and the internal. This is the true glory of heaven on earth.

Worldly man eventually becomes gloomy and discontent. He finds life full of trouble and sorrow, one deep disappointment after another. With no one to help him through his difficulty, he is without hope, and so he is likely to cry out, "All is vanity!"

But the Christian looks beyond the immediate. He has a joy which the world can neither give nor take away, and the longer he lives the stronger and brighter that hope becomes, for "character produces hope."

Look at those young people training in Christian seminaries. The more they know of Him, and the more they experience His presence deep in their hearts, the stronger their conviction becomes and the more radiant their hope.

What is this hope? It is simply knowing that we are already the sons of God awaiting our eternal inheritance, blessings so great that they pass all human understanding.

TODAY'S THOUGHT: *Tend as faithfully your ray of hope as the keeper of the lighthouse does his lamp.*

JUNE 3

Fragile Love—Life's Mightiest Force!

But I say to you, "Love your enemies and pray for those who persecute you." Matthew 5:44

One day the Master gave us a prescription for living. He said, "A new command I give to you, that you love one another." Love has tremendous power. Love gives a father the capacity to face untold hard work and temptation in business. He is willing to do it, because above all he wants to provide a living for his family. Love is the power sending the soldier into battle, willing to risk his life for his country. Love is the power sending the missionary into the far-flung places of the world to give himself unselfishly to those who live in darkness. Love is the power that sent Christ, the Son of God, to the cross in order that we might have forgiveness of sins, the abundant life on earth, and ultimately eternal life. Love is a bond holding up forever, because God is love.

An old woman came frequently to a certain bank. She would go into the back room, take out her safety deposit box, and spend about a half hour with it. Each day as she left the bank, people noticed a radiance in her face. No one could understand the mystery until the day came when the woman died. For when the bank officials opened the box, they discovered it contained a little pair of baby shoes, a tassel of hair with a blue ribbon around it, and a little pink rattle. They began to understand the significance of her visits. A little girl, the daughter of this woman, had preceded her to heaven. She had come to the bank to look at the little reminders of the great love she held for her daughter, and the love which her daughter had had for her. She had come to anticipate the day, which God had promised her, when they would be together again in heaven.

Not only did this handling of the precious mementos give her peace, but it spurred her to mother all the neglected children in her neighborhood.

Take a moment to look off to Calvary. God's great love for us stands revealed there. It is assurance enough that, not only do we live now, but we shall live forever. Love never faileth!

TODAY'S THOUGHT: *Place love's fragile plant in your heart, and spend your life cultivating a harvest of the heart.*

JUNE 4

Failure—a Stepping Stone to Heaven

So that we might be justified by his grace and become heirs in hope of eternal life. Titus 3:7

Sometimes we are inclined to wonder why God sends so much suffering and sorrow into the world. All suffering is the result of sin. If man had not yielded in the very beginning, there would have been no death and, therefore, no sickness. God does not cause the world's suffering, yet He can use any part of it for good. Your whole lifetime is a school where, if you learn your lessons well, you will know truth and humility and love. Just as stern, rigorous training makes our bodies strong and healthy, so trouble borne with Christian courage braces our spiritual nature, and trains us for heaven.

A particularly difficult form of trouble, which we experience at one time or another, is a feeling of failure. We work long days, yet never do we seem to approach success. Others pass us in the race, while we plod on day after day, seemingly getting nowhere. What we should remember constantly is that no one ever fails who tries to do his duty. Do not think you have failed because you have made mistakes, or because the world regards you coldly. In the world's eyes the crucifixion is proof enough of the greatest of all failures. The world expected a Savior who would rule all as an earthly monarch. They had thought of a Savior having great and far-flung armies under His command. They were certain He would use force to overthrow all tyrannical governors and kings, and set them all free from their galling bondage. They did not at all think in terms of a spiritual kingdom, nor could they understand the Master when He said, "My kingdom is not of this world."

From this, too, we should learn a lesson. For all too many of us values are judged in respect to money and power. Many of us believe too strongly in getting, and too little in giving. Too many people willingly lay claim to all the benefits of Christ's suffering, and give nothing themselves in return. We listen with feigned respect to His injunction, "Let him who would be great become the servant of all," and then turn right around to lord it over some underling. Let us remember that we live victoriously only as we follow the self-sacrificing example of Jesus.

TODAY'S THOUGHT: *If you are not sharing now out of your need, do not kid yourself that when you have more than you need, you will then be willing to give to a needy soul.*

JUNE 5

Courage—a Gem with Many Facets

For I, the Lord your God, hold your right hand; it is I who say to you, "Fear not, I will help you." Isaiah 41:13

Courage is a many-sided virtue. God-inspired courage braces us for any trial, gives strength for every day. Courage can also be a discipline. Many people are bewildered and unhappy because they lack courage to think of others first and of themselves last. They build high walls about their self-centered world, lest they see human need demanding some sacrifice from them.

There is a fine line between courage and faith and patience, yet at the same time the three are interdependent. They form an interlocking chain whose anchor, a steadfast belief in a divine Creator, holds within the veil.

There are times when people need to realize that they are wrong. It takes courage to listen to something very unpleasant to your ears, to a criticism or a fact you have steadfastly refused to face. And it takes a double dose of courage to admit you are wrong.

A man needs courage to live up to his set of high ideals, especially when they are different from those of Mr. Average American. It takes courage to break away from a pattern of living that does not fit God's purpose for your life. Some families, for example, send their children to Sunday school because they want to do what is right for them; yet these same parents continue to live on a completely materialistic plane. Their lives are geared to the frustrating and dangerous practice of keeping up with the Joneses. They have no time to practice the principles which the church is teaching their children.

One must have courage to resist the full-page advertisements which breed "wantitis," which make us covet what others have. An unhealthy stress on materialism breeds snobbishness in our children, and teaches them to think first of their own personal satisfactions and only incidently of other people's needs. Do you have the courage to sacrifice and share your possessions, when others are out to get as much as they can? Will you teach your children to sacrifice and to share through your example? With faith in God, you will have courage to dare to do not what you would, but what is right.

TODAY'S THOUGHT: *Dare this day to live a sincere, selfless life, and to love God above all things.*

JUNE 6

Millions of Hands Ready for Happiness

Happy are these your servants, who continually stand before you and hear your wisdom! 1 Kings 10:8

What do you desire more than anything else in life? Suppose this question were asked every man on earth. I am quite sure the answers would be almost identical. Man is seeking happiness, and he is restless until he finds it. It is one of the basic guarantees of America's Declaration of Independence. In it we are promised life, liberty, and the pursuit of happiness. Of course, America cannot guarantee happiness. It can only guarantee you the privilege of seeking it.

More than that, however, it is our heavenly Father's sincere desire that each of His children find this fervently sought prize of happiness. When Lord Horder, personal physician of King Edward VIII, visited this country, some reporters asked him what was being done to lengthen human life.

"Don't people live long enough?" answered Lord Horder. "How to live more happily would be more to the point. People are living longer, but what is the use of living longer if we aren't happy?"

One thing we must keep in mind: happiness is not a place or a destination. It is that spirit within man, springing from his faith that God is indeed present in one's life and that, having resources unlimited, he can handle any possible situation.

To be happy, we must remember that every single soul is precious and important in God's sight. Though we may have different talents, there is not one person who is not the object of God's care. To have happiness, we must develop a vibrant faith, one that can sing in the darkest night. We must dare to dream of better days ahead. We must be convinced that life's final day will be the most glorious of all. To have happiness, we must pray every day for the answers to the questions facing us. We must seek God's will in all things.

To be happy, we must practice the law of love in our day-by-day relationships. First this love for God will color all we say and do. Then follows a love of our fellow men which brings such satisfaction and peace that true happiness will abide forever and ever.

TODAY'S THOUGHT: *Ours is a double-barrelled opportunity: to love God and our neighbor.*

JUNE 7

Jesus—Our Daily Guide

He will be our guide for ever. Psalm 48:14

We ought always to rejoice over what the Lord does for us day by day. Not only does He lay out a pattern for life, but He helps us to live it. Our souls are glad in the knowledge of God's living presence. Day by day we can know what it means to be filled with the Holy Spirit who is willing to be our Ruler and our Guide. He is the One who so leads us through things temporal that we do not lose sight of things eternal. His power, channeled to us by the means of grace, gives us strength to live a holy life, and, therefore, a happy one.

Each person's path is different. For some it is more rugged and steep than for others. It is difficult to explain why this should be. But more important than that is this fact: to be happy, such differences in men's lives do not need to be explained. The man who tries to do his duty in the place where God puts him, and who daily seeks to walk with God, need fear no evil. Even in the midst of trouble he can rejoice.

No one ever will find life easy. It is at best a difficult fight. But, as soldiers in Christ's army, we can always rejoice. Remember the Apostle Paul? What a valiant Christian soldier he was! More than most men, he knew what trouble and hardship really meant. Into all his earthly battle he carried within himself the peace of God which passes all human understanding. When he entered the valley of the shadow of death itself, the Master walked at his side. He felt that God's rod and staff comforted him. His heart rejoiced in the presence of Christ and in the hope of eternal glory.

All of us should be more thankful than we are. Think of what Jesus has done for us! Remember what He is doing now as He guides us along the straight and narrow way of faith. Remember that Jesus lifts His holy and scarred hands to plead for our mistakes, for our sins. Look forward to all His promises. Feel thankful! And rejoice always! Let us daily resolve not to look only at our troubles, but also to the unnumbered mercies for which we owe God our gratitude.

TODAY'S THOUGHT: *Those who would give thanks must take time to remember and reflect on the specific blessings God has bestowed.*

JUNE 8

Today Is Cash in Hand

Jesus answered . . . "We must work the works of him who sent me, while it is day; night comes, when no one can work." John 9:4

Ken Smith, a bus driver in Baltimore, Maryland, knew that every minute could be used to good advantage. On every round he had to make with his bus Ken had to waste seven minutes at a dump about a half acre in area. Those seven minutes of waiting dragged until Ken thought of a plan. First he pulled the weeds and cut the underbrush, working seven minutes at a time, then he planted flowers and grass. Those seven minutes flew by, and his work went just a little farther between each bus round. Before long he had laid cinder paths in his little half-acre park. The next step was to build a barbecue pit for picnickers who would come after the job was done. Come they did, but not until the city formally dedicated the park, and everyone in Baltimore knew what seven minutes, well spent, can produce.

When we are going God's way, He will give us the desire to make the best use of every segment of time, whether it is a few minutes or a few days. When we give our time and our talents to the service of God, we shall see our work prosper and grow before our eyes, for it will have the blessing of the Master. When we take God with us wherever we go, and pause often to seek His guidance and ask for renewed strength, we can tackle jobs that would seem far too large for a mere human being.

When we do the work of the Lord, He gives us strength and power, first for the one job and then the next, and the next, until at last we have completed the colossal project set before us. It is not for us to pick our job, simply to dedicate our whole selves to God, and go wherever He sends us, and do whatever He asks. We can do things we had never dreamed to be possible, when we are yokefellows with the Lord, for we shall be undergirded by faith and the power of prayer.

Each day provides new opportunities for serving our Savior, for witnessing for Him, and for growing in our faith and love for Him. If we concentrate on today, we shall not have to worry about the other days. This is the philosophy of a woman who is 87 years young. She says, "Yesterday is a cancelled check. You cannot do anything about it—so forget it! Concentrate on today!"

TODAY'S THOUGHT: *Every day of your life should boost the sum total of the world's joy and light.*

JUNE 9

The Arm of Flesh Will Fail You

In thee, O Lord, do I take refuge; let me never be put to shame!
Psalm 71:1

One day there came to Jesus a father who had a child sick since birth. Every possible cure had been tried. The father loved his son, and wanted him to be well. Now, having reached the end of his resources, he turned to the Master and said, "If you can do anything, have pity on us and help us." The Lord answered him, "If you can! All things are possible to him who believes." He made no qualification whatsoever in his reply. And the man responded, "I believe; help my unbelief."

That indeed was a wise prayer, because it indicated that this man had reached the point where he recognized his own weakness. He realized that God alone had the power to channel into his weakness and failure new horizons for living.

Each morning, when you awaken, you can do one of two things. You can face the day by saying, "I can't make it today. There are problems to face that I just can't overcome. In fact, there are temptations that will bowl me over." Thinking such thoughts, you just cannot win. You are defeated before you begin.

But there is the other alternative you can choose. You can begin your day by getting in tune with the will of God, using these words: "I believe with all my heart. I believe your every promise. God, I know that you are going to be with me every step I take. I hug to myself that promise you have made, that 'all things are possible to him who believes.' I believe that you will give me power to spare, that I may be victorious."

No person who puts his trust in God has ever been put to shame. It is only when we put all our trust in our own strength, our own puny resources, that we fail. Wise is the man who by faith gets his eyes open to the power of God.

TODAY'S THOUGHT: *No one ever is a failure until he loses his courage. It is not that a hero has more courage than the other fellow. He is just braver five minutes longer.*

JUNE 10

Distrust Can Bring Distress

That was to make us rely not on ourselves but on God.

2 Corinthians 1:9

Eternal life is indestructible. It endures both the cross and the grave. It grows fuller and richer as the ages roll on. To the Christian eternal life is a present possession, a blessing he can enjoy now, and one he need not wait for by and by in the sky. To be sure, eternal life extends into a future state, but it is far more than mere endless existence. It is goodness and fullness of life, joy, peace and love. What must we do to possess it?

Faith is the sole condition of our salvation. Faith is accepting Christ as the only way leading through this world and its fleeting happiness to the lasting happiness in the world to come. Those with faith in the Master do His bidding and follow His teaching. *He* knows the way, having himself walked it, and we ought to trust our Guide. He holds before us all God's promises, which we ought to accept at His word. Faith is the act of staking our life on God. It means also being devoted to Him and opening our hearts to His influence.

Food will not save a starving man unless he eats. Schools and libraries will not educate him unless he studies. A check signed by the richest man will do no good unless someone has the faith to present it to the bank. The doctor cannot cure a distrustful man, who refuses to take the prescribed medicine. No guide can lead through a forest unless he is trusted and we follow him. A prisoner who will not believe in the offer of pardon cannot be released from prison.

Some people have the impression that Christ came to love men instead of to hate them. The fallacy is in the phrase, instead of to hate them, for this phrase is simply not true. If it were, it would imply that there was a time when God did not love man. God has always loved men. In the giving of His only begotten Son we see the highest expression of love. It was God's purpose that the love revealed in Christ should draw all men to Him.

His offer is unlimited. "Whoever believes," He said. The only condition is faith. God is not a "gate-crasher." The privilege of faith belongs to all of us. "By grace you have been saved through faith; and this is not your own doing, it is the gift of God."

TODAY'S THOUGHT: *Calm and confidence are among the fairest flowers in the lovely garden of faith.*

162

JUNE 11

Stop Pretending Independence

For God abases the proud, but he saves the lowly. Job 22:29

Life with God is worth while. Whether our circumstances be easy or difficult, with God life is always worth while. If the branch is attached to the vine, if we are in Christ and Christ is in us, then we resemble Christ more each day. This means we must correct certain values, must let other false values go, and hold fast to truth. If we really believe in eternity, then we should ultimately possess only those characteristics of life which have eternal meaning. The rest has little value, and will eventually be refuse for burning.

For example, we need to give up sham and pretense. Let us turn to God very simply and say, "God, I do not have strength myself. You have all that I need. I know that without you I can do nothing." Believing in God we must forget, leave behind, our fears and anxieties. There is nothing at all to be afraid of, absolutely nothing, just so we confidently believe that He walks the pathway ahead. Since He knows the way, we need merely follow.

Among life's eternal values there are two to which, above all, we must cling. The first is faith, and the second is the ability to judge what is important. Our faith must be pure and simple, in fact, childlike. Too many people are afraid to be childlike in their faith, foolishly thinking this seems to deny their maturity and reason. We make complicated what God has made so simple. We want to reason out everything, when in reality we do not need to "reason" faith. Faith is trusting in a God who is there, and ought to be accepted just as surely as the universe itself is accepted.

The second value, the ability to judge what is important, we must cultivate until it is second nature. Today in our complicated age there is such a mad dash after pleasure, power, and money. It is so noisy that few people hear any more "the still small voice." Tragically, we keep building bigger barns, without having anything to put in them.

A young woman on her deathbed said to her mother, "Mother, you taught me to sing and dance, and have fun. You taught me how to make a living. But, Mother, why didn't you teach me how to die?"

If we know how to live, we know also how to die. "For to me to live is Christ, and to die is gain."

TODAY'S THOUGHT: *Accept the heavenly Father's adoption, and one day you will walk arm in arm with Him in light.*

JUNE 12

Do the Best with What You Have

Has not God chosen those who are poor in the world to be rich in faith and heirs of the kingdom which he has promised to those who love him? James 2:5

A newspaper reporter traveled into the heart of Africa for a personal interview with the great medical missionary, Dr. Albert Schweitzer. Back again in this country, the reporter shared the interview with various groups. After he had talked to a particularly interested group, a member of the audience asked, "What, in your opinion, was the most outstanding quality in the personality of Dr. Schweitzer?" The speaker's answer was significant.

"I believe," he said, "it is his sincere conviction that his every task is equally important. He gives himself completely to each moment as God presents it to him. He considers his time a trust. And he uses every molecule of energy to be helpful in everything he does."

We, too, will begin to enjoy the serenity and power of the great men of God, when we believe that the most important task is to glorify God. He can be glorified in the most humble action. The secret of success in serving our heavenly Father is not in the number of talents we possess but in the divine power we possess. If God's energy flows through us, anything is possible, no matter how limited our talents.

Natural unaided man, without the power of God, can do but little. A sailboat may have her sails spread wide, but it cannot move until the wind comes. The lumber in a carpenter's house cannot frame itself into a ship without the skilled carpenter. A man living out of touch with God cannot be successful because he has no strength from above.

Not all of us can become famous like Dr. Schweitzer, but we can all serve God in our own humble way. From this great man we can learn that no task is so lowly that it cannot be a blessing, if we seek its accomplishment with the talents God has given. The man who does the most with what he has is a successful man in the sight of God.

TODAY'S THOUGHT: *Do simple things patiently, and in time you will do difficult things easily.*

JUNE 13

Leave the Rest to God

The Lord is my strength and my shield; in him my heart trusts.
Psalm 28:7

The Sunday school teacher was showing off her pupils to a visitor. She was anxious that everyone should recite well, so she asked only the questions she was sure they could answer correctly. She asked one of the slower students a question which appeared to have an obvious answer.

"Billy, is there anything that God cannot do?"

"Yes, ma'am," answered Billy confidently.

"Now think again," the teacher persisted, "I asked if there were anything too difficult for God to do."

"Yes, there is," came the reply, "God can't please everyone!"

The only reason that God cannot please everyone is that we fail to follow His instructions. We blame God for the difficulties caused by our own mistakes. Our heavenly Father has a plan for every one of us. If we seek to do His will and keep our lives in harmony with it, we will have happiness within our souls. It is only when we refuse to obey Him that we find ourselves in difficult positions.

If you bought a new electrical appliance and received an accompanying list of instructions, you would likely follow them in order that the appliance might give you the convenience you desire.

God brought us into the world, but He has not left us alone. He gave us a set of instructions to follow, and it is only when we disobey them that we find ourselves in trouble. If we follow them, we learn that He can supply our every need, and grant our heart's desire.

Every one of God's children has a place in His plan; no one is insignificant. Every task is important and should be performed as before God. And God is a partner who will help His children in time of need. The secret is to do all you can, and leave the rest to God.

These words are cut in stone over the entrance to the French College of Physicians: "I dress his wounds; God heals him." Never let us forget that all power is given to us through our daily partnership with God.

TODAY'S THOUGHT: *Do not trust to luck; instead seek the infinite power of God.*

JUNE 14

Silence the Voice of Temptation

The fear of the Lord is hatred of evil. Proverbs 8:13

An Indian was preparing a snare to catch a wild animal. A man who was watching was surprised to see that the Indian did not spring the trap the first time the animal appeared. Instead he let it come up to the trap several times. Then when the animal was familiar with the surroundings, the Indian set the trap and stood by to watch the animal walk boldly to its death.

Temptation works in much the same way. It does not expect to capture the victim at first. It deceives and lures a man on, until he is an easy mark for the final blow.

One certain way of defeating temptation is to stay away from it. In the days of the Civil War trading cotton was against the law. Many unscrupulous speculators made huge profits buying cotton in the South and smuggling it to the North. One of these speculators approached a Mississippi River steamboat captain, and offered him $100 to run his cotton up the river. The captain said that it was illegal and he would not do it. The man raised his price to $500, and still the captain refused.

"I'll give you $1,000," answered the black marketeer.

"No," said the captain, standing firm. The bid was promptly tripled, $3,000. The captain's hesitation indicated that he considered the figure tempting.

"Get off my boat," he roared, "you are coming too close to my price."

This is the only way to deal with temptation. Its voice can be most alluring. Often it promises gifts we would like to accept, but the pleasure of those gifts is short-lived and leaves us nothing but heartache and pain. The promised heaven becomes a present hell. Wise indeed is the man who remains so close to God that he cannot hear the siren voice of temptation when it calls.

Every day we should put on the whole armor of God. We are in the world, but we must not become like the world. God's strength is sufficient to keep us on the narrow way. The secret is to follow Him so closely that we see no other way; for the narrow way is the way to eternal life.

TODAY'S THOUGHT: *Do the will of God, and you will be too busy to dispute His plans.*

JUNE 15

Lanterns of Love

A new commandment I give to you, that you love one another; even as I have loved you. John 13:34

I once observed an interesting drinking fountain. It was an angel, beautifully sculptured in marble, looking toward heaven. The fountain bore an inscription with gilt letters. But I noticed that the water flowed through a small brass pipe, and that the people drank from an iron cup attached to an iron chain. After a moment I realized that the marble angel pointing heavenward would be useless without the brass pipe and the iron cup. What if the brass pipe had said, "I should be made of gold; I can't be part of this fountain." Or what if the iron cup had said, "I'm not silver; I am ashamed to be here." But this was not the case. They knew that the people would have water only if each part did its job. This is what they said, "They can't do without us, and we must do our part with the beautiful angel and the polished marble."

Just as each part of the beautiful fountain had different abilities and a different task, so every single soul is endowed with different abilities. Some of us think our tasks insignificant, and are tempted to shy away from them because they are not as great as we think they should be. But a common ordinary task can be sacred, if done in the spirit of love. It can bring rich blessings. Any labor of love, no matter how insignificant, will be triumphant when consecrated to Christ.

The love that is lit at the lamp of God never goes out. Jesus said, "A new commandment I give to you, that you love one another . . . By this all men will know that you are my disciples, if you have love for one another."

Years ago in England, lighted lanterns were hung in church steeples and in front of houses at night. These lanterns were the forerunners of the street lights we have today. Each night the watchman made his rounds calling, "Hang out the lights, hang out the lights." This is the call of Christ: "Let your light shine. Let the world know by your actions and words that you are a follower of mine."

TODAY'S THOUGHT: *God has a use for every tool in the kit marked Talents.*

JUNE 16

Set Aside a Quiet Time

For thus said the Lord God . . . "In quietness and in trust shall be your strength." Isaiah 30:15

A famous Scotch music master often told his students that the rests were just as important in music as the notes. New students thought he was exaggerating, but soon learned that without careful attention to the intervals, however brief, between musical phrases, the music lost half its beauty.

What is true of music is also true of life. For without intervals of silence, however brief, life would lose half its beauty. In a solitary walk through the silent woods, we note the glories of nature, and wonder at the wisdom and power of a God who created and maintains such a world. With awe at nature's beauty comes a reassurance of the Father's loving care. "Consider the lilies . . . they neither toil nor spin; yet I tell you, even Solomon in all his glory was not arrayed like one of these." If the duties of the day postpone the silent solitary walk until past nightfall, it can be to the good, for the puffed up self-importance of the day will shrink to its size when you walk under God's vast star-studded sky.

Though the American Indians did not know our heavenly Father, they knew the importance of taking time each day for silence and meditation. Indian mothers taught their children to go off by themselves at the end of the day, and make a place for the visit of the Great Spirit. Sometimes they built a fire and sat staring into the flames; sometimes they viewed a glorious sunset. The children were taught to reflect upon their actions and thoughts of the day. If there was anything of which they were ashamed, they were to say that they were sorry, and ask for strength to avoid the same mistake again. They found a great peace in this daily quiet time.

Our spirits desperately need such moments of prayer and meditation and Bible study, in order to be regenerated, just as much as our auto must be constantly refueled. If we do not take time to be renewed by prayer and meditation, we shall find ourselves without the inner resources that we need when we face one of life's difficulties. "But the pressures! You simply have no idea what pressures there were," said a senator to a constituent, taking him to task for a shameful vote. "Pressures nothing," he retorted, "man what about the braces?"

TODAY'S THOUGHT: *The mountains are mute—yet how eloquently they speak of God.*

JUNE 17

Extend a Helping Hand

Every one helps his neighbor, and says to his brother, "Take courage!" Isaiah 41:6

A Christian who is not making his presence felt in his home, his job, and his community is not very effective in helping others find the narrow way that leads to eternal life. We who love Christ must let our lights shine.

In one of Theodore Roosevelt's eloquent speeches, he asked, "Do you go out in a rowboat in a gale for the fun of it?" He answered his own question, "Never! You go out to save someone, but you fear the storm." A missionary was asked how he liked his work in Africa. "Do I like this work?" he replied. "No, my wife and I do not like the filth. We do not like crawling into vile huts, marching through swamps and forests in order to work with ignorant brutish people. But is a man to do nothing for Christ but what he likes? Liking or not liking has nothing to do with it. We have orders to go, and we go. Love constrains us." His words reveal the impelling power that brings out the finest and best in men and women as they help their fellow men.

A group of men working in a harvest field were sitting under a tree eating lunch, when they caught sight of a figure walking across the field with slow steps. From the way he walked, stumbling now and then on the uneven ground, all the while tapping a white cane, they knew he was blind. Ahead in the direction he was moving, was a precipice with the river 100 feet below. The blind man was walking steadily toward the brow of the cliff, piloted only by his cane, a man without a seeing guide. Nearer and nearer he came, unaware of what was before him. The farmhands watched silent and unmoved. No voice was lifted to caution him. No helping hand was extended to point out the danger. They stared, fascinated as he took the fatal step forward. The erect form toppled forward over the precipice. They heard a wild cry, and he was gone. Would they ever cease hearing that cry?

O how our heavenly Father loves us. This is so important to remember. The least we can do is to love Him in return, and sound the alarm to every straying soul about us. It is not that tomorrow's hell is so awful. What about the living hell of a life without God? Let us resolve each day to let our light shine for God!

TODAY'S THOUGHT: *Where there is no love put love, and you will find love.*

JUNE 18

God Knows Best

My lord has wisdom like the wisdom of the angel of God to know all things that are on the earth. 2 Samuel 14:20

An amusing fable is told about a Chinese farmer. He planted seed at the right time and eagerly watched each row, waiting for the first sprouts to push through the soil. When they appeared and the tender shoots began to point heavenward, he decided to help his truck garden to grow faster. Each morning he would pull the plants a little farther out of the ground, and he seemed to be ahead of the other gardeners, who just waited for their plants to grow. Then one day he found every plant in his garden drooping They all shriveled and died.

We would call this farmer foolish and would ridicule him. But are we not very much like him? We fuss because our plants do not mature fast enough, and fret when our work is slow in showing results. We cry to God, "Why aren't our prayers answered more quickly?" Indeed, we complain because God denies us the things we ask for. With a little patience, however, we shall learn the reason: Many things we seek would be harmful to us.

A mother was lolling on a sofa, while the maid was caring for her young son, playing on the patio just outside the door. The youngster, badly spoiled, threw a tantrum.

"Give him what he wants," called the mother to the maid.

Suddenly the child screamed louder than before.

"Didn't I tell you to give him anything he wants?" called the mother.

"Yes, ma'm," answered the maid, "he wanted that bee and he got it."

God who sees all knows what is best. He loves us as His children, and wants nothing to come into our lives bringing harm or discomfort.

The secret of victorious living is to remain in the presence of God, and to follow His instructions.

"Why is it our friend has such power in his life?" one man asked another.

"Because he lives so near the gates of heaven, he hears many things from God that we who do not get near enough cannot hear!" was the answer.

TODAY'S THOUGHT: *If you truly love God, you will make a time for kneeling in His presence.*

170

JUNE 19

The Meek Surpass the Mighty

Blessed are the meek, for they shall inherit the earth.

Matthew 5:5

To be meek, one must be gentle and mild of temper, self-controlled, and not easily provoked. In the spiritual sense, it means that one must submit to the divine will. Again, it means we give the Spirit the controls. Meekness implies great faith. It is not a weak but a heroic quality. "He who is slow to anger is better than the mighty, and he who rules his spirit than he who takes a city."

Only those of Christ's kingdom characterized by this quality of meekness shall possess the whole earth. The final conquest of the earth will not be by the force of world-conquering arms. Intellectual power or political shrewdness will never bring it about. It will come about by the spiritual power of the meek, by the gospel of the lowly Jesus.

Without Him, life becomes empty. The foliage of the trees of life may appear to us beautiful, but when we examine them closely there is no fruit to satisfy the deepest longing of our souls. On the other hand, the Christian has a tree laden with fruit that is good to eat, a tree that persecution and trial only serve to prune, until it bears more and more fruit. Truly here is the miracle for, the greater the adversity, the greater is the fruit bearing of this Christian tree of life. Here is a tree of trees, waiting to be plucked of its fruit, for God in His wisdom keeps replenishing the branches with richness and strength and love.

A Brahman once compared the Christian to a Mango tree. This tree puts forth luxurious blossoms and then weighs its branches with fruit. Is this fruit for itself? Never, but it freely offers it to the hungry who come to it for food. By and by the tree is assailed with clubs and stones, as men seek the fruit from the inaccessible branches. Its leaves are torn, its branches are bruised. But does it resent this cruel treatment, and refuse to yield fruit for another year? No, for the following year it is more fruitful than ever. Thus the Christian, in spite of persecution, in spite of difficulties and trials, yields himself to the will of God and becomes more fruitful the longer he lives. Victory over earthly strife may not be immediate, but eventually it always comes.

TODAY'S THOUGHT: *There is a spring for every winter and a victory for every defeat.*

JUNE 20

Keeping Watch Beyond the Stars

He made the stars also . . . And set them in the firmament of the heavens to give light upon the earth. Genesis 1:16, 17

In Arabia they tell the story of an American who had come there with a fancy, expensive telescope. One day he was seen peering into the heavens.

"I can see millions of stars with this one instrument that man has made," he boasted, inwardly marvelling at man's ingenuity to fashion this magnificent telescope which brought the heavens within his range.

A thoughtful Arab said to him, "We Arabs just use our eyes. We can see only a few stars up there in the heavens, but behind those stars we see God."

"Behind those stars we see God." This is the faith we, too, must hold. The tendency of our day seems rather to be to forget God and to deify man. We have led God to the rim of His creation and bowed Him out. We worship the means to the end rather than the glorious end itself.

Some would explain away the discipline of the Christian life and the Ten Commandments and all the rest. "Express yourself, just let yourself go. Rid yourself of all inhibitions. They cramp your personality and frustrate you. Instead, sin boldly! Eat, drink, and be merry!" Some people delude themselves, and think this to be the life! But that is to trade ashes for beauty.

There was once a man who came to a prominent European doctor and said, "I don't know what is wrong with me, but I do know that something is. Can you help me?"

The doctor examined him. "Physically you are all right. What you need to do is to have some fun. Go out and see that great clown, Rinaldi, that is in town. He will make you laugh."

The man turned to the doctor and said, "I am that clown!"

We find our definition of real life in the word of God, and no one can gainsay it. In Jesus' high priestly prayer our Lord reveals His purpose in coming to this world. He says, "This is life eternal, (Eternal means 'non ending')—to know God." There you have it: "to know God." That claims my soul, and I have made it the guiding star for my spirit.

TODAY'S THOUGHT: *You too will be introduced to God, if you will only listen to and follow through on the words of His Son, Jesus.*

JUNE 21

The Christian Is Transparently Honest

For we aim at what is honorable not only in the Lord's sight but also in the sight of men. 2 Corinthians 8:21

The story is told of a man called upon to repair a house. He did a very poor job, and it was not long before the place was falling apart again. When someone talked to him about the matter, he was quite embarrassed as he replied, "Yes, but it was done according to contract."

That man did not have God as his partner. If God had been with him, the man would have done honest work well, regardless of the careless specifications.

As we go about our daily tasks, we should remember the story of the ship owner who used to insure his vessels very heavily, and then, having repaired them with the cheapest and worst materials, would send them unseaworthy out to sea.

On one occasion he was obliged to be aboard one of his ships when it was overtaken by a violent storm. As the winds blew and the waves rolled, the boat began to strain. Water poured through the flimsy fastened timbers. Soon the owner was in an agony of fear. Previously he had felt utter unconcern for the lives of his sailors, going down to sea in his vessels. But now, with his own life at stake, it made all the difference in the world.

There are many people in the world today who loudly profess to be Christians, and yet who are sleazy in their actions in God's sight. Concerned only about themselves, they show no care for their fellow men.

There will come a day when every one of us must stand before the judgment throne and give an account of our life's work. We may have been able to fool our fellow men, but God knows all things. By living deceitfully we may think that we have been the gainers; but as we stand on the threshold of eternity, we cannot hope to deceive God, our Almighty Father.

The only way to conquer ourselves is to make God our partner in all things. If we will listen to His voice and let Him direct our way, our life will stand inspection and outride the stormy passage of Styx itself.

TODAY'S THOUGHT: *Every resisted temptation shoves the devil that much farther behind.*

173

Blest Out and Beyond All the Rest

With thy blessing shall the house of thy servant be blessed for ever. 2 Samuel 7:29

Every life has a purpose. And the best way to discover it is to lay your life before God in earnest prayer. Ought we not live every day in the assurance that someone needs our love, someone needs our help, and that God will open our eyes to our place of service if only we permit Him to?

One does not travel far in the world without realizing that we in America have so much more than any other people anywhere.

Visiting the Augusta Victoria hospital in Jerusalem, I looked into a ward of twelve baby cribs. In them I saw twelve pitiable bundles of bones not even resembling human beings. These little babies suffered from malnutrition. They were on the way to starving to death when brought in.

In Cairo, Egypt, I saw many crippled children hobbling in the streets. I asked my guide, "How come?" He told me that mothers crammed the little arms and feet of their children into milk bottles with the intention of crippling them. Then when the youngsters grow up twisted and crippled, the mothers carry them in their arms up and down the streets of Cairo to arouse sympathy, and to beg for money. They also rent the children by the night to other women, whose children are not crippled so that they, too, can beg for money.

I went to Africa and saw a little girl dressed in a freshly ironed dress, crisp and spotless. Her name was Kioti, which means, "Nobody loves me." This is how she got that name: She was set out in the bush to die, because she was so sickly and infected with sores that her family did not think it worth while to try to save her, since there were other healthier children to be fed and saved from starvation. A missionary found little Kioti and brought her home. Doctors dressed her sores, and helpers put a clean dress on her. But she withdrew within herself. The loneliest girl they had ever known, they tried to convince her that they loved her; but she did not know what the word "love" meant. One day, however, it dawned on her. She looked down on her freshly bandaged hands and her clean dress, and as she pointed to these concrete symbols of tender loving care she said, "Is this love?" Love is like that!

TODAY'S THOUGHT: *Have you learned yet what one hour a week spent in building a house of love could mean to another soul?*

JUNE 23

Made Lord of Your Life!

To the King of ages, immortal, invisible, the only God, be honor and glory for ever and ever. 1 Timothy 1:17

Life is purposeless to that man who has not found a faith that gives him courage and peace of mind. Without faith a man becomes bitter and full of the scar tissue of cynicism. One must find a faith worth leaving behind, if he would have a life worth living.

Have you found such a faith? Or are you blindly plodding along achieving nothing, until life is as dull as ditch water, and as meaningless. If, however, you are in possession of a vibrant faith, you have direction and purpose for living. What is more, you are walking as a child of God with peace and happiness in your heart.

Faith is able to work miracles. Martin Luther once told about two wonders he observed. The first revealed itself as he looked out a window and saw the stars shining in the heavens. Suddenly he realized there were no visible pillars supporting the firmament, and yet the heavens did not fall upon him. Then again he beheld great clouds hovering overhead, and he felt bowed down with a great weight like a mighty ocean. But in that moment he saw that the clouds rested upon no visible foundation, and yet, they too, like the stars, did not fall. After observing those two wonders, he came to this conclusion: there are people who, failing in their search for these pillars and foundations, go about in fear and trembling, as if the heavens must fall on them tomorrow, because they cannot envision these supports.

Faith is the only answer for such people, the faith that believes that we are in a world where God has the last word and is enthroned Lord of each individual life. Many have not yet accepted Him as such. But those who have, see His presence in everything about them. They know that God is not remote and detached from them beyond earshot of their call but ever present, upholding the mud ball of a world in which they live. All of man's real strength and driving force come from just such a faith. He who believes has the strength of ten. But he who doubts is weak. Only the man with strong convictions makes a dent in life or any kind of real progress. These convictions must be rooted in God. Buttressed by such a faith, a man can live courageously and unafraid.

TODAY'S THOUGHT: *Believe in God and you will see Him everywhere you look.*

175

JUNE 24

Faith and Work Go Together

They profess to know God, but they deny him by their deeds.
Titus 1:16

A man told about approaching the door of a building, and noticing from a distance that there was no latch. It appeared that it would be impossible for him to gain entrance. Yet on getting closer he discovered that the door was controlled by an electric eye that automatically opened it as one broke its ray. If he had stood off, and waited for the door to open, he would have waited in vain. But he went forward to enter, and the door opened for him without any effort at all on his part.

An active faith controls doors which would remain closed to us forever except we possessed it. We march forward stubbornly believing the door will open and lo, it suddenly swings ajar. To let doubt bring you to a standstill, however, is to let that door be closed forever.

Many are losing blessings today, because they do not go forward in faith to the new doors which open to ever widening horizons. Because of God's power there is no limit to what we can become. He has done all that is necessary for our salvation. Blessings await our claiming them, faith being the only condition. Faith does not mean waiting on God with folded hands, hoping for Him to hand us a blessing as by a miracle. A trusting faith in God means that we take God at His word, and then put our own efforts and talents into His hands for the accomplishment of His purposes.

A ferryman had painted the word "Faith" on one oar and the word "Work" on the other. Asked the reason for this, he said not a word, but took the oar with "Faith" on it and pulled with all his strength. The boat spun round and round, gradually floating downstream with the current. Then he put his hands on the oar marked "Work" and there was the same result. Finally he grasped both oars, "Faith" and "Work," and pulled them together, whereupon the skiff moved out of the current and across the stream.

We must always remember that it takes both faith and work to get anywhere in life. Faith brings us in touch with God to receive direction and empowering grace. As we follow His commands, yielding to His use of our abilities, we are led from victory to victory.

TODAY'S THOUGHT: *As the life in the seed is to the ripened grain, so is faith to our doing.*

JUNE 25

"In the Time of Trouble He Shall Hide Me . . ."

Do not hide thy face from me in the day of my distress! Incline thy ear to me. Psalm 102:2

One day the Master was asked, "Lord, teach us to pray."

In response He told a very interesting story about a man already in bed, the time being past midnight, when there was a knock at the door. Some people had come on a visit. He was taken unawares, and was more than a little embarrassed, for he discovered that the kitchen cupboards were bare. His visitors came to him from a long journey and had gone hungry all day. He had no food on hand to set before them. At this hour the village store was closed. What was he to do?

Finally he thought of a friend living two houses down the street. So, despite this midnight hour, he stumbled through the dark street to knock at his friend's door.

With the help of every dog in the village, he awakened the friend at last. He called out crossly, "What do you want?"

His friend said, "Can you lend me three loaves of bread? I am in an embarrassing situation. Friends have come from afar to see me. They have had no supper, and I have no food for them."

The friend gave him the bread; and he retraced his steps to his house to serve his guests.

Jesus wants us to learn a lesson from this little story. For one thing, it highlights the urgency of prayer. Why did this man turn to his friend? He turned to his friend when he was in a desperate situation, his own resources had all run out. Significantly his friend helped him. Not that the only time we ought to turn to God in prayer is in the time of crisis. We would do well to reflect on this: that as long as man is foolish enough to think he is all-sufficient and can do without God, God can hardly shower him with blessings.

Look at the Pharisee who struts into the temple stiffly to pray, "God, I thank you that I am not like other men." How could God possibly answer his prayer? Look at the Publican and hear the words he directs to heaven. "God, be merciful to me a sinner." Such a humble prayer draws out all God's heart, and opens His hands. Be thankful that God who stands behind the open door of prayer is, "our help in ages past, our hope for years to come."

TODAY'S THOUGHT: *There are times when, whatever other position our body may be in, our soul must be down on its knees.*

177

JUNE 26

In Quest of Faith

Then he said to Thomas, "Put your finger here, and see my hands; and put out your hand, and place it in my side; do not be faithless, but believing." John 20:27

A psychology student stood on a certain street corner. In his hand he clutched ten crisp one-dollar bills, offering one to each passer-by. After asking a score of men and women whether they wanted a dollar, he gave up. Only three had accepted.

"It was discouraging," said the young man. "Human beings do not seem to trust each other any more."

If we think that strange, what do we think of man's relationship to God? Our heavenly Father offers priceless gifts that no amount of money can buy. Yet daily we ignore the opportunities He freely offers. We are the intended joint heirs of heaven's riches. Yet we choose to live as spiritual paupers.

Still God does not give up. Through the ages He continues to offer us something of infinite value, something incomparable. Though comparatively few people accept His offer, He continues to give His children eternal life. He assures us that we belong to Him. He wants us to rest secure in the faith that He can be trusted.

One day a few summers ago a man and his ten-year-old daughter, both good swimmers, plunged into the Atlantic Ocean. When they were some distance from shore, the father realized they were being carried out to sea. He spoke to his daughter. "Darling, I am going to swim ashore for help. If you get tired, turn on your back and float. You will be able to stay up all day, if you do."

He swam away, and before long many people in their boats were searching the face of the waters for a ten-year-old girl. News of her plight spread to hundreds of onlookers on shore. Finally, far out from land she was found, floating on her back calm and unafraid.

The child was modest about the whole affair. She said simply, "My father told me I could float all day. He also promised he would return for me. So I swam and I floated for I knew he would come."

True wisdom is faith in our God who has never yet failed in one of His promises.

TODAY'S THOUGHT: *Faith helps to absorb life's shocks instead of resisting them.*

178

JUNE 27

Christ Is Our Captain

Jesus Christ is the same yesterday and today and for ever.
Hebrews 13:8

Even as we Christians believe there is a resurrection of the body
in the life hereafter, so we believe there can be a resurrection of
our spiritual life now. Each man has to die to sin and arise again
to righteousness. Every day should for us mean a death and a
resurrection. We sin by reason of the weakness of our mortal nature. We fall into the evil of some bad habit, some ugly thought
or word. When we truly repent we rise again and, regenerated by
heaven's power, we strive harder to climb higher. This is what
Luther meant by the expression, "the old man is to be daily
drowned and kept under."

The Apostle Paul says if you have been raised with Christ, you
are to seek those things that are above. In whatever measure we
partake now of the resurrection, in like measure we are strengthened by Christ to rise above our sins, to rise above all that is low
and mean, sordid and selfish. This is the true life of a Christian
every day of his life.

This means anything but not seeking to make the best out of
our life, or that we sit mooning with folded hands for "pie in the
sky by and by." We continue living happy, useful lives, firm in
the faith that we die only when our work is finished. We work
and wait as those preparing themselves for heaven.

We are called upon to be not only servants in the kingdom, but
soldiers in the battle of life. Our Captain is our Lord and Savior,
Jesus Christ. Our marching song is, "Onward Christian soldiers,
marching as to war." Think what it would mean if everyone who
professes Christianity followed the Master down the highway of
life, obeying His every command, willing to risk all in the service
of His kingdom. If this happened, it would not be long before the
forces of evil would fold up, and the devil would sue for truce
saying, "This is no place for me."

Resolve today that everything you do will be done to the glory
of God. Resolve to follow the heavenly pattern in your work, that
men may at a glance see by your manner of life that you belong to
Christ the King.

TODAY'S THOUGHT: *We can do nothing without God, and
God has bound himself to do nothing on earth except through us.*

179

JUNE 28

Selfless or Selfish?

Fight the good fight of the faith; take hold of the eternal life.
1 Timothy 6:12

A man hurried up to the church door one Sunday noon and asked, "Is the service over?" It so happened that the pastor had preached that morning on Christian service. The usher, who had taken to heart the pastor's words, made this reply to the man's query: "The worship is over, but the service is only beginning!"

Each day brings opportunities for practicing our faith in serving. We shall never be so near to Him as when we have given up our own plans, and poured out our self for the sake of others. Then only are we permitted to share humbly in the Master's sacrifice.

Jesus was the supreme example of love. He made it forever clear that the healthy life is one of perfectly unselfish service to others. He never worked a miracle for His own comfort. He hungered while He fed the multitudes. He mourned while He dried their tears, and He suffered that the world might rejoice. He gave His body to His accusers to be crucified on the cross that by His stripes we might be healed. The one great enemy of love is selfishness, our love of self that keeps us from loving our neighbors. We think so much of personal gains that we do not take the time to meet other people's needs.

If we would call ourselves Christians, let us love one another, help one another, and forgive one another. As the electric wire joins two hemispheres, enabling people to speak to each other across vast oceans, so love joins us to the Master in heaven. If we love God and our fellow men, God abides in us every day and gives our lives direction.

On our vacation trips we find it wise to carry a first-aid kit for emergencies. Let us keep close at hand the first-aid kit of the heart. It should carry alertness, compassion, sense of responsibility, active assistance and comforting words of encouragement. Always remember that doing something is more effective than saying something. But it is also better to say some kindly word of comfort than to pass by stolidly on the other side as did the priest and Levite.

TODAY'S THOUGHT: *The smallest package in the world is a man all wrapped up in himself.*

JUNE 29

Love Brings Serenity and a Sure Faith

Thou dost keep him in perfect peace, whose mind is stayed on thee, because he trusts in thee. Isaiah 26:3

Albert Schweitzer brings us this anecdote from the interior of Africa. Some young men were making fun of an old man who was a zealous reader of the Koran.

"You will soon know your Koran by heart," they said, "don't you get tired of reading the same thing constantly?"

"For me it is not the same Koran," said the old man, looking up into a circle of young faces. "When I was a young boy I understood it as a boy. When I was a young man I understood it as a young man. And now that I am old I understand it as an old man. I never tire of it. Though I read it again and again it always contains something new."

How wonderful it would be, if we felt the same way about our Holy Book! We can read the Scriptures all through life and never tire of them. With patient searching of His Holy Word, we grow in grace day by day as we learn to love God better.

We have all known someone who has affected our entire life, and made us better persons for having known him. Some people live so close to the Master's love that everything they do and say radiates inner warmth. Love is that kind of warmth, and it touches everyone we meet. It is born of an intimate companionship with the Master. Without this love there can be no mercy because love tempers all men's actions. It is the strongest bond between man and his neighbor. It is the foundation of peace. A heart that rejects love is in turmoil and is bitter about life, while the heart possessing love is at peace with the world.

Moreover, love can bring great happiness out of great unhappiness. A pilot who flew with Jimmy Doolittle, and spent many months in a Japanese prison said, "They were ignorant and mean, but we thought there was some good in them. The only way to develop that goodness would be by understanding and education—not by brutally mistreating them as they were doing us. Now I am going to a missionary school for training, and then I am going to return to Japan, and spend the rest of my life there, teaching the importance of love among men." Such is the way of Christian love!

TODAY'S THOUGHT: *May this be our ambition—to love always, to go a second mile, to create understanding, and to take a stand courageously.*

Do Something Worth While

Do your best to present yourself to God as one approved, a workman who has no need to be ashamed.   2 Timothy 2:15

Have you heard the story of the three stonecutters? Each was doing the same job. When asked what he was doing, the first said, "I'm cutting stones." In answer to the same question the second said, "I'm earning eight dollars a day." The third gave this reply: "I'm helping to build a temple."

This third man had vision, he was doing his small job and doing it well, but he had a vision of the beautiful building of which his small job was a part. Every one of us should cheerfully do the best we can with the work that we have before us. You may be scrubbing a floor, but it is just part of the job of maintaining a home for the family you love. It was Sir Wilfred Grenfell, the famous Labrador doctor, who said, "Real joy comes not from ease or riches or from the praise of men, but from doing something worth while."

Every day there are hundreds of worthwhile jobs which go undone. Some of them are not done because we are too blind to see the need. I remember reading about a 60-year-old business man who was alarmed to learn that there was not a dentist in the world devoting himself to caring for the teeth of Christian missionaries. In vain he sought and prayed for a young dentist who would provide dental care for missionaries at home and abroad. When no dentist came, he studied dentistry himself, and has now cared for the teeth of hundreds of young people studying for mission work. He has also made several trips abroad to provide dental care for missionaries in the fields. He has not charged a penny for any of his services. His only pay is the joy he finds in serving the servants of God. What a contrast between the attitude of this man, who was so concerned with missions and the welfare of the missionaries, and the attitude of many a complacent Christian, who does not have the concern to give of his means to mission work, or even to offer a prayer on behalf of missions.

We do not know what task we must face next, or into what field of service our God will send us. But we know that God can provide us with resources unlimited, and we can pray, "Lord, make me adequate for my task."

TODAY'S THOUGHT: *Why not tackle a big job and get it half done rather than trying nothing and getting it all done?*

JULY 1

Keep Your Eyes on the Stars

Lead thou me to the rock that is higher than I. Psalm 61:2

Theodore Roosevelt loved children, and took a special pleasure in seeing boys grow into strong, courageous men. Once he gave a group of boys this advice: "Keep your eyes on the stars and your feet on the ground."

If we look up at the stars, we shall find courage to continue, no matter what storms the changing days and years may bring. Sometimes the barriers in life seem immovable; we just cannot knock them over. Then we realize that the only way is to pierce the wall and tunnel through.

Many of us hesitate to ask for help when difficulties arise. Fears and doubts burden us, and force our eyes to the ground. Whenever this happens, our only hope is to look up and seek direction from above.

We have all known times when we were sure we were sinking under the weight of our sorrows, when the shore was far away and we were not strong enough swimmers to reach it. Knowing we could not survive through our own strength, we then sought the strength of the One who dwells beyond the stars. Miraculously new power coursed through our veins, and we breasted the turbulent waters to victory.

Have you ever stopped to watch children at the beach? Did you notice all the devices they have to keep themselves afloat? Gaily colored sea horses and whales have joined the old stand-by, the inflated inner tube, in keeping our children bobbing safely on the water. The children laugh and play, knowing they will stay afloat, relying on the bouyant toys their parents have provided for them.

Sometimes their mothers and fathers swim with them, and the children push aside their floating toys and ask their parents to help them swim. Parents are always nearby as they teach their children to swim.

We can rest secure in the knowledge that our heavenly Father is always with us. He has promised to keep us afloat, and later to carry us safely to firm ground. When difficulties come, He is there to lead us along the pathway to peace.

TODAY'S THOUGHT: *Some of us hasten to honor the great of the world, but neglect Christ, the greatest who ever lived.*

JULY 2

Trust the Great Physician

When I am afraid, I put my trust in thee. Psalm 56:3

The doctor was visiting his patient, and they were speaking of things of the spirit. The doctor admitted that he had been seeking for a long time to find peace with God. Convinced of his sinfulness, he felt that he needed something more than he had. He longed for the satisfactions that the world cannot give. He had material wealth and a wonderful reputation in the community, but he was not the happy man he wanted to be.

"I want you to tell me," said the doctor to his patient, "all about this believing and gaining happiness. What does it mean to have faith in Jesus? How do you get peace in your heart?"

"I'll try," said the patient, seizing the opportunity to witness for Christ. "I was sick. When finally I realized that I could not cure myself, I put my case in your hands. I'm trusting in you. That is exactly what every poor sinner must do—trust in the Lord Jesus Christ."

"Is that all," asked the doctor, "simply trust in the Lord?" He fell silent, then continued. "I see it now. I am spiritually sick. None of the medicines I have studied can possibly heal me. God is a Great Physician, and He can cure my troubled heart and give me peace and happiness."

We need to learn this lesson in trust, to believe that God can give us perfect peace. We must be absolutely sure that if we trust in the Lord forever, we shall find everlasting strength.

When children wade into the water to learn to swim, the teacher says, "Don't try to stay on top of the water. People cannot swim in the air; they swim in the water. Don't be afraid of it. The water is strong enough to hold you up. Trust the water. Let yourself down into it."

As we learn to live, we ought to remember too that God surrounds us. We cannot hold ourselves up with our own strength. Surely we should not be afraid. We must have the conviction that He is able to help us in our every need. We can trust Him. Calvary is proof enough of that!

TODAY'S THOUGHT: *Put Christ in the driver's seat, then your life will run more smoothly.*

JULY 3

There Is only One You

Being no hearer that forgets but a doer that acts, he shall be blessed in his doing. James 1:25

If in your garden you pick an armful of flowers, the kind with definite fragrance, wherever you go you will have that perfume about you. You will not be able to keep the fragrance a secret, for everyone will know you have been in contact with something sweet-scented.

If we live in the spirit of Christ and pray and meditate with Him, wherever we go people cannot but see the difference in our lives. Our every word and action will tell them some great power is ours.

Think what it would mean to the world if everyone who calls himself a Christian were a positive influence for good. How much happier life would be for everyone! We need not do great things to be helpful to God, but everyone should serve according to his ability.

Every evening a certain Christian visited the section of his city where the destitute sought temporary shelter. Every evening he provided at least one man with a bed for the night and breakfast.

One of his friends thought it a useless practice and said, "What good does it do in the face of acres of want and misery? It is only a drop in the bucket."

"You may be right," the Christian answered, "I am just attending to my little drop."

This was the prayer of a little boy in chapel at camp one evening, "Lord, that hill over yonder wouldn't be nearly as beautiful if there were only one pine tree growing there. But with so many pine trees growing straight and tall, it is a magnificent sight. Lord, help my life to be like a beautiful pine tree, always pointing upward, growing toward Thee. Help me to start other lives growing straight up to Thee, too, so that our world will be like that beautiful hill."

As you live each day, remember that although you are only one, there still is only one you. Do your very best with what God has given you.

TODAY'S THOUGHT: *Though you may be crippled in body or spirit, make it evident to the world that you are here to fight and not to run up the white flag.*

JULY 4

Explosions in Our Lives

May the God of steadfastness and encouragement grant you to live in such harmony with one another, . . . that together you may with one voice glorify the God and Father of our Lord Jesus Christ.
Romans 15:5, 6

Some time ago the newspapers carried the story of a violent explosion in a church in New York State. The boiler exploded and did a lot of damage, tossing the pews into all sorts of crazy positions. What a wonderful thing it would be to have explosions in the people occupying church pews, instead of in the basement under them. For if we open our hearts to Christ, He is capable of making us new creatures. If our faith is strong enough, it will be like an explosion in our lives. Tellingly a book binder rebound a worn Testament, labeling it by mistake TNT.

Many times that explosion takes the form of love, the kind of love that knows no limitations. That is the kind of love a certain well-to-do young couple demonstrated. They went to an orphanage to make arrangements for adopting two children. After filling out numerous forms, the director said she would show them the two nicest children in the orphanage. "Oh, no, please," the wife answered kindly, yet firmly. "We do not want the nicest children; we want two that nobody else will take."

This man and this woman had so much more than mere material wealth. They had a wealth of love which they wanted to share with two unloved, unwanted children. They had faith to believe the words of the Bible, "Love bears all things, believes all things, hopes all things, endures all things. Love never ends."

How wonderful it is when the explosion in our lives takes the form of devotion to our Savior. Some of the most striking examples of devotion come from across the sea. Charles Denby, an American minister in China, estimated that more than 15,000 Chinese Christains were killed in the Boxer Rebellion. Of those thus tested, only 300, about two percent, renounced their faith to save their lives. Would you remain faithful when faced by death? Surely the hope of eternal life was strong in these Chinese Christians; and so it should be in all of us. I can almost hear them repeating the Bible verse in their last moment, "I am the resurrection and the life; he who believes in me, though he die, yet shall he live."

TODAY'S THOUGHT: *The beginning of our belief in God is the end of our concern over life.*

JULY 5

Salvation Is Wonderful News

Again Jesus spoke to them, saying, "I am the light of the world; he who follows me will not walk in darkness, but will have the light of life." John 8:12

Without the presence of the Master in life, all is darkness. When He abides with us, what a difference it makes!

The hymn writer put it this way: "Sun of my soul, Thou Saviour dear, It is not night if Thou be near."

Christ is the Light of the world. He conquers the darkness of sin and despair, and brings to life the blessings of a new day. How grateful we should be for His gift of salvation. How we should yearn to share it with our fellow men.

Two blind, penniless, and illiterate men came to a mission hospital in India. Their curable ailments were treated, and after some time they were dismissed. Before leaving, one of them asked for a copy of the Jesus Book.

"Neither of you can read," the blind men were told, "what good will it do you?"

"We will take it to those who can read," they replied.

So they returned to their home village with the Bible. Incredibly enough the two were weavers, and whenever customers came to purchase fabrics from them, they were greeted with this request: "Before we will do business with you, you must read aloud to us a few pages from the Book."

When the doctor from the mission hospital visited that village some time later, he was amazed to learn that the heathen temple had been closed permanently, and a Christian church built. Almost every person in the village had been converted to Christianity.

Each one of us can be a witness, for we are possessors this day of the greatest news ever told. How many times have you seen someone burst into a room saying, "I have the most exciting news," and then proceed to tell that news, detail by detail? The news of Christ and Him crucified is exciting news, and we should not hesitate to tell that news, detail by detail, to our family and friends. How can we possibly keep it to ourselves? Wherever we go and whatever we do, we can seek to win others for Christ and His kingdom.

TODAY'S THOUGHT: *The army of the Lord would be the strongest in the world if every soldier were a recruiting officer.*

JULY 6

Your Life Can Be Transformed

For I came not to call the righteous, but sinners. Matthew 9:13

In his workshop an old sculptor had the model of a beautiful cathedral. It had been there for years, and was covered with dust. Nobody ever noticed it, although it was the exact model inside and out of a famous cathedral. Then one day his helper placed a light inside the model, and this light, shining through the stained glass windows, compelled every visitor to stop and admire the miniature cathedral's beauty. The change brought by the light was marvelous.

Many people in the world today believe themselves to be insignificant. They feel that their lives do not count for anything. But when the Holy Spirit comes to light them from within, they shine forth as the sun, and become an inspiration and blessing to all about them. Such is the transformation when God is given a chance. Christ has the power to transform lives.

A struggling artist had used all his canvas, and was too poor to buy more.

"Paint on this," a friend said, jestingly, and threw a napkin to him.

The painter took the napkin and painted upon it the beautiful face of the Madonna. That face now adorns the altar of a certain church and is known as the Madonna of the Napkin. So Christ, the great artist, can take an ordinary life and transform it, giving it immortal beauty by creating it in His image.

Others call Christ a master musician. A little girl visiting a summer resort was learning to play the piano and was practicing patiently, completely unaware that many of the notes she struck were unpleasant to sensitive ears. A brilliant pianist was also staying at the resort, and soon he hurried to her room to see if he could stop her discords. Offering to join her in a duet, he improvised beautiful chords to accompany the notes she played. The little girl's ears were thrilled; something stirred within her. The other guests listened enchanted, while the girl and the great musician played several such duets.

How wonderful it is to have Christ beside us, changing the discords of sin and doubt into songs of faith and hope.

TODAY'S THOUGHT: *God makes even a stagnant puddle to reflect the beauty of a sunset. He can bring beauty into your life if you will only give it to Him.*

JULY 7

Make God Your Life's Center

I would rather be a doorkeeper in the house of my God than dwell in the tents of wickedness. Psalm 84:10

Our lives perhaps resemble each other in many respects. All of us have different goals, and we get ourselves involved in so many activities that sometimes, I am sure, we stop to think, and ask ourselves the question, "Just what seems to be the matter?" We seem confused as we try to run in seventeen different directions at the same time. As a result, we cannot do anything well.

We all need a center in our life, a strong center of gravity. A rose has a center from which it unfolds petal after petal in different directions. Our lives can have many purposes, but all of them should be integrated around a worthwhile center.

Life is like a rose. If it is to have real meaning, at the center of it must be God. In the silent unfolding of each day's petal, God is there at the center supplying us with needed power to hold our lives together. If we do not have God we fly off at loose ends. "In him all things hold together," says St. Paul, meaning literally, "stick together." Who wants to be a "schizzo" anyway?"

Our highest quest is to satisfy the deepest hunger and yearning of our hearts. Certainly God satisfies even for all eternity. Faith is not a fly-by-night experience. It is granted that some things, some pleasures, satisfy for the moment. But very soon it is ashes to ashes, and dust to dust.

What we really yearn for is that which endures forever. We can find it only in God. At the top of life's totem pole is something which never dies, and we possess it when our soul is linked with God. The most important thing we know is that we have a personal God very much interested in us, a God from whom nothing can separate us unless, we choose to be separated.

A seven-year-old Indian lad was sent out by his father to spend the night alone in the forest. The father sought to test his son now to see whether or not he was a man. He gave him only a bow and arrow for protection. The boy, of course, was frightened. He waited through the long night until at last dawn came. As the light began to shine, the lad looked behind the very next tree and saw his father, who had been standing there all night with his mighty bow and arrow. So our heavenly Father cares for us.

TODAY'S THOUGHT: *God hugs us even closer than our shadow.*

JULY 8

Carry Your Cross Courageously

For I am not ashamed of the gospel: it is the power of God for salvation to every one who has faith, to the Jew first and also to the Greek. Romans 1:16

Some people, condemned to a life of weakness and ill health, are convinced that death is their only friend and the only one that can heal their ailment. Some are destined to lead a lonely life under a monotonous, dull, gray sky. Yet many of these bedridden folk come closer to the Lord than do others, and like the afflicted one in the crowd about Jesus, touch the very hem of His garment. Let those who are lonely remember the word of their Friend, "I will never leave you nor forsake you." This Friend is neither blind nor deaf to our seeking. He knows our state in life and is concerned about it. He gives the inner fortitude and strength to overcome anything, if only we put our trust in Him.

There is a story about a woman who was always lamenting about the weight of the cross placed upon her. She kept repeating that her sorrows were so much greater than those of her friends. One night in a dream she met an angel who led her to a fair and beautiful garden. There she saw crosses of all sizes and materials. The angel told her she was free to lay down her own cross and exchange it for any of those before her. Gladly the dreamer laid aside the cross which she found so heavy. She lifted up a much smaller one adorned with precious stones. To her surprise this small, beautiful cross crushed her to the earth with its weight, and she was forced to lay it down. Next she chose one wreathed with flowers, but there were sharp thorns in the foliage which tore her flesh, and the cross of flowers was more than she could bear. In vain she tried others, turning them all away. Finally she chose a plain cross on which was written one word: "Love." She found she could bear it easily. Then the angel whispered to her that it was her own cross which she had taken back again.

In a fit of madness Charles the Twelfth of Sweden drove a dagger into the breast of his faithful bodyguard. Quickly the aid drew it out, kissing its bloody blade. The shadow of affliction on our life, what is it but God's hand reached out to draw us closer! Will we be loyal enough to kiss that loving hand?

TODAY'S THOUGHT: *God sometimes sends us through a scorching desert, but we can be sure He is waiting at a beautiful oasis to refresh our spirits.*

JULY 9

The Father Knows Best

The Lord makes poor and makes rich; he brings low, he also exalts. 1 Samuel 2:7

A boy was watching an ant busily moving among the blades of grass on his lawn. He put a piece of sugar in front of the little creature, but the ant was intent on its own way. The boy laid his finger in front of it to guide it toward the sweet, but it remained unaware of the sugar. Only by interrupting its course again and again did the boy finally succeed in helping the ant find its prize. Often God puts His finger in our way to turn us aside from our own purposes toward the better things that He has prepared. But we must recognize His finger as an aid and not an obstruction. That is what we mean by the expression, "putting our wheels in line with the will of God." He has mapped out our course, but we must decide whether or not to follow it. Many times we rebel at the things through which we must go to reach the goal God has set. We fail to realize that passing through "the refiner's fire" will bring us greater blessings than we could otherwise receive.

A photographer takes his sensitive film into a dark room to develop the pictures. If he tried to develop it in sunlight the film would be ruined. Sometimes we ourselves must pass through the valley of the shadow in order later on to see clearly. Only when darkness falls can we observe the stars. Sometimes the Master must employ drastic measures to divert His children from the way of sin to the paths of righteousness. But after the transformation we shall join the blind ploughman who voiced his thanks to "God who took away his eyes that his soul might see."

A doctor told of a woman patient who swallowed too large a dose of morphine. In order to save her life he had to keep her awake.

"If I can just go to sleep, I will be all right," she insisted drowsily.

"Unless you stay awake, you will die," her doctor retorted.

Often we face the same danger. "If only my job were not so difficult. If I could just be relieved of this burden," we plead. "If life were just a little easier, I would be all right." The great Physician sees our need more clearly. Our souls must be awake and alert, if we are to live the vibrant, victorious life God intended.

TODAY'S THOUGHT: *Only the man whose back is bent low by a burden is stooped enough to see the beauty of the tiniest wild flower.*

191

JULY 10

Open Your Eyes to See the Lord

Come, behold the works of the Lord, how he has wrought desolations in the earth. Psalm 46:8

An eminent American sculptor tells of a summer holiday spent near a lake. Each night after the evening meal the family hurried outside to watch the sunset. One day the local girl who helped with the housework asked if her father and mother could come to see the sunset, too. She was told they would be welcome, but reminded that, since they had lived there all their lives, they had likely seen a thousand sunsets as lovely.

"Yes," replied the girl, "they have lived here, but they have never really seen the sunset."

Every day we are surrounded by the beauty of God's creation, by His power and strength. Yet often we miss these blessings simply because we do not take time to behold them. The things of the world throw sand in our eyes and blind us.

Have you ever cried out in desperation, "Why can't I find assurance in my faith so that my life can be abundant? Why doesn't God reveal himself to me?"

Thirty travelers climbed a hill in search of a cool stream where, on earlier hikes, they had quenched their thirst. But when they came to the place, the stream's course was dry. One of the men climbed higher to find out why the water had stopped flowing, and discovered that spring's source was clogged with leaves and twigs.

Sometimes, when our spirits pant for the living water, our thirst goes unquenched because worldly interests have clogged the channel between us and God. It may be only a combination of little things, like the sticks and leaves and pebbles that choked up the mouth of the stream. A leaky vessel can sink whether filled with heavy stones or little grains of sand. Flakes of snow, so fine that they can float in air, can snuff out a life if they cover a sleeping traveler.

Little sins can obscure our vision and hide God from our sight, even as a penny on the eye blacks out a beautiful sunset.

TODAY'S THOUGHT: *Even as a tiny unattended hole in a dike can flood a country, so a little sin, left unconfessed and unforgiven, can destroy an immortal soul.*

JULY 11

Wanted—Happier Christians

Look to him, and be radiant; so your faces shall never be ashamed. Psalm 34:5

I know a wonderful elderly Christian woman who loves to serve her fellow men. A skilled baker, she sometimes works from dawn to dusk to bring another person joy with one of her beautifully decorated cakes. Her personal life is complicated with tremendous problems, and there are days when she is oppressed on all sides; but she refuses to let them hinder her in this work of love. Instead, she busies herself with tasks of Christian love and service, prompted by a consuming love for Jesus. When someone reminds her of her own trials, she invariably replies, "Don't forget that all things work together for good to them that love him."

There are hundreds of unhappy people in the world today who have not learned to live life for what it is. Life is not always an easy road to travel. There is no escalator to happiness. Sometimes the only clear road is a roller coaster of ups and downs—a tortuous, boulder-strewn path up a mountain. Is it not misfortune that gives us a standard of comparison for appreciating good fortune? Some cross-country pikes plunge through long tunnels where we ride enveloped in darkness. Suddenly we emerge into the sunshine, and now we value the light as never before. Thus misfortune teaches us to recognize and appreciate the blessings which we have.

Are you counting your blessings day by day, naming them one by one to see "what the Lord hath done"? If we emphasize the positive, we shall be tipping the scale of life toward happiness. Do the lines about your mouth in repose show ten minutes of two or twenty past eight?

God gave us muscles so that we can turn our mouths either up or down, to smile or pout. He does not suggest that we clown through life, making jest of everything. But He gives the ability to master those muscles that give us a happy countenance. When we know the inner happiness of peace with God, our radiance is contagious. Wanted for this day and age—happier Christians!

TODAY'S THOUGHT: *Happy people are less for getting and more for giving.*

JULY 12

When Christ Appears, Darkness Disappears

The night is far gone, the day is at hand. Let us then cast off the works of darkness and put on the armor of light. Romans 13:12

Jesus came to earth in circumstances best fitting Him to be the Savior of man. Brought up in the small village of Nazareth, His life was humble and filled with honest toil. It was fitting preparation for His brief ministry. It enabled Him to become the friend of all men, and especially of the poor and suffering. The time of His birth was symbolic, since the 25th of December occurs when the longest night of the year has passed and the days have begun to lengthen. Whenever He comes into a life, the darkness disperses. He is the great light of life, casting brilliance into every human heart open to Him.

When He came it was said of Him, "There was no place for them in the inn." Too often in our hearts, in our business, crowds of worldly things are present, and there is no room for Jesus, no time to serve Him, no time for prayer and communion with Him. It is true that when He is present, worldly things are crowded out. But in another sense, Jesus does not "take up room"; rather He enlarges our sphere of living. Where He is there is room for all that is good. He transfigures, He blesses all things in His presence.

The coming of Jesus is living proof that there is a personal God, that He is our Father, that He loves us in spite of our sins, and that He cares for us. Jesus' coming proves that God will exert all His infinite love and wisdom and power for our redemption from sin and our entering the kingdom of heaven.

Some years ago the late Horace Mann, eminent educator, delivered an address at a reformatory for boys. He remarked that, if only one boy was saved from ruin, it would pay for all the labor and care of establishing the institution. After the exercises had closed a man challenged Mr. Mann on this statement. The man said, "Did you not color that statement more than a little when you said that all expense and labor would be repaid if it saved only one boy?"

"Not if that boy were my boy," was the solemn, convincing reply.

If you had been the only person in the world who needed saving, Christ still would have died for you.

TODAY'S THOUGHT: *Before a single man had sinned, God had laid the plans for man's salvation.*

JULY 13

The Perfect Rule—Love God

No one can serve two masters; for either he will hate the one and love the other, or he will be devoted to the one and despise the other. Matthew 6:24

An oriental prince once asked two of his wisest counselors how he might make his people happiest. He allowed them two months to prepare their replies. When the time had elapsed the two men appeared, one holding a bulky sheaf of papers containing over 200 written rules, the other empty-handed.

The first man read the 200 rules, and it was plain to see how the reading of them wearied the prince. The prince then called upon the other counselor for his reply. It consisted of two words: "Love God."

"Explain yourself," demanded the prince. "Did I not ask you how I might make my people most happy? And you direct me to love God?"

"True," answered the wise man, "this one thing I know. You cannot love God without loving your people also, as well as doing the things which will brighten their lives."

How different this world would be, if all of us would be more sincere in our devotion to God. Our Christianity would be so evident in our relationships with others. Too many of us only make a pretense of faith and do not follow Christ closely enough.

A Christian martyr was brought before a judge to be given the death sentence.

"What is your name?" the judge asked.

"I am a Christian," he answered.

"What is your country?" the judge asked.

"I am a Christian," he answered.

"And your business?"

"I am a Christian."

This man was so absorbed in the Redeemer that he had no name, no country, no way of life, except to be Christ's and to confess Him before men. We need that kind of Christians today. We need men and women who have the courage of their convictions, who are unafraid to confess Christ before others. A sincere faith will compel us to live it day by day. How possibly can we love God without loving our fellow men?

TODAY'S THOUGHT: *It may be more difficult to live humbly for your God than to die nobly for Him.*

JULY 14

Look for the Good

But test everything; hold fast what is good. 1 Thessalonians 5:21

Once in a far Eastern land a sinful woman was being dragged out through the city gate. She had been condemned to death by stoning. The noon sun scorched the stony streets, and on passing by a well she saw a sick dog lying motionless almost dead of thirst. Taking her sandal from off her foot, forgetful of her own impending doom, the woman filled the shoe with water and gave the suffering animal to drink. The king by whose order she had been condemned saw her kind act, and pardoned her. He was prompted by the same principle our Lord put in words, "Blessed are the merciful, for they shall obtain mercy."

This lesson all of us could well learn. Our world needs love. It is the only language that everyone can understand. Furthermore, we cannot find happiness for ourselves, unless we think of others. It is better to be deceived occasionally than to think everyone is bad or untrustworthy. Most people are not nearly as bad as they are reported to be, while many of our neighbors' faults exist only in our disordered minds.

So much depends upon our way of looking at things. A relative of mine brought his home into uproar, and even summoned the village constable to investigate a suspicious looking character peeping in the window. It turned out to be his own shadow reflected on a neighbor's wall.

Look for the good in God's world and you will discover it. Look for the good in God's people and you will find that, too. If we were half as ready to speak of men's virtues as we are to condemn their faults, the world would be a much happier place in which to live.

One of our greatest faults is that we love to boast of our own virtues, while at the same time we joyfully condemn others. How can we hope to find happiness in that? Using methods like these, we cannot win the battles of life.

Remember the fable of the sun and the wind. They contended to see which one could make a traveler shed his coat. The fierce wind only made him draw his covering closer around him, while the genial warmth of the sun forced him to lay his cloak aside. Just so, when harsh words have failed, the sunshine of a kindly manner will work wonders in the hearts of others.

TODAY'S THOUGHT: *Or best chance for a world at peace will come in our being kind to one another.*

196

JULY 15

Stumbling Blocks and Stepping Stones

For thou hast delivered my soul from death, yea, my feet from falling, that I may walk before God in the light of life. Psalm 56:13

"I wish I had never been made," is an often heard remark. The people who make that remark forget that we are not yet made. We are only being made. When we adopt the first attitude, we are questioning God's ways.

Life is a school. It is not always easy, and sometimes the assignments are difficult. But God has promised, "In the world you have tribulation; but be of good cheer, I have overcome the world." Though the assignment is difficult, God will help us complete it. In fact, we shall be strengthened by fire, for "through many tribulations we must enter the kingdom of God."

A visitor to a large pottery plant noticed a woman who was slowly, carefully painting a delicate flower on a costly vase. He watched as she patiently and tenderly bent over her task. She worked with painstaking care, intent on every touch of color.

"That is slow work," the visitor said to the woman, "You've been working for hours, and yet with one sweep of my hand I could wipe off every trace of it. What makes the impression remain there after the painting?"

"When I have finished painting the flowers, the vase is taken to the fire of the kiln," the woman replied. "After it has passed through the fire no power on earth can remove it."

Is it not true that after we have passed through difficulty, our lives are richer because of it? Each experience leaves a lasting impression, training us for future days. Many times our stumbling blocks are really steppingstones.

A little girl had been promised the privilege of climbing to a hilltop, which delighted her brother. But she drew back in dismay when she saw how steep the climb would be.

"Where is the smooth path?" she said. "It's bumpy and stony."

"We couldn't get up if it weren't," her brother replied. "The stones are what we climb on."

So often in life stumbling blocks become steppingstones.

TODAY'S THOUGHT: *Unable to grub out an unsightly backyard stump, some folks I know made it serve instead as a foot for their family picnic table. What personality stumps could you transform with the assist of God's Holy Spirit?*

Those Who Share Are the Happy Folk

Better is a little with the fear of the Lord than great treasure and trouble with it. Proverbs 15:16

Within the last half century medical research has added many years to the average span of life. Yes, although science can make us live longer, it cannot make our lives happier! One of today's real problems is giving people a purpose to live for.

Only God can give us real satisfaction. The dedicated Christian is the only happy person. The devil's minions are all sad sacks. The very essence of happiness is the security come from a perfect trust in Jesus, the knowledge that we are His now and are saved through all eternity.

The knowledge that we are saved leads us into fields of Christian service. We discover that to lose one's life is not to throw it away, but rather to give it away. Life is far too valuable to be sold at any price. We do not sell our most precious possessions. If we do part with them, we give them to a loved one. If, without thought of gain, we invest ourselves in some worthy cause simply because we love others, life rewards us in undreamed of fashion.

The newspapers carried the story of a prominent wealthy businessman who offered his services to a hospital board.

"I have spent enough time making money and enjoying myself," he said. "Now I'd like to have the pleasure of doing something for nothing."

The rewards of such unselfish service are limitless. Are you giving the best you have to Christ? Are you dedicating those things to Him that mean the most to you?

A certain art gallery once exhibited a picture entitled, "When earth seemed nearer heaven than now." It showed a little girl standing by a wayside shrine, holding up her tiny doll for Christ to kiss. This child felt sure that what she loved so dearly, Christ must love, too.

To consecrate the things we love by holding them up and sharing them with Him is the triumph of faith. What are you doing with your possessions? Happiness always comes to those who share.

TODAY'S THOUGHT: *Whatever we place in God's hands, we continue to possess.*

JULY 17

Your Life Can Be Beautiful

Every good endowment and every perfect gift is from above.
James 1:17

Have you ever thought of how many wonderful things in life are free? We pay absolutely nothing for beautiful cloud formations in the deep blue sky, for golden sunsets, or warming sunshine. Every aspect of God's creation thrills us, if only we have eyes to see. Our lives can be beautiful, too, when we work side by side with Him. We are God's channels through which His power flows to create harmony in other human souls. In dedicated service to others, our lives take on new meaning. God has a part for each one of us to play, and, in spite of His creative genius, if we do not play our part well, we shall find our lives in difficulty.

"I heard that you asked the Lord for a fine garden," said one man to another. "Is that right?"

"Yes, it is," the other replied proudly, surveying the garden which was his pride and joy. "But I never pray for a fine garden unless I have a hoe in my hand. I say, 'You send the sunshine and the rain, Lord, and I'll do the very best I can to keep down those weeds!' "

Too frequently we pray for a better world and a better community without saying, "Lord, here I am. Make me your instrument to help create that better world."

God has infinite power. All we need to do is allow Him to channel it through our lives. He will not send power into our lives, however, unless we are going to use it. Yet if we do use it, the more power we use, the more we have.

The magnet, for example, increases instead of decreases its force by constant activity. It loses its power when it hangs idle. Our Christian faith acts in the same manner, for the more it is used, the more active it becomes, and the greater is its influence. In speaking of the late Dr. Fred Winslow Adams, a pastor who was a vital channel of God's power, a young man said, "Whatever Dr. Adams did he always made beautiful." Another example of an active servant of the Master was a social worker who was said to leave a trail of happiness behind her wherever she went.

As we grow in grace every day, we become more effective in our witnessing power for God and our lives are happier!

TODAY'S THOUGHT: *God does most of His work for mankind through ordinary people.*

199

JULY 18

The Lord Bless Thee and Keep Thee—Going!

Whoever knows what is right to do and fails to do it, for him it is sin. James 4:17

A young man, having visited an elderly aunt, was about to leave her home when he saw it was beginning to rain. Noticing an umbrella standing neatly in a corner near the door, he was opening it when the old lady spied him.

"No, you can't do that," she exclaimed. "I've had that umbrella for 23 years and it hasn't been wet yet. I am certainly not going to let it get wet now!" Little good it would have been to hold out rain since the silk had rotted with the years!

Some people treat their God-given talents in the same way. They keep them stored away unused, thinking that by withholding them they will preserve them. Yet these people could multiply the worth of their talents a hundredfold, if only they used them along life's way.

A little girl, playing with her lettered blocks, spelled the word "good."

"Look, Mother," she said, "I can make two words out of this one word, good—'go' and 'do.'"

Corollary to this idea of "go and do" is this fact, that never can we be true children of Christ unless we practice our faith consistently.

A traveling missionary was speaking to some Hindu women when one of them got up suddenly and went out. In a few minutes she was back, however, listening more intently than before. When the service was over, the missionary asked her why she had left for those few minutes. Perhaps it was because she had not been interested in his talk at that point.

She smiled eagerly and said, "Oh, yes, I was so interested in the things you were saying that I went out to ask your driver if you really meant it, and if you put into practice in your life what you were saying. When he said you did, I came back to listen again."

This is the kind of consistent living that is necessary for our witness to have an impact on the world. Besides confessing our faith with our lips, we must live it in our lives. We cannot bury it within our hearts for true faith compels us to share it with others. We must go and do.

TODAY'S THOUGHT: *Our witness will plant in others a seed of hope from which will spring life's most lovely flower, Faith.*

JULY 19

A Moment's Prayer Can Change a Whole Life

I call upon thee, for thou wilt answer me, O God; incline thy ear to me, hear my words. Psalm 17:6

A minister was listening to the life story of a skeptic, a man who could not be sure that there was a God. He had made a fortune and lost it. Then he had made a second fortune and lost that, too. In dire straits, he could not even pay his rent. Furthermore, in his frustration he had to take sleeping pills every night. Seeing no way out of his predicament, in desperation he sought out a minister's guidance.

"Would you try an experiment?" the minister asked, "Why not try God?"

"You know I don't believe in God," the skeptic answered.

"This always helps people who do try it," the minister continued, "and I know it will help you, if you will only allow it."

"How can I let it help me when I don't even believe in it?" asked the skeptic.

The man of God then suggested that they kneel and direct some honest explanations to the unknown, and that the man say exactly what he felt.

"Well," the unbeliever replied, "I certainly couldn't be in a worse mess than I am now. I'm willing to try anything. O God," he began as he knelt, "if there is a God, send me help now, because I need it." Back in his chair, he turned to the minister, "Well, I don't feel any different."

The minister told him that it did not matter how he felt, just as long as he still was interested in following through. He suggested some chapters in the Bible for the man to read. He also asked him to attend church regularly, so that the spirit of faith from other worshipers might brush off on him. Above all this, he urged him to just keep praying.

That man later became an official of the church. God came back into his life as the man opened his heart, and it changed completely. His simple prayer, his stepping out in blind faith, was the first step toward that new life.

Such a transformation can happen to any of us. Through God's power all things are possible. When moments of doubt and despair come to you, why not turn to Him and say, "God, I need your help. I need it desperately, and I need it now." God answers prayer.

TODAY'S THOUGHT: *God and I are unconquerable!*

JULY 20

How Jesus Christ Is Like the Sun

I keep the Lord always before me; because he is at my right hand, I shall not be moved. Psalm 16:8

In the field of medicine there is continual evidence of the unlimited power of God. Dr. William James Mayo said, "The surgeon and physician realize quickly that they need religion to help them—I mean the personal realization of the individuals. I see patients who are dead by all medical standards, who we are certain cannot live. But then a minister comes to the bedside. He seems to touch some important spark within the patient and before long the patient is recovering, defying every diagnosis."

When one is willing to dedicate his entire life to God, things beyond human imagination can happen. In "Idylls of the King," King Arthur commands Sir Bedivere to cast the jeweled sword Excalibur into the lake. Bedivere thinks it sheer folly to throw away so valuable a sword, and in fact fails twice to do Arthur's bidding. The third time, sure that the sword would be lost forever, Bedivere threw it, and to his astonishment there . . . "rose an arm, clothed in white samite, mystic, wonderful," which caught Excalibur and "brandish'd him three times . . ."

By this the author, Alfred Lord Tennyson, encourages people to yield their lives to God. Some people consider their lives too valuable to present to an unseen God, but they fail to realize that the obedient person fulfilling the command is the only one who experiences the protecting power of God.

Tennyson himself cast his jeweled sword into the lake by putting his life completely at God's disposal. Because of his consecration he was the trusted voice of his people, poet laureate of England for 60 years. He expressed their fears, their faith, their trials, and their triumphs. In the same scene between King Arthur and Sir Bedivere the dying king from his barge said, "More things are wrought by prayer than this world dreams of." When asked what Christ meant to him, Tennyson pointed to a flower growing in the garden and said, "What the sun is to this flower giving it vitality and beauty, Jesus Christ is to my soul and to my life."

When we have such a faith as this we shall begin personally to realize the unlimited power of God!

TODAY'S THOUGHT: *With God as a partner, the impossible is possible!*

JULY 21

Tomorrow Is a New Day

Cast away from you all the transgressions which you have committed against me, and get yourselves a new heart and a new spirit! Ezekiel 18:31

In our everyday relationships we realize the difficulties in which people find themselves. Our hearts go out to those suffering bereavement or other tragedy. Some happenings crush even the bravest spirits. We must realize that, no matter how heavy the blow, it can be healed through faith in God's promises. "The darkest hour is just before the dawn." How often this proves true!

Here is the story of a courageous little boy. When this incident took place, child labor was still legal in our country. The boy, who was the sole provider for his widowed mother and four brothers and sisters, was taken to the hospital to have his leg amputated after it had been mangled in a severe accident. Following the amputation, his mother sat by his bedside and wept bitterly. Her son misunderstood the reason for her tears, and in his boyish way did his best to comfort her.

"Never mind, Mother," he said. "Don't cry, lots of kids get jobs sitting down."

Usually when we arise in the morning we expect to work uninterruptedly all day. Many times we have made great plans for the hours ahead. We want to get this done and that done, and then suddenly something disrupts our plans. The wind is taken out of our sails, and we must drop our work to unravel a serious problem. Our precious energy is spent coping with the unexpected, and when evening comes it seems half the day has been wasted. Interruptions spoil our plans, and leave us with a feeling of failure at the end of the day.

When such setbacks come we must keep going. There is always a tomorrow—a new day with fresh hopes and ambitions. We can carry on, if we have let Him set for us a definite goal, if we but follow our Guide, allowing Him to make even our mistakes to teach us, and bring some good from every tough problem that is faced.

TODAY'S THOUGHT: *Sorrow is the black slate on which God can legibly write His promises.*

JULY 22

"My Life Is a Weaving . . ."

Blessed be the Lord, the God of Israel, who alone does wondrous things. Psalm 72:18

A ship was being tossed about at sea. Breaking the rules, one of the passengers climbed to the bridge to look at the captain holding the wheel. He came back to report to his fellow passengers, "I saw the captain at the wheel and he smiled at me. Now I know everything is well."

If life's sea gets too turbulent, let us look up and let God smile down. Then we too shall know that absolutely nothing can daunt us.

A good friend of mine has had most of his stomach removed, as the result of three major operations. Throughout his whole life he has been busy doing good for others, all the time thinking very little about himself. One day he turned to me and said, "Will you tell me why God allows me to suffer like this?"

I said to him, "Have you ever looked closely at a piece of tapestry on the side which hangs next to the wall, the wrong side to us? Its pattern is indiscernible. There are multitudinous knotted ends and yarn crosses and criss-crosses in all kinds of crazy ways. Still, turn it over on the other side again, and there is the beautiful pattern. Life is so much like that. Now we see in a mirror dimly, discerning only snarled ends and long skips, but when we get to heaven and can turn over our life's tapestry, on the other side I am sure that the pattern will be understood. That is where our faith comes in. When one really trusts God there is glory in the most threadbare life, and any kind of day splashed with His glory can be beautiful."

A little boy awakened one night. It was raining hard and his mother and father started downstairs to take in the porch furniture. As the father went by the boy's room he observed his little lad, five years old, sitting in his pajamas, his nose pressed against the window screen watching the rain.

"Daddy, doesn't rain smell good? Daddy, isn't this a glorious night?"

Any kind of day can be wonderful, if God is in our hearts.

TODAY'S THOUGHT: *Reach for the sky, friend, for faith will lengthen your arms.*

JULY 23

Christ Can Change Your Life

Christ Jesus came into the world to save sinners. And I am the foremost of sinners. 1 Timothy 1:15

Lazily stretched out beneath a fig tree in the garden of Milan, lay a young man one warm summer day years ago. He had lived a wild life, daring to taste of every forbidden fruit. But now he was engaged in a bitter struggle with himself. Like the prodigal son, he had come to the end of his rope. He had thought earthly things could satisfy him, yet now it all seemed in vain. Seeking escape from his bitter struggle, he cried, "How long? Will not the answer come tomorrow? Is there not some way to end the sway of my lust and uncleanness and for me to find a new beginning for my life?"

As he lay there entangled in his dilemma, there came to him a voice of a child singing, "Take up and read." Opening a volume of St. Paul's epistle to the Romans, his eyes read these words: "Not in reveling and drunkenness, not in debauchery and licentiousness . . . But put ye on the Lord Jesus Christ, and make no provision for the flesh, to gratify its desires." Suddenly we see the prodigal, Augustine, come to his senses and changed into one of the holiest of God's saints. From this day on he would proclaim to the world from the testing of his own experience that man is forever restless, unless he finds his rest in Christ.

Each one of us should look to himself. How much there needs to be changed in your life, in mine. Our weak and wavering faith needs strengthening. Bad habits need to be broken. Flaring tempers need to be subdued. Selfish hearts need to be softened.

How is this change to come? Our part is to yield and surrender, letting God walk in to make the change effective and lasting. We cannot linger about the old haunts of sin, saying piously that we want to be changed, but that we just cannot help ourselves. "Denying Peter," said an old Scot, "had no business in the devil's territory."

Napoleon would have banished two words from our vocabulary— the words "I can't," and "Impossible." Exactly that is what the Christian should do. Has not God promised, "All things are possible to him who believes"? Wise is the man who accepts as his motto for daily living, "I can do all things in him who strengthens me."

TODAY'S THOUGHT: *God provides the power, but man sometimes drags his feet.*

JULY 24

Man Is so Richly Blessed

By his great mercy we have been born anew to a living hope through the resurrection of Jesus Christ from the dead. 1 Peter 1:3

Memory is one of God's greatest gifts. Man is the only being whose highly organized nervous system has the ability to recall events in their proper time setting. Life's events would form no story, no continuity, if the faculty of memory could not project the past into the present.

Man grows and develops as each new stage of life arises out of, and continues, a preceding stage. What will be is dependent upon what is. Each day we make our investments upon which we shall capitalize in the future. Years of training build the muscles of an athlete. Hours of practice perfect the technique of the musician.

Sometime we must pay the price for the mistakes we have made. Bruises to the leaf bud result in flaws in the leaf. Privation in childhood will stunt a man's growth.

As a man gives more and more of himself to God, he begins to reap the rich dividends of life's deepest satisfaction. Christ is the only hope for the world, and that means for every individual who makes up this world. We need the strength and hope that come only from above. When we live God's way, memory becomes to us what a rose is in December. It becomes the wonderful blessing which enables us to see the trail coming up from yesterday's past and leading forward to our glorious goal. And our sunset years will be beautiful, as we recall the countless blessings that have come to us from God's hand.

Did you ever, as a child, set out to count the stars in the heavens? Many of us tried hard, standing gazing skyward, until we had counted several hundred before wearying and giving up. We realized at long last that there were far too many stars for us to count. The unnumbered blessings of any one of us are like the stars, too! With Abraham we must say that they are more than can be numbered.

Chief among our blessings is Jesus' Calvary sacrifice, made so that we might live each day secure in the knowledge that, whether we believe or whether we die, we are the Lord's.

TODAY'S THOUGHT: *Fellow, will you still hesitate to give thanks, either aloud or silent, when you know they are heard in heaven?*

Life Is What We Make It

Multitudes, multitudes, in the valley of decision! For the day of the Lord is near in the valley of decision. Joel 3:14

God is forever making new mornings. Darkness comes repeatedly into our lives because of the sins that we commit. No matter how hard we try by ourselves, we are powerless to stop this vicious circle. Only the light of God's forgiving grace is sufficient. Without His assurance peace cannot be ours.

One night there was a terrible storm. A little girl awakened from her sleep, and called to her father, "What is God doing during the storm?" Then, as little children will, she answered her own question. "Oh, I know! God is making the morning."

When Christ was praying in the Garden of Gethsemane, when He was on trial in the courtyard of Pilate, and when He was being crucified upon the cross, I am sure the disciples, too, were asking, "What is God doing now?" Easter gave them their answer. He was making morning for man, giving His children the assurance of a day that would never end. He was setting loose a power that no force on earth could stop. He was proving that "in everything God works for good with those who love him."

From the lowest depths there is always a pathway leading to the loftiest heights. If we but seek God's will for our lives, and follow unrelenting in that way, we can never be defeated. Apparent reverses may come, but even in these we can, if we will, discover some good.

On the walls of an ancient temple there is the picture of a king and a slave. The king is forging his crown into a chain, while nearby the slave forges his chain into a crown. Beneath the picture are these words: "Life is what man makes of it, no matter of what it is made."

The apostle Paul knew how to forge chains into a crown. He knew how to transform his prison cell into a pulpit. He found in his troubles not only a chance to strengthen himself but also an opportunity to glorify God.

Many are they who follow in Paul's pathway, people who never despair, though it appears they have lost everything but God. For on reaching that point, they discover that God is enough.

TODAY'S THOUGHT: *If you must limit yourself to one companion on life's way, make certain it is Christ.*

JULY 26

Each Day Belongs to God

For a day in thy courts is better than a thousand elsewhere.
Psalm 84:10

An archbishop once said that the human heart is like a millstone. If you put wheat under it, it grinds the wheat into flour. If you put no wheat under it, it grinds on, but then it wears itself away. Many a godless man is grinding away his own life in drudgery, an existence with no higher purpose than to gain material wealth. As a result he never knows the only true joy there is, the joy of serving God and his fellow men.

Too often we forget that each day belongs to God. Awakening in the morning, we should remember, "This is the day which the Lord has made; let us rejoice and be glad in it." There is something for us to do today and every day. If we do not do our part, something will be left undone. We so often say, "I'll wait until tomorrow!" But tomorrow brings another duty for us to perform, and yesterday's is still undone. We should live one day at a time with God, for then we will surely become co-workers helping to build His kingdom. Every day has its appointed task. Every day brings man nearer the night that comes when no man can work.

Too many of us waste our time and energies planning and worrying about the future. The future belongs to God. We cannot foresee what will happen, and that is all to the good, too! But God knows. And if we live close to Him, we shall find His presence with us more than a sufficiency, come what will.

Let hope be our bread to give us strength. If we would be conquerors in life's fray, if we would fight the good fight of faith and lay hold on eternal life, we must have faith to believe in all the promises of our heavenly Father. Hope puts the rainbow in the soul's sky, and enables man to say, "Thanks be to God, who gives us the victory through our Lord Jesus Christ."

TODAY'S THOUGHT: *Keep the light of hope ever shining in your eyes as you walk the road of life.*

JULY 27

He Came to Teach the Way

And walk in love, as Christ loved us and gave himself up for us, a fragrant offering and sacrifice to God. Ephesians 5:2

Jesus came into the world to give the knowledge of salvation to all people; to set the captive free; to give dignity to every man; to wipe away the tears of the sorrowful; to bring men out of darkness and sin, and to set the joy bells ringing.

When first He came He was despised and rejected of men. There was no room for Him in the world's busy inn. Few paid any attention to Him, yet He went on to finish His mission, willing even to be abused in order to fulfill the will of God.

He came to teach the mighty and the great that, unless they became as little children, they could not inherit the kingdom of heaven. He came to tell those living uninhibited lives that a man is a slave if his lusts, his human appetites, control him. Moreover, He came to tell those who boastingly believed that they were the captains of their own souls, and be able to man their own salvation, that they were the foolish captives of their own minds. But even for such prisoners He brought release. Was there not a Thomas in His inner circle?

He came to cast off all these fetters that bind, and to lead His children into the glorious liberty of the sons of God. He came to open the doors of the world's gloomy prison house where men were held captive. He came to give release to any who call upon His name.

For the poor penitent thief there was freedom, pardon, and peace. For poor Mary Magdalene, broken in body and soul, for learned masters like Nicodemus, for simple folks like Bartimaeus, the prison doors were opened.

These were all His children. They belonged to Him and so do we, too, every mother's son or daughter of us! Each one of us can live in the hope that, if we turn to Him, He has the power to make us free.

TODAY'S THOUGHT: *God's children know the A, B, C's of salvation, and they will always believe in Christ.*

JULY 28

Man Fails, the Power Never

Behold, God is my helper; the Lord is the upholder of my life.
Psalm 54:4

It was the year 1876, and a group of men stood round a laboratory watching a young man conduct an experiment. He was using a glass bulb, electric wire, and batteries.

"Put out those lights," he commanded, pointing to the rows of candles and kerosene lamps. When they were extinguished, he continued, "I am going to pull a switch and when I do, you are going to see the first incandescent light ever devised by man." It was a dramatic moment. The switch was pulled, but the instantaneous flash of light was swallowed up immediately in darkness, and a groan of disappointment came from the group. When the candles were burning again, the scientist turned to his friends.

"I am sorry, I have a long way to go. The filament which I used was not strong enough to stand the heat of the electric current. It went up in a flash."

He did not know that it would take three more years and $40,000 before a loop of carbonized cotton thread would remain aglow in a vacuum for forty hours. But with faith and patience he perfected the incandescent lamp.

What do you suppose kept Thomas Edison going in spite of repeated discouragements? It was the knowledge that only his equipment had failed, for he had complete faith in the force with which he was dealing. He was positive that the power would not fail. It was just that the man who sought to harness it had been temporarily thwarted.

Often I recall this incident when I come to pray. Prayer is not the vital and meaningful force that it could be in the lives of so many of us. When there is no connection with God's power, it is human failure. Prayer has not failed; it never does. It is always we who fail. In order to receive His infinite power, we must honestly confess all our sins to God, for even small unrepented sins can clog the channel through which we receive His blessings.

TODAY'S THOUGHT: *Prayer changes things and people.*

JULY 29

Happiness Is Not For Sale

O taste and see that the Lord is good! Happy is the man who takes refuge in him! Psalm 34:8

One day Jesus told a story containing just 117 words. It is entitled, "The Rich Fool." The principal character in the incident talked about himself. He used about 65 of these words and 17 of them were in the first person, the big "I"! We remember the gist of the story: "I will tear down my barns, and I will build bigger barns. I will raise more crops, and I will be prosperous."

Too frequently we hear it repeated today: "I will build up my bank account, and I will buy more stocks and bonds, and I will find joy in the accumulation of things." Perhaps the Chamber of Commerce would award these people certificates as outstanding conservationists. But God issues His verdict in one word: "Fool!"

We must not say, however, that people who are wealthy are doomed to fail in the search for happiness. But we do mean to say that happiness will not come by just accumulating things. It is something that is not bought or sold in the market place. It is rather a by-product of a dedicated life. It comes when we allow the King to take up residence in the castle of our soul, and when we are assured beyond any "ifs" or "buts" that, even if all the world would be against us, we cannot fail, because God is for us. A mother was busy in her kitchen, and her two little daughters were playing in the living room. Finally one started to sing, "Safe in the arms of Jesus, Safe on His gentle breast; There by His love o'ershaded, Sweetly my soul shall rest." The mother turned to the older girl, the sister of the one who had just sung and said, "How do you know you are safe with Jesus?"

The girl answered, "I will tell you why. I am holding Him tight with my hands."

But the little sister asked, "Suppose the devil should come along and cut your hands right off?"

"Oh, I have made a mistake," the older girl said. "It's not I that am holding on to Jesus, but it is He that is holding on to me. The devil cannot do one thing to me then."

Do you see now what it means to know that you belong to God?

TODAY'S THOUGHT: *If we will only screw up our faces in a smile, God will pour joy into our hearts.*

This Is Not One of Our Four Freedoms—the Freedom to Sin

For freedom Christ has set us free; stand fast therefore, and do not submit again to a yoke of slavery. Galatians 5:1

There is much said these days about liberty, and the rising up of men and women everywhere to claim it. Liberty is a word that needs sharp defining. Every American has cause to be proud of his inheritance of freedom. But liberty does not mean license. It does not mean that we can do just as we please.

The decline and fall of the Israelites began when every man did what he thought right in his own eyes. The ruin of a soul begins the same way.

Christ came to the world not only to be the Savior of mankind, but to give each life the blueprints of direction. He came to set us free, yet we are not free to do as we please. Our freedom is the liberty of the sons of God, who know whose they are and whom they serve. As Christians we are not free to commit willful sin. Nothing we have is really our own. Jesus bought us body and soul and, while He freed us from the power of sin and death, we are not free to do wrong. We are free as servants of God, and as good servants we should be humble.

We live in an incredible age where everything and everybody moves rapidly. Education is making tremendous strides, industry is performing miracles, and science is making new discoveries every day. But the more we create with our own hands the less humble we become. When we set ourselves up as gods, we not only have not the humility that graces our attitudes one toward another, but we also lack the humility without which we become an abomination to God. There are some who think they are too clever to believe. Others, while professing to believe, refuse to walk humbly with their God. They would be masters instead of servants. Not content to travel the narrow road and learn a lesson each day, they prefer instead to find some new, quick short cut.

Pride is one of the seven deadly sins, and religious pride is the worst. We shall be happy only if we pray God to keep us humble and give us strength to follow His example.

TODAY'S THOUGHT: *Those who boast of their virtues seldom lead the parade.*

JULY 31

Caught in the Crook of His Staff

For no other foundation can anyone lay than that which is laid, which is Jesus Christ. 1 Corinthians 3:11

Some time ago a Negro died in Ohio. He had manned a shoe shine stand in a shop, working for 26 years without a holiday. He was well educated. Booker T. Washington once had asked him to be his secretary, but he had refused this offer, never explaining why. After his death the reason was disclosed. Beside him as he had worked were ten young Negroes, each attending school. He could have gotten along with fewer employees, but he always kept the number at ten. For 26 years this man, unhonored and unsung, kept ten boys in school. He dedicated himself to one task alone, the happiness of this continuing chain of ten young lives. The people around him felt he was the most vibrant personality they had ever known, a man who sincerely loved his God and, also, those about him. His faith in God was evidenced by his love for others and he, himself, was the richer for it.

Think of what faith can do. Not only is it a power which causes us to serve our fellow men, but it is a power that changes us from within. If our faith is strong, the day is sunny. If it is weak, the day is gray, regardless of the weather. A day may be wonderful or miserable, depending on our faith in God.

We who are young and active would do well to follow the example of those who have grown old in the faith. There is a wonderful story of an old man who lay dying. He was very weak, but his spirit remained cheerful. "When I am able to think," he explained, "I think of Jesus; and when I am unable to think of Him, I know He is thinking of me."

Every moment Christ is thinking of His children. If in faith we cling to Him, and show our faith in love and concern for our fellow men, then life will gain significance. Jesus demanded that we have faith if we are to inherit eternal life, a childlike faith. "Unless you turn and become like children, you will never enter the kingdom of heaven," says Jesus. We must join the little girl who spoke a great truth when she recited mistakenly, "The Lord is my shepherd, that is all I want."

TODAY'S THOUGHT: *Heaven is one dream which every soul can have come true.*

AUGUST 1

Resources Unlimited

Blessed are the men whose strength is in thee. Psalm 84:5

Suppose a very wealthy man gave you a blank check with his name signed in the proper place. You know he has unlimited drawing power at the bank, and you are merely to fill in the amount and present the check for payment. But you say, "The signature is all right, and this man has lots of money. But I cannot believe he means to help me. It is just too good to be true." So you frame the check, and hang it on the wall.

At the same time a friend of yours has the same wonderful courtesy extended to him. He believes that the check is good. He has cashed not one but many such checks, and he lacks for nothing. Still you remain skeptical. Occasionally you read the astounding words, "I promise to pay on demand," but you cannot bring yourself to do anything about it.

Jesus gave us such a check. Here are some of His promises: "Whatever you ask in my name, I will do it." "All things are possible to him who believes." These are powerful ideas. Many have believed and have enjoyed countless blessings, while others have just looked at His promises and failed to take advantage of them.

Of course, the greatest blessings are spiritual: "They who wait for the Lord shall renew their strength." We must recognize the source of spiritual power which we find in God through Christ. We must restore our connection with that power through the means available to us: Bible reading and meditation, worship and Christian service. By practicing these activities we start a flow of spiritual power which will give us resources unlimited.

Luther said, "Miracles take place, not because they are performed, but because they are believed." This is often true in life. The Wright brothers believed they could fly—and they did. Madame Curie believed in the existence of radium, and she discovered it. It is equally true in our spiritual lives. Then take God at His Word. His resources are unlimited. They are yours for the asking.

TODAY'S THOUGHT: *God's power was meant for global distribution, but only to men who will seek it.*

AUGUST 2

The Ever-Present Father

The Lord your God is he who is God in heaven above and on earth beneath. Joshua 2:11

We can be sure that God is with us. Sometimes it may seem that we are all alone, but if we look closely, we shall discover the One who has promised never to leave or forsake us.

Many a man wastes years before he finds God. Such a man was Count Leo Tolstoy. Though he was wealthy, honored and acclaimed, he was not satisfied. He reports in his biography that he ran through the calendar of sin without ridding himself of an annoying discontent. Then, while walking in the country, he saw a peasant and observed the look of peace and happiness on the man's face. Realizing that this peasant had no worldly possessions, and yet had joy in life, Tolstoy vowed to seek God. And one day in the forest he found Him. In God he found food for the inner hunger that was consuming him. Later Tolstoy concluded, "To know God is to live."

How wonderful it is to have God as our friend. He never asks us to go through anything that He would not go through himself. He never directs us to take a way upon which He has not traveled. We are never called upon to bear a cross that He has not borne. In all things He was made like us. He came into this world to blaze a trail. Wherever we are called upon to go He has been before. He was victorious even over the final enemy of man, death. As we follow closely after Him, we have nothing to fear.

We must remember that faithfulness to Christ requires discipline of the entire self—body, mind, and will. Holy Scripture has outlined that discipline: We must respect and use our bodies as temples of the Holy Spirit. We must think about things lovely and be truthful. And we must pray, not my will but Thine be done, O Lord.

Only total consecration to God will make us sure that we are with Him, and that He is with us.

TODAY'S THOUGHT: *Our profession of faith must be more than a whitewash on the exterior of the house in which our soul lives; it must penetrate every part of our spirit.*

AUGUST 3

God's Banner of Hope

Blessed is the man who makes the Lord his trust. Psalm 40:4

When you look at a rainbow what do you see? Those attracted by color and beauty see a wonderful display of brilliant hues. The scientifically minded see the refraction of the sun's rays into its component spectrum. Still others, touched with a bit of fanciful desire, see the rainbow as an arch of good fortune, at the end of which is the pot of gold.

In ancient times when a man looked at the rainbow he thought of God. He remembered God's goodness. He remembered God's mercy and His everlasting promise never again to wipe out the human race by flood.

The rainbow still is God's banner, flowing aloft on stormy days to remind man that every rain is sent not to destroy but to make the earth fruitful. It is an agreement between God and man which God has promised never to go back on, and which He will always keep in force, and that man ought therefore to remember. To those for whom God is real the rainbow is a sign of God's perpetual presence and promise. Ought there not be a corresponding banner of the rainbow flying in our hearts?

There was once a young man, a devoted Christian, hospitalized for a long, dangerous operation. Before the event he asked that there be held a brief service of prayer for his physical and spiritual strength. His pastor and a group of his Christian friends gathered at his bedside in a service where indeed God was present. They did not ask for the young man's physical healing, but rather that he might have that inner peace which alone would give him strength. As they left his room, a feeling of peace did steal into his heart and seemed to surround his very being.

The next morning before the operation, the hospital chaplain came into his room. "You are facing a serious operation," he said to the youth. "Would you feel better if I were to go with you to the operating room and stay by your side?"

The patient, his eyes shining, smiled calmly. "Thank you, sir," he said, "for your kind offer, but you need not go with me. There is peace in my heart because I know that God will be present there." We can trust His promise, "I will be with you."

TODAY'S THOUGHT: *The sword may subdue or destroy an enemy; the Spirit can transform him and make him your friend forever!*

216

AUGUST 4

Peace of Mind Is So Important

And he came and preached peace to you who were far off and peace to those who were near. Ephesians 2:17

It has been said that the need for security is a basic human instinct. It is a great comfort to know that security is within every man's reach. In security there is strength, just as there is peace in power.

Someone said, "Our outlook on life is the only thing that can fence us in or set us free." If we are at peace with ourselves, no fence is too high for us to climb. If we are aware of the true dimensions of life, we possess a courage that can open any gate. God has promised that we may lie down in green pastures.

These are difficult days in which to live. Many times we come home from work, completely exhausted, sometimes even in despair. We have a difficult time of it in the competitive struggle in the market place. And then sometimes when we turn home it is to find our loved ones there close to tears, saying, "I've really had a day of it." Perhaps the children are still quarreling when you arrive. Longing for peace and quiet, you are tempted even to want to run away. But there is no escaping it. If we have been so busy with the details of life that we have never had time to store up any reserve resources, we are indeed in a predicament.

But there is a way out of our trouble, and it is definitely not escape. It means instead staying to face the situation, and squashing the heresy that the grass is greener on the other side of the fence. After all, wherever we go we shall have to take ourselves along. You have to live with yourself! Every man can take refuge in his own resourcefulness. So be fit for yourself to know.

If we want a true and lasting peace that will help us in the days of crisis, we must have an inner wealth stored in a safe and accessible place, namely our souls and minds and hearts. If we have that peace, it will reveal itself in everything we do, in our manners, in our dealings, and in our dispositions toward others. For the peace that comes from God makes us more than conquerors through Him that loved us.

TODAY'S THOUGHT: *You need not ask a man if he is at peace—his life will tell it to you.*

AUGUST 5

More to Follow

So we do not lose heart. Though our outer nature is wasting away, our inner nature is being renewed every day.

2 Corinthians 4:16

A young boy was returning home from the lake with his father and mother. They had been on a fishing trip and had thoroughly enjoyed the days spent in God's great out-of-doors. The boy had hopelessly tangled his fishline, and was doing his best to untangle it as they rode home. The father soon noticed the boy's difficulty.

"Let me try it, Son," he said.

The boy handed him the line, and like magic it straightened out in his father's hands. In a few minutes it was back on the reel in working order.

In later years that boy often remarked on this incident to his friends, "That's a picture I'll never forget. To me it was a parable showing how God deals with His children and how we should deal with Him. We work with all our power and strength and get our lives nicely tangled up; then God comes along. With His great power, it isn't long before He gets it straightened out again. But the significant thing is that we must turn our problem over to Him. For us the difficulty seems so great. For Him the solution is so simple. Why are so many people struggling to solve the problems that God could so easily handle?"

The beautiful thing about our friendship with God is the fact that He gives us grace for every trial. He does not help us just once and quit. He is constantly by our side to bring us out of any dilemma in which we find ourselves.

Not only does He solve our problems, but He brings us joy as well.

A man decided to give some of his money to a person less fortunate than himself. Instead of giving the gift all at once he decided to send some each week, and to place in each gift a note which said, "More to follow."

This is the way God deals with us. We receive grace for today, but there is always more to follow. "And from his fullness have we all received, grace upon grace."

TODAY'S THOUGHT: *Just as the sun in warming our world never burns out, so God's love in changing our lives will never be used up.*

AUGUST 6

Victory and Joy for Keeps

For to the man who pleases him God gives wisdom and knowledge and joy. Ecclesiastes 2:26

The Christian should always be joyful, for he holds in his heart a peace which the world cannot take from him. No external force can possibly defeat him. We Christians are not always living evidences of victorious living. We act as if we had been dipped in vinegar. Sometimes people observing our actions must wonder what good our faith really accomplishes.

The joy that a Christian knows is not a stagnant pool, but a constantly moving stream which never runs dry. Because we have resources sufficient for any emergency, nothing should keep us from showing our joy to others. Too frequently happiness is regarded as the main pursuit in the Christian life, when it is really always a by-product.

Perhaps we are not as joyful as we should be because we are not well enough acquainted with Him who can give us the power we seek. After reading a new book, a young woman remarked to friends that it was one of the dullest books she had ever read. Not long afterward she met an author.

"I have a book written by a man with exactly the same name as yours," she said to him. "Is it a coincidence?"

"No," he answered, "I wrote that book."

After getting to know the author the woman re-read his book, and this time found it to be perfectly captivating. Now she put it at the top of her list of favorites. She had become acquainted with the author, and had come to be very fond of him.

In the Bible, the greatest book ever written, we find the secret of victorious living. Sometimes as we study its pages the story seems not as absorbing as it should. This is not because of the words, but because we are not well enough acquainted with the author. Once we make God's acquaintance we can say with assurance, "I know whom I have believed and I am sure that he is able to guard until that Day what has been entrusted to me."

Deep in an underground cave in Kentucky is a tablet which reads, "Out of the lowest depths there is a path to the loftiest heights." We find that path in God's Word, and it brings us eternal joy.

TODAY'S THOUGHT: *The Bible teaches the finest way to live, the noblest way to suffer, and the best way to die.*

AUGUST 7

The Power of Encouragement

Those who seek the Lord lack no good thing. Psalm 34:10

There is great power in encouragement. In an athletic contest sports writers usually concede to the home team a decided advantage, for cheers from the grandstand somehow compel it to victory.

It is true in life, too. Our Lord has commanded us to be kind to one another. Many times a few words of encouragement go a long way toward helping someone gain a victory.

A city tenement was afire, and a crowd gathered to watch the firemen bring it under control. Suddenly there was a shriek from a sixth story window. Someone was stranded in the building. A ladder shot upward from a hook and ladder truck, and a courageous fireman began to climb. Could he rescue that life? Fear welded the crowd into one body. Suddenly someone called, "Cheer him! Cheer him!" Thunderous cheers welled up from the onlookers below. The fireman moved steadily upward through the curling smoke, reached the window, and in a few moments descended with a woman secured safely over one shoulder. The dynamic power of cheering human beings had helped to drive him on.

Visitors to a certain hospital cannot miss a plaque bearing this advice: "Never utter a discouraging word while you are in this hospital. You should come here only for the purpose of helping."

Suppose we endeavored to speak only words of encouragement to those we met along life's way. How different life would be for them. How much joy we would gain from the knowledge that we had helped someone.

"It is a great morning, isn't it?" called a cheery businessman to an associate.

"Why, it is," the other replied as if he had not noticed before.

"It is a great day," said the lawyer greeting his stenographer one morning, and the girl's fingers flew and her eyes smiled happily all that day.

"It is a great day," says the Lord each morning as we awaken, and life is different because He has spoken. Why not, today, give someone a word of encouragement?

TODAY'S THOUGHT: *Speak a word of praise or encouragement when you can; it will cost you nothing, and will be priceless to others.*

AUGUST 8

Renovation by Faith

And Jesus said to him, "Go your way; your faith has made you well." And immediately he received his sight and followed him on the way. Mark 10:52

A man's faith is not what he holds but what holds him. When the depression of the thirties came, scores of people climbed to the tops of high buildings to hurl themselves down. Did you know that even the circular stair in the United States Supreme Court building has been closed because it became a favorite suicide spot? Why? Because peoples' gods had died. They depended totally on material resources, and when their money was gone, they had nothing to hang on to. Lost like a boat without a rudder in an angry sea, they preferred to end their lives. Without faith, they had no inner power holding their souls together.

Many people shy away from faith, thinking that if they commit their lives to God, no longer can they do as they please. Picturing a life of faith as one under a galling yoke of bondage, they seek the treasures that money buys. The fact that they miss is that doing what is pleasing in God's sight is the highest freedom of all. Only truth sets men free. Only God has the power to take a life battered and bruised by sin, and inject into it a meaning that enables it to become eternal.

Here is a story that parables that renovating process. A musician ordered a violin from the best violin maker he knew. When the instrument was ready, he came to the studio to try it. As he drew the bow across the strings it was obvious that he did not like it. Furious, he battered the violin to pieces, paid for it, and stalked out of the studio.

The violin maker patiently collected the broken pieces and set to work remaking the instrument. When it was finished, the violinist was called a second time; and this time it was perfect, just as he wanted it.

Life sometimes works that way. We are not what we ought to be. The keyboard of our life plays discords instead of harmony. As the years slip by, our lives become mangled and maimed. But if we willingly return the pieces to God, He will reassemble them into a living instrument that will play beautiful music. We simply must have faith in the Master for that to happen.

TODAY'S THOUGHT: *The terms of any settlement with Christ must read Unconditional Surrender.*

AUGUST 9

God Knows Best

Be still, and know that I am God. Psalm 46:10

Have you ever noticed that great plates of glass in the windows of unfinished buildings are always daubed with whitewash? Have you wondered why? It is because workmen save time wherever possible by throwing things through empty window spaces. If the glass were left transparent after it was installed, the workmen might not see it, and continue to throw things through it. For its own protection, the glass is besmirched and discolored.

Many times in life little troubles come to save us from larger ones. If we would concentrate on being thankful for all that is ours, instead of bemoaning our difficult way of life, I am sure each day would be more wonderful.

Why can we not trust in God, and believe that always He gives us what is best? An old tale illustrates this point. There were two monks each of whom planted an olive tree. One of them turned to God and said, "Lord, it needs rain that its roots may drink and swell. Send gentle showers."

The Lord sent the rain.

"Lord," the monk prayed then, "My tree needs sun."

The sun filled the earth with warmth.

"Now frost its roots to brace its tissues," he asked.

The little tree sparkled with frost, but in the evening it was dead. Then the monk went to his brother, who had also planted a tree, and told him his disappointment.

"I, too, planted a tree," said the other, "and see, it is thriving. I entrusted my little tree to God. He who made it knows better than I what it needs. I simply pray, 'Lord, send what it needs, storm or sunshine, wind, rain, or frost. Thou hast made it and Thou knowest best.'"

All life has come from God. So the man of faith turns his life over to Him saying, "God, whatever you decide is best. Your will be done."

TODAY'S THOUGHT: *It is both wise and needful to trust implicitly in God's wisdom.*

AUGUST 10

The Haunted House

No good thing does the Lord withhold from those who walk uprightly. Psalm 84:11

Every so often, when one is driving around the city, he sees an old house which was once a beautiful mansion. Now the windows are broken, the paint is dull and chipped, the foundation has begun to decay, and the weeds have overgrown the yard. It was once a well-kept home, neatly painted and well groomed with beautiful flowers in the garden. But now it is an eyesore to the entire community.

No one intended to do these things to the house and garden; but one day the owners moved away, and there was no one to take care of them. The wind and storms took their toll because nobody cared. Little by little beauty disappeared, as the weeds choked out all the flowers. It is haunted by the spirit of neglect.

There are lives much like that dilapidated house. Once they were pure and honest. But something happened, and they lost their goodness. The worthwhile things of daily life were neglected and, at first, quite unintentionally, a few wrongs took the place of right. Storms came along, the foundation began to crumble, and faith began to waver, until at last goodness and kindness had been lost.

It is not enough to say that we have found God, and then expect that our lives from that moment on will be immune from trials and temptations which try to discourage and defeat us. Even as we walk by the Master's side, our willful feet are tempted to stray. And if we once let go of His hand, we shall discover that we have lost our way, and are no longer traveling the straight and narrow path, but on a bypath leading nowhere. Every day we need to renew our allegiance to God. We need to listen to His voice as He speaks to us. We need to hear His commands directing our lives. If we try to go it alone, we soon discover that in our weakness we stumble and fall. But in His strength we are able to remain faithful and true.

Take a look at your house today—I mean the spiritual home in which you live. By your neglect of those things which matter most, have you caused it to be run down? Or are you daily seeking the advice of the world's greatest Architect, who will help you build a home on earth that will make you glad?

TODAY'S THOUGHT: *Every home built on Christ as the chief cornerstone withstands the gnawing tooth of time.*

AUGUST 11

When Scarlet Becomes White

For the law of the Spirit of life in Christ Jesus has set me free from the law of sin and death. Romans 8:2

While driving in the country, a minister found one of his parishioners working in the field. He stopped to talk, and finally remarked that the land did not look very productive.

"No," agreed the church member. "You see, pastor, this land is just like self-righteousness."

"What do you mean?" asked the pastor.

"The more a man has of it, the poorer he is," was the answer.

Too many seize every opportunity to parade their virtues before their fellow men. Too few realize how much they have done wrong and desperately need help. If only we would confess our sins, God is "faithful and just, and will forgive us our sins and cleanse us from all unrighteousness."

Two men were watching a parade of European soldiers.

"What color are their tunics?" asked one.

"Red," replied the other.

"Now look through this," said the first, handing his friend a piece of red glass.

The friend was amazed to see a white-coated regiment passing before him. It is just so with our sins. Though they be red as scarlet, Christ will make them white as snow. They shall be washed away forever from His remembrance.

Carrying a pail of white sand, a distraught woman came to her pastor.

"This is I," she said, gesturing toward the sand, "my sins cannot be numbered."

"Where did you get that sand?" the preacher asked.

"At the seaside," was her reply.

Gently he took her hand, and led her to the beach. With a shovel they scooped a mound of sand—more than a hundred buckets full. Then they stood back to watch the effect of the waves, as they washed over the pile of sand, completely annihilating it.

"I see now what you mean," said the woman. "The blood of Christ washes away all my sins."

In His infinite love, God allowed His only Son to shed blood to wash away our sins and make our scarlet souls as white as snow.

TODAY'S THOUGHT: *Our risen Lord's empty tomb is the source of all the joy in the world.*

AUGUST 12

Every Prayer Gets an Answer

And whatever you ask in prayer, you will receive, if you have faith. Matthew 21:22

In World War II, as our troops were about to invade Sicily, General Eisenhower stood with his staff on a hill overlooking the harbor of Malta. As he saw that great armada of ships, thousands of them, he straightened his strong physique, and saluted the men. It was a still night, and the moon was shining clearly. One could even hear the dip of the rowing oars. And then for a moment, without comment, the General dropped his head for a period of quiet prayer. After that little prayer to God, his Supreme Commander, he thought it best to explain to his staff his feeling. He turned to them and slowly he said, "There comes a time when, after you have used all the technical know-how available and every conceivable stratagem, there is nothing more left for you to do, nothing your men can do, but turn the whole matter over to God and let it rest there, and then have faith to believe that everything will turn out all right."

To me this is a classic example of faith, and from it we can learn a lesson. With God's help we must use well all the abilities He has given us, and then turn our task over to Him and be confident that everything will turn out all right.

Frequently people ask, "Does God answer prayer?" Certainly He does. There is not one prayer that has gone unanswered.

A little boy once chided his sister and said, "Sis, you believe God answers prayer, don't you? Answer me this, then! You prayed for a bike and He didn't give you one."

The little girl replied, "God does too answer prayer. But sometimes He has to say no."

We parents do not give our children everything for which they ask, knowing that such giving is not good for them. Sometimes they fail to understand our actions. Neither do we always understand God. But of one thing we can be certain. His loving arms are around us and beneath us, and He who understands our needs better than we do ourselves makes no mistakes. Should we want anything different from this?

TODAY'S THOUGHT: *Unless you wrestle with God in your prayer, it may be a nice prayer intended for human ears, but it falls short of the divine ear.*

AUGUST 13

The Lessons of Defeat

For the Lord disciplines him whom he loves. Hebrews 12:6

Life can be interesting for every one of us. It is not a voyage on a calm sea, nor a journey on a smooth highway without any bumps or detours. Any life worth telling about is a series of defeats and victories. Ought we be shocked at the thought that at sometime or another every one of us takes a fall. Life consists of falling down and getting up.

The experienced businessman anticipates losses. He expects to make mistakes. Therefore, in prosperous times he lays up reserves to cover misfortune, so that when adversity comes it does not break him. If he is wise, he learns from each experience, and picks himself up after each fall, a wiser man to rise to greater heights.

History tells us that the greatest conquerors have learned their lessons from their defeats. Frederick the Great lost battle after battle, campaign after campaign, before he made Prussia a mighty kingdom. Someone has said that there have been times in the history of nations when a defeat has been more valuable than a victory.

So it is in the Christian life. We who are trying to fight the good fight of the faith must expect many falls. Every day we sin and repent. We fall down, and by the mercy of Christ arise again. Someone has defined a Christian as one who has been knocked down and picked up. Every defeat in the battle of life should point out to us our own weaknesses. Every defeat should persuade us that we are not sufficient of ourselves, that unless God be our leader in battle, we fight in vain.

In the middle of the 17th century, 1666 to be exact, the great fire of London raged five days, destroying the old Gothic cathedral of St. Paul's. Only one single massive column still stood and amazingly enough it bore the motto: "I shall rise again." May that be our war cry! "Whatever happens to me today or any other day, by the strength and mercy of God, I shall rise again!"

TODAY'S THOUGHT: *If you are in despair, ask the Lord for a new lease on life.*

—

AUGUST 14

The Hand That Never Lost a Man

And to the centurion Jesus said, "Go; be it done for you as you have believed." And the servant was healed at that very moment.
Matthew 8:13

A little city boy, spending his vacation on the farm, had just seen a hen sitting on a nest of eggs. He was told that some day a little chick would break out of each egg. The child was so delighted at this dramatic idea, that every morning he went around watching for the miracle to occur.

Days passed and still nothing happened. The eggs still looked every day the same. Finally, the little boy's faith began to wane, until at last one day he gave up hope altogether. He told himself in disgust that he had been deceived, and that nothing would ever happen.

The next day, however, from habit he went around to see the nest, minus any real hope. Suddenly his heart leaped for joy, for as he came upon the scene, he saw a brood of fluffy, little chicks running in and about from beneath the brood hen.

All the time, of course, wonderful things had been taking place inside the little shells. But there had been nothing to show for it until the very last moment, when the little chicks suddenly appeared complete and perfect.

Some of our greatest demonstrations take place like this. For a long time there seems to be no change in the outer sphere. But if we keep our faith strong enough, despite appearances, the demonstration will come.

Two friends were once climbing the Pyrenees, and were caught by the coming of night. They pitched tent on a peak. Suddenly a terrific storm burst upon them.

"This," exclaimed one friend, "feels like the end of the world."

"Not so," replied the other, "this is how the dawn comes in the Pyrenees." Whatever be the trouble come upon us, it is but the prelude to the coming of the dawn, when our faith is securely anchored in God Almighty.

Someone has said, "When you reach the end of your rope, let go and drop into the waiting hands of God." What a safe place to be! His hands are underneath you. Has He not promised to keep them forever around us, if we but walk life's way with Him?

TODAY'S THOUGHT: *We toil tirelessly to gain material security, when all we really need is salvation's strong security.*

227

AUGUST 15

God's Love Reaches Me

And call no man your father on earth, for you have one Father, who is in heaven. Matthew 23:9

God's love is something from which no one can possibly become separated. It makes no difference what direction you travel, or how deep in sin you may fall, God is there. It makes no difference if you are educated or uneducated, rich or poor, a man of many talents or few, God still is love. No one can outgrow his need of that commodity, nor get so wise as to be able to do without it. God is love, and for every race and color. He loves each of His children in a very personal way.

A census taker once asked a woman how many children she had.

"Well," she said, "there is Willie, and Henry, and Martha, and . . ."

"Never mind the names," he said impatiently, "just give me the number."

His tone aroused the woman's indignation. "They haven't got numbers," she said sharply. "They all have names!"

God knows every one of us by name. Despite the fact that we do not deserve His love and mercy, He still showers it upon us. Patiently He gives himself to us, yet our reactions sometimes must sorely try Him to fling us to the side and out of reach of His bounties.

Some time ago in a doctor's crowded waiting room sat a mother with her little boy. He was about six years old and full of "insatiable curiosity." His questions flew thick and fast and he managed to "cover the water front" in the 30-minute wait. Yet to the admiration of all, his mother answered every question with loving patience.

Inevitably he got around to God, putting his hows and whys. The others seemed to wonder how she could continue to be so unruffled. But when she answered the little boy's final question, she had answered theirs, too.

"Why," he asked, "doesn't God just get tired and stop?"

"Because," she replied, after a moment's thought, "God is love and love never gets tired." Let us begin, continue, and end each of life's days remembering "God is love."

TODAY'S THOUGHT: *If you are tired at the end of a day, think then how tired God must be at the end of an eon, and still His love starts fresh with every new babe!*

AUGUST 16

Every Man's Friend

If any one walks in the day, he does not stumble, because he sees the light of this world. John 11:9

We discover in our Bibles that men in ages past were people much like ourselves. Some were bad and some were good; some proud, some humble. Some were rich and some were poor; some lived in doubt and some by faith. There always were those who lived in intimate friendship with God, discovering in their discouragement that He was the Friend who always helped. When defeat seemed inevitable, He was the one who saved them from despair. They talked to Him in prayer, and He heard and answered them. They trusted, and were not let down. Naturally they were happy in this intimate companionship.

Those who claim this opportunity to walk day by day with God are always the ones who gain the victory.

When the late Sir Ernest Shackleton returned to England to report on his Antarctic explorations, he told the king of his consciousness of the presence of God while traveling the frozen wastes never before visited by man. He said, "Bending over the oars, struggling through the snows, battling across the ranges, there was always with us, Another. He made the difference between triumph and disaster."

George Washington Carver, the noted educator and chemist, once was called before a senate sub-committee to testify concerning his work with the peanut.

"Where did you learn all these things?" he was asked.

"From an old book," he replied.

"What book?"

"The Bible."

"But what does the Bible say about peanuts?" asked a startled member of the committee.

"Nothing, Mr. Senator," replied Dr. Carver quietly. "But it tells about God who made the peanut. I asked Him to show me what to do with it, and He did."

Why not step out and claim His promise, "I can do all things in him who strengthens me." You will then discover amazing reaches of power.

TODAY'S THOUGHT: *Everyone who believes can enjoy the surprise that comes when God taps him on the shoulder and says, "I will care for you."*

AUGUST 17

First We Are Forgiven

In him we have redemption through his blood, the forgiveness of our trespasses. Ephesians 1:7

A soldier was once brought before his commanding officer for misdemeanor. He was a frequent offender and had often been punished.

"Here he is again," said the senior officer. "We have tried just about everything on him."

Then a subordinate officer stepped forward and excusing himself for the liberty said, "There is one thing that has never been done with him."

"What is that?"

"Well," he said, "he has never been forgiven."

"Forgiven!" exclaimed the commanding officer, surprised at the suggestion. But as he reflected for a moment his attitude changed, and he had the offending soldier brought in. The soldier stood before him ashamed and sorry, and awaiting the increased punishment he was sure would follow. To his utter amazement, the commanding officer turned to him and said, "We have tried everything else on you. There remains to us but this one thing. We are resolved to forgive you."

Tears welled up in the soldier's eyes. He could hardly find words to thank the officer. He retired in a daze from the interview, and from that day on he was a new man.

God's treatment of us guilty sinners is much like that. His forgiveness of sinners' mistakes is like the ocean swallowing up and cleansing filth and carrion, leaving no trace at all. Not only that, but God restores us again to the place of honor in the kingdom. We are made sons in God's household. The prodigal son became a stranger the moment he turned his back upon his father's house. He had never intended at the beginning that his final goal would be the far-off country. He had only wanted to be free of home ties which he felt inhibited him from doing the things his natural self desired. But the door of his home remained always open for his return. And in time the boy came to himself. Repenting, he retraced his steps to his father's house.

God not only waits but actively seeks for the lost. Today when He calls, will we listen to His voice?

TODAY'S THOUGHT: *As the sleeping mother awakens at the cry of her sick child, so God hears our feeblest plea.*

AUGUST 18

Jesus Conquered Death

You know that you were ransomed from the futile ways inherited from your fathers, not with perishable things such as silver or gold, but with the precious blood of Christ. 1 Peter 1:18

The greatest message ever proclaimed to man is, "He is risen!" How drab and hopeless life would be if there were no meeting beyond the grave. One would feel like spitting on life and fear any mention of death, were it not for the resurrection story. When Robert Burns read in Revelation, "He overcame the last enemy!" great scalding tears welled up and he repeated the words, "The last enemy is death!" Yes, that stone, too, is rolled away! This is even better news than that which the angels brought to Bethlehem at Christmas time. The message of Christmas tells us that Jesus was born, that He is willing, therefore, to suffer many things and be "crucified, dead, and buried." The good news of Easter tells us that Jesus has conquered sin and the grave, and that death has no more dominion over Him. It proves every outer claim He made; assures the fulfillment of every promise. What does this mean to you?

For the Christian it means that death has lost its sting. The heathen often decorated their tombs with the symbol of a broken column. An untimely death cutting a man down in the midst of his work, the cruel interruption of it all was visibly spelled out. There is no hopelessness as black and unrelieved as that of a godless pagan.

We plant our Christian graves with flowers which fade yet bloom again as a sign of the resurrection. We place a cross upon our tomb as a mark that we trust in Him who died for our sins and rose again for our justification. We repeat with deep conviction the words, "They that sow in tears shall reap in joy. He that goeth forth and weepeth, bearing seed for sowing, shall doubtless come again with joy, bringing his sheaves with him" (A.S.V.).

We all know that death is the last enemy we must face. Death without our faith in the resurrection is indeed an enemy, the death of all joy and song. What but the gruesome sign of the skull and cross bones can stand for such as have no risen Lord? But death seen in the light of Christian faith is transformed into an angel of light and love. For the Christian, death means dawn has come.

TODAY'S THOUGHT: *At death we do but leave our temporary dwelling to move into our permanent home.*

231

AUGUST 19

As a Man Thinks

For man believes with his heart and so is justified, and he confesses with his lips and so is saved. Romans 10:10

A mother sent her two little daughters out to play in a beautiful garden. She told them to look carefully around the garden, and then come inside and tell her what they had seen. One child came running and said in a sad voice, "Mother, Mother, all the roses in the garden have thorns!" Soon the other child came in radiantly happy; she exclaimed, "Mother, Mother, all the thorns have beautiful roses."

So much depends upon our attitude to life. If we adopt a negative attitude, we see nothing but the problems looming about us, and feel nothing but the heartaches brought by our failures. Life becomes a drudgery as we keep looking down rather than up. We may put in time at our jobs, but our hearts are not in them.

Attitude makes a difference. One gardener looks upon his job as nothing but digging in the dirt; the other gardener proudly proclaims that he is creating a place of beauty. One housewife is working in a maze of floors to scrub and dirty dishes to wash; the other wife is creating a haven of joy for her family. One student terms his schooling "an old grind"; another sees it as a great door into fuller living.

We need to look beyond the actual moment in which we are living. We must be aware, not only of what our job can do for us, but what it will enable us to do for others. The lives of the successful prove that working happily day by day adds up to the kind of accomplishments that all of us seek for ourselves. Any job at all, if done with consecration, can become significant in the sight of God. Your home or your place of business can become an altar at which you worship God by the way you work.

Confucius rightly said, "If there is righteousness in the heart, there will be beauty in the character." As you begin each day, look to the task ahead, and vow to do the very best you can. If you do, when you come to lie down to sleep at night there will be a great peace in your soul.

TODAY'S THOUGHT: *Happy is the man who does his work well, and blessed is the man who is worn with toil, for he shall taste the sweetness of rest.*

AUGUST 20

Someone Has Paid for You

You were bought with a price. 1 Corinthians 6:20

Pilate said of Jesus, "Behold, the man!" His heathen mind did not comprehend that this man was also God incarnate, who had come to die for our sins. What he could have said was this: "Behold the Shepherd, laying down His life for the sheep. Behold the Good Shepherd, dying for the weak and sinful. Behold the Bread of Life, broken on the cross for a starving world. Behold appalling cruelty and bloody lust of man, and learn the true nature of sin."

We often make light of sin, especially of our own. We like to decorate our pleasant vices, and call them by soft names. We need to turn to Calvary and see what these things really mean. What was the price of sin? The price was a nail-tearing, excruciating experience that caused our Savior agony of mind and body such as no mere man has ever experienced, nor ever will be called upon to experience. Such is the bitter fruit of our vices. When you are tempted to sin, remember that the eyes of Him who died on Calvary are alive to look upon you now.

I have heard about a certain person who had a picture of the crucifixion in his room. Whenever he was tempted into evil ways, he would draw a curtain across the picture before committing the sin in an effort to pacify his conscience and ease his mind.

Look upon three great facts—men sinning, men dying, and the world not caring a fig for their pain nor turning a hand to help. "What is that to us?" cried the chief priests sneeringly to the remorseful Judas. The world will help you sin, but it will not help you when your sin brings sorrow. Where shall we look for comfort then? Where shall we look for hope? Where shall we seek the peace which the world cannot give? Where shall we find that perfect love, that perfect sacrifice, which can bring us pardon? Where but at the cross of Calvary. "It is finished," cried Jesus as that colossal price was paid. Because of the crucifixion of God's only Son, you and I have a finished salvation, needing not so much as one good deed to open wide heaven's gate for us. Love so amazing, so divine, asks only our empty, uplifted hand to claim and lay hold of it.

TODAY'S THOUGHT: *If God is directing our defenses, the devil will be thwarted in his effort to break through and spoil our peace.*

AUGUST 21

"Even Calls Me by My Name!"

The Lord looks down from heaven, he sees all the sons of men.
Psalm 33:13

After hearing that God created the world in six days, a little girl asked her Sunday school teacher what business God has been in since then.

There are people who lose all hope every day simply because they feel that God is detached from the world He made, that He is not interested in the everyday lives of His children. They think that He wound up the world like an alarm clock and has gone off to let it run by itself.

Nothing could be further from the truth. God is just as concerned about us today as when He made us. Constantly He is trying to persuade us that following His plan will bring the more abundant life. Every day we see countless reminders that God cares for each and every child.

A strange African tribe is said never to count, not knowing arithmetic.

"How do you know if one of two sheep is missing?" a visitor asked one of the tribe. The answer was strikingly beautiful.

"Not because the number is less, but because I would miss the face."

We are more than numbers to God. Each one has been created as an individual, and even as a shepherd recognizes his sheep, so God misses the absent face of every one of His straying children.

He has provided ample resources for us. If a great king should issue an order that your needs would be supplied as long as you live, you would cease to worry because that king has authority and unlimited resources. How much more should the promises of the King of kings put a stop to our worry! He has promised every living mother's son or daughter the security of a heavenly Father's loving care.

Some years ago in a steamship disaster a father was carrying his six-year-old son into a lifeboat. The boy awakened, and looked up into his father's face, then snuggled closer in his father's arms and went to sleep again, unafraid.

In the storms of life it is not the boom of the waves that matters. What matters is the peace that we have in God's enfolding arms.

TODAY'S THOUGHT: *Man is on a search for security and there is only one place to find it—in God.*

234

AUGUST 22

"One Thing I Do!"

When you make a vow to the Lord your God, you shall not be slack to pay it; for the Lord your God will surely require it of you.
Deuteronomy 23:21

Many people have spent their lives striving for greatness, but hitching their wagons to a wrong star, they failed to achieve it. Some set their sights on a selfish ambition, or worked only for personal acclaim. Striving for such goals, however, man never achieves greatness, for a truly great man is one who has learned to walk humbly with his God. He looks to God for direction and follows Him wherever He may lead. Such a man, imbued with humility, knows that sometimes the hardest duty becomes the highest.

The pathway of the successful man is not an easy one to follow. To emulate the truly great, we must be willing to pay the price.

At a boys' school commencement a very famous man addressed the graduates. They were thrilled with his talk, and many of them told their class advisor that they wanted to be like this great man.

"Boys," the teacher told them, "that is a fine ambition. He is one of the greatest men in our country. God bless him for all that he does and the inspiration he is for many. But before you decide to be like him, you had better count the cost. I have known him personally since he was a boy. He has suffered privation, misery, misunderstandings, and many failures and disappointments. Are you willing to pay that price for greatness? If you are, it will be yours."

We are all inspired by great leaders, and many times the influence of their lives prompts us to take up all but impossible tasks. The best example of all is Jesus Christ. He went about doing good. He was kind and loving in all His daily relationships. He lived a lesson we should never forget. Common to all truly great men who have followed Jesus is the realization that they are their brother's keepers.

We need not have great talents to become great people. But, deciding to turn our lives over to God, for Him to use as He will, we can be sure we are on the pathway to success. That single decision can transform a mediocre life into a great one.

TODAY'S THOUGHT: *More important than gifts of mind and body is to make the right use of them. There is no flop quite as great as of a brilliant man cheating God of his life.*

AUGUST 23

He Has No Other Hands

And the hands of all who are with you will be strengthened.

2 Samuel 16:21

An unusual statue of Christ received much publicity. This figure of our Savior had no hands, and stood in a rebuilt church in Frankfurt, Germany. World War II caused this mutilation. After one of the most severe bombing raids the townspeople, rushing to survey the damage, found the statue still standing in place, undamaged save that Christ's hands were missing. When their church was renovated, they decided not to restore the hands. The people had come to realize that the statue spoke an eloquent message to all who saw it.

"Christ has no hands, but our hands to do His work today," it said.

Are you serving God by helping your fellow men? Does His love stimulate you to unselfish service? Do you inspire others by your dedication to Him?

A visitor went to the home of the village doctor. A young lad, evidently the doctor's son, was sitting on the porch.

"Is your father at home?" the visitor asked.

"No," replied the boy, "he isn't."

"Do you know where I could find him?" was the man's next question.

"Well," replied the boy thoughtfully, "you'll find him where people are sick or hurt. I don't know where he is, but he is always helping somebody."

The measure of a man's greatness is not the number of servants he has but the number of people he is willing to serve, for in serving others we serve our Christ.

The story is told of two doctors who went to a village in the deep South to die. One had tuberculosis and the other suffered from arthritis. Each heard of the other's plight, and decided to try everything to save that life. They became so absorbed in their work that neither of them had time to die.

In enriching the life of another person, the one most helped is one's self.

TODAY'S THOUGHT: *Our little, nameless, unremembered acts of kindness and love are the best part of our life.*

AUGUST 24

All Men Seek Security

The Lord is my shepherd, I shall not want. Psalm 23:1

Relief officers who went to Europe immediately after the conclusion of the last war found that there were little children dying of starvation in many refugee camps. After they had satisfied the children's bodily needs, they discovered that there were many who, because they felt insecure, needed a cure for their minds as well. Someone thought of a simple plan. After the children had been fed their dinner and were being prepared for bed, they were given another piece of bread not to eat but to hold in their arms as one does a doll. Hugging close this symbol of plenty for tomorrow, they dropped off to a dreamless sleep, their minds within saying, "I shall never be hungry again."

Faith masters every fear, if the faith we hold to is in God, who alone is able to give the security we so desperately need. We dare not forget for one day that God is sufficient to supply our every need. That conviction alone can truly chase black, nameless fear away. He is sufficient not only to provide for our physical needs, but also to direct us safely through every pitfall of life. Has He not gone that way before?

A little girl in a sight-seeing party was being shown some of the historic places of Rome. Late in the afternoon they walked through a dense garden where tall trees cast dark, heavy shadows. The little girl stayed close to the guide and occasionally asked him a question. After a while she walked more confidently and told her mother, "I am not afraid now. I discovered that the guide has been here before and he knows the way."

Followers of the living God have a Guide who knows the way all through this life.

Let us remember that there are 365 "Fear nots," in the Bible, one for each day in the year. Each one of them carries this message from God: "Fear not, I am with you. There is no force that can possibly defeat you."

TODAY'S THOUGHT: *How many talents are lost to the world each day, all because those who possess them bury them in the napkins of fear, lacking the courage to put them to work?*

AUGUST 25

Here Is a War from Which There Is No Surcease

Break off your sins by practicing righteousness, and your iniquities by showing mercy to the oppressed. Daniel 4:27

As Napoleon stood on the field of Waterloo and saw the battle going against him, he cried out urgently, "Night or despair!" He knew that his only hope was darkness to save him from defeat.

It is not so for the Christian in the battle of life. He walks in the light as a child of the light, and marching to victory he cries out, "Daybreak and Jesus!" "Thanks be to God, who gives us the victory through our Lord Jesus Christ."

The peace which we have is not the safety of the coward who has fled the battle or run up the white flag of disgraceful surrender. The peace of God ruling in our hearts is the peace of those sticking at the post of duty. We must wage unceasing war against sin. Just as the boy, Hannibal, was brought to the heathen altar to swear eternal vengeance against the Romans, so every Christian is pledged to a lifelong contest with the world.

What then is "the world" against which we must fight? "The world" means everything false, or mean, or selfish, or cruel. It means whatever is contrary to the gospel of the Master. When we say "the world" we mean the evil lurking in our nature. "The world" inside of us is often worse than the world without, for in the former we hear the murmur of self will. It is there we fight the battle of conscience and develop either the coward spirit that draws us back from conflict, or the victor spirit that asks and gives no quarter.

No, this is not God's world. When God "created the heavens and the earth" then He looked on "everything that he had made, and behold, it was very good." But the fall into sin made a mess of that. In the blessings of our baptism the Holly Spirit helps us to choose a life for God, and our heavenly Father gives His gift of happiness in loving Him and one another. Sin is the serpent lurking in that Eden, and from the cradle to the grave the war must be waged.

Let us take courage from knowing that victory can be ours, because those who are for us are greater than those who are against us.

TODAY'S THOUGHT: *Follow Christ and you will be led safely out of your maze of trouble.*

AUGUST 26

Your Life Is a Lantern

God does all these things, twice, three times, with a man, to bring back his soul from the Pit, that he may see the light of life.
Job 33:29, 30

Before we can become the kind of witness God can use, we must be willing to pray the prayer of the Psalmist: "Create in me a clean heart, O God." Otherwise our light will not shine.

A clever minister once took an old-dirt-smeared lantern to church and put it in front of the pulpit. Some of the audience laughed when they saw it, wondering why it was hanging there. In the course of the sermon the minister asked his congregation what good the lamp was in such condition. They replied that it was good for nothing. When he asked them what was the matter, they promptly answered that the lantern needed to be cleaned and to have a new light put in it. The minister then reminded them that the lantern could not clean itself or put in another light. He compared the dirt-blackened lantern to a man with a sin-smeared life, a man who was a useless good-for-nothing. If ever he would allow God to cleanse him from sin, to direct him, to light within his heart the lamp of love, this same individual could serve God and his fellow men.

Though our talents may differ, we can all serve God. Our heavenly Father does not expect us to show forth any more light than He has given. But we each possess a certain amount of candle power, and if we allow God to keep our lanterns lighted and to redeem our living, the darkness of the world will vanish.

How is the lantern of your life? A motorist was struck by a train at a grade crossing. The gate tender who was supposed to give the warning signal was subpoenaed to appear in court. During the long trial he testified repeatedly that he had frantically waved his lantern but with no result.

"I was afraid at first that your testimony wouldn't jibe and hold up," his superintendent said the following day, as he congratulated him for winning the case for the Railroad.

"Boy, was I afraid that the lawyer would ask if my lantern was lit!" replied the signal man. He escaped because the key question was unasked; but we cannot escape God's question, "Did you allow Me to keep your lantern aglow?"

TODAY'S THOUGHT: *How many of those who fall on life's battlefield are wounded running away from their problems?*

239

Building Palaces Under God's Own Eyes

O sing to the Lord a new song, for he has done marvelous things! His right hand and his holy arm have gotten him victory.

Psalm 98:1

Many of us are far too selfish. We are concerned only about our own personal happiness. Too seldom do we think about God's plan for our lives. The great principle we should remember is this— not my will, O God, but Thy will be done. We can find happiness if we find the place that God has assigned to us, and if we abide and work with Him to the best of our ability.

In a frightful storm a coast guard squad received word of a vessel breaking up on the reef close by. The wind was off shore and howled its vengeance. The captain, fully aware of the danger, ordered the men to the boats. "But," protested one fearful of his life, "we will never make it back!"

Roared the old salt, "We have to go out, we don't have to come back; to your boats!"

Man's real greatness will not be revealed, if he seeks only his own creature comforts or fame, his own enjoyment and security. It will never come by his whimpering, "But a man must live!" or by his trying to save his own life, or seeking his own glory. It will come only as he seeks to do God's will today. He puts his life under God's direction, as he comes to the conclusion, "Whoever loses his life will preserve it."

This is equally true for the man of high or low station, for the rich or the poor.

Let us seek the will of God for our lives. Let us face the fact that we will never on this side of heaven be able to side-step the struggle between God's will and our own, and intrepidly launch our lifeboat into the teeth of the gale. But let us hold before us the truth that, if we run our race with patience, if when struggling our own gardens of Gethsemane we will turn to our heavenly Father and say, "God, not my will but Thine," we too shall have angels ministering to us, and the devil leaving us as we emerge victorious.

TODAY'S THOUGHT: *As the builder must have a design for the house he constructs, so God has a plan for each individual life.*

AUGUST 28

Prayer Makes Jesus Real

He told them a parable . . . that they ought always to pray and not lose heart. Luke 18:1

Most of us wait until we are in trouble before we call upon the Lord. We drift along until we face some desperate problem, and then run crying to Him for help and strength.

Prayer is more than asking for things. God is always willing to help us, but how wonderful it would be, were we to say each morning as we awaken, "Lord, is there anything I can do for you today?" An old gospel song begins, "I'm satisfied with Jesus." How about a second verse to run like this, "Is He satisfied with me?" As we become better and better acquainted with Him, we build within ourselves power and strength to withstand anything that happens. Then, too, the better we know Him, the more likely it is that His strength will uphold us in moments of trial or weakness.

A little boy wanted a new suit of clothes. He begged his mother to ask his father for the suit, but his mother suggested that he ask for it himself.

"I would," said the boy, "but I just feel I am not well enough acquainted with him."

The better acquainted we become with God, the more rewarding the friendship. Some excuse their prayerlessness saying, "The reality of God has left me." May it not be that because you have left off praying, God has become distant and unreal? When a genuine partnership develops, each partner does as much as he can for the other. God is our senior partner. We must learn to trust Him at all times, and believe firmly that He has the power to fulfill our every need. We must remember, too, that His judgment is always right.

"Everything goes against me," said a man to Luther. "None of my wishes ever come true. My plans never work out."

"That is your own fault," replied Luther. "You never pray to God, 'Thy will be done.' You ask Him to help you according to your own wishes. God knows best, remember that."

Many Christians forget that tribulation often works patience and that God answers prayer in His own way. But God never fails. Whatever His answers are, they are always right.

TODAY'S THOUGHT: *Prayer is the key that opens the door to God's goodness and guidance.*

AUGUST 29

The Master Is Come and Calls You!

Let me dwell in thy tent for ever! Oh to be safe under the shelter of thy wings! Psalm 61:4

"Doctor," asked the dying man, "tell me about eternity."

"Do you hear that scratching at the door?" the doctor said. "That's my dog trying to get in. He doesn't know a thing about this room except that his master is in it. That is enough for him."

God's word tells us that heaven has many mansions. It assures us that our hearts need not be troubled if we believe in God. Though now we see through a glass darkly, and know little of the details of eternity, it is enough to know that the Master is there, and that we have the promise of His presence throughout all time. With that promise we can look forward to the life to come. We will have the courage to walk the narrow way knowing that one blessed day, by the mercy and love of Christ, we shall thrill to that glory prepared for us before the beginning of time.

How foolish we are to fear death, for the cross has bridged the valley of its black shadows. Faith will enable us to walk triumphantly into the heavenly mansions. Armed with faith, we can scale the jagged rocks and surmount life's mountains of difficulty.

Helen Keller speaks of the magic light in her heart. Though she has been blind and her pathway on earth dark, she says that her faith became a strong spiritual searchlight. That searchlight illumines the way and she walks unafraid, knowing in both life and death the Lord is always present.

He is always present, though sometimes we allow the clouds of sin to separate us from Him. On my first visit to Japan I wanted to see Mount Fujiyama. For several days it was hidden by a thin haze of low lying clouds, and then one day the sun broke through, the clouds parted, and I beheld the glorious snow-capped mountaintop.

So shall it be, at the end of time, when we see Him face to face.

TODAY'S THOUGHT: *Just as every blind man imagines dreams of how earth must look, so every believer ought to have a vision of paradise.*

AUGUST 30

Sin Can Paralyze

Let not sin therefore reign in your mortal bodies, to make you obey their passions. Romans 6:12

One day a man sick of the palsy came into the presence of Jesus. When Jesus saw the faith He said to the suffering man, "Son, your sins are forgiven." First He gave to the man healing of soul. He told the man his past faults were completely forgotten. He was told he was received back again to the heavenly Father's favor and love, as the prodigal son was to his father's home. The forgiveness received doubtless was the very thing which above all others the man needed and desired. Jesus was reading his heart. No doubt his sickness and the near approach of death had awakened his conscience and made him see his guilty condition in the sight of his heavenly Father. He was unprepared to meet God, and so unprepared to enter heaven. Hence, he needed and desired most the forgiveness of his sins. Jesus grants the greater blessings first.

Then Jesus proves His power to forgive by His power to heal. He said to the man, "Rise, take up your bed and go home." Here was a living witness to the power of Jesus. The cure was a visible illustration of the work He was able to do for the souls of the children He loved.

Sin in the soul takes on all the forms which paralysis does for the body. Sometimes it takes away or dulls the sense of feeling. Its victims are insensible to the greatness and goodness of God, the appeals of reason, and the truths of religion. They are, as the apostles say, "past feeling." It sometimes weakens the will so that when men would do good, evil is present with them. They put off the duty at hand. They know what is right, but they will not come to a decision.

Sometimes sin produces an affixed condition of evil with intense tortures of conscience. If you are caught in this kind of dilemma, what is there for you to do? Like the paralytic, you must desire to be cured. He had heard of Jesus, and had great faith in Him. That is the beginning point. He knew he could not cure himself. He had no way to go to a physician without the help of his friends, but he determined nothing would stand in his way to a cure.

If we turn to God in faith, He will surely come into our lives, and give us the peace that comes from knowing that we are free.

TODAY'S THOUGHT: *Character is the result of the choices we have made in life.*

243

AUGUST 31

"Tell My People to Go Forward"

For we walk by faith, not by sight. 2 Corinthians 5:7

God has invited us to be His followers. What does this imply? Surely this means obedience, purity, and adoration.

Have you ever taken your children on a vacation, and told them to follow you on a new way to the country? Well, then you know how perfectly they believed in you. Though they had never been that way before, they did what you told them, without fear or doubt, but with simple, childlike faith, absolutely assured that you knew the way. If we are followers in God, we must do the same, knowing that what our Father does is well. With the arrival of each new day, we discover a new bit of road we have not traveled before. As long as we follow Him, we remain assured that all will be well.

Following God as His children means there will be purity in our lives. Whenever a child accompanies his father to some special place he feels it a privilege, and he cleans up carefully and wears his best clothes. Knowing we are companions of God and remembering that no unclean person has any inheritance in the kingdom of God, we must ask Him every day to cleanse our thoughts and to make us pure. "Everyone who thus hopes in him purifies himself," says our Bible. Though we cannot be cleansed by our own merit, we must have the faith to believe that God through Christ has provided each one with the white cloak of righteousness.

Being a follower of God means walking, that is to say movement, advancement, growth. If we stand still, we shall lose sight of God because we are not following. He is forever going forward. He is never satisfied with the present, for there is always more beyond. If we are not better people than we were a year ago, if we are not less selfish, less easily provoked to anger, then we have not been walking in the right way. Then Jesus of Nazareth has passed by, and we have not risen to follow Him. In the Christian life there can be no standing still. Either we are growing better or worse, growing in grace or increasing in sin, getting nearer to God or farther from Him. There are but two paths for us to choose—life or death. On which path are you walking?

TODAY'S THOUGHT: *We cannot make heaven real by speaking only of earthly things, for each one of us dwells on what really possesses his heart.*

244

SEPTEMBER 1

All Things Work Together

Rejoice and be glad, for your reward is great in heaven, for so men persecuted the prophets who were before you. Matthew 5:12

Long ago a German baron made a great harp by stringing wires from tower to tower on his castle. When the harp was ready, he listened for the music. But the air was still and the wires hung silent. Soon autumn came with its billowing breezes, and there were faint whispers of song. Then as the powerful winter winds swept the castle, the harp answered with the most majestic music ever heard, and the baron was happy.

So it is with the harp of the human heart. Sometimes in the summer days of joy it yields pleasant soothing music. But the full, rich symphonies leap forth only under the striking of the winter winds of trial. Some of the sweetest songs ever sung have come forth in the midst of darkest sorrow. Many of the richest attainments of character have been reached through pain. Jesus himself was made perfect through suffering.

There are times when we complain to God about the hard things that happen to us. At the moment we cannot understand their meaning. It is impossible for us to see how they can work together for any good.

A certain village church owned a well-toned bell. All the people in the community were very proud of it. But an accident cracked the bell, and a blacksmith was called to repair it. He riveted it so skillfully that when he had finished the repair, the crack was barely visible. Back in its tower, the bell was given a test ring and the listeners were greeted by an appalling sound. The only hope was to have the bell recast. When that was done, to the surprise and pleasure of all, the new bell had a sweeter tone than ever the old one had.

Men may devise clever schemes to try to cover up the ravages of sin in a heart. But a wholly new heart re-created by God himself is the only remedy. We should rejoice rather than rebel at the burdens He places upon us. For when we walk into the freedom of a new day, we shall realize He has allowed us to suffer only in order to make us possessors of a more vibrant faith.

TODAY'S THOUGHT: *Many have emerged from the school of sorrow to reveal to the world the beautiful songs of heaven they learned while there!*

245

SEPTEMBER 2

The Sugar-Coated Poison

Resist the devil and he will flee from you. James 4:7

One day when his mother was away from home, a little boy climbed up on a chair, and reached into the shelf of a certain cabinet. He found a small white package, tasted its contents, and found them sweet. He took some, then returned the package to the shelf. Moments after his mother's return the boy became violently ill. She asked what he had eaten and he told her he had tasted some of that sweet sugar in the bathroom cabinet. She looked for herself and learned, to her horror, that he had swallowed poison. Hurriedly she called the doctor, and he was able to save the boy's life. That little boy never forgot that some sweet-tasting things can be very unpleasant, and even lead to tragedy.

So it is with sin. Frequently it is very attractive, and we are fond of it for the moment. But if, having sinned, we reject the healing emetic of the Great Physician, we are surely doomed.

There is only one way to everlasting joy in this world, and to life in the world to come. It is to have faith in God. We must realize that when we have lost faith, we have lost everything.

A small boy visited Sunday school, and was thrilled with the picture card he received. On it was written this text: "Have faith in God." On the way home his precious card was caught by the wind, and fluttered out of the open bus window.

"Stop the bus!" he cried, "I've lost my faith in God. Stop the bus!"

The good-natured bus driver obliged and the card was recovered, much to the delight of the other riders. A thoughtful passenger remarked that many lives would be happier, if people were wise enough to call a halt whenever they were in danger of losing their faith in God.

Faith is our most valuable possession. As long as we keep it, nothing need concern us. Let us guard it carefully.

TODAY'S THOUGHT: *Temptation seldom comes while we are hard at work earning our bread or serving others.*

SEPTEMBER 3

This Detour Leads Home

Sorrow is better than laughter, for by sadness of countenance the heart is made glad. Ecclesiastes 7:3

Many are hesitant about following the Christian way because they think it is far too difficult. It is not that Christianity has been tried and found wanting, but that it has been tried, found hard, and given up. People shy away from crosses and crucifixions, from troubles and tribulations. They forget that passing through the fire of difficulty is the only way to gain something worth while.

A family was on an outing in their car when they came to a place where a new road was being built. They were in a narrow mountain pass between two cities, and the old road was uneven and full of holes. Nothing was being done to repair it; it was merely being kept passable until the new road was completed. As they hit bump after bump, the children complained bitterly. It was as trying a trip as this family had ever made. They fretted; they blamed the state for leaving such a road, and because of their annoyance, the trip seemed much longer than it actually was. The father's patience was nearly exhausted, when he caught sight of a sign which some thoughtful construction worker had set up along the road where the ruts were the deepest. "Be patient while we build you a better road, friend," it read.

Traveling the highway of life, we frequently complain to God because the way is not smooth. Even the disciples could not understand why the Master had to go to Jerusalem to suffer and die. We cannot understand why we must pass through trials and temptations to reach glory. Life is a school and we must learn day by day the lessons it offers. Out of any situation in life a blessing can come. Adversity is always overruled by good.

Two men were watching a boat steam up a river.

"There was a time when no boat could pass through this channel," said one. "The channel wasn't deep enough, and had to be blasted out."

It was possible for the river to carry large vessels only after deep blasting had been done. When the sands of difficulty sift in on your way, remember it is only by turning to God for help to deepen the channel that you will be made a better servant of the Lord.

TODAY'S THOUGHT: *Many a lasting friendship has been forged in the furnace of human difficulty; how wonderful it is when the Friend is Jesus.*

SEPTEMBER 4

The House of Tomorrow Is Being Built Today

But when the sun rose they were scorched; and since they had no root they withered away. Matthew 13:6

Every Christian should bear this motto in his heart, "Hope in God." It is this "hope set before us" which lights our path and gives us strength to fight the good fight, to keep the faith, and to finish the course. Our hope is grounded in the fact that our Lord has gone to prepare a place for us that where He is we may be also. Hope reminds us that heaven is our home and, although for a little while on earth we cannot see our Lord except through the eyes of faith, hope assures us that again in a little while we shall see Him and be with Him forever.

Our hope of heaven will make us aim high in life, even as it has the saints who anticipated becoming citizens in the City of God. In a sense each one of us is building his own house in eternity while living here on earth. The evil habits of the slave of sin build for him a dungeon for his future torture, while the earnest servant of God, who seeks His strength every day to climb higher, builds here a vestibule to the paradise of a happy eternity.

There is a legend telling of a certain king who determined to build for himself a tremendous palace. He secured a famous architect who was first and foremost a man of God's church. Having entrusted to him great sums of money, the king departed to a far country. The architect spent the money in feeding the hungry, clothing the naked, and teaching the ignorant. When the king returned and found that no palace had been built, he became angry and had the man imprisoned. One night the king had a vision in which an angel carried him to paradise, where among the many mansions, he saw one far more beautiful than the rest. The king asked the angel to whom the glorious home belonged, and he learned that the architect who had spent his money had built for him a home in eternity. In that moment the king learned something all of us should learn. The wisest man is the one who builds, not for the day that is only, but also for eternity.

TODAY'S THOUGHT: *A man who knows the true meaning of life will not hesitate to plant a tree under whose shade he knows he can never sit.*

SEPTEMBER 5

Accept Then Christ's Invitation

Jesus said to them, "I am the bread of life; he who comes to me shall not hunger, and he who believes in me shall never thirst."

John 6:35

"What do you seek?" asked Jesus of the two disciples who first followed Him.

The answer each person makes to this question both tests and determines his character and his destiny. What do you seek—truth, character, usefulness, love, the kingdom of God? For what port are you steering? Holding out his empty cup, man can get it filled only to its capacity. By his willingness to surrender, and the measure of his consecration, man determines what keys he will hold, what treasure houses he will open.

"Come and see," was the Master's invitation. Learn the facts. See what Jesus has done for others. See what He has done for the world. The best, most convincing proof is to go to the Master. Then you will learn how incomplete life has been as you have tried to travel your way alone.

Hawthorne compares Christianity to a grand cathedral with divinely wrought windows. Viewed from without, these windows give not the slightest conception of the beautiful forms and radiant colors which are manifest to those looking at them from within.

Some fail to find Christianity because they do not see the real facts. They only see incidental evils and outward appearances. Mr. Spurgeon tells the story of a man who was invited to come into an orchard to eat some fruit. He refused for he said that he had picked up some of the apples that had fallen by the roadside, and they were of poor quality and tasted bitter. The owner replied that those border trees had been placed there on purpose so that boys would not be attracted to the orchard to steal. "Come inside," he said, "for here the apples are delicious."

Whenever one accepts the invitation from Christ and allows Him to come into his life, what a change takes place! The disciples accepted Christ. Simple fishermen became Christ's apostles, leaders in a kingdom which has been transforming the world, changing the soft, base charcoal of life without Christ into rarest diamonds. The disciples were far from faultless. But because of yielded lives they became powers for good. This can be so for each of us.

TODAY'S THOUGHT: *He who enters the service of the Lord has a job with an unlimited future.*

SEPTEMBER 6

Prayer Brings Release and Inner Peace

Is any one among you suffering? Let him pray. James 5:13

Have you ever watched tightrope walkers? If you have, I am sure you have been amazed at their ability to keep their balance on that thin taut wire high in the air. I am sure, too, that you have noticed they carry a long pole in their hands. By this means they are able to keep their balance at great heights. If the pole were taken away, these skilled performers would never be able to make the trip from platform to platform. In life we all need something to hold on to, some kind of balancing pole to keep us from falling. The memorizing of verses of Scripture or hymns or prayers gives a man a balancing pole. Each day we have a journey to make. Sometimes it is as difficult and precarious as the journey of the tightrope walkers, but we can always be assured of safe arrival at the end of day, if Christ our companion is helping us keep balance. We cannot, however, leave it all to Him. There is something we must do, also.

During the war the chaplain of a bombing squadron frequently got together with the men before the planes took off. One morning a crew newly arrived from the States was to make its first flight. The chaplain let them have it straight from the shoulder. He said, "Prayers cannot hold you up, boys, but your knowledge of aviation will."

A frightened young pilot replied, "You mean we shouldn't pray? You mean prayers aren't worth anything?"

"I do not mean that at all," said the chaplain. "Prayer has brought many a plane home safely, not because it gave the craft a magical immunity, but because it gave the crew peace, and courage, and faith, and enabled them to bring their plane home safely."

When we possess the inner peace which comes from knowing God, tremendous energies become ours, energies that we never realized were ours.

TODAY'S THOUGHT: *Since time began God has been the source of all power.*

250

SEPTEMBER 7

The Divine Multiplication Table

Do not neglect the gift you have. 1 Timothy 4:14

Whatever we have is a gift from God. Our many talents, our time, our influence—or whatever else it is, came from God and should be dedicated to His service.

No one ought to think lightly of God's gift because it is small. Remember the significance of the widow's mite, or the cry of the penitent thief on the cross, or the loaves and fish of the little boy.

Perhaps you are wishing that your mite could be a great offering for the church you love. But you only have a very little to give, and you feel it is insignificant. Give what you have, and God will use and bless it as much as, or more than, some of the greater gifts which He has received. You are thinking it would have been glorious to have lived with Jesus back there in Judea, and to have had the privilege of ministering to Him as Martha and Mary did. What an escape from reality! You need not have lived then. You can minister to Jesus now. Go, help your neighbors. Hold out a friendly hand to those you meet who are in trouble. Always be kind in your judgments of others. Living like that, you will be ministering to Jesus.

The Master does not ask us to do great things, unless He has given us great talents. All that He expects is that we do the very best we can. If we have been given only a little, He will not expect from us the same as from those whom He gave much. What you have is significant to God, and that is the important thing. Perhaps you alone are called upon to do a very special work, an assignment unknown to all other people. If you do not carry it through to completion, it will never be done. Seek the will of God for your life today. Try to find your purpose for living, and then go out and fulfill it.

Of one thing we all can be certain. All about us there is a hungry multitude of God's needy children. Many of them are starving for want of the peace and comfort of religion. You who have found peace, you who know the blessings of your Father, take time to minister to those who are less fortunate. By the grace of God you can direct them to Him who is the answer to every one of their needs. Doing so will lead into a wonderful way of life.

TODAY'S THOUGHT: *If you would satisfy the deep hunger of your soul, enlist for service, and distribute your love in generous helpings.*

SEPTEMBER 8

Faith Overcomes Fear

For in it the righteousness of God is revealed through faith for faith; as it is written, "He who through faith is righteous shall live."

Romans 1:17

A young father wanted to teach his two-year-old son what faith is. So he boosted him up on a table, stood back several feet and commanded, "Jump, Son, jump."

"I can't, Daddy, I'm afraid," replied the little boy.

"I'll catch you," said the father. "Look right at me and jump."

The boy drew himself up, ready to jump, but stopped to look at the floor below and hesitated again, "I'm still afraid."

"Darling, didn't I tell you I would catch you? Do you think Daddy would let you fall? Now look me right in the eye and jump. Don't take your eyes off me. Don't look at the floor. Jump!"

The boy leaped into his father's arms.

Delighted, he said, "Daddy, let me jump again." Now his boy had faith. He was confident that his father would surely be there to catch him.

How many times have we not doubted God? Although He promised us that His everlasting arms will receive us, we still have feared the darkness around us and have not dared to venture forth. The secret is to look away from the difficulty we fear, and instead keep our eyes fixed on Him who never fails. How strong then will not our faith in Him become!

A ship was tossing on a stormy sea, and angry waves were washing the deck, when the passengers heard the loud speakers blare, "Abandon ship. Man the lifeboats." But the boats seemed such tiny and fragile things in which to entrust their lives! Even the bravest passengers were desperately afraid. One of the first to step down into a lifeboat was a delicate woman with a child in her arms and a little boy clinging to her dress.

"Are you afraid?" a man nearby asked the boy.

"I don't like the storm, but Mother is here," the boy answered.

Turning to the mother, the man asked again, "Are you afraid of the storm?" She shook her head, pointed upward and said, "God rules the storm, sir, and I am not afraid, for He is my heavenly Father." Peace will flood our hearts, if once we stop to let faith remind us that God is in His heavens, ruling our world.

TODAY'S THOUGHT: *Does it take courage for you to place your life in the hands of Him who holds up the world?*

SEPTEMBER 9

Happiness Is Twice Blest When Shared

Each one must do as he has made up his mind, not reluctantly or under compulsion, for God loves a cheerful giver. 2 Corinthians 9:7

A recent magazine article, entitled, "Don't Be Afraid of Sentiment," told the story of a Scottish minister who came to his first church very young and inexperienced. As he began his work, he felt as if he were not doing a good job. He imagined that his people were looking upon him with pity and contempt. Then one day to his chagrin the stern Scotchmen who were his church elders filed solemnly into his vestry. But they had not come to reprove. They had come to persuade him not to be afraid.

"Next Sabbath before you begin to speak," they said, "we ask you to say to yourself, 'they are all loving me' and it will be true. From the oldest to the youngest we will be loving you very much." This act of kindness was the start of a happier, more confident life for this man, and for all who looked to him for guidance.

One writer put it this way: "We are all lonely under the stars, all strangers and sojourners here upon earth." We will accomplish a great deal if we, each one, make a place of warmth and comfort for one another.

Too often we fail in our duty to our fellow men. We miss a chance to bring them encouragement and joy, because we are spending all our time complaining about our problems. We would all enjoy life more, if we remembered our good fortune, saying, "I have so much for which to be thankful. I will look to the bright side, and not let life's misfortunes crowd out the joy of living."

Why not ask yourself, "How much do I want happiness? Do I want it enough to do something about it, to live and share it with everyone I meet?" Remember that such everyday things as a pleasant voice, a cheerful smile, and a constant practice of the Golden Rule are simple means of sharing peace with others. Try bestowing these easy-to-give gifts on your friends. You will soon receive happiness and all the other satisfactions which you desire. You will be a living illustration of the words of our Lord: "It is more blessed to give than to receive."

TODAY'S THOUGHT: *Sing with happiness, and you will harmonize with your world.*

SEPTEMBER 10

Purpose Yields Power

For God did not give us a spirit of timidity but a spirit of power and love and self-control. 2 Timothy 1:7

Many live today without hope. For them life has no purpose, no meaning. They start constructing palaces, only to have them tumble in ruins, all because they do not possess the sufficiency to finish the task. We too often fail because we do not realize that living is not merely existing twenty-four hours a day, but rather living is to live "for" something—to live for God.

Life has a divine purpose, and we must seek it out and make it our own. Our lives ought to become God-centered, otherwise there will be nothing to show for them but a series of disappointments. Our dreams will come and go, and never be fulfilled.

When a man is dedicated to a goal, and then reaches up for the power of God, he will be given strength to fulfill that goal. No matter how weak and insignificant may be his state, if he feels that by the help of God he is doing something worth while, he will surmount every difficulty and ultimately gain the victory.

Think now of a buoy fastened securely to a rock in the sea. No matter how the winds may rip up the sea, the buoy's position remains constant. The angry waves splash harmlessly around it. The tide rises and falls, but the buoy is still there. The billows rush upon that little object, and for a moment you think it has been swept away, submerged in the rushing torrent, but suddenly it bobs up on the surface again. It is in its place again, unmoved and unharmed.

Here is a real picture of the conquering life! By the power of God the soul is enabled to rise above an opponent, conquer any fear, overcome any difficulty. The time may come when it will seem as if the battle is lost, but suddenly God will give us the strength needed to rise again, and to live on from victory unto victory.

TODAY'S THOUGHT: *The anchor of your life will hold if it is tied to Christ. You cannot but triumph.*

SEPTEMBER 11

Both Joy and Sorrow Will Come

Restore to me the joy of thy salvation, and uphold me with a willing spirit. Psalm 51:12

The life of Jesus is meant to be an example for His people. What He does, we ought to do. Does He suffer? Then we too must suffer. For Him there was a lowly birth, a tedious path of patient learning and the apprenticeship to a carpenter's bench, a stormy three years of ministry, fraught with temptation, and opposition, a cruel cross. Then came the glorious resurrection and ascension, and the opening of those everlasting doors of heaven.

So it must be for all of us, cut off from the visible presence of Christ. Whatever our rank, regardless of whether we are poor, sick, and helpless, or favored and pampered, we must at last all pass through our school of experience and sorrow. We must bear His cross, and we shall be tempted. Lent comes before Easter. The blasting storms of sin and their trials always precede the crown. Sorrow endures for the night, but joy comes in the morning.

Even as the Master was led by the Holy Spirit into the Judean wilderness to be tempted by the devil, so we too are led through the wilderness of the world to face daily temptation. Sometimes the devil may leave us "for a while," but even as he tempted Jesus throughout His life, so he will tempt us as long as we live.

We would be wise to note that it is after great spiritual blessings that we should especially be on our guard. For blessings are likely to be followed by the most severe temptations. The devil is happiest when he conquers those most deeply committed to the Lord. Whenever our hearts have been strongly moved by a deep experience, it is then the devil likes to attack and conquer. It is during sessions of spiritual discipline that the evil one is more active. Constantly we must be on guard, and never relax our vigil. When we succumb to temptation and fall into sin, we are most miserable. But when we seek God's help in order to stand, a great joy and peace diffuses mind and body. "Great peace have they who love the Lord!"

TODAY'S THOUGHT: *Salvation is the costly pearl and faith in a Calvary Christ is the price to claim it.*

Love Shall Reign Immortal When the Worlds Lie Dead

Who shall separate us from the love of Christ? Shall tribulation, or distress, or persecution, or famine, or nakedness, or peril, or sword? Romans 8:35

Jesus gave us a pattern for living when He told us that we should love one another even as He loves us. We ought always to remember that low hill, and the slivered cross whereon Jesus was crucified. Never once in life or in death did He ever show any hatred or bitterness toward His fellow men. For His love encircled both those who were His friends and those who were His enemies. When He taught us to pray He said, "Pray then like this: . . . 'forgive us our debts, as we also have forgiven our debtors.'" What the world needs today more than anything else is a people determined to practice the gospel of love as lived by the Master.

Love is a tremendous thing. It is the only language the whole world understands. It must be the foundation stone of every home. It alone is the power that can create citizens who will stand strong and resist temptation and become leaders in our community.

The students of John Hopkins University made a survey. They went into the tenement districts of New York City, and chose 200 children whose lives they would follow as they grew up. They assumed that most of these children, because of their socially depressed environment, would some day end up in a reformatory or a prison. Some years later when the survey was completed and the case histories checked, of the 75 they were able to follow, they were amazed to find that only five had any kind of prison record. When they asked these people what had most influenced their lives, they all gave the same answer. They said, "We had a teacher." The university researchers discovered her to be a tiny, old lady with little education, who had given her entire life to this school in the slums. So they went to her and asked her to show them the methods she had used in teaching these children.

She replied, "I didn't use any method. I just loved them!"

That was Christ's method. It is still the only method that will solve the unfolding problems of an individual in today's world.

TODAY'S THOUGHT:
> "The night has a thousand eyes, And the day but one;
> Yet the light of a whole life dies When love is done."

SEPTEMBER 13

God Will Never Forsake Us

But I call upon God; and the Lord will save me. Psalm 55:16

There are times in our lives when we must pass through the fiery furnace of trouble. If we live in the assurance that the Son of God is with us, we can be brave in our trials. There are times when the battle of life becomes severe, and the temptations of the evil one attack us like a cloud of arrows. Our spiritual enemies surround us. It is then that we need courage to fight bravely, lest we fall and suffer the remorse of sin.

One of the saddest of all sights is that of a man who wants to do right and yet who does not have the fortitude to withstand falling into sin. The really happy people are those who have decided to do right at any cost. Constantly they listen to the voice of God, and follow His directions in every area of their lives.

Our hope must be something more than the world can give us, for if it is not, we shall remain forever unsatisfied. Man's soul will be restless unless the clear light of heaven floods his being. I hope you answer the question, "Where is your hope?" in this confident manner: "My hope is in God. He has never failed me, nor has He ever forsaken me. He is the one person who can be trusted. When mountains of sorrow overwhelm me, He is there. He will lead me through. Though my enemies attack me, His forces are stronger than all those of the world. Though I am called upon to walk through the valley of the shadow of death, He is there, and I will fear no evil, for He will be with me to lead me on." This is an assurance that a man can live by.

In our lifetime we may lose our health, our money, and even most of our friends. But there is One whose friendship we need never lose, One who gives riches that are more than all the money in the world, One who is able to give us eternal life. He has assured us that we need never give up our hope in Him.

There is a little flower which forces its way through the deep snows of the Alps and hangs its tiny, bell-shaped blossom over the icy cleft. Our hope should be like that Alpine flower. It should help us force our way through the sorrows of life, and lift us up above the wintry snows of trouble toward the heavens. In heaven Jesus promises a home where we shall be like Him and see Him as He is.

TODAY'S THOUGHT: *When the worst has happened, then ask God to help you wrest the best from out of it.*

SEPTEMBER 14

To Follow HIM Means to Take Up a Cross

Do not boast about tomorrow, for you do not know what a day may bring forth. Proverbs 27:1

Following our Master on the way to Golgotha, we meet Simon the Cyrenian, who was compelled to bear the cross of Christ. On some errand of business or pleasure, Simon was on the way from his country home to Jerusalem. Little did he exepect to meet Jesus or to have to bear His cross! Yet that day was to be the turning point of Simon's life. There can be little doubt that, having borne the cross of Christ that day, Simon became from thenceforth a Christian and carried that cross throughout his life. He is spoken of as the father of Alexander and Rufus, and we find Paul some 25 years later greeting Rufus in these words: "Chosen in the Lord." Thus from this seemingly accidental meeting, as he was coming out of the country, Simon of Cyrene and his entire household became Christians.

It often happens just that suddenly. When we least expect it, and are coming out of the country to our business or pleasure in the town, the cross is laid upon us. The letter or telegram brings bad news. The shadow of sickness or death falls on our home. In all this we see that we have been asked to bear a cross. Sometimes it seems so difficult to bear. And yet how glorious it becomes for us, when it brings us closer to God.

Simon found a cross, but he also found a Savior. So, we may be sure, we are nearest Jesus when we are treading the way of the cross, that narrow way which leads to life eternal. In every true Christian's life there must be a crucifixion. If we would partake of Christ's glory, we must share His suffering. We must go with Jesus to Calvary.

We have all known sorrows, but perhaps we have not recognized them as the crosses through which we may find God. A business man may spend his time striving for gain, but misfortune descends upon him and failure appears to be his lot. Perhaps in his love of earthly treasure he built a barrier separating him from his Christ. So it could be that his cross of failure could become his resurrection.

Apparent defeat becomes ultimate victory, if we but allow God to reveal His intended lesson.

TODAY'S THOUGHT: *The larger the island of your faith becomes, the longer will be the shoreline of patience demanded.*

SEPTEMBER 15

Our Lord Demands Unquestioning Loyalty

Blessed are those servants whom the master finds awake when he comes. Luke 12:37

History tells the story of Cassabiansia, a brave boy, who was placed at a certain shipboard spot to perform a particular duty in the battle of the Nile. He was bidden to remain there until relieved by his father. Unknown to Cassabiansia his father was killed. The ship caught fire and the sailors began to desert the doomed vessel. Again and again the boy cried out, "Father, may I go!" But no answer came. The child stood alone on the burning deck and perished at his post.

A Christian must show a like loyalty to his heavenly Father, if he is to know the meaning of victory. But to conquer we must know the proper weapons. David refused to fight Goliath clad in borrowed armor which he had not proved. Just so we should mistrust the world's untested protections against the day when we stand in judgment. One voice in the world will say, "You don't need God or the church. Just lead a good life. Be a respectable person. That is all that is necessary." Another will say, "You have always been generous to those in need and have given them money. You can be sure heaven will welcome you. The victory is yours."

There is only one tried and tested way, and that is to believe in the Lord Jesus Christ, to keep in constant touch with Him, and to obey His orders, though it may even mean the sacrifice of your very life. To fight this kind of battle, we must keep in training. It will not do to run the race for a while and then fall back into idleness, sloth, and sin. To keep ourselves fit by training will mean giving up certain things our sinful flesh likes. It means casting off the impediment which hinders us from fighting the good fight.

A soldier forgets his own comfort in his eagerness to gain the victory. When a certain Roman general determined on a conquest he would put his troops ashore, and then burn his boats to prevent any possible retreat.

If we are to conquer in the life and death struggle with our old nature, we ought to cut off every avenue permitting retreat to the old habits. We must burn our boats. If you knew the cunning of your adversary, you would give up all hindrances to gain the victory.

TODAY'S THOUGHT: *Let the shadow of the cross fall between you and the vain world.*

259

"Whoever" Means You

For a man's ways are before the eyes of the Lord, and he watches all his paths. Proverbs 5:21

Some years ago many a mountain climber lost his life by reason of defective ropes. At a crucial moment when the full weight of the climber drew it taut, the rope would sever and so another climber would plunge to his death. Finally a mountain-climbing club decided to do something about the problem of insecure ropes. Their efforts brought a marked improvement in the quality of rope making materials, as well as in the way the ropes were made. Today ropes that pass the inspection of this club are guaranteed to hold, and these ropes are uniquely identified by a crimson thread running through them.

As we climb the mountains along the highway of life only one rope is safe, the one having the crimson thread of Christ's blood woven through it. No matter what enters our lives, that rope is sure to hold because it has been tested on Calvary's cross. Whoever holds fast to this rope, will never be lost. This rope is free for the asking and every climber of life's steeps may possess it.

A missionary was working with a group of underprivileged city children. He put a dime under a book on the table.

"Whoever believes, let him come and take it," he said. He waited. Nobody came. Finally a ragged little lad came up, took the dime, and thanked the missionary.

"What is your name?" the missionary asked.

"Tom Jones," was the reply.

"Did I say Tom Jones could have the dime?" the man continued.

"No, sir," replied the boy, "but you said 'whoever,' and that means me, doesn't it?"

"It surely does," answered the missionary. "You get the dime. I want you to remember always that when it says 'whoever believes in the Lord Jesus Christ will have eternal life,' that means you, too."

We live in doubt because we have failed to appreciate how personal are the promises God has made. We can be everlastingly rich, if we will only accept the things which God offers us every day.

TODAY'S THOUGHT: *God has offered us His friendship, and that includes comfort and companionship.*

SEPTEMBER 17

"Swing Low, Sweet Chariot!"

Truly, truly, I say to you, he who hears my word and believes him who sent me, has eternal life; he does not come into judgment, but has passed from death to life. John 5:24

Of some things we can be certain, if we believe God's Word. Death for the Christian will be a victory. The Apostle Paul was ready to be offered, because he knew that what seemed like death was really the crown eternal. No more would he know the hard warfare, no more the bitter struggle with temptation and sin, no more the weary watching of the long campaign of life. His earthly life had been like a beseiged city, with inward troubles and with outward foes; but in death he would hear the trumpets of the angels. He would hear their song proclaiming, "Thanks be to God, who gives us the victory through our Lord Jesus Christ."

We who belong to Christ and believe His Word know that death will bring us rest. "Blessed are the dead who die in the Lord . . . that they may rest from their labors." It will not be the resting of idleness, however, but the rest that we all crave, the knowledge that care and anxiety are gone, that the pain of suffering is removed, and that doubts and fears are impossible.

To those who believe in the promise of God's Word, death means a continuation of life in a higher, nobler form. We live in an earthly school, filled with petty jealousies, selfish desires, narrow horizons, and divisive elements. At death we pass into the company of saints and angels. At death our eyes close to all earthly things, but to reopen to see what earthly sight cannot behold. Though eternal life surpasses anything that man's understanding conjures up, we can only dimly picture the glorious freedom of the sons of God in Paradise. All thought of self will be lost in the contemplation of His glory. There we will do His will perfectly. The ruling principle will be love, and consequently we will love our fellow men as God loves them. It is not important to know the details of the future. If we love God, we know that all will be wonderful. Our main concern should be that we are prepared when He calls us home.

TODAY'S THOUGHT: *Think earnestly for one minute of your chances to get to heaven! "Three surprises await me that day," said Luther, thinking about heaven. "One, I will miss some I felt certain would be there; two, I will be amazed to see others I was so cocksure would not be there; and, thirdly, and the greatest surprise of all, is that I, miserable sinner, was granted an entrance."*

SEPTEMBER 18

Revenge Is No Remedy

Forbearing one another and, if one has a complaint against another, forgiving each other; as the Lord has forgiven you, so you also must forgive. Colossians 3:13

An old proverb tells us that "The remedy for injury is not to remember it." He who suffers from mental or spiritual injury inflicted by another has the choice of doing various things. He may seek vengeance; he may let the matter work as a cancer in his mind; or he may follow Christ's way of forgiving and forgetting. Vengeance is never a remedy, for it always acts as a boomerang, and the result is harder on the one seeking vengeance than on the on who receives it. If when we are hurt we harbor ill will we are robbed of peace of mind. Only if we seek reconciliation, will we be relieved of our distress. In reconciliation there is also the distinct possibility of our regaining a lost friend.

The Norwegian writer, Johan Bojer, in his book, *The Great Hunger,* tells of a man whose little son was killed by a neighbor's dog. Revenge could not satisfy this man. He found a better way to relieve the agony of his heart. When a famine plagued the people and his neighbor's fields lay bare, the man with a bleeding heart knew thereby that his neighbor had no corn to plant for the next year's harvest. So he set out under cover of night to sow his neighbor's field with corn, explaining, "I went out and sowed seed in my enemy's field that God might exist."

An old Arabian proverb says, "Pardon is the choicest flower of victory." We who expect God to forgive us certainly should ask Him for grace that we might forgive others. We should forgive not only because we know it is God's will that we do, but also because we cannot be happy unless we forgive. No man holding a grudge against others can have the peace of mind and heart which comes to people who live as did our Master, and who are willing to love even those who despitefully use them.

Whenever you are tempted to seek revenge, think of your Master, of the perfect example when He, being tormented by the pains of hell on the cross, prays for His crucifiers saying, "Father, forgive them; for they know not what they do."

TODAY'S THOUGHT: *We cannot do everything, but we must do something, even if that something is only to speak a word of forgiveness.*

SEPTEMBER 19

The Time Is Now

This is the day which the Lord has made; let us rejoice and be glad in it. Psalm 118:24

When someone is discussing a great personality, do you ever say to yourself, "I would like to live that kind of life. I want my life to count for more, but where do I begin?"

The old adage about burning the candle at both ends is, generally speaking, not good advice. But Henry van Dyke has well said, "It is better to burn the candle at both ends and in the middle, too, than to put it away in the closet and let the mice eat it."

Like a poor boy with a shining coin, who takes it out again and again to look at it, we should look often at Jesus' Word, "Whoever would save his life will lose it." We are saved to serve. It is wonderful to light our candle early in life, so that God can enjoy the full benefit of it. It is sad to see people waste most of their lives and then, coming late, fling the snuffings at the Master's feet. They let youth's vital, hot flame dissipate into thin air, missing out on the true joys of living.

A neighbor influenced a 90-year-old man, who had never had any use for the church, to attend an evangelistic service one evening. The old man was deeply touched, and when the minister invited his listeners to come forward and dedicate their lives to Christ, the old man struggled to his feet.

"I was a long time coming," he said in a quavering voice, "but I guess I am still in time."

There is joy in heaven over every lost soul that turns to Christ in repentance, even as there was joy when the penitent thief turned to Christ in the last moment of his life. It is a great comfort to know that it is never too late for a man to mend his ways.

But how much more meaning would come into our lives, if we lived for Christ all the time! Think of the happy days we miss because we try to run our lives alone. Think of the joy we never know because we do not realize that He will forgive our sins and lead us to victory. Think of the moments of satisfaction that are not ours because we fail to serve our fellow men.

Now is the time to give yourself to God.

TODAY'S THOUGHT: *Walking alone, we can lose our way even on a well-marked path; taking God's hand, we can travel on the super highway.*

One Step Enough

I tell you, do not be anxious about your life . . . Is not life more than food, and the body more than clothing? Matthew 6:25

Our goal of being like Christ is always far out ahead of us. The most mature Christian has something to attain. The Christian life remains constantly a growing promise, and the real fulfillment does not come until we arrive home in glory to be perfected by our God. This is one of the great challenges of our Christian faith. It is the glory of our religion.

A teacher tells of a small boy who, on his first day in kindergarten, wandered around examining the low tables, the chairs, the cupboards, and the coat racks. Everything was just the right size for a five-year-old. Finally he walked up to the teacher and said, "I don't like it here. There is nothing to grow up to."

A man is spurred on and challenged by having dreams, objectives, and goals. We should not complain because they are there. Rather we should strive unceasingly to attain them. So often, however, life becomes a burden, and because our objectives seem so impossible to reach, we let life grind to a standstill.

Some time ago in California a man who loved the out-of-doors began to cut down trees to build himself a log house. A friend who knew of his purpose and also of his extreme age said to him, "Isn't it too large an undertaking to one who is no longer young?"

"It would be," answered the naturalist, "if I looked beyond the chopping of the trees and the sawing of the logs, and pictured myself laying the foundation there, erecting the walls, and putting on the roof. But why carry the whole load all at once and let myself be exhausted? It isn't much of a job to cut down this little tree, and that is my only job at the moment."

The man was wise in concluding that he must do only one thing at a time. His objective was large, but he knew that it could be attained, if he faced tasks as they came to him.

So it can be with us. Nothing is impossible, if we face our challenge one day at a time.

TODAY'S THOUGHT: *In giving us the gift of time, God has also given us with it an opportunity to explore the glorious deeps of a lifelong friendship with Him.*

SEPTEMBER 21
Worship Tends the Life Line

I call upon the Lord, who is worthy to be praised, and I am saved from my enemies. Psalm 18:3

The Dutch have a legend about a spider. Now this spider was a respectable, well-behaved creature living high in the rafters of a barn. One day it looked down from its rafter and said to itself, "I wonder what the world below is like." The adventurous spider then swung downward on its long, sturdy thread, and came to rest on a beam far below. Pleased with its new surroundings, it spread its web and set up a home. There it lived, spending long days catching flies and growing fat and prosperous.

Then it noticed the long, sturdy thread running into the darkness high above. The puzzled spider said, "I wonder what that thread is for. I cannot see its purpose; I will do without it." So the spider broke the thread and its little world collapsed.

Like the forgetful spider, man grown fat, prosperous, and self-sufficient cuts his ties with God. He acts as if he were the only god he needs. But when that tie is severed, his whole world tumbles down about him. How many times have you heard people say, "What good is there in going to church or reading the Bible or spending time in prayer?" Ought they not remember that these acts of worship build a tie between the security of heaven and the instability of earth? Church worship gathers spiritual reserves that brace us in times of trouble and bring us out again into the sunshine of His smile.

A party of inexperienced men once climbed a mountain in Switzerland during stormy weather. They made their ascent on the sheltered side. At the top, exhilarated by the thought of the view before them, they stood up to survey the beauty about them. They were almost blown over by the wind. The guide caught them and pulled them down.

"On your knees, men," he said, "you are only safe when you are on your knees."

So it is when the fierce winds of misfortune sweep down upon us; prayer to God and faith give power to keep our footing. Wisely we keep intact that precious tie twixt heaven and earth.

TODAY'S THOUGHT: *No hour is ever so full that a minute cannot be spared for guidance and help.*

SEPTEMBER 22

Look Closer at the Face Beside You

Truly God is good to the upright, to those who are pure in heart.
Psalm 73:1

It is so difficult for our finite minds to understand the infinite love of God. And yet, when we think about human love and remember that God's love is much greater than that, we catch a glimpse of God's love.

The daughter of a certain poor widow followed bad companions into the paths of sin. She ran away, leaving her mother alone in their modest home. The mother then turned to her only resource: prayer. But that was enough. Her petitions were heard because she had faith to believe they would be. One day, close to midnight, the daughter returned home and was surprised to find the door unlocked.

"My child," said the mother, "the door has never been locked since you left. I knew you would come home some day, and I didn't want to keep you waiting a single minute."

God never keeps us waiting. When we commit sin and wander away from the household of faith, He keeps the door to the Father's house unlocked, hoping for our return and waiting to receive us, if we repent.

God not only awaits our return, but seeks us anxiously, hoping with His great love to bring us back.

Here is an experience which changed the life of a tramp begging on the streets. He touched a passerby on the shoulder.

"Mister, please give me a dime," he said.

Their eyes met and the tramp recognized the face of his own father. "Father, don't you know me?"

Throwing his arms around the son, the father answered, "I have found you. At last I have found you. All I have is yours."

Think of it! A tramp begging his own father for ten cents, when for years the father had been looking for him, longing to give him all that he had.

Like that is the great love of God, your heavenly Father.

TODAY'S THOUGHT: *Let the love of God be the stabbing spotlight to guide you out of the land of doubt and despair into the land of faith and hope.*

SEPTEMBER 23

Heaven Is Our Hope

For I know the plans I have for you, says the Lord, plans for welfare and not for evil, to give you a future and a hope.

Jeremiah 29:11

The hope of heaven should cheer us in all time of disappointment and loss. It is very difficult seeing things for which we have long labored suddenly fade away as does a dream when one awakens. It is hard to see the prize for which we have striven so hard snatched from our grasp. It is hard to see our friends dropping one by one from the path of life and leaving us to journey alone.

But the thought of heaven brings comfort. At bedtime the child is reluctant to part with its playthings, but it cheers itself with the thought, "I shall find them in the morning."

We, too, should be cheered. We should be satisfied to lose for a moment what we love so much, when we know for certain that we can find it again in the morning.

The hope of heaven should remind us of our unfinished work. "Work while it is called day," advised our Lord. How much work for God remains to be done and how short is the time left to us to do it in! How many evil habits there are needing to be conquered! How many sinful desires needing to be crushed! How many mistakes to be corrected! How many sins for which to seek forgiveness before the time comes when we can lie down to rest.

Today let us humbly ask ourselves these questions: "When our life is finished, what will it be? The end of a selfish existence? A life lived for pleasure and gain instead of for God? Or in faith and humility will we be able to say, 'I have finished my course. With your help, Lord, I have done the very best that I could'?"

The faith by which we know that our Lord has prepared us a place should make us fearless to meet death under any circumstance. Our faith teaches that death is but the swinging door opening to the Lord's palace, that we do not take that last journey alone, for even through the valley of the shadow of death He will be walking at our side. We need fear no evil. He will not leave us nor forsake us.

TODAY'S THOUGHT: *In this world we are always just one step away from death; in the next, death will be shut out forever from the Father's house.*

SEPTEMBER 24

Love So Amazing Demands My All

For to this end Christ died and lived again, that he might be Lord both of the dead and of the living. Romans 14:9

Some years ago a farmer in North Carolina drove his team of horses pulling a wagon full of hay to a small village where he had a few errands to do. The horses, young and skittish, were tied to a hitching post. As the man entered the store, he glanced back and saw that the horses had broken loose and were charging down the street. Shouting desperately he sprinted after them and managed to grasp with one hand the bridle of the nearest horse. Pulled by the man's weight the horses swerved sharply and, neighing in fright, reared high in the air on their haunches. The farmer lost his grip on the bridle and tumbled to the ground just as a heavy front hoof came down upon him. Several villagers rushed in and led the shying horses away, while a crowd gathered around the crumpled man, mortally injured. As he lay there dying one of the men stooped down close to his ear and said, "John, why did you give up your life for a pair of horses, a wagon, and a mere load of hay?"

John's eyes opened briefly and he whispered, "Go look in that hay."

The people looked and found a sleeping boy, the man's son for whom he had given his life. And when these people gathered several days later to lay John to rest, not one thought his sacrifice too great.

One day I stood on a hill overlooking Jerusalem. I recalled the time when Jesus had come up over that hill to that very spot, marveling how the view of the city below and its people literally breaks into sight. He had come to be a sacrifice for them. Oh, what pain He knew in His heart when He remembered it was a sacrifice they would pass unheeding. "Would that even today you knew the things that make for peace! But now they are hid from your eyes," was the cry wrung from His grieving heart.

Today is our acceptable time for salvation. The sacrifice was made for every living human being. There is nothing we can add to it. We need only to open our hearts to Him, and give Him His rightful place as King of kings and Lord of lords.

TODAY'S THOUGHT: *Some give Christ a place in their thinking, others even accord Him a prominent place. But since He is satisfied with nothing short of a pre-eminent place, will you give it to Him?*

SEPTEMBER 25

Only One Place for Sin's Crushing Weight

Blessed are those whose iniquities are forgiven, and whose sins are covered. Romans 4:7

One of the great merchants of our day tells an interesting story about his life. As a young man he was a tremendous success, and built up a vast financial empire. But he made the mistake of relying on his money rather than on God. So naturally when he lost his personal fortune, millions of dollars, he thought all was lost. This was in the depression days of the early 30s. Suffering a nervous breakdown, he was hospitalized. When only a shadow of his former self, and seeming to be at death's door, he attended a simple chapel service where he heard the words of this hymn: "Lean, weary one, upon His breast. God will take care of you." He also heard the familiar words from Scripture: "Come to me, all who labor and are heavyladen, and I will give you rest." The inspiration of this service led him to pray, "O Lord, God, please take care of me."

He relates that almost in a moment the crushing weight was lifted from his spirit. He came forth with a soaring sense of relief from the bondage of gathering death, throbbing with the pulse of living hope. His recovery was assured. Since that time he has regained his fortune. And today wherever he goes he witnesses freely about prayer as the sole source of his strength, and the mainspring of his life. God has come to be his first love.

Love knows no limit to its endurance, no end to its trust, no fading of its hope; it can outlast anything. It is in very truth the one thing that still stands when all else has fallen. Our Father's infinite love can reach through to every area of life, helping those who are in desperate need and seek His help. There is only one thing more amazing than His love, and that is our reluctance to claim it.

Constantly God is seeking the sinner to forgive him and to set him in the right direction for his life. By himself man is not able to give life any real meaning. Man is merely a blackened unlit lantern awaiting the flame of God's Holy Spirit, before he can help another soul on the way. God's light will never fail. His love will never let a man go. "Take hold of the hand that never lost a man." cried a veteran Alpine guide to a trembling beginner seeking footing at a dizzy height. A loving Master's hand is reaching for yours!

TODAY'S THOUGHT: *If you will but choose Christ and learn how precious He is, it cannot help but be the choice of a lifetime.*

SEPTEMBER 26

The Holy Spirit, My Advocate

Now there are varities of gifts, but the same Spirit.

1 Corinthians 12:4

You cannot see the wind upon the strings of the Aeolian harp, but you know it is there because of the music. So with our lives. We cannot see the Holy Spirit working in us, but we know He is with us. There are certain gifts which come to those who are led by this strange but significant power.

One of these is faith. How can we believe the doctrines of the church, the tremendous mysteries of the creed, and the difficult sayings of the Bible? How can we believe that God is three persons, yet one God; that Jesus Christ, the everlasting Son of God, became man and is man as well as God; that He died and is alive again, and that although we shall die, we shall rise again and live forever? How can we become so certain of all this as to stake our life on it? By faith, which is the gift of the Holy Spirit! We will never in a long lifetime come to believe by ourselves. St. Paul says, "No one can say 'Jesus is Lord' except by the Holy Spirit."

There are some people who do not believe these truths, because they will not receive the gift of the Holy Spirit. They have never asked for it, and therefore, have never had it. If in spite of all our losses and afflictions, we can believe in God's mercy and love; if only we will trust God for tomorrow, we shall know that God the Holy Spirit is teaching us, guiding us, and giving us the faith.

When we are led by this strange power, we do have courage and endurance. The early Christians suffered for the sake of Christ, enduring tortures too horrible even to think of or speak about. Now, in these easy days, we are not called upon to such martyrdom. We are not thrown to the wild beasts because we are Christians. Yet, in another sense some of us must be martyrs every day. Some must bear the world's scorn and its abuse because they go to church and pray and read their Bibles. Others must bear their troubles bravely, losing neither heart nor faith when sore difficulties are come upon them. All of us know such martyrs. What is the secret of their victorious lives? It is that they know they are not alone. There is the presence of God the Holy Spirit at their side. He is our Advocate, which means "one called to your side."

TODAY'S THOUGHT: *No child of God ever fears the dark, nor the deep darkness of death's vale, nor yet the darkness of despair.*

SEPTEMBER 27

"Father, Forgive Them"

God be merciful to me a sinner! Luke 18:13

The greatest outshining of love the world has ever seen took place on a certain Friday many years ago. Indeed, it was a Good Friday for all those who have anchored their lifesaving peace in the crowning event of that day and so have come to know the salvation through Christ.

When Jesus was dying upon the cross so that, "whoever lives and believes in me (Jesus) shall never die," an angry mob swirled round Him all the while. Yet, there was no fleck of revenge in His heart. Instead, He revealed His love by praying to God in the last moments of His earthly life, "Father, forgive them, for they know not what they do."

Does He not pray that identical prayer now for those among us who thoughtlessly sin and shut Him out of their lives? Although they live in a Christian land, moving past the open doors of thousands of churches as they go to and from their work each week, they live in unbelief and open sin.

Unfortunately, as did the multitudes of old, there are many in our day who come to the cross as mere spectators. To such people the crucifixion of the Son of God was nothing then and is nothing now. Men of old and men of today gaze on the agony of Jesus, and read the same story of His sorrows, yet no feeling of remorse strikes them. No conviction of sin crushes them. They do not see their own handiwork in the crucifixion. There is no stern whisper of conscience to say, "You have a share in this dastardly thing. You crucified Him!"

What kept the Pharisees and governors, the Scribes and priests from kneeling at the foot of the cross, there to receive its blessings? Why did they remain only indifferent spectators instead of joining with the captain of the guard crying, "Surely this was a righteous man!"

Was it not pride in their intellect and education, and also their ignorance? These things kept them back. The same pride keeps so many men from the cross today. Think of what pride can lose for us! The greatest blessing any of us can have, and the only one that can secure for us eternal salvation beyond all shadow of doubt, is that of having faith as a little child!

TODAY'S THOUGHT: *Take care that you do not become full of yourself, for then Christ will have to send you away empty.*

SEPTEMBER 28

The Christian Wears Chains of Love

If I speak in the tongues of men and of angels, but have not love, I am a noisy gong or a clanging cymbal. 1 Corinthians 13:1

All of us belong to God. Because He has been so good to us, we are obligated to work for Him as His faithful servants even to life's end. At this point in your life ask yourself these questions: "What account can I give of my work for Him? Has it only been a part time proposition? Has it been just a matter of church attendance? Has my faith permeated my life, so that each day men have seen that I am a Christian? Have I made of my profession a pulpit?"

The Apostle Paul once called himself the "slave of Christ." But we must remember that Christian slavery sets men free. It leads us into perfect freedom, and soon we discover that the only chain is the chain of love. The Master bought us with His precious blood. "You are not your own; you were bought with a price."

Some time ago there lived a faithful woman working in a mining-country hospital, whom everyone affectionately called Sister Dora. One day a poor pitman was brought in with his right arm shattered. Examining it the doctors decided to amputate. But Sister Dora with rare intuition felt that, with careful nursing, the arm could be saved. She persuaded the doctors to spare it, and after long, faithful care the shattered limb grew well. Soon after this incident, the nurse herself was stricken with illness. Every day the grateful pitman walked miles from his work to inquire about Sister Dora's condition, for he was deeply concerned about her welfare. Always he sent her the same message through the attendant: "Tell her that 'her arm' knocked at the gate to inquire about her well-being."

We belong to God, for He has redeemed our soul. We are not our own. He has every right to expect certain things from His children. Unless we fulfill His hopes for us, we cannot possibly attain peace within our lives. He needs us so that He can be sure His work in the world will be done. But most important, we need Him if life is to have true meaning.

TODAY'S THOUGHT: *God's love is the one thing in the world we can depend upon.*

SEPTEMBER 29

Life's Battle Demands Our Best

Fight the good fight of the faith; take hold of the eternal life to which you were called when you made the good confession in the presence of many witnesses. 1 Timothy 6:12

In olden times when the Greeks fought the Persians they entered the battle willing and even eager to die for their country in order to gain the victory. The Persians, on the other hand, were slaves, and had to be driven to the field by the whips of their leaders. We can easily understand why the Greeks conquered the Persians.

If we want to do our work well, and make it pleasing in the eyes of God, we must do it cheerfully and willingly. God has not chosen to treat us as slaves to be driven to our duty. We must choose to serve Him. He has given us perfect freedom. If we choose Him, He intends our lives to be full of glory.

There are actually many good but mistaken people who never seem to grow in grace because they leave out the sunshine. They fight the battle of life after a fashion, but they are like sick slaves. They do not know the glorious freedom belonging to those who are sons of God.

So often we hear people talking about the miseries of life. If only they tried to do their duty, if only they were conscious of the Master's presence and looked forward to the hope of tomorrow, they would not find the world such a sad place in which to live. There are many people who find living, nothing "but a long headache on a noisy street" because they are not doing faithfully the work God has given them to do.

Truly, no man is lost until he despairs. Every living person is capable of possessing God's eternal, sustaining hope. And this is one of the greatest and most important of Christian graces. We should live and work in this spirit.

TODAY'S THOUGHT: *No matter how impossible your task for tomorrow may seem to be, be hopeful, and you will find it already half-done when faced in that spirit.*

SEPTEMBER 30

Strength from Above

Turn to me and take pity on me; give thy strength to thy servant.
Psalm 86:16

The coming of the Holy Spirit into the world is a great mystery, yet it is one of tremendous significance. The Lord promised that He would not leave us comfortless, that He would send Someone to us, so that we would never again be alone. The presence came at Pentecost, the birthday of the Church. And whenever it enters into our lives, we receive that extra strength to meet dangers and temptations. No other strength will suffice. Education will not give it nor can it provide the means to obtain it. No mere method of man is sufficient. Only as we yield to Christ, our Savior, will we receive the blessing of His presence through the Holy Spirit.

How was it possible that the first disciples were able to carry on His work, to preach in spite of persecution, and to plant the Church far and wide? Think of what these men once were. At one time, afraid to acknowledge Christ, they forsook Him and fled. They hid themselves in an upper room behind bolted doors.

What changed those eleven disciples? What made the denying Peter bold as a lion, and doubtful Thomas faithful and true? What made all of them ready to meet death and persecution for the gospel's sake? One thing: the presence of Christ after the Resurrection, and the coming of the Holy Spirit at Pentecost. These men, ordained to carry on the work of the Church, were empowered with strength which came to them from God. They had a message to preach that enabled them to show people how their lives could be changed.

This message gives anyone the strength to fight temptation and conquer sin. Whoever comes to God earnestly seeking help will find it. If we ask, we shall receive. If we come knocking at the door of mercy, it will be opened unto us. Though we cannot see physically the One who has promised to forgive us, He is as real as our best friend. We cannot see the Holy Spirit coming into our hearts and lives, giving us the power which Christ promised. Here, as always, the kingdom of God comes not with observation. The kingdom of God is within us. Here, as always, "God moves in a mysterious way, His wonders to perform."

TODAY'S THOUGHT: *The Holy Spirit, given the channel of dedicated Christian lives, can perform amazing wonders in this our day.*

OCTOBER 1

Follow the Print of His Wounded Feet

And he said to them, "Follow me, and I will make you fishers of men." Matthew 4:19

Every one of us is following one of two guides and walking one of two ways. Either we are followers of God, as He intended us to be, or we follow the evil one, who leads us down sin's slippery ways. We are walking either the narrow, forbidding way upward toward heaven, or the broad, glamorous road of destruction which leads away. There is no middle path whatsoever. No one of us is clever enough to emulate the circus rider, with one foot on each steed when it comes to plotting our lives. There is but one Master for us to follow, God or Satan. We must all realize the importance of discovering early just who is our ruler and guide and what road we travel, so that, if we have chosen the wrong leader and missed our way, we may be able to turn back before it is too late.

When we were baptized we started on the narrow way and became followers of God, but there are many people who begin a journey and never finish it. A child starts off to school in the morning, but temptations to stop and play and the urging of mischievous companions meet him on the road, and occasionally he turns from the narrow path of duty and never reaches school at all.

In like manner we all began as followers of God. The question is, whom are we now following? We can truthfully answer that we are followers of God only if we have put our trust in Him. Then we will choose to remain close to Him, and pay no heed to the tempter's voice. I like the old Scot's comment about Peter cursing and denying his Lord while mingling with Christ's captors at the fire: "He had nae business with the flunkies." We know God has just the right answers for the many questions that loom in our minds. Knowing that He has traveled the way before, and so knows where He is leading, we can feel deeply confident. So we are unafraid.

If we truly repent, we can know that Jesus will be faithful and just to forgive our sins. Banking on Calvary, change your status from a "hope so" to a "know so" Christian.

We really are not followers of God at all, unless we trust Him all in all.

TODAY'S THOUGHT: *Some of us find it hard to carry the heavy burden of our sins, but why struggle with that load when we can turn it over to God?*

OCTOBER 2

One Plus God Equals a Majority

O my strength, I will sing praises to thee; for thou, O God, art my fortress. Psalm 59:9

Every single human being is important in the sight of God. Each of us is here to do something in this life, and if we do the best we can with what we have we will succeed. If we fail, not to all eternity will that work be finished.

Too often we do not try the task at hand because it seems so insignificant. We refuse to tackle a job unless we feel it is worthy of our talents, thus robbing ourselves of the joy of a job well done. This motto is easy to remember: "I am only one, but yet I am one; I cannot do everything, and yet I can do something. Because I cannot do everything, I will not refuse to do the something that I can do."

A woman standing in front of a magnificent cathedral heard someone behind her say, "Didn't we do a fine piece of work here?" She turned and saw a man in working clothes. Obviously he was not the architect or the contractor, and he seemed so insignificant that she wondered what job he had done.

"Sir, what did you do to help erect this building?" she asked.

"I mixed mortar for two years," was his cheerful reply. The world today needs cheerful, patient, diligent mortar mixers in every area of life. It may not be the easiest task. Mixing the mortar is one of the dirtiest, most disagreeable jobs in constructing a building. But no building could ever be constructed without this kind of help!

It is amazing what God can do with our limited means, if only we turn them over to Him. During a concert the great violinist, Nicolo Paganini, broke every string except one on his violin. Then this gifted musician turned to his audience, lifted his instrument to his chin and began to play, as if to say, "I will bring you music even with one string."

Paganini's experience can teach us a lesson. When you feel deserted and everything seems to be going wrong, why not see what Christ and a poor human soul can do? You will find that the two of you are a majority. With Him you are always victorious, whether you are building a magnificent cathedral or improvising on one string.

TODAY'S THOUGHT: *With one hand cling to God, with the other reach out to your fellow men.*

OCTOBER 3

Harden Not Your Heart

Blessed is the man who fears the Lord always; but he who hardens his heart will fall into calamity. Proverbs 28:14

One of the special marks of a sin-hardened heart is cruelty and indifference to the pain of others. In the heathen days of Rome women and children looked unmoved upon sins of cruel agony. The popular idea of a holiday was not to watch a football game in the arena, but rather to see bloody gladiators battling to death, or the sufferings of Christians being mangled by the hungry lions. People by the tens of thousands gathered to witness these cruel spectacles.

It was much the same at the greatest of all tragedies, the crucifixion of our Lord and Savior, Jesus Christ. The crowd gazed unmoved at the agony of Him who had nothing but good, even praying in His death throes for His crucifiers. They stood there and looked at those strong but gentle hands, a carpenter's hands, which had raised the dead, cleansed the lepers, opened the eyes of the blind, and healed the sick. Those same hands were now torn by the cruel nails. They saw the tender eyes which had looked lovingly on many a sad mourner now glazing with the film of death. They saw the lips which had spoken those wonderful words which rang throughout all Judea, and Galilee, the lips which uttered those peace-bringing words, words which told of the welcome the father had for his wandering prodigal just come home. They saw these lips now cracked and parched with agonizing thirst. The feet which a Magdalene had bathed with her penitential tears, because she had been forgiven, these were now pierced and bleeding.

Yes, it was all nothing to them. Neighbors passed the time of day jesting and gossiping beneath the very shadow of the cross. Gamblers cast dice for the stainless robe of the Master, while the learned ministers of that day's church stood ground, discussing doctrine. The latest news from Caesar's palace was traded for choice bits of guard-room ribaldry by the Roman guard. Traders hawked their wares, while Jesus hung there through the leaden hours on the cross. The prophets words surely match the scene, "Is it nothing to you, all ye that pass by?" We should ask ourselves: Is it any different now than it was that black Friday with a suffering greater than anyone before or after has ever known?

TODAY'S THOUGHT: *Will you look up to that cross? Take your eyes from off the things of the world, and look up at your wounded Savior taking your place.*

OCTOBER 4

Your Life Deserves a Foundation of Solid Rock

Built upon the foundation of the apostles and prophets, Christ Jesus himself being the chief cornerstone. Ephesians 2:20

The commissioner who investigated the bursting of a certain dam near Los Angeles, California, reported that the collapse of the structure was due to faulty foundations. The collapse of that dam cost more than 450 people their lives.

Faulty foundations—in these two words we have the explanation of the moral collapse of so many lives. In building a life a good foundation is even more necessary than in the construction of an actual building. During the early formative years of a child's life parents are responsible for everything their youngsters do—eating, sleeping, working, playing, learning, thinking, feeling, believing. Time and time again investigations indicate that most of the women and men who have gone wrong have lacked early religious training in the home. No attention was given to the moral foundations of their lives, and the children grew up without any instruction in the A-B-C's of character, wholly without reverence for God or man.

Jesus declared a wise man will build his house upon living rock, but the foolish man erects his house upon the sand. Now a rock represents integrity. It is substantial, and does not shift. It will not give way when the storm is up. It is a symbol of permanency, impervious to pelting rains and lashing gales. It can support an enormous weight and withstand vast strain. A great life likewise sinks its shafts down through irritating problems and change. It bears up under periods of crushing strain. It possesses the secret that defies even death, because the good is imperishable like love, which will reign supreme when stars snuff out like candles.

In His word God has promised that He will provide the solid foundation on which to build our lives. It is the Rock of Ages. We can choose this if we will, or we can reject the solid footing He provides, and choose instead our own piece of shifting sand. Maybe it seems to you that the land which God offers seems too expensive a plot of ground on which to build. But unless we are willing to pay the price, and choose to build there, we face nothing but ultimate loss of all. Yet, following God's advice, we shall gloriously succeed.

TODAY'S THOUGHT: *He is mighty foolish who plays truant from the School of Gods Love.*

OCTOBER 5

Open Wide the Windows of Your Soul

For once you were darkness, but now you are light in the Lord; walk as children of light. Ephesians 5:8

Windows have always fascinated me. We can look out through them into the streets of life. The sunlight from God's heaven shines through them into our homes. One can draw the shade to keep the light out, or one can raise it high to let the light in. If we choose, windows can bring the world of loveliness and endless fascination into parlor or kitchen, giving immeasurable space even to the tiniest room in the humblest dwelling. As we look through windows, we are assured that life surrounds us and we are not alone. We look up and we are reminded of our heavenly Father, who is always present to supply our every need.

The soul, too, has its windows through which it may look to see the countless blessings which God has prepared for all who love Him. Sadly enough, however, many of us keep the blinds drawn, failing to claim our rightful heritage.

An old story tells of a man who in a dream had the opportunity of visiting heaven. An angel guide showed him all the beauties of the place. Suddenly he came to a special room where he found many beautiful wrapped packages, and he asked the angel about them. "Why are these here? Are they for some special person, or are they to be given away on some great occasion?"

"No," replied the angel, "these are the blessings which God has provided for His children, but for which they have never called."

The promise of God's Word is this: Ask and ye shall receive. But the secret is that we must ask in faith. If we are really joint heirs with Christ, all of the blessings of heaven will be ours. Then our opportunity is limitless, for God is able to provide anything that we need.

Life will be more abundant if we will only keep the windows open to heaven, and if in faith we seek, for then we shall find. Daniel prayed three times daily at his open window, and what a life his story unfolds. Look! Why not let God show our day what He could do with a soul that really flung wide the shutters of his life!

TODAY'S THOUGHT: *A man has no more right to a faith he does not practice than to a meal he does not pay for.*

279

OCTOBER 6

Share That Love

And above all these put on love, which binds everything together in perfect harmony. Colossians 3:14

We do not have to have one worry about the past. That is, if we will trust in Christ our Savior. One day a little boy went to his pastor and said, "There is one thing God cannot see."

The pastor replied, "No, that cannot be true, for God sees everything."

"But He doesn't," insisted the boy, "He doesn't see my sins when they are covered by the love of Jesus Christ."

We trust God to forgive our mistakes. We can trust Him to give us a glorious future. Whatever be our circumstances, life can have rich meaning for each. We may ride in an old jalopy, but if we have a destination we can be happy on the road. We can be riding in the finest car that money can buy, but if we do not know where we are going we can be the most unhappy person in the world.

There is so much in the world that needs to be done. Most of the world's people do not have enough to eat. So many people are living in tattered tents and under conditions of extreme poverty. There are unnumbered sick people, looking for a doctor's help and medicine to cure. There are acres of lonely people who have never heard of the love of God or of friendship with Christ.

Think of what your own faith means to you. Not for anything in the world would you want to be without it. This thought should inspire us all to share our Christ with the world.

Randy, a U. S. pilot in the Korean War, was shot down and killed. Friends and neighbors came to Randy's parents, bringing flowers and words of sympathy. Meldina, a Negro nurse, lived in a little cottage in the back. She had raised Randy. Friends went to her, too, to give sympathy. But as they came they were surprised to find Meldina smiling. They said, "How can you smile when Randy's gone?" The reply of this truly great Christian soul was, "Mr. Randy has wings that will never fail." On a shaft on the grave of Kermit Roosevelt, a flier downed in World War I, a broken-hearted father, a former president, had inscribed, "He hath outsoared earth's shadows."

This is life eternal to know that God has given us wings that will never fail . . . no never!

TODAY'S THOUGHT: *In dying for our sins, Christ made possible a precious new world citizenship after death.*

OCTOBER 7

Begin Where You Are

And though your beginning was small, your latter days will be very great. Job 8:7

A recent survey asked people to pick their most nagging worry. "I worry most about finding a goal in life," about one-third of the people answered.

Of course, unless we have a goal we cannot hope for victory. Many times, setting our eyes on some distant objective, we begin well, but our goal soon fades and grows obscure. Daily circumstances block our view. We need help beyond ourselves to be led to victory.

A man applying for a position began to apologize for a slip in his past.

"I don't care about the past," the interviewer said. "Start where you stand."

We learn much from past mistakes, but thank God there is always a day of beginning again. If you start where you stand, you will write a new chapter in the Book of Life, or take a new pathway you never would have discovered if, like Lot's wife, you kept continually looking back. As we begin each day there is always One at our side who says, "Take courage, friend. Take courage and push ahead. Start where you stand." In spite of all our sins, our mistakes, and our failures, if we are truly penitent, God's love and enabling power will help us to wrest profit from the most tragic and broken past.

On a hill outside Florence, Italy, in a park overlooking the city, stands a famous statue by Michelangelo. The statue shows David about to slay Goliath. The figure of the young shepherd is graceful and strong, as he lifts his arm to hurl a stone from his sling. But the marvelous fact about the statue is that it was carved from a castoff block of marble, which another artist had worked on and thrown away as useless.

Even so the Great Artist is able to disentomb something of beauty from our mistakes, from what we supposed to be our useless past. He asks only that we turn our lives over to Him.

TODAY'S THOUGHT: *Do you think G. Studdert-Kennedy's observation would match yours, when he said that he never knew yet a man who had changed his life out of fear of hell-fire, but he could count many whom the love of Christ had redeemed from sin and loss?*

OCTOBER 8

God Comforts and Cares for Us

Blessed are those who mourn, for they shall be comforted.
Matthew 5:4

In its original interpretation the word "comfort" means, "called to one side for added strength, encouragement and consolation." It is one of the names given the Holy Spirit, "Comforter." Our word "comfort" is derived from two Latin words, "con," together, and "fortis," strength—made strong together. It pictures the drawing away of sorrow by the transforming and transfiguring infusion of God's Holy Spirit in a human soul. Sorrow literally is compelled to bestow blessings that otherwise would never be. It is not so much soothing sympathy as it is a strengthening and inspiring of the soul thus indwelt. Courage and fresh life pour in like early sunlight into a darkened room.

With God as our partner, our work for the salvation of others wins stubbornly fought ground. Someday the whole world will be redeemed. The kingdom of God will come. Every time we pray the Lord's Prayer we shine afresh that glorious promise. And they who have sown with care over the unbelief and sin of the world will reap and rejoice with a joy unspeakable.

Then God comforts those who mourn by giving forgiveness and cleansed consciences and a hope that is pure. The burdened find in Jesus a comfort beyond all expectation. In all our sorrows He comforts us by making them work out for good, ennobling our character, enlarging our sympathies, and giving us the power wherewith to help others.

He comforts us also by revealing to us, through the eternal word, the world beyond, for which life's hard training would prepare us. When standing on heaven's brighter side we see God's meaning in all, we shall be comforted. Many of the choicest blessings of life can come in no other way. How dull and blind he who never mourns for himself and for others! For one not to care about the sorrows of others is to be as unfeeling as a boar eating his own offspring and as far away as possible from greatness, from heaven and God's angels. Such a person misses the sweetest music which can come to him, the music of being able to lift someone who has fallen along life's way, bearing his "thank you" for the comfort of God.

TODAY'S THOUGHT: *You cannot keep the bats of sin and sorrow from flying close over your head, but you can keep them from nesting in your hair.*

OCTOBER 9

Rejoice in Your Blessings

May the God of hope fill you with all joy and peace in believing.
Romans 15:13

Happy is the man who does not grieve over what he has not, but rejoices in what he has. If we take inventory of ourselves, it is amazing how rich we really are. When one concentrates on his blessings, they not only seem more numerous, but our whole attitude toward life becomes different. So often we wish we were somewhere else or possessed what somebody else has. How few of us know the joy of being deeply grateful for what is ours.

The Red Cross is saving a treasured dollar bill until they find someone who needs it more than Aunt Jenny did. Aunt Jenny, born in slavery, claimed to be 110 years old. She lived alone in her two-room house, doing her own housekeeping and cultivating a tiny patch of cotton in her backyard. The year she gave her dollar to the Red Cross, to help the poor, Aunt Jenny's cotton crop brought in $18. This is what she said, "God told me if I lived a good life, He would prosper everything I planted, and He has." How does our devotion measure up to this act of sacrifice?

Another touching story of sacrifice came out of the American depression of the early 1930's. When news of the depression came to a Christian girls' school in Africa, the Negro girls held an all-night prayer meeting for the poor Americans. Out of their thankfulness for their salvation and for their school, these new Christians decided to give up the goat meat they had twice a week and send the money to America. One dollar and seventy-five cents was actually sent! Which of you ever made such a sacrifice?

Besides material possessions we have countless other blessings. When he was approaching the summit of his life, John Burroughs said that the longer he lived, the more his mind dwelled on the wonderful gifts God has given us in the beauty of His creation. "I am in love with this world," he said. "It has been my home. I have tilled its soil. I have gathered its harvest. I have waited upon its seasons. Always I have reaped what I have sown."

We always do. If we invest our life in the Lord's work, we shall have a bountiful harvest, for He has the power to give the increase. Those who daily walk with God sing and rejoice as they work.

TODAY'S THOUGHT: *"To love" would probably be selected as the most beautiful verb in any tongue, but "to help" should be a close second.*

283

OCTOBER 10

God and You Unlimited

Two are better than one, because they have a good reward for their toil. Ecclesiastes 4:9

South America is the home of the "pitcher" plant. On the stalk below each leaf is a little cup-like growth that is always full of water. The cup keeps full from the time the plant is hardly more than a slender stalk growing until it reaches maturity.

Here is a parable of life. Each person is created differently. Some have many talents, some but few. Yet all God asks is that we use our talents, many or few. We must open our hearts that they may be filled with His love, whether ours is the tender heart of a little child or the full-grown heart of man.

God is present everywhere. If only we open our eyes in faith, we cannot help being affected by His power and strength. Here is an interesting description: "My God is so tall you can't jump over Him. He is so low you can't duck under Him. He is so wide you can't squeeze around Him. You must come in through my Lord." The simple miracle is, you cannot come in through the Lord without a bit of Him rubbing off inside you. And when this happens, you will discover how wonderful it is to have God a part of you.

One author writes of two people attempting a great climb. Their friends tried to hold them back, but they were determined to go.

"There is no precipice too steep for two," shouted one of the climbers back to those who had meant to detain them. That thought is worth remembering. If God is your companion, there is no precipice too steep, no road too rough, no difficulty too perplexing, no sorrow too upsetting, and no duty too arduous. It is wonderful to walk with God whose power is always sufficient to meet our every need.

In His presence there is nothing to worry about. Someone has said, "The eagle that soars in the upper air never worries about crossing rivers." With God as our partner, fear has said its prayers and become faith.

TODAY'S THOUGHT: *If you want a good test of memory, try for instance to remember last week's worries.*

OCTOBER 11

What the World Is Dying for Want of

Swear to me . . . that as I have dealt kindly with you, you also will deal kindly with my father's house. Joshua 2:12

If we are to be happy and useful workers in God's kingdom, we must love not only God but also our neighbor, for this is pure religion and undefiled before God. All too often we think too highly of ourselves, and look down on others. In those moments we need to turn our eyes to Calvary, and see God dying for all His children. We are so onionskinned, easily taking offense and resenting all sorts of imaginary and real injuries inflicted upon us by our fellow men. In moments like these we should turn to Calvary, and listen as Jesus prays for those who despitefully use Him.

Whenever we are impatient and peevishly want things to go our way, we should think of the Master's agony in the Garden of Gethsemane. How He prayed that the cup of suffering might be taken away from Him! How submissively He called upon His father to relieve Him in this moment of sorrow! Yet in the still watch of that night, He was able at last to lift His eyes to heaven and say to God, "Not my will, but thine be done." What a glorious victory that was for man's immortal soul!

When we are tempted to become proud, we should think of our Savior taking the form of a servant, despised and rejected of men.

How do we best show our love? Love can manifest itself in many ways, one of which is kindness in judging others. Some people rejoice when others experience misfortune. There are people who get their greatest pleasure from the heartaches of others. How ready we are to pass harsh judgment on the acts and motives of our fellow men. How difficult to praise another's accomplishments!

If we could look through a microscope at our human world, we should see men and women who ought to love each other as children of God are in bitter conflict in a selfish battle for life. Instead of joining hands for the common good, they fly a banner which reads, "Every man for himself."

Wrapped up in ourselves, we can all too easily be unmindful of our fellow men. So let us resolve to stop in our busy occupations for a moment and turning to God say, "Lord, what would you have me do?"

TODAY'S THOUGHT: *Do not be afraid to utter a little word of kindness just because you feel you cannot preach a sermon on brotherly love.*

OCTOBER 12

Reaching Up in Prayer

But when you pray, go into your room and shut the door and pray to your Father who is in secret. Matthew 6:6

Someone suggests that our prayer life can resemble either a fire extinguisher or fire proofing. Prayer life of the fire-extinguisher type means one used only in emergency. But when it is of the proofing kind it enables us, if we pray without losing heart, to surmount any problem whatsoever. The latter is the only prayer life worth having.

Not long ago a survey was made involving 63 college students. All of them were given four questions to answer. The first question was this, "If you had a child dying, would you pray?" Sixty-two out of the 63 college students answered, "Yes."

The second question was this: "If you were on a boat and the boat was in a storm at sea, would you pray?" Fifty-two out of the 63 said, "Yes."

The third question asked, "If you took a walk one day in the beautiful woods, and the sun was shining and the flowers were blooming, would you pray?" Only 39 of the 63 said, "Yes."

The final question asked, "If you were trying to accomplish something great in life, some great achievement, some great invention, and you finally succeeded and completed it, would you pray?" Only 19 out of the 63 said, "Yes."

Just what do we think prayer is? It is a Christian's vital breath. Prayer is a man reaching his hand toward God, and God reaching down to receive it. Prayer is not just saying, "God, give me . . ." It is saying, "Thank You, God, for the power and strength You give me, rendering my life so fireproof that none of hell's searing fires can reach it to destroy it."

But how should we pray? I have had people come to me and say, "I don't know how to pray."

My reply is this: "Do you mean to tell me you don't know how to talk?"

Prayer is walking and talking with God, as good friends should and do. Our lives would be so different if, counting our blessings, we would only spend more time thanking God in prayer.

TODAY'S THOUGHT: *Go to God and spread out before Him your good news and your bad news, your happiness and your heartbreak.*

OCTOBER 13

Your High Calling

The hope of the righteous ends in gladness, but the expectation of the wicked comes to nought. Proverbs 10:28

Since only the pure in heart can see God, it is important that we strive to live a holy life. The great mark of a Christian is not giving our faith lip service only. Nor does it mean merely the outward observance of forms and ceremonies, such as churchgoing or stewardship. All of these things are important to an end. The mark of marks of a Christian is his striving to lead a holy life. Many who call themselves Christian look back, and secretly long for the desires of the old life. We are loath to empty our hands of the things we should not be doing in order to have God fill them.

Are you trying hard to serve two masters, trying to hold on to the Master and the things of the world at one and the same time? Let us search the secret corners of our hearts to see if some of our Christianity is mere front. Are we consistent in our lives, activated by the same principles in business, in work, and in the home, as we are in God's holy church?

What are the sure marks of a Christian? You are correct in emphasizing that the beginning of everything in our faith is believing on the Lord Jesus Christ. But from then on out we ought to remember every living moment that our believing will lead into righteous living.

There are people who go smugly to bed at night, secure in the thought that they are saved by the simple fact that they believe. Yet all that day they intentionally committed sins which had the Master's disapproval. We would do well to remember His words: "Not every one who says to me, 'Lord, Lord,' shall inherit the kingdom, but he who does the will of my Father who is in heaven."

We must be more than name Christians. We must convince the world that we bear the marks of our Lord, Jesus Christ, especially the one great proof of a consistent life of holy desires and deeds. This is God's will for you, "even your sanctification."

TODAY'S THOUGHT: *Everyone needs something to live for. Why not live for Jesus?*

OCTOBER 14

Surrender Unconditionally to Him

For godly grief produces a repentance that leads to salvation and brings no regret, but worldly grief produces death.

2 Corinthians 7:10

Many wires stretch across our land, carrying unnumbered thousands of volts of electricity for light and power. These wires are carefully insulated at every pole and held aloft so as to be well out of man's reach. If we could reach up far enough to touch one of these wires, death would strike as swift as lightning.

Yet birds light upon them and are not harmed. They rest on the wires safely and contentedly. They are safe because they touch nothing else as they swing on the fully powered wire. The wires are dangerous to us by reason of the fact that, touching the wires also touching the earth, our bodies close the circuit and the current burns us to a crisp.

God would have us seek our safety in complete surrender to His power and love. It is only when we reach out one hand to Him, while still holding fast to the things of earth, that we are in danger.

When we learn that by committing ourselves totally to God we find not only complete safety but also the answers to the questions man is asking, we have learned an important Christian lesson.

A colored woman in Africa came to a missionary and said, "I want to learn to read. Please, I want you to teach me to read Jesus first."

"Why do you want to read the word, Jesus, first?" the missionary inquired.

"If I learn to read Jesus first, everything else will come easier," she replied.

She was precisely right. When we put Christ first in our lives, we find the answers to the questions which baffle us.

Putting Christ first means a total surrender to Him. One woman remarked that it took her a long time to learn that she was unhappy, because she had not handed over the whole keyboard of her life to God. She had tried to play one of the notes herself, and that was enough to turn her life's music into discord. You will never know what beautiful music lies concealed in your life until you surrender it to the great Master, Jesus Christ.

TODAY'S THOUGHT: *Those who love Christ have a vision of heaven constantly before the eyes of their souls.*

OCTOBER 15

When We Know His Peace We Have Unlimited Power

And let the peace of Christ rule in your hearts. Colossians 3:15

A young, misled lad was listening attentively to a man in a rescue mission, forcefully quoting the lines from Kipling's poem, "If" . . . "If you can keep your head when all about you are losing theirs . . ."

After the speech the lad looked up, and referring to those two lines audibly asked, "But what if you can't?"

Many people are asking that question today. Certainly we have discovered our puny strength when alone. But thank God, many others know the unlimited power that comes when we open the door of prayer to receive it. Nor does anyone need to go on an intensive search for that kind of power. In recent years folk have been buying Gieger counters to search for uranium. Many make great personal sacrifices in order to possess them, but few find the costly ore. How frustating to spend one's all in such a search, and then never to find it.

Far different is man's quest for the power of God. It may cost him a price. He may have to give even of his physical life, but in giving his life he receives dividends which make him an heir to eternal life. God's power assures every Christian of victory and the certainty that, linked with the Almighty, no earthly force can prevail against us.

An English psychiatrist wrote, "With peace in his soul a man can face the most terrifying experience. But without peace in his soul he cannot manage a task as simple as writing a letter." The most urgent question of our time is whether man can bear to live without God, because all the problems of life find their solution when man has peace in his soul.

There is only one way to gain that peace. We must turn to the God who made us, so that the Great Physician can create in us His living image.

This motto identifies the desk of a distinguished businessman: "How great a God we need, and much greater is our God than our greatest need."

TODAY'S THOUGHT: *God does not demand great talents, only an honest and obedient heart.*

OCTOBER 16

A Little Talk with Jesus!

You will make your prayer to him, and he will hear you.

Job 22:27

Driving along one day, I came to a billboard with this slogan. Advertising gasoline, it read: "The stop that keeps you going." As I saw it, I was reminded of the embarrassing times when I had run out of gasoline. I would look at the gasoline gauge and think, "There must be a few gallons left and why not go to the next town before I refuel." No time was gained by such reasoning. In fact, I found that time was lost because I ran out of gasoline. Sometimes it took me as long as two or three hours to get started again because of the foolishness of not making the stop that keeps one going.

Then I thought of the slogan in relation to people. Many try to work around the clock, seven days a week, some even robbing themselves of sleep at night to increase their earnings. Ultimately they have a breakdown. They always protested that they must get their work done first before taking time out for rest, or for church going, or for prayer to God. They are all too busy accumulating things of the world. They keep on pushing until finally there is a breakdown. Then they may be hospitalized for as long as six months, paying through pain and confinement their neglect of "the stop that keeps you going."

No man ever is his own king. Trying to follow his own orders, and to use his own reasoning without seeking counsel from God, his life always ends in tragedy. We are children of God and are made to commune with Him. He offers to be our guide and to point us along the pathway we should travel. Life without Him is like a house without windows. It matters not how much of the worldly things we may accumulate, they will not be sufficient. An automobile may be very beautiful with its snappy color scheme, and it may house a powerful engine, but if there is no gasoline in the tank, the car will stand stock still despite appearances.

A person may be talented and live in a beautiful home, but unless he takes the time to make the stop that keeps one going, unless he receives power from within to live as he should, that life cannot be successful, nor can it ever be the life abundant.

TODAY'S THOUGHT: *Christ wants to be the sun of your soul, but you must expose yourself to His rays.*

OCTOBER 17

Prove Your Faith by a Consistent Life

As the outcome of your faith you obtain the salvation of your souls. 1 Peter 1:9

Think of the time we spend on ourselves in comparison to what we do for God. Think of the time we spend gathering mere things in contrast to the few and intermittent moments we spend pursuing the life eternal. In our day we want religion to come easy. Denial is a word we would prefer to exclude from our vocabulary because it means giving up something. Who wants to do that? We are primarily interested in the forms of religion. It is all to the good, we think, and want our children to be trained in the church, nor do we object too much to attending ourselves. But if challenged to make a practice of faith, that is a vastly different thing.

Unless your faith is out and out, unless it is evident to friend and foe that you are willing to really sacrifice in its behalf, it is a thing of sham. That was true of the Pharisees in days of old. Our Lord censored them for making a display of their phylacteries, i.e., strips of parchment on which were written certain passages of scripture. They were enclosed in a case and worn on the forehead and left arm. Certain of the Pharisees tried to make these outward signs as conspicuous as possible, so that they might become walking advertisements of their own holiness when, in reality, their lives were cruel and sinful.

Before we become too severe in our judgment of them, had we not better turn the spotlight on ourselves? Do we have true faith in our hearts?

History tells about the ladies who went to church in Alexandria wearing a copy of the gospel around their necks. They wore splendid clothing and their skirts were embroidered with the story of the rich man and Lazarus. Yet their empty, vain lives proved they had not put on the yoke of Christ, for right at their gate lay starving beggars.

History repeats itself today. We can find plenty of people willing to wear an ornamental cross, but how rare it is to see those who wear Calvary's old rugged cross in a sacrificial life.

Let us be transparently honest about our faith. Only then can we become effective in our service to others.

TODAY'S THOUGHT: *You alone hold the key to whether or not you will give Christ your life or your lip service.*

OCTOBER 18

Speak Well of Your Neighbor

What does the Lord require of you but to do justice, and to love kindness, and to walk humbly with your God? Micah 6:8

A woman confessed to her minister that she had gossiped about her neighbor.

"One day I saw her staggering across her yard," she said, "so I told some friends that she was intoxicated. Now I know that her staggering was caused by a leg injury. How in the world can I stop the malicious talk I've started?"

The minister excused himself for a few minutes. Returning with a pillow, he asked the woman to follow him outside. There he cut a big hole in the pillow with his knife, and let the wind scatter the feathers. Some of them caught on trees and flowers nearby, others flew across the street, while some were carried out of sight by the wind. Fascinated, the woman watched them disappear.

"Now," the minister said to her, "will you go out and gather up every one of the feathers?"

"That's impossible," she protested.

"Exactly," he answered, "and so it is with your gossip."

Once you have said something malicious about another person, it is humanly impossible to make full amends for it. How much happier we would be then, if we looked for the good in our fellow men. We all have our weaknesses and our strong points. Let us focus our attention on the strong points in our neighbors. Why not look for the good?

A certain woman had a reputation for refraining from criticizing other people. Some of her friends tried to tempt her by talking about a person known in the entire community to be good for nothing.

"Well," the kind woman said finally, "I know he's the best whittler of kid's willow whistles in the whole village. At least we can give him credit for that."

As the Master ministered among men, there were many things that disturbed Him. He hated sin and never hesitated to point that out. But let us also remember that Jesus always loved the sinner. He made a conscious effort to meet sinners in order to release them from the grueling bondage of sin. He expects us to do likewise.

TODAY'S THOUGHT: *Today it is true that many men hunger for bread, but it is incontrovertible that many more hunger for the gospel's good news.*

OCTOBER 19

Work While It Is Day

For the works which the Father has granted me to accomplish, these very works which I am doing, bear me witness that the Father has sent me. John 5:36

We Americans are about the busiest people in the world. We are a nation of workers. Every day in the newspaper we read of new engineering projects, of bridges being built, or of scientists making new discoveries. As we perform our daily tasks, the roar of workers is all about us, as if we were standing in some vast factory. Most people, being gainfully employed, work very hard for a living. Therefore, when we hear the Lord asking a certain question, we do not think it applies to us. The question is this: "Why stand ye here all the day idle?"

We are to think for a moment of three workmen. The first, works for money alone. He will have nothing to show for his efforts, come to the end of his life, because what good will money do him then? He leaves the world as poor as he entered it. The second man works for fame. But the time comes when a man's fame is as nothing to him, when his story can only be written upon his coffin after his earthly course is run. The third man works for power and becomes a ruler of men. But when his eyes are dim and his voice feeble, another takes his place and nothing remains, only his burial in the city of his fathers.

But there is a higher and better goal to work for than these three, a work which the grave can never swallow. It is the work that God has sent us into His vineyard to do. It is work for our own souls and for the souls of others, a work for eternity, a work that is our Father's business. This work of salvation, this race for the prize, this struggle after holiness is the greatest of all. When every monument of the earth has tumbled into dust, and the great noble names have been forgotten, the one who has humbly dedicated his life to God, whatever were his gifts, will continue to live on in heaven.

As Christians we must do the work of Him who sent us. We must be about our Father's business. There is much to do in our workaday world. There are too many sitting idly by in the comfort of their firesides. Will you do your part today?

TODAY'S THOUGHT: *The light of God has been put in the hands of men to carry as in a torch relay.*

OCTOBER 20

He Who Hesitates Is Lost

Commit your work to the Lord, and your plans will be established. Proverbs 16:3

One day Jesus was tempted as He drew nigh to an exceedingly high mountain. There Satan showed the Savior the kingdoms which our Lord had come to redeem from sin and death; and he offered to give them to Jesus if He would fall down and worship him. This temptation was by far the most dangerous that Jesus had to face.

It was the temptation which faces us so frequently, the temptation to obtain good by evil means. Jesus stood there, and His loving heart yearned for the kingdoms of the world that they might be saved from their sin. Here was Satan, offering a short cut to the salvation of all. There need be no self-denial, no fasting, no agony in Gethsemane, no pain nor injury, no crucifixion, if only Jesus would bow down and worship the evil one. Indeed this was the supreme temptation to turn aside from the path of duty.

Jesus was silent a moment. Then He turned and with unbelievable, quiet power He said, "Begone Satan! for it is written, 'You shall worship the Lord your God and him only shall you serve.'"

Today the devil frequently takes us, too, up into a high mountain. He gives us a glimpse of the world's wealth and beauty, and intentionally he whispers to us, "All this will I give you, if you fall down and worship me." To one he gives a vision of riches earned, not by patient toil and faithful industry, but by the short cuts of dishonesty and lust of the world.

To another he paints pictures of ambition, encouraging him to aim for high place. "Elbow your way to the top," he says. "Think first and only of yourself. Just climb and climb, and never pay any attention to whom you trample under foot as you're on the way up."

Perhaps some of you are listening to the tempting voice. You too are at the crossroads. You are hesitating, trying to decide which way to go. Before you plunge be sure to count the frightful cost.

TODAY'S THOUGHT: *Everyone must make this life or death decision: Shall I live for Christ or not?*

OCTOBER 21

God Knows Even Our Unspoken Needs

As for me, I am poor and needy; but the Lord takes thought for me. Psalm 40:17

In the early months of infancy a little baby cannot talk. He can only cry and hold out his arms. He cannot tell his mother what he wants, and often perhaps he does not even know. It is the mother's business to find out what he wants, and get it for him as long as it will not hurt him.

We cannot thereupon conclude that an earthly mother can be kinder than her Creator, God. We believe that God does not wait for us to put in words our wants, when yet we are not mature enough to have the words to express what we want, if indeed we even know what we want. Often the only thing we know is that we are dissatisfied and unhappy. Within us is a vacuum that must be filled, a desire that needs satisfying. We must believe that God is always patiently thinking about our possible desires in order that He may uncover and fulfill them. We must remember His promise that, "I came that they may have life, and have it abundantly." Day by day He seeks to give us that life. But we mishear His directions, involved too deeply in the pursuit of worldly things. His still small voice is drowned out by the burly roar of our lusty lives.

A French peasant was accustomed to sitting quietly for a long time in church at the end of his day's toil. When a priest asked him what he prayed about, he answered, "Oh, I just look up at Him and He looks down at me!"

The answer to our complex problems and to the confusion of the days in which we live is to be found in God. We need to look up at Him and He down at us. He then can resolve the conflicts in our hearts. Only through unceasing prayer and devotion can life be kept in balance. Constantly there are forces trying to drag us down, voices calling for our attention, temptations and problems weighing heavily upon our shoulders. Only by having the upward pull of the power of God can life be kept on an even keel. Without His mercy and strength we are helpless, and hopeless, and will be ultimately defeated. Only in Christ can we be victorious.

TODAY'S THOUGHT: *Just as a young child learning to walk moves the more steadily when holding its mother's hand, so man walks straightest and best when holding the hand of God the Father.*

Stay Out of the Devil's Territory

My son, if sinners entice you, do not consent. Proverbs 1:10

We are all reading much these days about modern miracles which are fast becoming a part of our daily life. It is now possible to fry eggs by electronics. An automatic device now shuts the windows as soon as it starts to rain and manages the shades. No longer do we need to expend energy in opening the door of many stores. An electric eye does the task for us. Soon, we are told, we shall be able to span the Atlantic Ocean in a matter of three hours by commercial jet aircraft. Thousands of inventions have revolutionized living in our day. But these things alone do not make us happy. We have taken good care of our bodies, but what about our souls?

As I was talking to a friend one day about these matters, he said, "Wouldn't it be a wonderful thing, if there were some kind of automatic device that would pull down the shades of the soul, and prevent our yielding when temptation came?"

I turned to him and said, "There is." If we really want a sensitized conscience, an electric eye within to alert us on the least approach of sin, we need only to reach out to God for His companionship. With Him we have power to resist sin and to eliminate much of our human misery.

In spite of our mechanical advance, we of the twentieth century are subjected perhaps to more temptation than were people of any other age. We talk about "Faith of our fathers," but in our motorized age we need more faith than they of the horse and buggy day. However, we need not be concerned about being defeated, if we will only build into our lives the consciousness of Jesus being a living bright reality, that constantly He is by our side, cheering us on to choose the real thing rather than false living, true values rather than empty ones.

We say we are seeking the best. What is the best? It must not only be that which satisfies the deepest hunger of our souls, but it must satisfy all our needs. Among the people who came to Jesus during His ministry, no one ever asked Him, as one might today, "Lord, make me a millionaire." No one ever said, "Lord, make me great and famous, so that my name may be spread afar." But many prayed, "Lord, be merciful to me, a sinner." This is the key that unlocks the door to all the resources of the Savior.

TODAY'S THOUGHT: *Strike hard against every known sin, for it first brings despair, then bitterness, and finally death.*

OCTOBER 23

Like the Compass Needle Points North, Seek God

Oh send out thy light and thy truth; let them lead me, let them bring me to thy holy hill and to thy dwelling! Psalm 43:3

What does God promise when we pray to Him? He gives this assurance: "Knock, and it will be opened to you." All of us need to spend more time in prayer. It would make our lives richer and happier. We should begin each day by turning to God for guidance through the hours ahead. Then intermittently through the course of the day we should talk to God as good friends should and do. If we believe Him to be our best Friend and capable of helping us in any situation, certainly we should stay on the most intimate and friendly terms with Him. Too many of us believe that God is found of us only in church. We respect and honor Him while we are there, and then go off to leave Him there, forgetting that He wants always to be with us wherever we go.

We live in difficult times. Problems and temptations assail us on every hand. Yet think what it would be like, if every day without fail all Christians in every position and area of life sought the strength which comes from communion with God. What a different world it would become! Think how different our lives would be, if the Lord became so real to us that whenever we were faced with any temptation or sin, we had a little quiet time and said, "God, what do you want me to do?" If we did this, our lives would become more vibrant and our thinking more sound. With God as partner we would be more effective in our work, for there is absolutely nothing He cannot help us do. How foolish we are to walk life's road alone when this tremendous power, this spiritual energy, is available for each one of us.

We would be wise, too, if we spent more time developing the prayer life of our children. It is good discipline and worth while to teach them the simple prayers which most of us know. No matter how old we become, we never forget them—prayers like, "Now I lay me down to sleep." But that is not to say that you cannot talk to God in language of your own. No prayer ever goes unheard, even the lisping prayer of a child. Children need to be taught that they can talk to their heavenly Father even as they speak to their loving parents. Never need we be concerned about the future, if we claim our richest inheritance—the power of prayer.

TODAY'S THOUGHT: *Let us put prayer first. Start each new task with a prayer.*

OCTOBER 24

Cover Hatred with Love

Having purified your souls by your obedience to the truth for a sincere love of the brethren, love one another earnestly from the heart. 1 Peter 1:22

The truly forgiving spirit cannot be a halfway matter. It must be all out, if it is to give us satisfaction, and if it is to pass muster with God. In His model prayer Jesus prayed this petition, "Forgive us our trespasses, as we forgive those who trespass against us." God's forgiving spirit toward us is dependent upon our forgiving spirit toward others.

We think that it is a sign of defeat to admit we are mistaken. More often we need to humble ourselves under the mighty hand of God, and to discover that "None is righteous, no, not one." Few of us can be deeply proud about the way we live. We are in such need of goodness. Our lives are threadbare and shoddy. Truly, without the love of God, our lives would be hopeless.

Love can perform miracles. The story is told of a delinquent boy, who early in life had missed the experience of being understood and loved. He expressed his resentment in actions that finally brought him into court. The court understood his case, and assigned him to live with various families in the hope that he would be helped. But it was to no avail, until a certain man and his wife requested the opportunity of helping this boy.

In a short time the boy began to show such signs of improvement that the court could not understand the reason for the miracle that was taking place. When the foster parents were asked how they had accomplished the unbelievable, they replied humbly, "We didn't do anything especially. We only made it plain to him in the beginning that nothing he could do would make us stop loving him."

Love "covers a multitude of sins," and if when you try to cover hatred with love and still it does not work, just keep doubling the dose, and you will at last be successful in what you are striving to do. Love never fails, for God is love, and God is power.

TODAY'S THOUGHT: *Get on fire with faith and love, and you will soon melt the icy indifference about you.*

OCTOBER 25

Give According to Your Gifts

According to their ability they gave to the treasury of the work.
                                                            Ezra 2:69

Some years ago a wealthy man gave considerable equipment to a mission hospital across the seas. He was standing on the pier watching the vessel depart with his cargo, when it seems he encountered an acquaintance of his to whom he mentioned his contribution.

"That is splendid," his friend commented, "I am certainly happy that you made this generous gesture." Then he added, "I, too, have a gift on that vessel. My only daughter is on her way across the seas to serve as a missionary to those who do not know Christ."

The wealthy man winced as he replied, "Thinking of what that sacrifice means to you, I feel I have given nothing."

The size of the gift is not important, for God expects all of us to give according to the way that we have been blessed. If we fail to be good stewards of that with which God has entrusted us, we ourselves are the ones who are shortchanged throughout both our mortal and eternal lives.

There are many variations of the story about the lady getting her call home to heaven. She had been a very wealthy person with a beautiful home, and as she was being led about in the House of Many Mansions she saw a lovely place.

"That is the house I want to live in," she exclaimed.

She was told that the home was occupied by a little lady who had been very poor on earth. Finally, the wealthy woman came to her assigned place.

"I can't live in such a home as this," she said.

"Well," the answer came, "this was all the material you sent up to us to work with, so we couldn't build a more beautiful home for you."

When man tries to rob God, he is only robbing himself. Each day we are building our earthly home, and in building whatever kind of life we choose, we must remember—it is the very life we must live with forever.

TODAY'S THOUGHT: *If you want to be thoughtful and kind in eternity, be thoughtful and kind today and every day.*

OCTOBER 26

Taking Time Out to Let God in

My soul waits for the Lord more than watchmen for the morning.
Psalm 130:6

All of us are so constituted as to need time for meditation and prayer. We need moments of quiet in order to prepare ourselves for the tasks ahead.

Consider the life of John the Baptist. He was born in the hill country of Judea. John was a child of prayer and prophecy. Scripture tells us that he was filled with the Holy Spirit at birth. The history of the first 30 years of his life can be written briefly. He grew in stature. He grew strong in spirit and character, and through his devotional life developed powers of spiritual insight. Firmness of will characterized him. All this time he lived in the desert, a sparsely inhabited, barren region of jackals and wild beasts, a little removed from the hill country of his home.

The object of this long period of retirement seems to be clear. It was growing time for him, wherein through deep communion with God he readied himself to properly fulfill his mission as a forerunner of the Lord.

All of us need ample spiritual resources and the firm foundation of faith if our life is to be secure. The buds that open and grow in the spring were formed in the autumn and conditioned by the long cold winter. The hyacinth bulb must be kept in darkness for weeks, if it is to be a perfect bloom.

In observatories astronomers have discovered a new way of spotting stars. They place a highly sensitive photographic paper under the telescope and leave it there until it records a perfect image of the starry sky. Sometimes upon removing it, they uncover new stars, which previously had escaped notice, and which they never would have discovered merely by gazing through the telescope. Now in order to make that highly sensitive photo paper do its work, all has to be in perfect stillness. The least noise or vibration of the air would have marred the impression of the heavens which the paper was taking.

Just like that our souls must have times of stillness, if they are to receive the impressions of heaven.

TODAY'S THOUGHT: *Those priceless moments in God's presence avail to do more than ever you think.*

300

OCTOBER 27

Love's Acid Test

None of us lives to himself, and none of us dies to himself.
Romans 14:7

In the world today there is a veritable babel of voices crying for many things. Most of these voices are calling for love. Without love life becomes a barren desert. Love is gladdened by good, is always hopeful and patient, and never fails. If a man really believes that love fails, his whole life would be changed. This pitiful note was found left behind by a suicide on the banks of the Thames: "Do not think me even temporarily deranged. But the loneliness at the end of the day was like a grey ghost." Every morning repeat those three words to yourself: "Love never fails."

During the past few years we have made wonderful progress in developing a brotherly love reaching around the world. We have had many opportunities to share our resources with those less fortunate than we. By our contribution through fund drives we pool our love for our fellow men, regardless of their color or creed, and fulfill His command that, "He who loves God should love his brother also."

Love must be a deep, personal experience in the life of every one of us. If a child in infancy is taught the meaning of love, he will have a prize that never can be taken from him.

Love is a discipline. So often a parent says to a child, "This hurts me more than it hurts you." Children find this hard to believe. But as parents we come to know the deepest depth of parental love when we find it necessary to discipline our own children.

Love is also a longing and a hunger. We want to know more and more about the person whom we love. So should be our feeling for God, our heavenly Father. If it is a true love, we will want to know more and more about Him, never tiring in our search for His truth. As we become better acquainted with Him, we grow more willing to make sacrifices for others. We realize, too, what a short time we have to help.

An unknown writer's inspiring words should pace us: "I shall pass through this world but once. Any good, therefore, that I can do, or any kindness that I can show to any human being, let me do it now. Let me not defer nor neglect it, for I shall not pass this way again."

TODAY'S THOUGHT: *Kindness has brought far more sinners to Christ than eloquent preaching.*

OCTOBER 28

Strike a Balance for Life

For with thee is the fountain of life; in thy light do we see light.
Psalm 36:9

Your physical body is like a bank account. A man who maintains a safe balance in the bank can live comfortably without fear, because he is protected against a measure of adversity. He is prepared for the rainy day. But if he overdraws his account and creates a deficit, immediately he is in trouble both at the bank and with himself.

So it is with your body. If you overdraw your physical bank account of endurance and nervous energy, you are likely to find yourself in trouble. Spiritually speaking, the story is much the same.

By living in daily prayer and communion with God, we can build within ourselves reserves of power to help us when adversity comes. If, however, we do not take the time to be with God and make His acquaintance in times of prosperity, we shall not have the joy of His intimate friendship when times of difficulty appear.

God is the best friend that we have. He knows each one of us. He knows us far better than we understand ourselves. He does not expect more of us than we are able to take or to give. He knows our weaknesses and frailties, and He handles us tenderly, because He knows the weight of each cross we must bear. He is a wonderful God, wonderful in patience and redeeming love! He stands by at all times to be a very present help to us, and offers His hand in friendship to lead us on our way.

The way of God is the only way. None other really works. God has a purpose for us in the world, and we had better try to find it, if we are to be happy. Life will work out only one way, and that is God's way. If we willfully choose our own paths, however successfullly we may appear to be making out, we shall find that the road leads either to a precipice or a dead-end street; and to achieve lasting happiness, we shall have to turn around and retrace our steps.

The wise man seeks each day God's will for his life. As he talks to God in prayer throughout the course of the day, he receives his directions, not only in times of sorrow but in times of happiness too. He finds God the greatest Companion a man can have.

TODAY'S THOUGHT: *Life's boat without Christ at the helm is either sinking or sunk.*

302

OCTOBER 29

Play Square with God

Cast all your anxieties on him, for he cares about you. 1 Peter 5:7

Many people today are afraid to use prayer power. Yes, they are afraid of what it might do to them, afraid of the commitment they might have to make, of the things they might have to give up. They forget the glory that is by-passing them as they walk alone, without the help of the power of prayer.

The greatest men and women this world has ever known are those who walked and talked with God. We all can be great in the development of our individual gifts, if we allow His divine Spirit to touch our lives.

Whenever we pray, we can be certain that the One who holds the universe in His hand is giving us His undivided attention. What a thrill to know that this Almighty God is giving His complete attention to our problem! Yes, we can come in contact with that tremendous power. All we need do is approach Him sincerely, and we shall become channels for that power. And when we think of the countless hours some of us have spent apart from Him, trying to run our lives singlehanded, we marvel at His patience.

To receive God's help we must be absolutely honest with ourselves and with Him. Whenever we visit our family doctor we describe our pains specifically, for if we do he has a better chance to diagnose our ailment and prescribe the right medication. In like manner God urges us to be honest with Him. There is not an ailment that He cannot cure. There is not a problem that He cannot solve. There is not a worry that He cannot banish, for His presence is the cure for all troubled hearts.

The only condition He imposes on us is that we be honest with Him. If we come in honesty and penitence, He will forgive us all our sins. If we have faith, He will fill our hearts with power. He will trade despair for hope. We must yield our lives to Him, saying, "Here is my life, Lord. Without your help I am completely defeated. Take my places of weakness and fill them with your strength."

How strong we would be, if we made that commitment!

TODAY'S THOUGHT: *Only God can add the mark which changes minuses to pluses in our lives.*

OCTOBER 30

Strike Those Chains from Your Soul

Then my soul shall rejoice in the Lord, exulting in his deliverance. Psalm 35:9

Sin means a wall of our own making between us and the very source of life. God never intended that His children should be apart from Him. We are the ones who have broken the bridge. In His own great mercy and love God restored it at Calvary; but He does not force anybody to cling to the cross and so be saved. It is His hope and desire that we should, but the choice remains ours, and when we turn against God we set our little wills against the great will of the Father.

Our deepest awareness knows that the time will come when we realize the folly of our mistakes. What must happen first? The wall which our sins created between us and our God, that barrier of resistance inside ourselves, must be broken down.

I have heard many a man ask, "What must I do?"

This is how he should think: "I ought to turn to God to whom I have been saying 'No,' acknowledging that my attitude is the greatest sin of all. I ought to throw myself upon His mercy, for He alone can create in me a clean heart and put a right spirit within. Did not the Son of man come seeking to save that which was lost? The fact that I am lost puts me in a position to be found. Remember, it is not God who is confused. It is I. I can find Him wherever I find myself. He has pursued me even to the far-off country, seeking His prodigal's return. If I choose to I can now say, 'Yes,' instead of 'No' to this overflowing life which He offers me through His grace. I can be restored to the father-son relationship which He desires to be between us."

Lois Chrysler when asked what was the most beautiful thing she had ever seen in the Rockies, gave this reply: "Up there it is so clear that as I look it unprisons my soul."

That is exactly what redemption does. It is the unprisoning of the soul. It brings us out of bondage into freedom, out of darkness into life, out of doubt into faith, and out of despair into glory. It gives us courage to keep going in spite of every difficulty. Nothing outside of myself can stop the progress of my soul. Through faith we are "becoming" the children of God, with each new day more wonderful than the preceding one, from glory to glory.

TODAY'S THOUGHT: *The believer measures all advancement in terms of goodness rather than in terms of goods.*

OCTOBER 31

Keep Looking Up

One Lord, one faith, one baptism, one God and Father of us all, who is above all and through all. Ephesians 4:5, 6

A platoon of soldiers was drilling in the open square of their village under the command of a leader who was directing their movements.

Finally, nearing the end of his patience, he barked, "Men, quit looking down at your feet! Keep your eyes front. Your feet will always follow your eyes."

As we look steadily at what is good we move toward it. Our feet will always follow our eyes. If, however we fix our attention on what is wrong, we will find ourselves drawn to it. If we run the race of life looking up to Jesus, we shall come nearer to Him and every day grow more like Him.

The familiar hymn, "My Faith Looks Up to Thee," was written by an author only twenty-two years old whom sickness and poverty already had begun to hound. Several years after writing it he said that he had composed the words deeply conscious of his own needs, and had finished the last line with tears in his eyes. Never did he dream that the poem would become a hymn used for Christian worship. He was simply trying to forget his own problems by focusing his attention on God who was the cure.

Such action is a remedy for all our needs. Looking to Jesus, we find the answers to the problems we face. Following Him day by day, we become increasingly aware of the tremendous spiritual energies available to us because we belong to Him. All that He expects of us is our looking up, our striving for higher goals than we have reached before.

In the Alps a memorial has been erected in memory of a guide who died attempting to scale a certain mountain. "He died climbing," says the inscription. That is a fitting tribute to a heroic man. He died in the line of duty, striving to reach a higher goal. That tribute will be paid to us, if we do the very best we can with the gifts we have been given. We must keep climbing day by day, drawn upward by the power of Him who said, "And I, when I am lifted up from the earth, will draw all men to myself."

TODAY'S THOUGHT: *Do your best consistently, and the worst will never happen.*

NOVEMBER 1

What Sons of Privilege We Are!

But lay up for yourselves treasures in heaven, where neither moth nor rust consumes and where thieves do not break in and steal. Matthew 6:20

This is the month of Thanksgiving. Let us resolve here at its beginning to take inventory of ourselves each day in order to discover how grateful we should be. It could lead to more positive thinking all the year through.

The first thing our Pilgrim fathers did when they got off the Mayflower was to kneel down under the open sky to thank God. In that Presence each listened for His voice speaking within, and each resolved earnestly to live His way. They worshiped Him not only on Sunday, but always and everywhere. Writing a constitution for their new free land, they prayed for guidance from the greatest Lawgiver of all.

How privileged we are to live in this great land, we who enjoy the fruits of the pioneers and trail blazers. Someone has been here before us. Let us repeat it like a creed each day: "Someone has made my world more beautiful for me. Such a trust asks that I be found worthy, and that I too leave something in return."

Perhaps you have been wont to complain, and to wonder why life should be so difficult for you. But you have only to stop to think how happy you would be if, having lost everything you had, you then got it back again. Think of how fortunate you are compared to so many others who walk life's way with you.

There is a Thanksgiving story that never grows old. It was told long before the Pilgrims ever landed on the shores of this new world. It came from the lips of a wise oriental, Confucius. It seems that a Chinese beggar wallowed in self-pity because he had no shoes. He burst into a bitter tirade every time a rich man happened by in fine, leathern sandals. One day he clapped a wrinkled hand over his mouth, and resolved never to complain again. He was a smiling, contented man from then on. He had seen a man who had no feet.

Let us take stock of ourselves today and every day of our life. How about beginning each day saying with the hymn writer, "Now thank we all our God With heart and hands and voices"?

TODAY'S THOUGHT: *Begin by rating yourself at zero, and then consider every single talent or possession or friend a degree above that point and a reason for thanksgiving.*

NOVEMBER 2

Why Not Really Live Today?

For a day in thy courts is better than a thousand elsewhere.
Psalm 84:10

A certain farmer and his family worked hard year after year. As his sons and daughters grew up and married, they left home. So the father and mother came to live alone, worn out at last by their arduous efforts throughout a long lifetime. Then one day the wife collapsed over her wash tubs and died quickly.

At the funeral her husband did not weep or show any sign of grief as he plodded to the grave. When the service was over he stayed behind to talk to his pastor, and held out in one hand a small shabby book.

"It's a book of poems," he said quietly, "and she liked them. Would you read one for her now? She always wanted me to read them with her. I never had time. Every day there were always things to do on the farm. But I got to thinking, nobody's doing the work today, and it doesn't matter. I guess you don't know what time it is until it is too late."

How wise we would be to take forethought and spare ourselves the remorse for things we left undone. Too often we postpone to some distant time in the future the moments of joy and happiness we could have now. Sad indeed are the words, "Too late." Why not live to the hilt today?

One writer declares that the hillbillies are the happiest of all Americans. They live to enjoy today, and accordingly they live twenty years longer than the rest of us do.

"Many a hillbilly," this writer said, "doesn't know the meaning of worry; and if he does, he refuses to heed it. They just inhale and exhale one day at a time. As a rule they are very happy people who have learned to relaxedly enjoy the simple things in life. Although their houses may be cluttered, their lives seldom are. They just take one day at a time and try to live it to the fullest, instead of postponing the enjoyment of a particular stroke of good fortune to a time that may never come."

The secret of victorious living is to take time each day for happiness and joy. This does not mean improvidently omitting to plan for tomorrow either.

TODAY'S THOUGHT: *If you want to be happy tomorrow, begin to be happy today.*

NOVEMBER 3

Where Are You Going?

Teach me thy way, O Lord, that I may walk in thy truth.
Psalm 86:11

Dean Swift, an eminent English cleric, one day took a train to London. He was late for an appointment, so he jumped into a cab outside the station. "Get going as fast as you can," he ordered the cab driver. After they had gone some distance, he called to the driver, "Are we there yet?" "Where?" the driver said. "You didn't tell me where to go!"

Many people are living like that today. Many are suffering because life is so "every-dayish" and routine. They are doing the same things over and over again without feeling any joy or satisfaction. People are looking for happiness in the wrong places, and so are not finding the joy that everyone wants. They search the ends of the earth, only to discover they could have found what they were seeking at home.

A man went into a restaurant and ordered a cup of coffee. The waitress observed that he put several spoons of sugar into it. "Why don't you stir the sugar?" she asked.

He growled at her intrusion. "Who wants it sweet anyway?"

In our hurry-scurry lives we go through unthinking, needless motions that leave us breathless and tired, when with little reflection the sweetness of life could be stirred up.

Life has meaning only as we seek every day to find God's will for our lives. It is part of our erring human nature to postpone enjoying and appreciating what we have right now. Anticipating some magical garden of tomorrow, we overlook the beautiful flowers growing outside our very window. Every day can have meaning for the Christian, if he is attuned to it.

What is life? Many and varied are the answers that we give, but most of them do not satisfy. Some people would say that life is simply to enjoy our inventions—all the things that the mind of man has created. But this kind of living would never satisfy an eternal soul, for life's richest qualities come out when a man is quickened with the dynamics of God. When that happens, life will always have a driving purpose.

TODAY'S THOUGHT: *Those who have knowledge only but no driving purpose know the meaning of the word, dilemma.*

NOVEMBER 4

In Whom Do We Really Trust?

O Lord of hosts, blessed is the man who trusts in thee!
Psalm 84:12

One day a little girl came running to her mother. She was in tears.

"Oh, Mommy," she said, "how can I untrouble trouble?"

Many of us ask that question today. How are we to untangle all the snarls which irritate us so, and make life unpleasant? Jesus only can answer that question. He can help us as easily as He made the towering waves lie down like dogs at their master's feet. Moreover we shall find the answer when we come to trust Him and believe in His power.

Whom do we trust most? A mature Christian, who has served the Lord effectively for many years, tells of the experience which changed his life. He needed financial assistance from time to time in his business. He often was very worried about where the money would come from.

"One day," he reports, "I realized that I slept better when some powerful financier had underwritten my loan. So I came to ask myself why so nervous then, when I had the Lord's sure word, 'I will supply all your needs'? I decided, therefore, to trust in the Lord with all my heart. So now I have the kind of peace the world cannot give, the peace that comes with the knowledge that your underwriter is the Almighty who has all power in heaven and earth."

Where do we seek our refuge and strength? During an air raid in China some years ago a native Christian, his wife, and their six-year-old daughter could not get to the air-raid shelter. They took refuge under the dining room table and, as the bombs burst nearby, they prayed.

"Daddy," said the little girl, when the danger was past, "our Lord Jesus Christ is the best air-raid shelter, isn't He?"

Here is such a One as we can depend upon. God's lights never cease shining. He never blows them out, and then turns in to sleep. Why not say with the old Christian, who tossed on his bed as he worried, and then stopped to think of the foolish pagan he was, and said to himself, "No need both of us staying awake," and leaving all in God's hands, he fell into a child's untroubled sleep.

TODAY'S THOUGHT: *Dare to say to God: "Use me as Thou wilt in Thy service."*

NOVEMBER 5

What Then Is Faith?

Now faith is the assurance of things hoped for, the conviction of things not seen. Hebrews 11:1

Faith is the root from which spring the flowers of assurance. But you cannot have the flowers without the root. Faith guided a poor woman's trembling hand as she touched the hem of Jesus' robe, and received forgiveness and peace. In faith the penitent thief cried from the cross, "Remember me," and received the answer, "Today you will be with me in Paradise." Faith prompted Peter's cry, "Lord, save me!" as he began to sink into the sea. Faith egged on the timid voice calling, "I believe; help my unbelief!" How great are the blessings of faith! It is the bridge that can span any chasm in life.

While God's power is always available, man has the choice of taking or leaving that power. Can you picture a locomotive standing there at the station like an iron war horse? That engine is capable of pulling a long chain of cars to their destination. All of its parts are in working order, the starting signal has been given, but still nothing happens save that the engine chugs off by itself. The train of cars will not move as long as the coupling that connects the cars with the engine is separated. But when it is joined like two great hands clasped, the train will move. Without that coupling or link, the chain of cars would stand and rust on those rails.

So it is with our faith in Christ. It is not our faith that saves us, but Christ. Our faith is a coupling, linking us to His power.

One cold, snowy day a man was feeding birds. He crossed his porch, and threw them a handful of crumbs. The birds just sat, cold and afraid, because he was a new face and his movements strange. They did not trust him.

God is like that man feeding the birds. He offers us all the blessings we could ever want. He watches, waits, and hopes that we will take them; but He cannot force us to accept. Once we do, we shall have discovered the abundant life.

TODAY'S THOUGHT: *God has set His pastors and teachers as watchmen to awaken the people to their opportunity for an abundant life, replete with spiritual blessings.*

NOVEMBER 6

You May Be Looking at the Wrong Side

For you were straying like sheep, but have now returned to the Shepherd and Guardian of your souls. 1 Peter 2:25

Wireless messages are always heard best in the stillness of night. In the same way, people passing through the midnight of trouble and bereavement are often more responsive to the voice of God. When a panorama is to be shown to an audience, the artist darkens the room to focus their attention on the screen. God sometimes darkens our little world. One light after another fades out. Many times we are ready to rebel at what is happening. Then, suddenly, a vision of beauty passes before our souls, and we see more clearly the glories of another land.

Frequently we become dissatisfied with life, for it can be such a complicated tangle. It seems altogether meaningless. Nothing seems to turn out right.

A little girl was weaving busily, when a stranger came into her room.

"What are you doing?" he asked amiably. "I see only tangled webs and confused knots."

"You are looking on the wrong side," the little girl said, unperturbed, turning the piece over to display a beautiful design.

That man never forgot that lesson.

Often we are confused all because we look at the wrong side of things. "In everything God works for good with those who love him." We may not understand steps A and B and C in God's plan, but can we not trust that things will eventually turn out right? The secret is to follow closely after Him. It is easy to trace a man's footprints if we stay close behind him. But if we lag some distance back, and others walk the same path, we may not be able to find the footprints at all. So each day we ought to live close to the Lord. It is only when like Peter "we follow afar" that we get into difficulty. Then the voices of worldly temptation have their chance to start us down a wrong path. Only one way leads to life, and that is the narrow way. It is also the only happy way. There can be no true joy unless we walk hand in hand with God.

A saint was asked why he was always smiling.

"Because no one can take my God from me," he replied. That thought is worth hugging to your heart.

TODAY'S THOUGHT: *Walk ever close to the Master in this world, and you will walk forever with Him in the next.*

NOVEMBER 7

Do You Climb the High Road?

Whoever seeks to gain his life will lose it, but whoever loses his life will preserve it. Luke 17:33

In these restless days when we live in such a ferment of chance and adjustment, it is helpful to look back to the early days of our country. How faithful and courageous our forefathers were who pioneered an unknown land and transplanted a civilization. They tackled monumental tasks, yet they put first things first. They accomplished much because they prayed and kept in touch with the Infinite. They made God their ever-present help. He held His hand protectingly over them in Indian attacks, through disease, and crop failure, and plagues.

I do not want to appear to minimize that we should work hard while it is day. You can never regain a moment of life, for each new minute pushes the preceding one into the bourne of history, forever beyond our recall.

We all want progress, to move toward the place where we want to be. But if you have once taken a wrong turn, mere forward motion does not bring you nearer your destination. If you are on a wrong road, you must eventually do an about-face, and retrace your steps back to the right path. Accordingly the man who turns back the soonest will be first to reach his destination.

This is so true in life. I have seen it happen on the job. Having made a mistake, I discovered that the sooner I started over again, the faster I moved along. There is nothing progressive about refusing to admit a mistake and begin again.

Our difficulty, however, is that we become so reliant on our own strength that we keep making these mistakes and taking the wrong roads. If we only would take more time to pray and to read God's directions, we should soon discover His plan for our lives, and find that taking time for devotions is definitely not time lost, but gained.

Although man is lost and cannot find the way by himself, there is a Hand ready to lead him on. But man must first admit his own weakness. He must find someone beyond himself upon whom to depend. That someone is God. He stands ready to guide us through each day that we live.

TODAY'S THOUGHT: *There is no such thing as trusting God too much.*

NOVEMBER 8

Just What Are You Living For?

The fool says in his heart, "There is no God." Psalm 14:1

It has been said: "Life can only be understood backwards, but it must be lived forwards." For abundant living we must have the vitality of courage and the strength of love. In any journey we take, we must be alert to the warning signs set up for our safety on the highroad. There are warnings in our spiritual travels, too. Let us today set up a warning of the danger in misplaced values.

An efficient shopkeeper checks sales progress by taking frequent inventories. Let us look inward to take a personal inventory, just to see if our values are properly priced and ticketed. Misplaced values are particularly common today because of the over-abundance of material comforts. Accordingly, what do you think is really important in life?

A well-known minister on the west coast was invited to address some college students in their fraternity house at commencement time.

"What are you living for?" he asked one of the young men.

"I'm going to become a pharmacist," the student replied.

"Yes," the minister said, "that's how you're going to earn your living, but what are you living for?" The youth bowed his head for a moment.

"Sir," he answered, looking up, "I'm sorry, but I haven't thought this thing through." Soon they discovered that only two of the 30 students present had asked themselves this vital question. They all knew how they were going to earn their living, but only two had discovered the central purpose of life.

The spiritual values which we develop are far more important than the material things we seek to gain. Silver and gold must be left behind, and we must live forever in the house we build within ourselves. Take time for God today that you may build that house wisely.

TODAY'S THOUGHT: *The central purpose of life is to love and serve God.*

NOVEMBER 9

That Mighty Hand to Guide!

Blessed is the man who trusts in the Lord, whose trust is the Lord. Jeremiah 17:7

Children give us the most striking illustrations of trust. A little girl went down to her father's office, and cheerfully informed him that she was going home with him. The two were on their way when suddenly the girl said, "Let's pretend I am a poor little blind girl, and that you must lead me by the hand. You just guide me along and tell me where to go."

Her father agreed. The little girl shut her eyes, and the journey began. As they walked he directed her: "Now step up—now step down." Before long they arrived safely at home.

"Wasn't that fun, Daddy?" asked the little girl, climbing into her father's lap. "I didn't open my eyes once."

"But, dear," said her mother, "weren't you afraid you would fall?"

"Oh, no, Mother, I wasn't afraid. You see, I had a tight hold on Daddy's hand, and I just knew he would lead me safely over the bad places."

God will lead all His trusting children over the bad places. If we are but willing to keep our hold on Him, He will guide us safely into the unknown tomorrow. No one knows what a day will bring forth, but we need not be concerned, if we stay close to the Master. Let us learn to live each day as it comes, to take one step of the journey at a time. Remember you are always safe, if you hold your heavenly Father's hand.

Why is it that we will not trust God? In one of the darkest moments of Luther's life when he was anxious about the future, he looked out his window, and saw birds gathering in the branches of the trees cheerfully chirping. As he thought of their trust in the heavenly Father, he was ashamed of his anxiety. He thought of how they slept in their tiny nests, free from care; how they rose in the morning to let every drop of blood, every nerve and muscle rise to pour out their praise to God. Then they turned to search for food, and invariably they found it.

"Shame on me," Luther said, "an old fool am I who has so much grounds for trusting God and yet do not do so!"

Let us trust in God for a change.

TODAY'S THOUGHT: *Though men may call you poor you may be rich if you have faith in God.*

NOVEMBER 10

The Strength of Ten

The conduct of the pure is right. Proverbs 21:8

A Christian gives himself away by the purity of his life. Its tremendous power is garnered through discipline, and the resolving of inner conflicts by the strength that comes from above. He conquers the temptations that would otherwise make his life a continual battleground. It was said of King Arthur's knight, Sir Galahad, that, "He had the strength of ten because he was pure." There is no strength like that of a pure heart. Those who allow God to come into their lives subdue the fiercest thrust of sin. Those who seek to keep themselves pure, who consistently turn their backs on temptation, and ask God's help to keep their lives free from sin, have indeed "the strength of ten men."

We are too easily attracted by worldly voices drawing us away from God. Their promises are so alluring. We would be wise, however, always to keep in mind that these are but empty promises, and cannot bring lasting peace. Today it is fashionable to make light of certain sins. But while the world says one thing, God says another. God tells us in plain language, "Do you not know that . . . God's Spirit dwells in you? If any one destroys God's temple, God will destroy him." Each one is in desperate need of the spirit of God. In proportion to our asking, God will give to each of us those gifts most suitable to our special needs.

Are we in doubt as to the right? Are we anxious, unable to see our way, concerned about the future? Pray God to be enlightened, for strength on the way, and the assurance that His way is the right way.

Are we in sorrow and affliction? Pray God to send you the Comforter. How much we need His comfort! The world is full of troubles and worries, great and small. The dark and cloudy day comes for all of us when we bemoan our losses and the crushing burden of our sins. Walking through that dark and cheerless valley, we want and we seek His comfort.

The unbeliever tells us that we are alone, that there is no one to help us, that our case is hopeless. The Christian says there is always the spirit of God, and that if in penitence we will turn to Him, He will give us a comfort which the world cannot give, "the peace of God, which passes all understanding."

TODAY'S THOUGHT: *Those who have found Christ have a new plus in their lives.*

NOVEMBER 11

Being a Christian Is No Part-Time Job

As therefore you received Christ Jesus the Lord, so live in him, rooted and built up in him and established in the faith, just as you were taught, abounding in thanksgiving. Colossians 2:6, 7

A young woman with much artistic talent asked a fine sculptor to accept her as his pupil. In reply to her request he said, "Sculpture is not a part-time occupation. Your friends will urge you to stop. Are you willing to pay the price of being a pupil of mine?"

She said, "If I begin, I will not stop."

He persisted. "Soon your family will tell you that you are wasting your time, that you would be wiser to invest it in something else."

"I do not believe they will. But even if they did, I would keep on. I am determined to make sculpture my life work."

"Then I shall be glad to teach you," replied the sculptor.

The young pupil worked hard, seldom leaving her teacher's side. She was worthy of his faith. Today she is a success, and he is naturally proud of her. He works happily, knowing that in her strong hands his art will live on.

You who wish to become something in Christian life, who wish to feel its abiding inspiration and who want Christianity to live on to God's eternal glory, will find that it comes at a price. What will attaining this Christian life demand of me?

It means following the rules. It means bowing under the yoke that creates freedom. It means listening as God's Holy Spirit speaks to you through conscience. It means wholeheartedly following His teachings, and making the shaping of a Christian character your life work. It ought not be a Sunday faith, merely attending church and its activities. It should penetrate every area of our daily living. We may leave no secret place in our heart for the things which the natural man wants to do. We must be totally consecrated, willing to battle the evil one the rest of our life.

As I direct a youth camp in the summer, I have opportunity to see the competitive spirit of youth at work. It is equally keen whether it involves boys or girls. This spirit of excelling is in their very blood. They simply do not know the word, "Quit."

If we are to reveal a Christian life that has deep meaning, we mature folks, too, must have the will, the will to become.

TODAY'S THOUGHT: *A good beginning is necessary in life, but it is also important to keep growing.*

316

NOVEMBER 12

A Christian Gives, Gives, Gives

I looked for pity, but there was none; and for comforters, but 1 found none. Psalm 69:20

There was a good farmer who loved his Lord. Since he believed in sharing any success with his Lord, he lived a very happy life. His extreme generosity prompted his friends to ask how he could give so much and yet thrive so well.

"We can't understand it," they said. "You give more than we do, and yet you continue to have greater prosperity."

"That is easy to explain," said the farmer. "I just keep shoveling into God's bin, and God just keeps shoveling into mine. And God has a bigger shovel!"

How often have we complained about the constant demands made upon us by the church and worthy charities?

"As far as I can see this Christianity business is just give, give, give," said a wealthy, influential man. After a moment his minister answered him.

"I wish to thank you for the best definition of a Christian that I have ever heard," he said.

Keep in mind that God never asks us to give beyond what His enabling makes possible. Whenever we complain about the ever enlarging demands made upon us, let us look to the cross, and see there the picture of God giving His only Son. No amount of worldly wealth could possibly pay for the gift of salvation. No matter how long we might live, we could not do enough for God to repay Him for what He has done for us. Nor does He expect that we should.

Yet the Christian life, too, makes certain demands. Our Savior asks that we consecrate our lives to Him. Once He gets our life, He has all there is of us—our time, our talents, and our possessions. Having made such an investment, we are assured of fabulous dividends. The more we give to God, the more we receive back in spiritual peace and satisfaction. One of the unfailing laws of life states that, as we give, so shall we live.

TODAY'S THOUGHT: *Few men have attained greatness who have not given themselves to others.*

317

NOVEMBER 13

"On Earth Is Not His Equal"

For he who has pity on them will lead them. Isaiah 49:10

Some years ago the rector of a parish in one of London's lowliest districts visited occasionally a poor widow occupying a garret in this dirty, noisy slum. Among her few possessions was a flower pot containing a stunted geranium, which she tended with anxious care. On one of his visits the clergyman asked her why she took such pains to keep the puny plant alive.

"It keeps telling me," she said, "that God is here."

What a difference in our lives when we know that God is present wherever we are. How hopeless life would be, if we had to make our way without Him beside us. For He alone can conquer every foe, brace us against any temptation, and lead us through the darkest night. Without this assurance of His unfailing help, life would not be worth while. We need to develop a more childlike faith. How boundless our satisfactions and happiness, if only we fully believed and trusted God's promises even as does a child its affectionate parent.

One day a grandmother asked her grandchild how many had been present in her Sunday school class. The little girl replied, "Grandmother, counting God, there were fifteen of us."

That is the kind of faith we need!

Are you always conscious of His presence whatever you do and wherever you go? This awareness will hold you back from sinning and doing those things which are contrary to the will of God. Certainly, if He walks with you, there are places you may not go, there are things you may not do, there are words you may not speak, and thoughts you may not think. But also if He leads, there are those things you must and should do, which otherwise you would sidestep. There are burdens you will willingly shoulder, crosses you uncomplainingly will bear, and journeys you will take at His prompting.

Unable sometimes to see the road ahead, we become afraid. We stop stock-still. All forward progress ceases, and it appears that we are on a dead-end street. If in that wavering moment of indecision we would only summon up our faith and move on, we should discover anew that God again has opened up a way for us to walk dry-shod through the Red Sea of difficulty.

TODAY'S THOUGHT: *Faith is the soul daring to go farther than the mind of man can see.*

318

NOVEMBER 14

We Are Infinitely Rich

Blessed is the man who trusts in the Lord . . . He is like a tree planted by water, that sends out its roots by the stream, and does not fear when heat comes, for its leaves remain green.

Jeremiah 17: 7, 8

Someone has said, "Praise is the rent we owe to God, and the larger the farm, the greater the rent to be paid."

Each of us has been given certain talents. We only are expected to produce according to what has been given us. Yet all of us are infinitely richer than we think. I am not thinking now of material wealth, but of those blessings which we easily forget. Take a look, therefore, at yourself. How rich are you?

Most all of us have eyes to see. In a world of total darkness you would gladly pay all you possess in order to have the ability to see. Without your eyes you could not see the sunny smile of your child, the colorful array of spring flowers, the red and gold splashes of sunset, or any other glories of nature.

Most of us have ears to hear. In a world of silence, you would borrow all you could to buy the ability to hear. Without your ears you would be denied the trill of birds, the rippling laughter of children, and the soft strains of an orchestra over water.

Most of us have minds that think. In a world of incoherent madness, you would give the gold of Midas for one rational thought, one hour of sanity and contentment.

Most of us have limbs to use, legs with which to walk, and arms with which to work. In a stationary world, how much would you willingly give for the thrill of a brisk morning walk or the pride of doing things for yourself?

Yes, we are all infinitely rich. Hardly any among us but has friends, those who will stand by us, come what may. All of us have God—a God who has promised to be with us always, even to the close of the age, a God who has invited us to come to Him, if we are weary and heavy-laden, a God who has promised to guide us along the highway that leads to eternal life.

To whom much has been given, of him much is expected. Think how infinitely rich you really are; and then resolve to dedicate your life to Him, to show your gratitude for what He has done for you.

TODAY'S THOUGHT: *Every plant is known by the kind of fruit it bears.*

NOVEMBER 15

Burdens Can Be Blessings

Cast your burden on the Lord, and he will sustain you.

Psalm 55:22

Several years ago a young college student had to make his way from class to class on crutches. Though awkward in his actions, he had a genius for learning and for making friends, and a spirit of unquenchable optimism. During his four years this crippled young man won every scholastic honor. His friends, out of consideration and respect, had never asked the cause of his handicap. But one day a friend had courage enough to approach him.

"John," he asked, "why are you crippled?"

"Infantile paralysis," was the brief answer.

"Then tell me," continued the friend, "with an affliction like that, how do you face life so confidently, and without any trace of bitterness?"

The young man smiled, then tapped his chest and replied, "Oh, I never let it touch my heart."

God will grace us to endure any hardship we encounter. We taste defeat only when we permit the trouble to get inside us. All the water in the world will never sink a ship unless it gets inside. Our problems cannot overcome us unless we let them topple the inner man.

Many times our difficulties are spurs to urge us on. At other times they actually can be safeguards to prevent still more serious trouble.

An African explorer reports that the natives burden themselves with a heavy load before crossing a swift stream. If nothing else they carry a rock. With the load balanced on their heads they wade into the water, the load's solid weight helping them keep their footing, and preventing the rushing waters from dragging them downstream to destruction.

The only time we are really in trouble is when we push away the power which Almighty God holds out to us from above, adequate strength to continue no matter how heavy life's burdens may be.

TODAY'S THOUGHT: *Today our burden may seen unbearable, but come tomorrow you will discover that you have a new strength because you bore that burden.*

NOVEMBER 16

We Must Deny Ourselves

He who trusts in his riches will wither, but the righteous will flourish like a green leaf. Proverbs 11:28

Over the young Napoleon's bed in Corsica hung a beautiful tapestry on which had been intricately worked the Homeric story of the Greek heroes. Seeing mighty Achilles and many another hero, Napoleon felt his heart take fire. He, too, determined to become a conquering hero.

The history of the church of Jesus Christ holds before us a far grander picture of the brave men and brave women, the saints who fought, conquered, and died for the cause of Christ. The battle roll of the saints is the most heroic of all. As we read the names of each good soldier of Christ we should feel, "I, too, have a work to do, a battle to fight." Think of the glorious examples set by others before us.

"Since we are surrounded by so great a cloud of witnesses, let us also lay aside every weight, and sin which clings so closely, and let us run with perseverance the race that is set before us, looking to Jesus, the pioneer and perfector of our faith."

What is involved in this race we are asked to run? How may we work for Christ? I think self-examination will uncover that no one of us has denied himself as God has commanded. Not long ago I heard of a young man who considered himself a good Christian. Still he confessed he could not remember that he had ever once denied himself. What an example our Master has set before us! He who could have been king took the form of a servant. He humbled himself, and became obedient to death on the cross.

Look around God's vineyard. Look at all the work there is left for us to do, all the people that need help. Let no man say there is no work for him to do. Every person has something to offer, from the tenderest child to the oldest father. Every bit of work done in the name of God is significant.

What is involved in being a disciple of the Master? "If any man would come after me, let him deny himself and take up his cross and follow me." If we accept His challenge, we will discover we are traveling on the glory road.

TODAY'S THOUGHT: *The hand that clasps the Lord's hand cannot at the same time reach for riches and things.*

NOVEMBER 17

Turn to Him Today

Do thou, O Lord, protect us, guard us ever from this genera-
tion. Psalm 12:7

People often say they do not have time to read God's Word and
to pray. There are just too many things to do. Life is too busy.
Suddenly an emergency is upon us. Then, no matter how busy we
are, we are compelled to seek God's help, and to try to find a
way out of our moment of despair.

How unfortunate that it takes an emergency to stop most people
on their busy rounds of getting and spending. Do they really want
help? Will they ever voice an honest regret and a plea for a second chance? Catering only to the busy things of life, they have
taken no time to be still and commune with God.

I have often thought of the familiar mechanical device which
sounds emergency. A siren means business. When it blows, it is
the sound of desperate urgency. You have no choice, when the
policeman's siren sounds behind your car, but to stop. When the
fire truck races down the avenue, you shove on the brakes for a
stop. And when the ambulance siren screams, you pull to the
curb. Whether you like it or not, whether you have time or not,
you stop. All traffic comes to a halt. No one attempts to argue,
because somewhere there is desperate urgency—life or death.

It would be well if we did not wait for the sirens to blow before
we decided to pause in our busy occupations, and take time to commune with God and so gain strength as we learn from His Word.

It is possible to fortify ourselves against adversity. Remember
the old gospel hymn that sings of the time when "sorrows like
sea billows roll." It assures us that, whatever our lot, if we have
God, we can say, "It is well, it is well with my soul." It tells out
the message of faith's solid foundations, undergirding life in spite
of what storms may assail. Whatever storms the world may hurl
against the inner castle of the soul, we can successfully withstand
them, if anchored to the Rock of Ages.

TODAY'S THOUGHT: *It is the set of a sail, and not the force of
the gale, that decides which way the ship will go; like that is faith
to a man's life.*

NOVEMBER 18

Faith Foils Despair

The Lord is my light and my salvation; whom shall I fear?
Psalm 27:1

The happiest people in the world have been those who have given their lives to others. They are the ones who, instead of making material gain their chief goal, have rather sought to serve others.

Think of Madame Curie. One day she sat in a classroom and heard a teacher say, "There are stars at some of your fingertips." She could not forget it. Later, she married Pierre Curie, and worked side by side with him in the laboratory. They were not thinking at all of making a fortune for themselves, but rather of setting out in search of radium, hoping that this discovery would alleviate the sufferings of some of their fellow men. One dark night they entered the poor, ill-heated room in which they were working to discover that the empty cups were glistening. They had made the wonderful discovery for which they had been searching! They found that the stars were indeed at their fingertips because they were willing to work in utter abandon for an unselfish goal.

Consider the Pilgrim Fathers. They came to this country not in search of gold, but in search of God. Although their cemeteries grew faster than their gardens, they never lost their faith. They found joy not in material security, but in the peace that came into their hearts as they remained in tune with the living God.

I think of a great song writer. His heart was broken because he was rejected in love. Moreover he had become blind. All circumstances seemed to turn against him. But he did not accept his inner promptings, which were like to the advice given to Job centuries before, "curse God and die." Rather, he sat down and wrote a hymn that will not be forgotten. Its words are addressed to God and its title is, "O Love That Wilt Not Let Me Go." His name was Matheson.

When that faith becomes ours, we shall find the joy and the happiness that we are seeking. Life will become more wonderful, the longer we live it.

TODAY'S THOUGHT: *If we only have faith in Christ, we have everything.*

NOVEMBER 19

Strip Off Your Tunic!

Even a child makes himself known by his acts, whether what he does is pure and right. Proverbs 20:11

During a certain revival a young man was asked by an evangelist if he were saved. This was the young man's answer: "I have been a Christian for several years, but no one has found it out."

This is impossible! You cannot really be a Christian, and conceal the fact that you belong to God. Remember Peter when he was denying the Lord? They said of him, "Your accent betrays you." You cannot long remain in the presence of the Master without a vast change taking place.

If Christ dwells within our hearts, His beauty will be seen in our words and deeds. How different life would be, if more people became living epistles, if, rather than trying to cloister their faith and so rendering themselves utterly ineffective, they allowed themselves to become the good leaven, transforming this soggy lump of mortal life into lightness and joy of spiritual reality.

The Master teaches His followers that they, although they must be in the world, need not be of the world. They are to be the salt of the earth. If, therefore, His followers are to be effectively contagious, they must come into contact with human need wherever they find it. Jesus teaches His followers they are to be bright, shining lights, set on a lampstand, and not hidden under a bushel. A world of darkness would vanish overnight, if all who profess the name of Christ would live up to all that His name implies.

So often we do not do the little that we can because we feel that only the many-talented person can be effective in his community and in world service. Such thinking is a tragic mistake. Friend, open up your eyes today and see all there are about you who need a touch of friendship or sympathy. There is so much for all of us to do. Without question there are lonely people nearby who need your companionship. Maybe you have a free evening with which to serve as a volunteer in a social agency. Maybe a lonely body in some old people's home would have something to look forward to, if you cultivated a friendship, planned a shopping trip, or car ride, or a visit to a movie together. Why not seek out your task today and do it? It will help make your life worth the living.

TODAY'S THOUGHT: *The aim of the Lord's host is: No on-lookers please; strip off your tunic and into the fray!*

NOVEMBER 20

Kneel at Heaven's Gate Today

Blessed are the poor in spirit, for theirs is the kingdom of heaven.
Matthew 5:3

Blessedness has ever so much more to it than mere happiness. It is closely identified with character. It is joy growing out of the soul. It is part and parcel of the soul's very nature, and indestructible by any outward power. Blessedness is the fire within that gives light and warmth, whatever the outward circumstances of life may be.

We discover in the first beatitude the kind of character which can be called blessed—"the poor in spirit." These are the people so acutely aware of their sin, their need, and spiritual incompleteness that they seek the aid that only God can give. They are the ones who reach beyond themselves toward the eternal, and so each day they kneel at heaven's gate, asking strength for the hours ahead. The poor in spirit are the opposite of those who are proud, self-righteous, and conceited. Being poor in spirit corresponds precisely to the attitude of becoming as little children. We must be willing to learn, to ask, and to seek.

It is not mere poverty of worldly goods that makes one poor in spirit. One may be both poor and proud. It is not one who lacks self respect, nor one who cringes before his fellow men. It is rather a humble estimate of one's self in view of the goodnes of God. It is the humble man's feeling when he looks deep into the ideal character of Jesus, and sees himself as in a mirror, unworthy to be in the company of one so pure and holy.

The reward for such souls is this—"theirs is the kingdom of heaven." This does not refer only to a locality, but to the character or state where God rules, where all dealings, all feelings, all hopes, are heavenly. It is heaven on earth. It is heaven forevermore.

To the poor in spirit belongs this kingdom, because they only are in a condition to receive it. They only want it and seek it with all their hearts. They alone have the heavenly spirit begun in them. It is a present as well as a future blessing. Our pride, conceit, and selfishness lock and bar the gate to the temple of heavenly blessedness. The poor in spirit have entered the door like children, to live henceforth in the kingdom of heaven.

TODAY'S THOUGHT: *Man's power is to the power of God as the beam of a ten-cent flashlight is to the light of the noonday sun.*

NOVEMBER 21

You Can Be a Lifeline to Others

Anxiety in a man's heart weighs him down, but a good word makes him glad. Proverbs 12:25

The day King George VI of England was to broadcast a message of peace from London to the United States, a sudden break occurred in a transmitting wire. The trouble was spotted just a few moments before "air time." A quick survey revealed that it would take at least 20 minutes to make the repairs. But hundreds of thousands of people waiting to hear the King would be disappointed. Without hesitating, one of the engineers of the station grasped the ends of the broken wires, one in each hand, to restore the circuit. The shock of the leakage of current shook his arms and burned his hands, but he held on while the King's message of peace was broadcast.

We, too, are called upon to be links in a broken line, transmitting the message of life to our fellow men. No matter what our occupation—parents at home with children, doctors with patients, teachers with students, or executives with employees—we all have the opportunity to grasp some severed life line, and so keep the current flowing.

Jesus is our supreme example. He put His body in the breach, letting hell's fire sear and burn it, all so that the line of communication between heaven and earth might be restored, in order that our heavenly Father and His children might be brought together again. They nailed Him to the cross, and it sufficed to bridge the gap between a holy God and the sinner, allowing the forgiving love of the Eternal Father to flow freely once again to the hearts of those who will receive it.

Are you willing to stand still and let the current of God's love flow through you, even though it may mean sacrifice? True love of God always means service and sacrifice. A wealthy man was an official of his small country church, and was known as one of the most zealous and self-denying Christians in the community. A friend asked why he pursued such a course.

"When I became a Christian," he said, "and began to read and understand my Bible, I read that I was called into the vineyard of the Lord. I realized that I was not there to eat grapes, but to hoe, and I have been trying to hoe ever since."

TODAY'S THOUGHT: *Do what is right and, as your reward, God will give you the power to continue to do right.*

NOVEMBER 22

Stand in God's Smile

May God be gracious to us and bless us and make his face to shine upon us. Psalm 67:1

A number of years ago there lived a man whose chief aim in life was to attain great wealth. Business success gave him much that money could buy, including a fine residence. He retired to enjoy his wealth, his home, and his family, but it was not long before tragedy struck. First it took from him his children, one by one, then his wife. Thus the day came when he turned from the cemetery to an empty and desolate house.

These rapidly occurring events started him thinking. He saw that he had realized his ambition, but that in so doing he had neglected life's most important thing. One day, as he was sorting over some treasured things, he came upon a trunk—the one he had used when he went off to school. He found among other things in it, a pair of tiny shoes, his baby shoes, which his mother must have put there. On the sole of one of them he found writing in his mother's hand which reminded him of a story she had told him long ago.

One day when he was a little lad he and his mother were in the parlor together. Suddenly the sun tipping in at the window made a bright spot on the floor. The little fellow had cried out, "What is that?"

Mother replied, "It is God's smile."

Busy, she left the room for a few moments. Upon her return she saw her little boy with feet planted close together standing on that spot of sunlight.

"I am standing in God's smile!" he told her proudly.

Turning the shoe over in his hands, the man smiled wistfully to himself, and felt a tug in his heart as he read these words: "This is the pair of little shoes my baby wore the day he stood in God's smile. May he always stand in the smile of God."

Suddenly he dropped to his knees, seeking forgiveness from God. For he saw as in a flash of sunlight that he had not put first things first.

We would do well, if each of us would stop and ask ourselves whether or not we are today the kind of people our mothers and fathers wished us to be. Have we remained true to the faith, and are we growing in spiritual stature as we live the gospel daily?

TODAY'S THOUGHT: *Serve God faithfully, for earth is the overture to the symphony that is heaven.*

NOVEMBER 23

Prayer's Mighty Miracle

He (Jesus) said . . . "My house shall be called a house of prayer."
Matthew 21:13

People do not wait to understand the physics of sound before they turn on the radio, or the mechanics of video and audio before they turn on the television. As children we do not diagram our parent's affection before we take advantage of it. As gardeners we do not fully expect to understand nature before we plant seeds and later enjoy the fruits of our labors and our faith in that seed.

This process of acceptance without understanding applies also in focusing our attention on God. We do not have to explain the full nature of God in order to learn that He exists, and that we can reach Him. We just start experimenting. Soon we discover how simple it is to receive God's infinite power, a power that will flow through our lives and make for us the kind of glorious life we are all seeking. It is as practical as turning on the faucet to see if the water is running, or plugging in a lamp to see if the electricity is available.

Everyone has the power to commune with God in prayer. Some people are disturbed and say that praying is like playing with fire. "There is a power available," they say, "but what do you do with it when you find it? Are you sure you can bend it to your own uses? What if it bends and breaks you?"

These questions that people ask about prayer deserve worthy answers, for they deal with the most powerful weapon on earth. Yes, it is more powerful than any bomb man has developed. By all authentic records, splitting the atom is a small energy release compared with the power that prayer generates. Through prayer lives have been changed past all recognition, communities have been transformed, the course of civilization has been diverted. Through prayer all things are possible—not only for the world in which we live, but for the people who live in that world. Prayer can do wonderful things for you.

TODAY'S THOUGHT: *Launch a ship of prayer each hour, and the world of your life will be a different place.*

NOVEMBER 24

Serve Him with Thanksgiving

Enter his gates with thanksgiving, and his courts with praise!
Psalm 100:4

Growing on cliffs at the edge of the sea is a plant called samphire, and though it is near the salt water, it always stays above the reach of the tide. One day a group of shipwrecked sailors was struggling up the face of a rugged cliff, desperately afraid that the advancing tide would overtake them. Then one of the men spotted some samphire growing serenely among the rocks. He shouted for joy and assured his companions that they had reached a safe place. He knew that the sea would come near this spot, perhaps even soak it with spray, but that the waters would never reach it.

Christ is our refuge from the advancing tide of life's problems. Because we have been created in His image and belong to Him, we may be sure that although we live in full sight of the world's angry waves, if we but remain close to Him, we are perfectly safe. What a joy to know that such security can be ours every day!

The enjoyment of God's protection, however, places a responsibility upon us. In our thankfulness for God's loving care we will want to serve Him in all that we do. This service should not be born of a sense of duty, but should spring up from our love and gratitude for Him.

Suppose a son or daughter, returning home at regular intervals to visit a widowed mother, should say, "Mother, I really do not want to come. I have many other things I prefer to do, but duty compels me to see you."

How would the mother feel? I am sure she would tell her child to stay away rather than visit her out of a sense of duty.

How many of us, as we go about our Lord's work, think "I will do this because I have to. I have no love for it."

Only as we serve God in love and thanksgiving can we merit the reward of happiness.

TODAY'S THOUGHT: *Those who do the Lord's work never work in vain.*

NOVEMBER 25

He Lent Dignity to Work

For the works which the Father has granted me to accomplish, these very works which I am doing, bear me witness that the Father has sent me. John 5:36

Most everyone knows that story of Jesus, when at the age of twelve He was found with the doctors in the temple, asking and answering questions. Only a few verses sum up what we know about His boyhood, but these are significant. "And Jesus increased in wisdom and in stature, and in favor with God and man." We see Him for an instant in the school, and then He passes into the obscurity of the workshop. Every true life must be one of learning and labor. Every day we should be learning something, and every day we should be working for something. Every field produces a crop, whether it be good wheat or some worthless seed pod. And so it is with life, for each day produces its particular fruit toward the ultimate harvest.

The fact that Jesus spent those years in the carpenter's shop in Nazareth gave great dignity to work. The touch of God's own hand has consecrated labor. If God is with us in all that we do, work becomes a virtue. We are best prepared to receive a special message from heaven when we are about our everyday business.

Look into the history of the past. The shepherds were watching their flocks by night when the angel brought the message of Christ's birth. Amos was taken from the herdsmen of Tekoa to become a prophet of the Lord. The first disciples of the Master were called from the fishing boats and from the customs house.

Happy is the man who rejoices in his work, certain that he has the best position in the world. Happy is the man who labors honestly, and does his best even at routine tasks. This man, be his work lofty or lowly, is about his Father's business, and he is supremely important in God's sight. God shows no partiality. If we do our appointed tasks well, we all stand as equals in His sight.

TODAY'S THOUGHT: *You expect an honest day's work from those under your charge; are you thinking of what God has the right to expect from you?*

NOVEMBER 26

Make Your Life a Thank-You!

And this, not as we expected, but first they gave themselves to the Lord and to us by the will of God. 2 Corinthians 8:5

On a visit to a native village, a missionary found a little lad all alone stretched out on a simple straw mat. His eyes were closed, and it seemed that death was near. Very slowly the man of God whispered this verse from Scripture into the boy's ear, "God so loved the world that he gave his only Son, that whoever believes in him should not perish but have eternal life." He repeated it five times without any apparent response. The boy did not seem to hear.

On hearing it the sixth time, however, he opened his eyes and whispered, "And I have never thanked Him, but nobody told me!"

Do we ever show God the appreciation that we should? "There was no other good enough To pay the price of sin; He only could unlock the gate Of heaven, and let us in." Do you appreciate what these words mean?

A group of boys was arrested in a Southern town for presenting a minstrel show without a license. The case was brought by the owner of the old building which they had used without permission. They were all found guilty, and the judge pronounced the sentence.

"I find the prisoners guilty and fine them one dollar each," he said. "The alternative is one day in jail." The little offenders were greatly disturbed until the judge added, "But I was a boy once myself and I remember breaking the law in much the same way. I will pay the prisoners' fines."

Does not this incident remind us of Him who was touched by our infirmities, and who became the expiation for all our sins? Should not the knowledge of God's great love inspire us to dedicate our lives to His service? We need to thank God for Calvary more frequently in our prayers, but more than that, we need to thank Him with our lives. There is so much work for all of us, that His love should be the inspiring force helping us create His kingdom on earth.

TODAY'S THOUGHT: *The one who works for the love of it, rather than for fame or fortune, has already been blessed by God.*

NOVEMBER 27

Life Offers a Crown

He who sows to the Spirit will from the Spirit reap eternal life.
Galatians 6:8

Christ offers us a crown of righteousness for our days on earth, and He promises a crown of glory in heaven. God is constantly seeking us. We are His children and the sheep of His pasture. He provides spiritual food as He feeds us with the bread of heaven. To each one belongs the precious crown given because of His grace and mercy. He offers strength to lead a life like His, for only in living such a life do we wear the crown He intended we should. If we share this gift generously, we shall find a more glorious one in future time, when we receive the unfolding crown of eternal life in heaven. Now, each day we must live a sincere, a holy, self-denying Christian life, if ever we are to receive the crown prepared for all those who love the Lord Jesus, and if we are to look forward with joy to His second coming.

What are the chief characteristics of this Christian life, the jewels of this earthly crown which we dare not lose? God enumerates them in His word—"love, joy, peace, patience, kindness, goodness, faithfulness, gentleness, self-control." Each time one intentionally sins he loses one or another of these jewels from his crown of righteousness.

Indeed, in the parable of the lost coin it is supposed that this was one of the coins from a woman's bridal tiara, lost through her carelessness—as chastity is lost to a passing lover.

May this persuade us to be careful lest we yield to temptation. May this thought give us the courage to withstand the tempter's voice when he bids us sin. Whenever we recognize that we have fallen, may His love lead us to true repentance which can restore that lost jewel or coin of our spiritual heritage.

Each time we turn to God in true penitence we can be sure that new joy will fill our hearts as the jewels of the crown become brighter.

Let us cling securely to the wonderful gift that God has given us, that no man may take away our crown of life.

TODAY'S THOUGHT: *Lean, weary soul, against the granite pillar that is Christ and sense the thrill of renewed strength.*

332

NOVEMBER 28

Every Man Needs a Savior

For by grace you have been saved through faith; and this is not your own doing, it is the gift of God—not because of works, lest any man should boast. Ephesians 2:8, 9

One day a leper came to Jesus and said, "If you will, you can make me clean." No one ever need doubt Jesus' willingness to cleanse us of our unrighteousness. He stands always ready and willing. The question is, are we? It seems that most people want the forgiveness of sins only when they realize that "the wages of sin is death." Is it not true that some of us fear the consequences of sin much more than sin itself? How many of us recoil at the hurt that a loving God knows at our sin? Is it not the hurt and shame of being found out and punished that gets us most?

God is willing to help only if we are sincere in our request. Too many of us presume on receiving God's pardon, and then flippantly go out to repeat the same mistakes again. Too many of us, like a certain man of old, are asking God to change us but not yet, and so are merely trifling with the Almighty. Too many of us want the world and Christ at the same time. Too many of us are proud in our own conceits and do not recognize all of our wrong doings.

A certain nobleman who died a long time ago use to mutter aloud in church as each of the commandments were read, "I never did that." In his own thinking he had no need of a Savior. But for him there was also no abundant living.

Let us be honest with ourselves. Let us ask God where we have broken His laws. Let us not sort out our virtues only, but rather the many mistakes and sins which we commit each day.

Are we willing to be made clean? Before you will ever receive pardon or know the peace that comes from it, and feel at last the power for living which follows, you must not only see your sin, but you must hate it. It must lead you to recognize your need for Christ the Savior to redeem you.

Today Jesus of Nazareth passes by. Turn to Him, sinner, and plead, "Jesus, Son of David, have mercy upon me." If we are sincere in this cry, He will certainly hear our cry. He will give us too the blessed assurance, "I will; be clean." And then we shall have found the gate to a new life and enter into the glorious fellowship He means us to enjoy.

TODAY'S THOUGHT: *Christ's love can wipe away the rust of sin on the shield of a man's life.*

333

NOVEMBER 29

Who Is Indispensable?

And they sing the song of Moses, the servant of God, and the song of the Lamb, saying, "Great and wonderful are thy deeds, O Lord God Almighty! Just and true are thy ways, O King of the ages!" Revelation 15:3

Christ with His disciples have just left the upper room, singing a hymn. Now they are walking together up the hill toward the Garden of Gethsemane. As they walk along the olive grove Jesus called attention to some of the heaped up branches that had been cut off because they were fruitless. He commented that ultimately they would be gathered together in one huge pile for burning. Then Jesus said to them that apart from Him they would become such a branch for withering and ultimate burning.

The good branches, however, bore fruit. So they deserved to stay on the vine. They proved their worth, taking of the trunk's strength only to put it to the ripe fruit.

So it is in the Christian life. True faith demonstrates itself in work. Without God it is impossible really to live. The parable of the vine says that, if true life is in our hearts, if God is there, then our hands are bound to move in Christian service, and our feet to walk in Christian love. It follows as naturally as day follows night.

God is indispensable for living. If we refuse to take Him into our lives, we shall continually face problems which not only will break our own hearts, but also sadden the heart of God.

It is a disturbing experience to watch a Memorial Day parade and see different uniforms from many wars. They attest to the fact that we have not yet learned to put our trust in the Prince of Peace. As a consequence our homes know vacant chairs, and thousands of citizens suffer with mangled bodies, minds distressed, languishing in some veterans' hospital instead of being usefully employed. No, we cannot possibly solve the world's problems without God. How great our wisdom would be, if we transformed this realization into the conclusion that God is indispensable.

Sometimes I marvel that God can be so long-suffering, that He can wait patiently so long in dealing with His children. God wants us to know that life lived with Him is really worth while. He is truly indispensable.

TODAY'S THOUGHT: *Alone and unaided, man gets nowhere, but grasping God's proffered hand, he will make it all the way to heaven.*

NOVEMBER 30

Man Makes His Choice

While you have the light, believe in the light, that you may become sons of light. John 12:36

A certain writer says that our soul is a machine, that God is a force, and that man's future is a coffin. Thanks to God, the Christian can reject that dolorous creed. We believe God has given us free will with which to choose either good or evil. Our hope is in a God who is a living Father, an omniscient Guide. He is an unfailing Friend, a very present help in time of trouble. We believe the important future we head for is not death, but life eternal. Man is not called on to work out his own salvation, for God provided the plan fulfilled in Jesus, our Savior. But God does look for that salvation to result in godly living and attitudes.

But in our hands is the power of choice. Every man decides which way his soul shall go. By the things we say and the things we do, we make our decision.

Let us closely examine our life today. Does our every word and deed work to the honor of God? Do men know by the way we talk that we are Christians? Other lives are much affected by the words we speak. Many are the broken hearts caused by the tempers of men with unbridled tongues. Cruel words cut like a sharp razor, and make wounds that are difficult to heal. The unjust charge is the hardest judgment of all for the sinner to bear. The unjust charge hardens us more than the heaviest blows administered to the body. One of the saddest of all sins, and one we are all guilty of, is the sin of foolish talking.

In our speech we sin also in another way. Too frequently we ask, and too seldom do we thank God. Let us think more of God's goodness and less of our real or imagined troubles, and soon all that we say will be filled with love and gratitude. Why not think positively today of all the blessings God has given? You will soon discover your life full of prayer and thanksgiving.

TODAY'S THOUGHT: *Take time each day to consider just how really fortunate you are.*

DECEMBER 1

Bound for Heaven

Instead, seek his kingdom, and these things shall be yours as well. Luke 12:31

You will be glad tomorrow, if you refuse today to be earth-bound. Jesus came into the world to point us in a new direction, to show men the glory there can be in living. He came with power to transform our lives. Instead of pointing only to earth, our lives should be tri-dimensional—downward to earth, as we live a wholesome natural life, outward to our fellow men, and upward to heaven. "Ah wears dis world lak' a loose garment," said a simple soul. Just so, we can live as though we have not here an abiding city, assured that some day we shall share the ultimate glory in the House of Many Mansions.

Some build personal empires of wealth and broad estates. Many accumulate things, and believe that these can bring them happiness. What a false assumption! A gold horse will never pull a load of hay. God alone put the right key in our hands in the words: "Whoever does the will of God my Father," "Seek first his kingdom." God means that we should live according to the pattern of His life.

Consider James Garfield. He was always second in school until one day he discovered the reason why. The young chap ranking ahead of him rose 15 minutes earlier every day to study, and that 15 minutes made the difference. So James Garfield resolved to get up half an hour earlier. The extra 15 minutes he gained on the other student made him the leading scholar in the entire school.

How many of us spend 15 minutes a day, and that is only 1/96 of a day, in prayer and meditation, or in the reading of God's Word? Just 15 minutes a day! If we are still, and open our hearts to God for at least so short a time, we can expect the glory that Scripture tells us of. If a sick man refuses to use the medicine, how can he ever expect to become well?

The time has come for us to quit staring at the steps. The time has come for us to start climbing them by doing the will of God. We shall never finish anything that we do not begin. If God is allowed to come more and more into the consciousness of the soul, there will be increasing glory. Is there a rainbow in your soul, a rainbow that gives hope for this day, hope for tomorrow, and hope for all eternity?

TODAY'S THOUGHT: *There is no inconvenience or trouble in having a sure hope.*

DECEMBER 2

Turn Away from Temptation

And do not fear those who kill the body but cannot kill the soul;
rather fear him who can destroy both soul and body in hell.
Matthew 10:28

Take a look at the second temptation of Jesus which took place
on the very pinnacle of the temple. The true God of the temple
was being tempted, standing atop His own holy house.

Immediately we can learn a lesson. Although we come to God's
house filled with reverent thoughts and feelings, we may have to
slug it out with the evil one even in His holy place. An evil heart
of unbelief Luther calls a "great and shameful sin." There can be
the wandering thoughts and the indifference to holy things that
render a heart callous.

The second temptation was to presume upon God's love and
mercy. Satan tried to make Jesus place himself in the dangerous
position of putting His heavenly Father to the test as to whether
or not He would save Him. We likewise are tempted when the
devil seeks to make us disregard the voice of conscience, as when
he whispers that God will take care of us despite our neglecting
our health, so vital to our well-being, and when he fills our
thoughts with purely worldly concerns. He tempts man to injure
his health by overindulgence in things harmful to the body. Moreover he stands at man's elbow, assuring him that all is well despite
his callow disregard of soul, that he is quite safe, and that certainly
God will preserve him, however deeply he plunges into sin.

How then shall we meet temptations? Jesus gave us the answer,
when He each time turned the devil away saying, "It is written!"
Hold fast to this, and remember some one of the precious promises
of God when the next temptation comes.

Never purposefully put yourself in the way of temptation. Often
we excuse ourselves by saying the devil has come to us, when
actually it is that we have of our own free will gone to him. Therefore, stay close to the Lord Jesus Christ. He alone has the power
to help.

TODAY'S THOUGHT: *Every traffic light is a reminder to us
that the devil should get our Stop, and Christ our Go.*

DECEMBER 3

With Christ, for Christ

For as many of you as were baptized into Christ have put on Christ. Galatians 3:27

Dr. Livingstone's motto was, "Fear God and work hard." It is a good motto for every Christian. We are to be workers together with God. He always stands ready to indwell us and work through us, but we must do our part by yielding and surrender.

Our various gifts are to be put at His bidding, for God has given gifts to each in some measure. There are so many different ways we can do this work. We must take care to use our gift, our particular talent, to the best of our ability. One man can preach, while another man can build the pulpit in which the minister stands. Some are called to go forth, taking the gospel message to the heathen in faraway lands. Others are called to preach the gospel through the power of God on the street where they live. Wherever we are and whatever we do, each of us can prove to the world that he is God's servant.

Whether our life be as brilliant as the sun, or seemingly insignificant as a candle, above all we should take care each day to show our light, to let it shine before men, that our Father in heaven might be glorified.

So many of us are wasting our lives in idle dreams. We think noble thoughts, but fail to fulfill them. Living in a dreamworld, we say continually, "I wish I could do something great for Jesus rather than just be a flunky."

Why not do something for Him today, however humble it might be? Wherever you are you have a work to do. You can show your faith in your daily occupation. Whoever does best, whatever he is called upon to do, can make of his life a pulpit from which are preached the world's finest sermons.

Let us resolve today to begin using every single opportunity to be God's witness to our fellow men. As we invest our lives in service, we soon shall discover our reward in the deep satisfaction such a life can give.

TODAY'S THOUGHT: *A faith shared is a faith doubled.*

DECEMBER 4

Saved by Faith

This is the victory that overcomes the world, our faith.
1 John 5:4

The story is told of two men who were boating in the rapids above Niagara Falls. They lost control of their boat, and soon were being carried swiftly downstream. It seemed they could not escape being dashed to pieces, but shortly before they reached the falls, someone on shore threw them a rope. One man grabbed it and was pulled to safety. Just as the rope was thrown to the other man, a log floated near him. Terrified and confused, he grabbed the log instead of the rope. He made a fatal mistake.

Both men were in imminent danger. One of them was pulled safely to shore by the rope, his saving connection with the people on land. The other man went to his doom, clinging to the loose, floating log.

Now faith is a saving connection with Christ. No matter how firmly or tightly we may cling to our own virtues, they cannot help us at all. If we trust only in ourselves, there will be a time when, because of our folly, we shall be led to destruction. We shall be like disconnected logs which have no contact with the heavenly shore. Only as we put our faith in the help God offers, can we be drawn out of our difficulty to a position of security and safety.

"What is your faith?" you ask. Let this little boy answer.

"How do you know your brother has gone home to heaven?" he was asked.

"Well, sir," he said, "my brother was dying, and he seemed afraid. I told him simply to trust in Jesus. He asked me what to do. I said, 'Pray to Him.' My brother answered, 'I am too weak. I can't.' Then I said, 'Well, just hold up your hand. Jesus will see you and know what it means.' And that is what he did."

I often think of that dying lad with his uplifted hand as a beautiful illustration of the simplicity of faith.

TODAY'S THOUGHT: *As the stranger follows carefully the directions of the native, so a man ought to taks his directions from the Son of God.*

DECEMBER 5

Repent and Be Forgiven

Repent, for the kingdom of heaven is at hand. Matthew 3:2

As we think of the suffering and death of our Lord Jesus Christ, there are many lessons to learn from the incidents surrounding this event.

We can learn a lesson from the fate of Judas. His sin had been found out. The money which he coveted had become hateful to him and, driven by remorse, he cast it away and took his own life.

There are many like Judas in our world. They begin well but their lives end in ruin. There was a time when the traitor loved his Master and saw glory in His footsteps. So, there are some who put their hand to the plow but who then look back. In the beginning they take the yoke of Christ, only to let it slip from their shoulders. They begin by being loyal to Jesus, but end by betraying the Lord of glory.

Judas had never considered the full consequences of his sin, and when he saw the awful result of his weakness, it drove him to despair. No man deliberately would commit sin if he weighed the consequences. Let us think before we act, lest we ruin our souls.

It is true that the Master will always forgive us, but let us remember that repentance can come too late. Mary Magdalene came in time, and so did the dying thief as he called to the Lord for mercy. But for Judas the door was shut.

Let Pilate also teach us a lesson. He declared Jesus to be innocent and yet he delivered Him to die. He washed his hands in token of his innocence of Christ's blood. Likewise, we often wash hands from the responsibility of our guilt. We sin and try to throw the blame on someone else. We say it is the way things are in this world, and we just cannot help ourselves. We insist that we got into bad company, and that being overwhelmed we did wrong. We even have the temerity to say that we committed sin from a good motive. These excuses do not offer escape because they are not honest. Nothing can be hidden from an omniscient God who knows all things. "Whatever a man sows, that he will also reap." If we sow a life of evil and deceit, we must suffer the consequences. If we allow the Lord our Savior to help us sow a life of goodness, we will find happiness and peace.

TODAY'S THOUGHT: *Christ died to straighten out man's zig-zag path of sin and death.*

DECEMBER 6

You Too Can Build for Christ

Jesus then said to the Jews who had believed in him, "If you continue in my word, you are truly my disciples." John 8:31

Hundreds of years back a poor man lived in a wretched mud hut in a wild and desolate district far across the seas. Being a godly man, he thought if he could only build a church, people would be less savage and wicked. So day after day as he returned home from his weary day's work, he would pick up a large stone and carry it with him, until he had gathered a great heap around his cabin. With staunch faith, this poor laborer told his doubting neighbors that one day these stones would be a church. The man grew old, and the heap of stones grew bigger; but at last he became mortally ill. Before he passed into the Great Beyond, he spoke these words, "Some day this heap of stones must build a church to the glory of God."

Having heard of the poor laborer's pious zeal, the lord of the manor undertook to carry on the work the old man had begun. The church rose on the foundation of those very stones which the humble peasant had collected.

Each of us can do something to build up the living church of Christ. We need not have outstanding talents or extensive means. If it is consecrated to Him, God has a miraculous way of taking our little gifts and using them for tremendous good.

"What can I do?" you ask.

Have you ever stretched out a helping hand to try to lead some soul into the kingdom? That is one way to carry a stone, as it were, for the pile from which will be built a little more of God's house! But you say you haven't the talents, and you wonder how you can do this. Your prayers, your sympathies, and, above all, your example can do it! If you are to win others for Christ, you must follow Him yourself. If you wish others to march with Christ's soldiers, you must yourself keep step.

Too few of us have been willing to make the total consecration of life necessary to be an effective witness. Even at home we expect more of our children than we do of ourselves.

Let us resolve today to run the race of godliness, and lay aside every weight that can cause our defeat. Let us press on toward the prize, knowing that with the help of God we shall be victorious.

TODAY'S THOUGHT: *Discard the old patched cloak of self-concern, and instead wear the cloak labeled "others."*

DECEMBER 7

In God's Eyes No Job Is Insignificant

There is nothing better than that a man should enjoy his work, for that is his lot. Ecclesiastes 3:22

One day Martha Barry called on an architect and asked him to make plans for a new barn on the campus of the Barry Schools. There was a farm attached to this campus where students got the opportunity to work their way through school by helping to raise their own food.

When the architect showed Martha Barry the completed plans she looked at them and was pleased. But she said, "I would like to have you make one change. I want a spire on that barn."

Shocked, the architect said, "But, Martha Barry, that would be sacrilegious."

"No," she answered, "you are wrong. This is the way I feel. When the students bring in the hay and the crops from the fields I want them to see that spire pointing heavenward, for it will remind them that there is no occupation in life so commonplace and menial that it is insignificant in the sight of God."

God has given us each the great gift of life. Sometimes on receiving gifts we push them aside and say, "Why didn't I get something else?" Then again we may treasure so much the things we receive as to put them away, waiting to use them in the future. But life is one of those rare things that, although it be used extensively, it nevertheless will not wear out. In fact the more we use it for good, the more wonderful life becomes. Instead of the well running dry, its resources only become greater the more we use it.

Side by side on the highways of life walk all God's children. Some are living abundantly and some are not. Some have been touched by the hand of the Master, while others will have nothing to do with Him. The results are very apparent.

In a Belgian art gallery, side by side, are two pictures by Rembrandt. One is the first effort of his youthful genius, a simple sketch, imperfect and faulty. The other is a great masterpiece which all men admire.

Each one of us can be a portrait touched by the hand of the Master. As we grow in His grace, we become increasingly fruitful in the service in the eyes of God and of our fellow men.

TODAY'S THOUGHT: *To the man who loves God and serves Him, life appears to have wings.*

DECEMBER 8

Put Your Heart in Your Work

A man's mind plans his way, but the Lord directs his steps.
Proverbs 16:9

The motto of one of the world's greatest persons had two words: "I serve." Every faithful servant of God shares this objective. The secret of all true service is to put your heart into it. We shall not find any work too hard, or any sacrifice too great, if we love our Master.

The story is told of a nobleman and his wife who were traveling through a Russian forest, attended by their faithful servant. Presently the air was filled with terrible cries, and they knew that starving wolves were pursuing them relentlessly on all sides. The master fired the only shot in his gun, but still the wolves came nearer and nearer.

"Give them one of the horses," cried the servant.

It was done, and for a time the wolves were checked. But soon the savage pack returned to the chase. Seeing the only hope for his master's safety, the servant said, "I'll throw myself to the wolves, and so give you time to escape." Quickly the servant who loved his master cast himself to the wolves, and the travelers escaped. On that forest path the nobleman erected a pillar inscribed with the name of his devoted servant, and then these words: "Greater love has no man than this, that a man lay down his life for his friends."

God has drawn many of us near to Him and, having come into His presence, we have heard His gracious voice. Thus favored, ought we not then turn and lend a helping hand to others? In this great world there are servants of many different degrees, some of high estate and some of low. Yet not one of us can stand alone. We ourselves need help, and ought to be quick to help another. Let the strong help the weak and the well the sick.

Let the Christian seek out his fellow man who is still a stranger to God, and help him to see Him. Let us do our level best to serve God. For as we do that, our kinship with the Master will grow daily more discernible. Our faults and failures daily diminish, and we shall know at last His blessing in the kingdom prepared for us from the begining of the world.

TODAY'S THOUGHT: *The best work is done without hesitating, without difficulty, without boasting.*

DECEMBER 9

Accept These Gifts so Freely Offered

Christ . . . gave himself up for us, a fragrant offering and sacrifice to God. Ephesians 5:2

When traveling, we come frequently to a sign which reads, "Travel at your own risk." Sometimes we see other signs, "Road under construction," or, "This bridge is condemned." These signs are used by states and counties to warn travelers, and so clear themselves from responsibility for accidents caused by the condition of the highways.

There are two roads open to every human being—the broad road, or the narrow one. The sign by the broad road reads, "Travel at your own risk." This is the way of the world. He who walks this highway, must rely solely on his own strength. There are many pitfalls along the way, and, worst of all, this road has no destination.

The second road opening to us is the narrow one. Here are no warning signs. But instead Jesus meets us, speaking softly and tenderly words to this effect: "Follow me. If you do, I will lead you to abundant life." His voice assures us, "I will give them eternal life . . . and no one shall snatch them out of my hand." Think of the riches His promise offers.

A missionary was preparing to leave for his church's foreign mission when a rich friend said, "You are going a long way from home to serve Christ and His kingdom. You may need more money than you have. Here is my checkbook. Take it with you. The checks are all signed. Fill out as many as you need."

Imagine the elation and gratitude of the missionary to have such confidence placed in him. He had behind him the resources of one of the community's wealthiest men.

We, too, have a Friend who has placed at our disposal the riches of His promise. He says that if you follow Him, He will provide sufficient strength for every emergency; every crisis that can possibly happen to you. What hope and confidence must be ours as we follow His way. Why are we so slow to accept these gifts freely offered? There is but one condition imposed upon us if we are to receive these gifts, and it is that we take Him who is the possessor of all things into our hearts. If God has our hearts, then, regardless of where we go, we possess resources unlimited.

TODAY'S THOUGHT: *The man who has formed a friendship with God is unbeatable, unless he himself first gives in.*

DECEMBER 10

The Kindness Cure

One must help the weak, remembering the words of the Lord Jesus, "It is more blessed to give than to receive." Acts 20:35

One who keeps his eyes open cannot travel around our world today without forever remembering thousands on thousands of sick, starving people pleading for help, love, and mercy. Their physical suffering they could endure without whimpering, if they only could know that there were countless loving outstretched hands of mindful Christians. It is difficult for us who are strong and healthy, and who live in a land of great economic prosperity, even to picture those unfortunates with insufficient food, clothing, and shelter, with only a straw pallet or even the hard ground itself for a bed. It seems hard to believe that many suffer needlessly, simply because there are no doctors to minister to them and no medicines for healing. It is difficult for us in a land of infinite educational opportunity to accept the fact that many, many of God's children are illiterate and lack any educational opportunity whatsoever.

When Florence Nightingale attended wounded soldiers in the Crimea, they blessed her very shadow as it fell upon them when she passed. We may not be able to do the spectacular work which she and many others have done. But all of us can do something. We can help to feed the needy, the suffering, the outcasts, sharing what we have.

One afternoon some years ago a little six-year-old boy went out to play with a younger companion. The two of them rambled along until they left the houses of the town behind, and found themselves in the open country. Looking for landmarks after a while, they discovered they had lost their way. Night was approaching and it was stormy and cold. Chilled and hungry, the younger child began to cry, but his brave companion cheered him on. Night finally fell, and they were forced to finding shelter in a field. By this time the older lad could not bear his playmate's crying. He took off his own clothes and used part of them as a bed and the rest to cover his little friend. Together they said their prayers. In the morning they were found. The younger lad had survived the rigors of exposure, but the older one was dead.

As we dedicate our lives to others in unselfish service we help God build His kingdom.

TODAY'S THOUGHT: *No amount of money can ever take the place of a kind word or a thoughtful deed.*

DECEMBER 11

Love Will Outlast the Stars

Love bears all things, believes all things, hopes all things, endures all things. 1 Corinthians 13:7

A man visiting a chrysanthemum show stood amazed at the beautiful blossoms. He noted the wide variety of colors and forms, but was impressed most of all by their size.

"How do you produce such marvelous blooms?" he asked one of the gardeners.

"We concentrate the strength of the plant on just one or two blossoms," the gardener replied. "If we allowed the plant to bear all the flowers it would like to, none of them would be worth showing. If we are to have a prize-winning plant, we must be content with one or two blossoms instead of a dozen."

This gardener spoke a parable of the way God works. In order to help us grow more like Him, He cuts away the useless buds of conceit and pride, so that we may have singleness of purpose. As we allow Him to prune away the things harmful to our spiritual lives, our faith is strengthened until we become flowers fit for the gardens of eternity.

Through this growing process we are nurtured by three helpers, Faith, Hope, and Love. A time will come when we can part with two of them, but one will last forever.

Faith, the first helper, is defined in the Bible as the assurance of things hoped for, and the conviction of things not seen. Faith makes real our belief in God, even though we have never actually seen Him. Some day we shall no longer need faith, for we shall see our Savior face to face.

Our second helper is Hope, a virtue that carries us through countless hours of trial and days of distress. Some day we shall reach a place where all promises and expectations are fulfilled.

Our greatest helper is Love—the powerful force that unites us with God and binds us to our fellow men, the element that gladdens our earthly pilgrimage. Love never fails. Love will never be left behind, for it goes with us into the gardens of eternity. Truly, God is love.

TODAY'S THOUGHT: *Life has no wounds that love cannot heal.*

DECEMBER 12

Spiritual Food Is God's Good Gift

Truly, truly, I say to you, he who believes has eternal life. I am the bread of life. John 6:47, 48

One of the significant phrases found in the story of Jesus feeding the five thousand is often overlooked. When it came supper time the Master discovered He was facing the problem of there not being enough for the multitude to eat. This is what He did: Jesus lifted up His eyes. Of course He lifted them up to His heavenly Father who supplied His need.

When we hunger and thirst after righteousness, having discovered that the ways of the world do not satisfy, let us lift up our eyes to ask God for spiritual food. This alone gives the satisfaction we crave. When we experience trouble and sorrow, let us lift up our eyes. Look above the world for that peace which the world cannot give. When we are faint and weary with the burden of our sins, and long for strength to do better, then let us lift up our eyes to the cross of Calvary and discover its cleansing power.

All the money in the world cannot satisfy a hungry soul. Many of us spend our gold trying to gain that which it cannot give us, namely, spiritual satisfaction. In a feverish pursuit of gain we forget God. What would a bag full of gold do for a man lost on a desert and dying of thirst? Again and again we need to remind ourselves that gold cannot buy food for our souls. Spiritual food is a gift from God—the bread coming down from heaven.

There is another lesson we can learn from this miracle. When the disciples saw the five barley loaves and two fishes, they asked disparagingly, "What are they among so many?" The unbelieving of the world, looking at the seemingly insignificant things of the Christian life, sneeringly ask, "What good can these things do?" They see a little water used in baptism, a little bread and wine distributed at Holy Communion, a hand laid on the head at confirmation, and they wonder, "What good can these things do?" They see a child offering its simple prayer, they observe a man reading his Bible, and they laugh at a religion which consists of such small matters. But the faithful find a meaning that the unbeliever can never find. The secret of the Lord is with them that fear Him.

TODAY'S THOUGHT: *The price of food for the body goes higher and higher, yet the price of food for the soul remains ever the same. It is trust in God.*

DECEMBER 13

Talk About Heaven

Not every one who says to me, "Lord, Lord," shall enter the kingdom of heaven, but he who does the will of my Father who is in heaven. Matthew 7:21

In a certain city there lived a little girl who was born blind, and had never seen the beauties of the world. Then it was discovered that surgery would restore her sight. After the operation her eyes remained bandaged for weeks and then for several days she was kept in a dark room. For her first sight of the world she was taken outdoors after dark and the bandages were removed from her eyes.

"Oh, Mother, is this heaven?" she cried as she beheld the stars and moon in all their glory.

"No, this is earth and that is the sky above us," her mother said.

"Why didn't you tell me it was so beautiful and so grand?" the girl asked.

"I tried to, my darling," the mother answered, "but you have to see it for yourself."

Many people wonder what heaven will be like. It is described in God's Holy Word. We know it will be a place without sorrow, suffering or death, where we shall have everlasting life. We know that there we shall be reunited with our loved ones, never to be parted again.

If we observe the world about us, we cannot help but anticipate the world to come. There are so many things here that God has given us to enjoy, and we wonder how heaven can possibly be more wonderful. As we look heavenward at night we are prompted to say, as did the little girl seeing the star-studded sky for the first time: "If the wrong side of heaven looks like this, what must the right side look like?"

The doors of eternity are open to anyone accepting the promises of God and having faith to believe them. A mother heard her four-year-old son talking to himself about heaven.

"I will get a ladder," he said, "and put it at the top of a tall tree, and climb up and knock at the door, and God will say, 'Who is there?' and I will answer, 'Willie.' And God will open the door and say, 'Come in, Willie.'"

Oh, that we might have the faith of a little child!

TODAY'S THOUGHT: *Just as a boy knows his kite is flying high because there is a tug on the string, so we know God is with us because there is courage in our hearts.*

DECEMBER 14

When Little Makes Much

Am I not allowed to do what I choose with what belongs to me?
Matthew 20:15

You need not be endowed with great talents to make your gifts significant in the eyes of God. The African native is unbelievably poor. For a house he has a mud hut, for furniture only a reed mat, no dishes at all, only clay pots. Many natives have no clothing except goats' hides, and only corn for their pitiful diet. Very few have machines or farming implements. From an economic point of view you would have to say that the African native has nothing to make life comfortable or secure.

Yet, it is interesting to note how he gives instinctively to God's work. At the out-station he helps build a church, the schoolhouse, the pastor-teacher's house, and place for the missionary to live when he visits the station He gives from whatever little money he can earn. He gives grain or anything else he may possess. One day, for example, a native brought in a fine helmet, the pride of his life, which he had bought with his hard earned money. Yet, after hearing of Christ's sacrifice for him, he gave that which he loved most.

A man in a New England town had been unemployed so long that he had but one dollar left. On Sunday he went to church, and placed 50 cents in the offering plate. The following morning he heard there was a possibility of his obtaining work in a neighboring town to which the railroad fare was one dollar. It looked as if he should have kept the 50 cents he placed in the offering plate, but he took the remaining half dollar and bought a ticket halfway to his destination. At the mid-point he stepped off the train, and started walking toward the town. But there was something better in store for him. Before he had gone a block he learned of a nearby factory that needed help. In 30 minutes he had a job paying five dollars more per week than he would have received, had he gone to the other town. The first week's pay returned his 50 cents ten-fold.

Not always does our giving result in a visible material return here upon earth, but it is surely the soundest and best for eternity. It brings into being spiritual qualities that help make living rich.

TODAY'S THOUGHT: *Use your gifts, tangible and intangible, in such a way that you can make a good report when the Giver appears.*

DECEMBER 15

Present Your Life to God

You shall walk in all the way which the Lord your God has commanded you, that you may live, and that it may go well with you. Deuteronomy 5:33

There is a beautiful garden chapel, built on the outskirts of one of our great American cities. It is very simply laid out, being little more than a narrow pathway winding through pleasant lawns and flowers. At intervals there stand attractive notice boards, each with a message showing us the journey we must take, if we are to do God's will.

First we come to the word Vision. Underneath are the words, "I saw the Lord sitting upon a throne, high and lifted up." All of us need vision in our lives. We need to look beyond the trials to see the glory that shall be.

A child was standing with her father one day on the summit of a high mountain. The two were standing above the clouds, and a thunderstorm clashed and rumbled below. Where they were it was perfect calm and sunshine, and their eyes, looking up, saw nothing but the deep blue of heaven, while all around their feet were bare rocks.

"Well, Lucy," said her father, "there is nothing to be seen here, is there?"

But the child exclaimed, "I see the Doxology all around me, and I hear it say, 'Praise God from whom all blessings flow.'"

A little farther along the pathway of the garden chapel you come to a second board with Confession as its theme. "All we like sheep have gone astray. We have turned everyone to his own way." All of us are guilty and need the forgiveness of sins. We have been given the assurance that "if we confess our sins he is faithful and just, and will forgive us our sins."

A third sign post calls for Renewal, for there is a promise: "They that wait upon the Lord shall renew their strength." Human resources ultimately run out. Constantly we need the renewing of strength which comes from God. Finally at the point where the garden must be left behind, and the noise of the great city greets us, we are confronted by this challenge: Dedication. "Here we offer and present unto Thee, O Lord, ourselves, our souls and our bodies, to be a reasonable and a living sacrifice to Thee."

TODAY'S THOUGHT: *The Holy Spirit stands ready to plant the seed of faith but is our heart's soil prepared?*

DECEMBER 16

Overcome the Day's Problems

In the world you have tribulation; but be of good cheer, I have overcome the world. John 16:33

Most of the world's people awaken each day to face a particular problem or concern, and they are doubtful that they will be able to conquer it. If they would only look in the right direction, they could find the help they desperately need.

What is your problem today? Are you remorseful because of the many wrongs you have done, and concerned about the consequences of your sin? Turn to God's Word and believe the promise He gives the penitent, "He is faithful and just, and will forgive our sins and cleanse us from all unrighteousness."

Are you worried about the days ahead? Are you so fearful of tomorrow that you are losing all joy in living today? Turn to God's Word and heed its advice. "Do not be anxious about tomorrow." God will take care of you.

Do you feel that nobody cares? Are you nervous, restless and jittery, not finding calm anywhere? Turn to God's Word, hear its invitation and accept it. "Come to me all who labor and are heavy-laden, and I will give you rest."

If you follow God's plan, you can discover a treasure finer than gold and more precious than sparkling gems, which no one will ever be able to take from you.

Through the ages, people have overlooked the Savior and forgotten the promises He made. To all of His people He offers a treasure, the richness of living free from doubt and worry, with the assurance that Someone greater than ourselves guides and protects us every step of the way.

If you would enrich your life, give your heart and soul to Christ today. Remember this admonition: "Do not lay up for yourselves treasures on earth, where moth and rust consume and where thieves break in and steal, but lay up for yourselves treasures in heaven . . . For where your treasure is, there will your heart be also."

Live this day rejoicing because great are the riches of heaven which belong to you.

TODAY'S THOUGHT: *Look full at the light of faith, and walk toward it down the narrow way.*

DECEMBER 17

Courageously Show Your Colors

Only be strong and very courageous. Joshua 1:7

Are we ready always to be on the Lord's side? Have we the courage to declare our principles, to stand up and speak the truth to the unbeliever or to those who sneer at sacred things? Do we always show our colors? Or, do we turn heel and flee rather than stand up for Christ?

We wonder why during Jesus' crucifixion all the disciples forsook Him and fled. And yet we do the same thing over and over again. When it comes to suffering loss, insult, or contempt for the sake of our Savior, and when it comes to giving up our way and sacrificing our wishes, too often we forsake Him and flee. We join the crowd of those who helped crucify Him on the cross years ago. Every mean, selfish, wicked device that we employ helps to crucify the Savior afresh.

Do not ask yourself what you would have done, had you actually lived with the Savior. Rather ask yourself how you are acting now toward Him who is with you always, even to the end of the age. Have we not frequently, like Peter denied Him, like Judas betrayed Him, and like the people of Jerusalem chosen Barabbas instead of Him? Have we not often made the fatal choice between sin and Christ? Have we not everyone faced the situation wherein, on the one side, was the meek and gentle Jesus, knocking at the door of our hearts, and saying, "Come to me, and I will give you rest," and on the other was bad company, the door to sin, and the whisper of impurity? What was your choice at that time? Was it right or wrong? Barabbas or Christ?

We, too, by our sinful acts have joined in the crucifixion. We, too, have caused suffering to come upon our Lord. Whenever we lead sinful lives, and thus influence others who follow after us to do the same, again we have crucified the Lord Jesus. We ourselves share the guilt of that dread word—"His blood be on us and on our children."

TODAY'S THOUGHT: *Follow the straight and narrow way of God, and your influence will take care of itself.*

DECEMBER 18

A Bright Light for a Dark World

Give light to those who sit in darkness and in the shadow of death. Luke 1:79

Today we pause to consider one of the most exciting days in the world's history. We are preparing to celebrate the anniversary of the birth of Jesus, our Savior from sin. Think of the darkness that enveloped the earth before His coming.

At the beginning of time man had his chance. God created a beautiful home for him, and he could have lived there forever without the cruel experience of death. But man chose sin, and as a result was destined to die. From that time until the coming of Christ all was despair, except for the joyous news of the promise of the Messiah. There was no land of beginning again, no opportunity for forgiveness of sin, no hope of eternal life. But God was not satisfied to see men die, and so He planned Christmas and the giving of himself once more for the family of man.

An artist was painting a picture of a wintry twilight. It was a dark and desolate scene, depicting a raging storm. Looking at it everything seemed hopeless, even as the world looked before Christ came. Then with a stroke of yellow he put a light in the window. The effect was magical. The entire scene was transformed by the addition of a ray of comfort and cheer.

The birth of Christ was just such a bright light for a dark world. His coming did not mean that we would no longer have sufferings and heartaches. We would still be in the world. But shining through our problems would be the presence of One who would conquer all. He was the One who gave us the courage to say, "Though there is thundering and lightning there are also stars in the sky, the stars of hope, faith, and love, breaking through the black and frightening thunderheads, giving us the strength that no one can take from us."

Let us resolve not only to celebrate Christmas for a day, but to keep its spirit and message throughout an entire year. Life will become more wonderful, as with the wise men we, too, follow the star lighting the way to the Prince of Peace. The peace He gives, the world can never take from us.

TODAY'S THOUGHT: *Though Christ be born a thousand times in Bethlehem, if He is not born in our heart, we are still forlorn.*

DECEMBER 19

Do Not Play with Dynamite

Be sober, be watchful. Your adversary the devil prowls around like a roaring lion, seeking some one to devour. 1 Peter 5:8

A true believer would not dive into the Niagara River above the falls and expect God by a miracle to save him from being caught in those roiling waters and plunged over them. A reasonable man would not set a match to a keg of gunpowder, and then turn to God, asking to be kept from being blown to bits. Would a man run into a busy intersection and fling himself into the path of an on-coming car, and then expect God to spare him injury?

Yet there are men and women who, paying only lip service to God, brazenly walk the way of temptation, expecting God to de-liver them. Not long ago a newspaper told of some children found playing with sticks of dynamite. Unwittingly they had stumbled upon a cache of them secreted by desperados. Everyone who read of it gasped.

We grownups ought to avoid the "fire sticks" of the devil instead of playing with temptation. Every time we pray to God, "Lead us not into temptation," we ask Him to keep us from doing those things that stir up the evil that is in every man's nature. We can lead ourselves into situations where temptation is certain to strike and where sin is sure to maim. In our willingness and carelessness, once we enter the avenue of temptation, we may not be able to resist the evil enticing us. We should avoid those lure-laden situa-tions which are certain to harm us.

Temptation flows like a river through the life of man. It has been here from the beginning of time, yet it is as new as today. It touched the Perfect Man, but He resisted. His example proves that we, too, can have the strength to conquer temptation with the power that is His.

The battle with temptation is a constant one. Though we make an effort to avoid it, it is always present in our lives, like a shadow hounding a man wherever he goes. Never can we relax, thinking we are safe from it.

The Bible counsels: "Therefore let any one who thinks that he stands take heed lest he fall." Before we yield to temptation, we should compare the heartaches and misery of those who fall into sin with the peace and joy of those who are faithful to God.

TODAY'S THOUGHT: *You cannot keep temptation from knock-ing at the door, but you need not invite him to dinner.*

DECEMBER 20

Trust God for a Single Day

If you will not believe, surely you shall not be established.

Isaiah 7:9

A minister was enduring a long illness. Finally when it seemed as if his faith were beginning to falter, he received these words from a loyal friend: "It seems to me that you are making the mistake of examining your faith rather than the promises on which your faith should rest.

"If you were traveling a new highway and came to a bridge which did not seem strong enough to satisfy you, would you stop to examine your faith in that bridge or would you get out and look at the structure itself? Common sense would tell you to get out and examine the bridge. When you were satisfied with its strength you would cross with confidence.

"Look away from yourself to the promises that God made to you," he continued. "Remember you have always been able to trust Him. No matter what happens, never forget that His promises are true. Remember the bridge."

Too often our faith falters simply because we are not content to trust God for one single day: Constantly we keep looking to the future, wondering what will happen next. We borrow and multiply trouble by trying to live too many days at a time.

A missionary with very little financial support was bound for a foreign land, and on the way she had a dream. She was standing on a tiny plank, floating in a vast ocean. There was absolutely nothing in front of her, or behind her, or on either side. Then she discovered that when she lifted her foot to step forward, suddenly another little plank appeared in front, ready for her to step on. God taught her this lesson: she was to trust Him one step at a time. She was to serve Him, knowing that if she did, there would always be another job for her to do, together with the grace and power to do it.

Whenever a disaster occurs aboard a British naval ship, it is the bugler's duty to play, "The Still." When the men hear it they stand perfectly quiet for a moment collecting their wits, preparing for the emergency. We, too, need moments of stillness day by day to enable us to face life as it comes.

TODAY'S THOUGHT: *Ponder the power and love of God until it permeates every nerve and fiber of your being and becomes your second nature.*

DECEMBER 21

Surrender Your Whole Self

Man is bowed down, and men are brought low, and the eyes of the haughty are humbled. Isaiah 5:15

As I talked with a man about a problem he faced, he confessed, "The trouble is that we have so much pride, so much that we will not admit to anybody, that we have a problem."

The first step in conquering a problem is to admit that we are baffled, and that we have not within ourselves the power to overcome our dilemma. In that spirit we surrender to a power beyond ourselves. And then we discover strength sufficient for any problem that we have to face.

Our difficulty is that often we are not willing to pay the price. We expect our Christianity to come far too cheaply: "Unless a man deny himself, take up his cross, and follow me, he cannot be my disciple." The Master put that severely. Too often people try to get religion at a bargain counter.

One day a woman who had shopped at a sale came home with a dress she considered an outstanding bargain. As she was exclaiming to her maid about the bargain she had made, she discovered some flaws in the garment, a ripped seam and some buttons missing. They looked at each other, and concluded that it had not been such a bargain after all. And then in her own peculiarly wise way the maid said, "It ought to teach you a lesson that you don't get nothin' for nothin' except *nothin'*."

That is true of life. "We don't get nothin' for nothin' except nothin'." Unless we are willing to pay the price, we are not going to enjoy a full measure of worthwhile living. If we wonder why life does not hold more meaning for us, let us think about a few questions. During the last week how much time did we spend praying? How much time did we set aside for the reading of the Word of God? How much did we practice each day our Christian faith? These are the processes by which we grow. And if we do not do these things, how can we possibly expect life to be worth while?

"Apart from me," said Jesus, "you can do nothing." "And when the sun rose it (the seed) was scorched,, and since it had no root it withered away." But once your life is rooted, it becomes a wonderful unfolding process.

TODAY'S THOUGHT: *A man without faith is like a car without a motor; it cannot move forward.*

DECEMBER 22

A Star in His Window

Where is he who has been born king of the Jews? For we have seen his star in the East, and have come to worship him.

Matthew 2:2

Over 1900 years ago God placed a star in His window, just as lonesome parents in the various wars placed a star in their windows to show that a son had gone to war. The twinkling rays of God's star pointed to a little manger where His Son was to be born, the Son destined to become the Savior of the world. This was the greatest gift ever offered to man. God proved His love by giving us His only Son.

Sometimes the gifts we receive are not as significant as they seem. A jewel was submitted to an expert for appraisal. He tested its weight, cut, and color. His final valuation was just a fraction of the figure the customer expected to see, and the owner of the jewel was obviously upset.

"This isn't a first-rate stone," repeated the man who had tested it.

"It must be. It was a royal gift," said the owner.

"I have examined many royal gifts," replied the jewel expert, "and I learned long ago that kings keep the best for themselves."

His conclusion may be true of earthly rulers, but it certainly is not true of the Lord of lords and King of kings. In His wondrous love He gave the best He had or, as Phillips translates John 3:16, "the only son He had." Jesus' life was not to be a life of ease and luxury, even though the most royal blood flowed in His veins. He was part of the very being and power of Almighty God, who flung the galaxies of stars into the sky, who created the mountains, scooped out the seas, and blew the breath of life into the soul of man. He was to be the one to live a perfect life, and mark a pathway on earth for His children to follow. Finally He was to die upon the cross—the complete payment for the sins of man. He was to live in the hearts of His children not only during His life on earth, but "even to the close of the age."

The star in God's window shows that He has given a Son, a sacrifice for each of us in the great war against sin.

TODAY'S THOUGHT: *Many a pride-swollen mortal has regained normal size out under the vast star-studded sky.*

DECEMBER 23

Immanuel—God with Us

How precious is thy steadfast love, O God! The children of men take refuge in the shadow of thy wings. Psalm 36:7

The true meaning of Christmas is found in these words: "God is with us." If Christ had come to earth for a brief spell, only to go away never to be heard of again, that would not have been tidings of great joy. The early disciples would never have won men to His way of life, if they had preached the way of a Master who absented himself from life, who left His church and went on to heaven, leaving man to go it alone. A merely historical Christ, whose record in the Bible came to its end at His ascension, could not be of comfort or help. The fact that Christ showed himself to a few people in that little spot almost two thousand years back would not give us reason to rejoice today.

The great secret of Christian joy lies in our believing not in a Christ who absented himself from the world, but in one who is ever-present, one who is Immanuel—God with us. He made a promise He has always kept: "Lo, I am with you always, even to the close of the age." He will never leave nor will He forsake us. If He had gone away leaving His children alone and comfortless, do you imagine that the early disciples would have changed from the cringing cowards of Good Friday to the flaming evangelists of the Resurrection? What nerved them to face any fear, to bear any persecution? It was that they were never alone and that, having the Master's presence in every conceivable situation, they in turn were masters of every changing circumstance.

Having descended into the catacombs of Rome, and seeing grave after grave of the early Christian martyrs who sacrificed their lives rather than give up their faith, I asked myself the question, "Why were they willing to be thrown to the angry beasts and to suffer such horrible martyrdom?" The only answer that makes sense is, they believed that Jesus was with them. They grounded their faith in His promise: "I will not leave you desolate; I will come to you." Daily they worshiped in His presence.

Where would they find that presence? In the Word and in the sacraments. These mediated to them, and will to us, the knowledge that He dwells in our hearts each day, to direct us in the way we should go.

TODAY'S THOUGHT: *God gave man three unspeakable gifts: Life, the Savior, and the Word.*

DECEMBER 24

He Came to Save His People

That whoever believes in him may have eternal life. John 3:15

Before Jesus there was darkness upon the face of the earth. Men had lost sight of God. They had corrupted themselves with false idols, until the God of their fathers had become to them a dream. The whole world lay in the shadow of death. Men had lost sight of personal dignity, and of their own divine creation. The strong oppressed the weak. The poor were slaves of the wealthy, and degraded women suffered as mere beasts of burden. Selfishness reigned supreme. Worldly pleasures occupied men's thoughts.

One class of people held this creed: "Let us eat, drink, and be merry, for tomorrow we die." Another group thought that life was emptiness, that pleasure was real joy, that indifference was bravery. And so the cruel world which Rome had conquered grew more cruel, more selfish, and farther away from God.

Yet, there were still a few thoughtful minds looking and longing for better things. Not only in Athens, but in other places as well, had there been erected altars to unknown gods. The question which remained in the minds of these peoples was this: "Where is He?" Slaves longed for a god who could set them free. Sinners wanted pardon and release from their bondage. "Where is God that we may believe, and have peace?"

The answer came at Christmas. In Bethlehem's stable there was born the Savior of the world, and His name was called Jesus, because He was to save the people from their sins.

At His first coming there were many who failed to believe in Him. But today we have the advantage of seeing just what He has done in the lives of people for almost two thousand years.

Are you asking today, "Where is He"? You do not have to look for Him. He is right beside you, closer than the air you breathe.

TODAY'S THOUGHT: *Christ came to fill our world's greatest need—the need for a Savior.*

DECEMBER 25

Christmas—Freedom's Birthday

And she gave birth to her first-born son and wrapped him in swaddling cloths, and laid him in a manger. Luke 2:7

A little boy had lost his father in death. He had loved his father dearly, and missed him very much as the days went by. Often he would go up and look at his picture which was on the library table. Christmas was approaching and his mother lifted the little lad to her lap and turned to him and asked, "What do you want for Christmas, Son?" He got up and stood before the picture of his father.

"I wish Father would step out of that picture," he said with tears in his eyes.

This is the meaning of Christmas. God has stepped out of the frame of heaven and come to earth in the form of man. He was to be called Immanuel, which means, "God with us." When the appointed time came, the star pointed its finger to the stable in Bethlehem saying that God is on His way to earth that He might offer himself as a sacrifice for all mankind. "You shall call his name Jesus, for he will save his people from their sins."

And so Christmas is Christ for the world, the Christ of justice and charity, freedom and peace.

The joy of Christmas is for everyone. It is the true joy of the soul, and the soul cannot die, so Christmas belongs to all ages. No force or power in the world can destroy it, for it means a union with Him who has overcome the world.

God is the supreme ruler of the world. When men begin to acknowledge that fact, greed, pride and hatred will vanish, and once more men will travel to Bethlehem to discover the light which will cast out the shadows and illuminate the world.

This is the birthday of freedom, for it is only in following Christ that we can find freedom—freedom from tyranny of sin, the anguish of doubt, the heartbreak of loneliness, and the fear of everlasting death. Because of Christmas the everlasting day of eternity is possible for all men. Believe in Christ, and you will be saved.

TODAY'S THOUGHT: *God gave Christ two tasks: to atone for man's sins and to change man's nature.*

DECEMBER 26

Christ Conquers Fear

Be not afraid of them, for I am with you to deliver you, says the Lord. Jeremiah 1:8

Fear is one of man's greatest enemies. It can hold him captive, and cause him to forfeit the victorious life which God intended for him. When man becomes separated from God and forgets His power, fear strikes the hardest. When our faith looks up to God, we can hold a song in our hearts, and with His song we are helping not only ourselves but others as well.

A small boy, walking home, whistled in the darkness. When asked why he whistled he replied, "I thought if there were some other little boy out in the dark, he would like to hear me whistling to know I am not afraid."

We pass people every day who need our help. As our faith grows deeper, remember, we can be an influence on others, too.

A shipwrecked sailor was thrown on a rock where the waves were high and dangerous. With all his strength he clung there until the tide went down. After he had been rescued, one of his friends asked, "Didn't you shake with fear when you were hanging on that rock?"

"Yes," he replied, "but the rock didn't."

Christ is our Rock of Ages, our security, though storms seem to overpower us. He is the Captain of the storm, and if we trust Him, He will see us through.

In our trials He reminds us that all things work together for good. A little boy's boat sailed beyond his reach, and he shouted for help. His older brother came, picked up some stones and threw them out beyond the toy boat, starting miniature waves which carried the boat back to the shore until it was within the boy's reach. How happy the little boy was with his boat in his hands again.

Sometimes certain things coming into our lives seem out of place, as though not being part of the plan. But if we wait we will see that each new trial, each striking of the stone upon the quiet waters, has brought us nearer to God.

TODAY'S THOUGHT: *The faithful can walk into nothingness, and always find a path blazed for them.*

DECEMBER 27

Gone the Crushing Weight of Worry

When you are in tribulation, and all these things come upon you . . . you will return to the Lord your God and . . . he will not fail you. Deuteronomy 4:30, 31

Every day has its trials, its tribulations, and its worries. There is never a moment when we do not need courage. We need it as much for daily living as the soldier needs it on the field of battle. We need it to be honest in all our daily relations. We need it to resist temptation, to speak the truth, and to refrain from pretending to be what we are not. We need courage to overcome the obstacles that we face. Everyone's life is a battlefield where many a hard struggle has to be fought. Even as nature's storming elements can rage about our heads, so within our souls rages temptation. Sometimes we lash out wildly, blindly seeking we know not what. If only we possess the assurance that Jesus is with us, and that we are trying humbly to do our duty, we need fear no evil. The only time we need fear the storm is when we lose our faith in God.

We may have worries of every description. We can be concerned about the security of our job, about our children's future. Carefully made plans crumble to the ground like a house built on the sand. We dream dreams only to discover they do not come true, and subsequently we begin to doubt. We wonder about God. Is He not concerned about our troubles? If only we will remain receptive to Him, soon His voice will be sounding in our hearts: "Why are you afraid, O men of little faith?" Trust God and do your best.

Two kings were engaged in battle. In the midst of it one stalled for time under the pretense of seeking help from his god. The other, without leaving the field, called for divine aid, continued to lead on his forces, and won the victory! "Ora et labora" was the watchword of a saint. Who could put it better, "Pray and work"?

So it should be with us. God expects us to trust Him, but He also expects that we shall do our best.

TODAY'S THOUGHT: *Trust in God, put Him first and foremost in your life, and you will be amazed at the adventure your life will turn out to be.*

DECEMBER 28

God's Door Is Always Open

Are not five sparrows sold for two pennies? And not one of them is forgotten before God. Luke 12:6

The teacher sent a boy to the principal to be reprimanded for misbehaving. The principal, a kind and understanding man, listened carefully to the facts of the case.

"You have never been in this office before for doing something wrong," he said finally. "In fact, I don't know you very well. You may be a very good boy, because even good boys sometimes make mistakes. Now watch as I write your name in my records with the date and the reason. You see, I'm writing this in pencil, very lightly. If you remain a good boy, and are not sent to me again this year, I will erase this from my book, and no one will ever know anything about it."

So it is with our loving God. He gave Peter another chance after the Resurrection, and He will lead us to the land of beginning again, if we sincerely repent our sins and mistakes. The door to the heart of God is always open to receive us, when we seek forgiveness for wrongdoing.

This story is told of President Lincoln. One day he was ill and refused to see anyone—senators, judges, or diplomats. The greatest and most distinguished people in the land could not gain admittance to the White House. Then came a poor woman whose clothes were plain and worn, whose face was thin and sorrowful, and who was carrying a tiny spindly baby. She was told that the President was ill and could not see her. But she begged so persistently for a moment of his time, that finally her request was taken to Lincoln.

"Show her in," was the answer.

Though he had not seen the important people who had come to honor him, he could not refuse to see this poor woman who came to him in distress.

Is it not thus with Christ? Day by day He gladly sees the penitent, suffering children who come to Him in need. The door to the heart of God is always open.

TODAY'S THOUGHT: *God can mend anything that is broken, even hearts and promises.*

DECEMBER 29

Living Above

For the wages of sin is death, but the free gift of God is eternal life in Christ Jesus our Lord. Romans 6:23

Jewelers know that an imitation diamond is never as brilliant as the real stone, but inexperienced eyes cannot detect the difference. If you wish to test a diamond, simply place the stone under water. An imitation is practically invisible, while the genuine diamond is clearly visible and even sparkles. Held under water, the difference is apparent to anyone.

Many of us fail the water test. Sometimes God places us in stormy seas, and when trouble comes no longer do we shine for Him. But if our faith is genuine, we will witness, no matter how severe the adversity may be. We must believe we are never alone in any problem, that God knows best, and is with us always.

A little boy was helping his father unpack some boxes of dry goods. The father was taking out bolts of cloth and piling them in the boy's out-stretched arms.

"Don't you think you have a big enough load?" a passer-by asked the boy.

"Father knows best," the lad replied. "He knows how much I ought to carry."

God will not allow us to carry too heavy a burden. When our strength runs out, He will add His strength to ours. He endows us, too, with the capacity to live above the difficulties of the world.

Over the door of a little cabinet maker's shop in London there hangs a sign—Living Above. This man's customers know that he can be found above his shop, if the door is locked. It is a wonderful thing for a man to be able to say that he is living above his work, that his life's dreams and hopes are above the level of his day's labor. He may have to work amid the world's tension and turmoil, but at least he can live above.

We are called to be in the world, but not of the world. If we seek it, God gives us grace to resist every temptation to hide our colors. God witnesses our every thought, word and deed as evidence of our love for Him. Can you pass the test? Does your faith ring true?

TODAY'S THOUGHT: *God accepts no counterfeits. He demands the love and devotion that has the true ring of the genuine.*

DECEMBER 30

"Closed for Inventory"

He who is faithful in a very little is faithful also in much; and he who is dishonest in a very little is dishonest also in much.

Luke 16:10

Every wise man pauses periodically to take inventory. But, contrary to a general impression, this process should not be confined only to those in the business world. All of us should use our opportunities to discover what our present position with God is— or whether or not we have lost or gained ground in the race of life during the past year. Each time the year ends we stand on the threshold of a new one, and it becomes a solemn occasion indeed when we hear the voice say to us, "Son, daughter, give an account of your stewardship."

The most obvious feeling we have is that of the swiftness with which time passes. Such a short time ago this year began. We think of the many things we failed to do, and of those things we did that were wrong. Why did we not weave in better fashion the pattern of our daily life, knowing that the kind of life we lived helped to construct the materials of our house for tomorrow? Each of us creates his future in a definite pattern, and every daily act adds something to that pattern.

Are we working only for earthly gain, or are we remembering to work also toward eternity. Shall we be happy when God asks us to look upon the weaving of our hands? Shall we care ourselves to look upon this handiwork? If ever there were a purgatory—and Scripture never even hints at there being one—would it not be to have to walk among the records and products of our sleazy, shoddy living? Will we dare stand one day to have unveiled a life record giving no sign of divine guidance?

We would be wise to start weaving into the fabric of our living such things as love, peace, kindness, goodness, meekness. Salvation is God's gift of grace to the believer; when saved, he is eager that God directs his doing. Even now we can repent of our mistakes; for if we are sincere in our confession, then we can be positive that all the past is forgotten.

Let us accept this promise in faith, and resolve that by His grace every day of the new year will for us be God's day.

TODAY'S THOUGHT: *Make Christ the sun of your soul, and your sunny days will last from here to eternity.*

DECEMBER 31

The Only Reward He Asks Is Your Love

For this is the love of God, that we keep his commandments.

1 John 5:3

A little boy worked long, tedious hours making a model ship. When it was finished he delighted in sailing it along the river. One day he left the model tied to a tree along the river bank and returned to find it gone. He was very unhappy because he treasured the little craft, particularly since he had made it with his own hands.

Not long afterward in a little town he passed a store window and saw in it his boat marked, "For Sale."

"That's my boat," he said. "I made it with my own hands."

"I am very sorry, but it was brought in here," the storekeeper replied. "I bought it, and to get it you must pay for it."

The boy asked to have the boat saved for him and went out to earn money to buy it back. Later, with his precious boat under his arms, he told the storekeeper, "Now it's twice mine! I made it with my own hands, and I bought it back for a price."

God has not only created us but also bought us back for a price, the beautiful life and atoning death of His only Son, Jesus Christ. It was not by His carelessness, however, that we were lost, but instead because of our sinfulness. Even though it was not God's fault, His love for us was so great that He purchased us a second time with the life of His own Son. Think of the claim He has upon us. No fact in history is so great as the fact of the infinite love of God—a love that will never let us go!

What does He expect in return? This anecdote gives us a clue.

Excitement ran high at the orphanage the day little Jane was to go to her new home. When her new mother arrived, she said to the little girl, "I am going to dress you in beautiful clothes, and you will have a room all your own, a little chair and table, and a doll and buggy. Are you ready, now?"

Little Jane hesitated, then turned to the woman and said, "But what can I give you?"

"You can love me," the woman answered with a warm smile.

So it is with God. For all that He has done for us God asks only that we love Him.

TODAY'S THOUGHT: *The Great Physician is never discouraged, He never gives up, for He knows that love can win where all else fails.*